Organizational Ecology

Organizational Ecology

Michael T. Hannan
John Freeman

Harvard University Press
Cambridge, Massachusetts
London, England
1989

Library of Congress Cataloging-in-Publication Data
Hannan, Michael T.
  Organizational ecology/Michael T. Hannan and John Freeman.
    p.   cm.
  Bibliography: p.
  Includes index.
  ISBN 0-674-64348-8 (alk. paper)
  1. Organizational change. 2. Organizational behavior.
I. Freeman, John, 1945– . II. Title.
HD58.8.H363 1989   88-15470
302.3'5—dc19   CIP

For Susan and Diane

Contents

Preface   *xi*

Part I   Theory

1 Organizations and Social Structure   3

Organizational Diversity   7
Perspectives on Organizational Change   10
The Demography and Ecology of Organizations   13
Population Thinking   15
Evolution of Organizational Forms   17
Dynamic and Comparative Analysis   24

2 Theoretical Background   28

Organization Theory and Sociology: Missing Connections   28
Comparison of Contemporary Approaches   33
Controversies and Misunderstandings   35
Managerial Implications and Applications   40

3 Boundaries of Forms and Populations   45

Approaches to Defining Forms   48
A Focus on Boundaries   53
Boundary Dynamics and Diversity   60
Implications for Research   62

4 Structural Inertia and Organizational Change   66

Structural Inertia   70
A Hierarchy of Inertial Forces   77
Variations in Strength of Inertia   80

5 Competition and the Niche   91

The Principle of Isomorphism   93
The Niche   95
Classical Competition Theory   97
Niche Overlap and Competition   103

6 Modeling the Dynamics of Organizational Populations   117

Variations in Intrinsic Founding Rates   117
Effects of Environments on Carrying Capacities   123
Conceptualizing the Size of Populations   129
Carrying Capacities and Density Dependence   131
Rate Dependence and Diversity Dependence   141
Dynamics of Selection   143

Part II Methods

7 Designs of Empirical Studies   147

Defining Events   147
National Labor Unions   153
Semiconductor Merchant Producers   164
Newspaper Publishers in San Francisco   175
Comparison of Data Sets   176

8 Models and Methods of Analysis   178

Describing Organizational Histories   179
Models for Transition Rates   184
Counting Process Models   192
Estimation and Testing   194

Part III Empirical Findings

9 The Population Ecology of Founding and Entry 201

Core Questions 201
Founding Rates of Labor Unions 207
Entry Rates of Semiconductor Manufacturing Firms 224
Founding Rates of Newspaper Firms 238
Comparisons and Contrasts 243

10 Age Dependence in Failure Rates 244

The Liability of Newness 245
National Labor Unions 247
Exits of Semiconductor Manufacturing Firms 267

11 The Population Ecology of Organizational Mortality 271

Disbanding Rates of Labor Unions 273
Exit Rates of Semiconductor Firms 293
Failure Rates of Newspaper Firms 305
Comparisons and Contrasts 308

12 Dynamics of Niche Width and Mortality 310

Niche Width and Mortality of Restaurants 314
Niche Width and Exit Rates of Semiconductor Firms 323
Comparisons and Contrasts 329

13 Conclusions 331

Implications of the Research 332
Problems for Analysis 336

References 343
Name Index 359
Subject Index 363

Preface

The ecology of organizations is an approach to the macrosociology of organizations that builds on general ecological and evolutionary models of change in populations and communities of organizations. The goal of this perspective is to understand the forces that shape the structures of organizations over long time spans.

Our interest in developing an ecology of organizations began in the mid-1970s at a time when the sociology of organizations began to emphasize the effects of environments on the structure and functioning of firms, bureaus, and other kinds of organizations. Most theory and research in this period treated organizations as rational, flexible, and speedy adapters to changing environmental circumstances, and thus variability in structures was accounted for by local adaptations to short-term environmental fluctuations.

We did not find this approach to be useful in explaining the structures we observed. We hardly recognized in these accounts the concrete organizations of our experience or those described in detailed accounts of life in particular organizations. The organizations we knew did not seem to have unitary, stable preference structures and simple mechanisms for implementing them in the face of changing conditions. Rather, they were composed of subgroups with differing interests (meaning that there is no unitary "organizational" preference structure). In our experience, subunits and coalitions commonly engaged in political contests for control over decisions and resources. Such political processes, along with various kinds of sunk costs and legitimacy constraints, caused these organizations to be anything but flexible and quick in collective response to changing opportunities and constraints in the environment. Put simply, we thought it was a mistake to build models of organizational change that rely on anthropomorphic images of organizations. Thus we decided to build a perspective that treats organizations as complicated systems with strong limitations on flexibility and speed of response.

Following the proclivity to think anthropomorphically about organizations, theorists and researchers in this period also focused on action by individual organizations. They used what we have called a "focal-organization perspective"; that is, they sought to describe and explain the actions of single organizations facing specified environmental problems. But this perspective too seemed problematic. The success or failure of any tactic or strategy for dealing with an environmental problem presumably depends on the tactics and strategies adopted by the other similar (and dissimilar) organizations in the system. Thus we decided it would be productive to shift the level of analysis to the population level, which means considering the actions of all organizations of a particular type.

We also concluded that the organizational theory of the 1970s was leading the field to an isolated position within sociology. Both the tendency to reason anthropomorphically about organizations and the focal-organization perspective greatly limited the usefulness of organizational theory for explaining large-scale social change, for reasons that we explain at length in the first two chapters.

In preparing to develop a different kind of theory of organizational change, we considered two kinds of analytic structures. The first was the theory of the firm in competitive markets. This collection of theories has the appropriate population focus: its distinguishing characteristic is an emphasis on the consequences of simultaneous actions of all parties in a market. However, this approach relies on theories of action and of organization that seemed to share many of the defects of the organization theory of the 1970s. Firms were viewed as rational, unitary actors with broad behavioral repertoires. Therefore, following the example of formal models of the behavior of firms dealt with only one of the two broad problems that concerned us.

A second analytic structure, evolutionary models of population and community ecology, seemed more promising. These theories sought to explain how selection processes shape adaptation at the population level to environmental variations. The individual actors, biotic creatures, are assumed to have relatively fixed repertoires of action (coded in the genome). So the motor of change is selection—the excess of births over deaths of actors that possess a certain fixed strategy. In a pair of papers (Hannan and Freeman 1974, 1977) we proposed an approach to analyzing organizational change using particular models drawn from population ecology.

Since invoking selection processes in the social sciences violates an implicit taboo, as we discuss in Chapter 2, it is worth noting our motivations. We did not seek to use biological theory to explain organizational change; nor did we propose to develop metaphors between biotic populations and organizational populations. Rather, we wanted to explain a variety of sociological phenomena that could not be explained satisfactorily with existing social science theories. We relied on models from population biology because these models appeared to clarify the social processes of interest. This was very much a "modeling strategy." As we explained initially, in describing our use of Lotka-Volterra models, "No known population (of animals, or of organizations) grows exactly in the manner specified by this mathematical model . . . What the equations do is to model the growth path of populations that exist on finite resources in a closed system. Neither protozoa nor bureaucracies behave exactly as the model stipulates. The model is an abstraction that will lead to insight whenever the stated conditions are approximated" (Hannan and Freeman 1977, p. 961).

In moving in the direction of an ecology of organizations, our thinking was influenced by Amos Hawley's (1950, 1968) neoclassical theory of human ecology. This theory, modeled on the bioecology of the 1930s and 1940s, sought to explain patterns of adaptation of human communities to ecological settings. It relied on a principle of isomorphism which holds that, in equilibrium, "units subjected to the same environmental conditions, or to environmental conditions as mediated by a given key unit, acquire a similar form of organization" (Hawley 1968, p. 334). We thought that the organization theorists of the 1970s were searching for such a principle but lacked the rigorous logic of Hawley's theory. It seemed useful to us to try to extend Hawley's approach in two related ways. First, we were mainly interested in dynamics rather than the comparative statics of neoclassical human ecology because we doubted that organizational populations are often observed in equilibrium. Second, we thought it was important to think about isomorphism in settings in which the environment is spatially and temporally heterogeneous.

Our thinking was also influenced strongly by Stinchcombe's (1965) insightful analysis of change in the world of organizations. This essay suggested that cohorts of organizations are "imprinted" with the social, cultural, and technical features that are common in the environment when the cohort is founded. Because imprinted characteristics are highly resistant to change, the current characteristics of populations of organizations reflect historical conditions at the time of founding rather than recent adaptations.

We thought that Stinchcombe was right about the historical facts, and we have suggested that his reasoning was strongly consistent with a population ecology theory of organizational change. Developing the implications of Stinchcombe's argument led us to emphasize rates of founding and rates of mortality in organizational populations and to consider processes over long historical periods.

In the time following our initial proposal that sociologists build an ecology of organizations, this approach has become an active field of research. Carroll's (1988) recent collection of research papers and the references to this volume testify to the breadth of effort.

This volume reports on our theoretical and empirical work since the late 1970s. Several features are noteworthy. First, it should be clear that we use ecological models as frameworks within which to study *sociological* processes. For example, Chapters 6, 9, and 11 develop models of the consequences of competitive interactions and of processes of legitimation in shaping change in populations of organizations. In no sense do we limit our attention to processes that have clear parallels in bioecology.

Second, our work focuses on dynamics, especially on the local dynamics of processes that shape rates of entry and exit in populations of organizations. And we study such processes over long periods of time.

Third, in the course of studying such dynamics, we consider entire populations of organizations over the full histories of the populations. This strategy of research departs radically from most research on organizations, which tends to focus on the largest and longest-lived organizations and on cross-sections or very short time series.

Fourth, we depart from a long tradition in organizational analysis separating theory from empirical research. Most important treatises on organizational theory contain no empirical research and make only passing reference to empirical studies. In contrast, this book develops tight links between theory, models, and empirical research. We have tried to develop theories and models that lead reasonably directly to comparative research. Consequently, research findings play a prominent role in this book. We have studied dissimilar populations over long periods: national labor unions in the United States from 1836 to 1985 and manufacturing firms in the semiconductor industry from 1945 to 1985. We have also reanalyzed Glenn Carroll's data on the population of newspaper publishing firms in the San Francisco Bay area from 1840 to 1975. Finally, we have collected data in a three-year panel study on samples of restaurants in eighteen cities in California. This mix of populations includes market and nonmarket organizations as well as high-tech and low-tech firms. A principal goal in our research is to learn whether similar processes have characterized these dissimilar populations. Part III reports our findings to date.

In the course of a decade's research on the ecology of organizations we have received inspiration, advice, and support from many colleagues and students and financial support from several sources. Although we cannot list all of those to whom we are indebted, we would like to acknowledge some of the leading actors, individual and corporate.

As will be clear in the pages that follow, we have profited greatly from collaboration with Glenn Carroll. We refer frequently to his joint work with Jacques Delacroix. He also collaborated with us in reanalyzing his data on American newspapers in order to explore some new themes introduced here. Moreover, he has provided useful critical comments on the entire manuscript.

We have also received helpful comments from many others. Susan Olzak provided detailed comments on more drafts of the entire manuscript than we would like to admit. David Weakliem also provided comments on the entire manuscript. Heather Haveman went over the manuscript with unusual care to detail in the course of preparing for Ph.D. qualifying examinations. Paul DiMaggio, John Dumont, Paul McLaughlin, Walter W. Powell, James Ranger-Moore, W. Richard Scott, and Jitendra Singh provided useful criticisms of a draft of Part I.

We have benefited from suggestions and criticisms at many stages of the empirical projects from former colleagues at Stanford and Berkeley and current colleagues at Cornell. In addition, we receive excellent research assistance from Warren Boeker, Jack Brittain, Charles Denk, Barbara Dohrn, Lauren Edleman, Michael Fischer, Jerry Goodstein, Nancy Langton, James Ranger-Moore, Douglas Roeder, Kim Voss, and Douglas Wholey.

Major financial support for this project was supplied by the National Science Foundation (grants SOC-78-12315, SES-81-09381, ISI-82-18013, and SES-85-10227). In early phases of the project we benefited from the support of the Organizations Studies Section of the Institute for Mathematical Studies in the Social Sciences at Stanford University and the Institute of Industrial Relations at the University of California, Berkeley. Since our move to Cornell, our research has been generously supported by the College of Arts and Sciences and the Johnson Graduate School of Management. Computing support came from the Cornell Supercomputer Facility, which is supported in part by the National Science Foundation, the state of New York, and the IBM Corporation. In the final stages of the project,

Michael Hannan was supported by a fellowship from the John Simon Guggenheim Foundation and had the pleasure of working in Karl Ulrich Mayer's research center at the Max-Planck-Institut für Bildungsforschung in Berlin.

A number of chapters draw on materials that have been published separately. Earlier versions of parts of Chapter 1 were published in Michael T. Hannan, "Uncertainty, Diversity and Organizational Change," in Neil Smelser and Dean Gerstein, eds., *Social and Behavioral Sciences: Discoveries over Fifty Years* (Washington, D.C.: National Academy Press, 1986). An earlier version of Chapter 3 was published as Michael T. Hannan and John Freeman, "Structural Inertia and Organizational Change," *American Sociological Review* 49 (1984): 149–164. A version of much of Chapter 6 appeared in Michael T. Hannan and John Freeman, "Where Do Organizational Forms Come From?" *Sociological Forum* 1 (1986): 50–72. A portion of Chapter 9 is based on Michael T. Hannan and John Freeman, "The Ecology of Organizational Founding: American Labor Unions, 1835–1985," *American Journal of Sociology* 92 (1987): 910–943. The middle part of Chapter 10 is based on Michael T. Hannan, "Age Dependence in the Mortality of National Labor Unions: Comparisons of Parametric Models," *Journal of Mathematical Sociology* 14 (1988): 1–30; and a portion of Chapter 11 is based on Michael T. Hannan and John Freeman, "The Ecology of Organizational Mortality: American Labor Unions, 1836–1985," *American Journal of Sociology* 94 (1988): 25–52. Finally, part of Chapter 12 is drawn from John Freeman and Michael T. Hannan, "Niche Width and the Dynamics of Organizational Populations," *American Journal of Sociology* 88 (1983): 1116–45, and John Freeman and Michael T. Hannan, "The Ecology of Restaurants Revisited," *American Journal of Sociology* 92 (1987): 1214–20. We thank these publishers for permission to excerpt these materials.

M.T.H.
J.F.

I | *Theory*

1 | Organizations and Social Structure

Most sociological theories emphasize the actions of individuals, interest groups, social classes, and institutions. Yet almost all modern collective action takes place in *organizational* contexts; and organizations are the main vehicles for action in modern society (Coleman 1974). When interest groups and social classes take collective action, they do so using organizations such as labor unions, political parties, or national liberation fronts. Even relatively amorphous social movements have a higher likelihood of success if they can utilize existing organizations (Tilly 1978). The state, which has become the focus of so much social action, is itself an organizational apparatus. Struggles for power and control in modern societies typically involve struggles among organizations for privileged positions in the state structure as well as struggles between the state and other kinds of organizations.

Organizations develop formalized roles and procedures for enforcing their rules. Therefore, institutional rules have most force when they are codified as explicit, legitimated organizational rules. Examples include codes of professional ethics and employment contracts. Professional codes of ethics become significant constraints on behavior when professional associations succeed in obtaining licensing requirements as part of their effort to secure monopolies of practice. Employment contracts have more continuous and binding effects when labor unions monitor compliance and resist their abrogation.

Because organizations play key roles in modern societies, the speed and direction of social change depend on the dynamics of organizations. In particular, the ability of society as a whole to respond to changing conditions depends on the responsiveness of its constituent organizations and on the diversity of its organizational populations.

The problem of matching the outputs of an educational system to the needs of a changing economy illustrates the issues. It has long been evident that American school systems are failing to teach enough mathematics and science to all but the richest and ablest students. A series of national commissions has dignified this failure as a national problem and has urged immediate and far-ranging reforms of U.S. public education. Some commissions urge more attention to teaching (and requiring) more mathematics, science, and computer skills; others emphasize attention to writing. All agree that the quality of teachers should be upgraded and that more time must be allocated to teaching. A broad consensus seems to have emerged on the definition of the problem. Federal and state officials, school district officials, legislators, school employee unions, and parent groups all urge reform.

How quickly can the national system of public education be reformed? There are a number of reasons for suspecting that change will be halting at best. First, the demographic and institutional constraints on change in this system are very powerful. Consider the problem of upgrading the technical knowledge of teaching staffs. In a period of declining enrollments, school staffs have been shrinking. Given the "last in, first out" policies favored by bureaucratic logic and demanded by teachers' unions, change in the composition of teaching staffs will be glacially slow without some radical change in employment policies; but any such radical change is sure to encounter stiff resistance from unions and legal challenges as well. Radical change in policy may also mobilize previously quiescent groups.

The complexity of interorganizational networks compounds the problem of educational reform. There is no unitary chain of command; rather there are multiple, partially overlapping jurisdictions of local, state, and federal agencies, with no central planning mechanism. Change in any one sector is hampered by overlaps with others. The seemingly simple problem of changing textbooks in public school systems is made very complicated by the nature of the organizational arrangements. Many different organizations and individuals must be consulted. Any one of them can block or at least forestall the change. Implementing a broad and powerful mandate to change the educational system thus means changing many organizations and their interlocking connections. The speed of response of the whole system is constrained by the speed with which the slowest of the component organizational populations responds.

Similar issues pertain to industrial change, although the processes differ. During the late 1970s and early 1980s, leading firms in a number of highly concentrated American industries such as agricultural and construction

machinery, automobiles, and steel stumbled in the face of the more efficient methods of scheduling, performing, and evaluating production used
by foreign competitors. These giant American firms had adapted structurally to earlier technical and social conditions and have been ponderous at
best in responding to new challenges. The tendency of these firms to rely
on their political muscle to obtain favorable government intervention to
limit competition has served to forestall radical change in industrial strategies and structures. Global national policies of reindustrialization imply
massive change in the structures of thousands of organizations in the economy. Whether such policies can proceed quickly enough to meet the international competition and rapidly changing technologies depends largely
on the responsiveness of the existing firms in the economy and the
rate at which new firms can be created and brought up to speed. Analysis
of such policies requires knowledge of the dynamics of organizational
populations.

The discussion to this point portrays organizations as passive brakes on
social changes initiated by interest groups in the society. But organizations
are more than passive actors; most social changes begin with actions of
organizations. Indeed, organizations are constructed as tools for specific
kinds of collective action. Individuals and groups invest resources in hospitals or armies, for example, in the hope of achieving specific kinds of
performances.

Organizations are far from simple tools, however. Among other things,
they consume substantial resources in simply maintaining their structures.
Because great quantities of organizational resources are used for building
organizations and for administrative overhead, rather than for production
or collective action, creation of a permanent organization is a costly way to
achieve social goals. (In Chapter 5 we discuss why such expensive solutions are used so commonly in modern societies.)

Organizational politics complicate the relation between technical needs
for production and the actual distribution of resources. Subunits strive to
protect and expand their budgets and staffs. The resulting competition
between units for fixed resources is especially severe in times of contraction or decline (Freeman and Hannan 1975; Hannan and Freeman 1978).
Because allocations within organizations spark intense political contests,
organizational action depends on the history of prior allocations and on the
nature of current political coalitions. Organizations develop lives of their
own, with action at least partly disconnected from ostensible goals, from
demands of relevant environments, and often from the intentions of organizational leaders.

Even when organizational action unfolds in an orderly and rational way (when viewed from the perspective of public goals) as in Weber's image of bureaucracy, organizations develop momentum that goes beyond the intentions and interests of key actors. Weber (1968, p. 345) made the point as follows: "If a group pays someone to act as a continuous and deliberate 'organ' of their common interests, or if such interest representation pays in other respects, an association comes into being that provides a strong guarantee for the continuance of concerted action under all circumstances . . . . The pattern of intermittent and irrational action is replaced by a systematic 'rational' enterprise, which continues to function long after the original enthusiasm of the participants for their ideals has vanished."

Although Weber argued that organizations take on lives of their own, largely independent of the wishes and interests of those who created them, he thought that organizations would invariably carry out their initial programs and purposes. The tradition of organization theory begun by Michels (1915/1949) leads to a different position. Michels identified a set of processes by which organizational goals are displaced in favor of the goal of simply maintaining the organization and its hierarchy of power and privilege. The private goals of powerful members of organizations tend to dominate its public goals as an organization ages. For these and other reasons cited in Chapter 4, organizations are at best recalcitrant tools, as Selznick (1948) put it. The politics of resource allocation in organizations prevent them from responding quickly to pressures to alter organizational practices or to initiate new kinds of action.

Despite the fact that inertial tendencies seem to be strong, especially for old and large organizations, populations of organizations have changed markedly over time: the forms flourishing today differ dramatically from those that held sway at the turn of the century. Chandler (1977) gives a vivid account of the changes in organizational forms in industry over this period. Similar changes can be found in the structure of labor unions, medical care organizations, and government agencies.

Changes in social, economic, and political systems do affect organizational structures and practices. Changes in organizational populations also affect social systems, though such effects go beyond the scope of this book. The major gaps in our understanding of the causes of organizational change concern the actual dynamics: Exactly how does change in larger systems affect the forms of organizations in society?

The applied literature on organizational behavior often assumes that attempting to change the motivations of managers and workers and the details of the organization makes a difference for profits and the attainment of other goals. The theory and research we report emphasize the replacement of outmoded organizations by new forms when environmental conditions and competitive relations change. Both processes appear as change or favorable innovation, though at different levels of analysis. It is important from both theoretical and practical points of view to understand the limits on these processes.

Addressing this issue requires knowledge of rates of change of various types: rates of reorganization, rates of creation of new forms, rates of organizational disappearance, and so forth. At this point we know very little about these rates. The theory and research reported in this book attempt to remedy this problem.

Organizational Diversity

The ecological-evolutionary approach developed in this book directs attention primarily to organizational diversity. It seeks to answer the question: Why are there so many (or so few) kinds of organizations? Addressing this question means specifying (1) sources of increasing diversity, such as the creation of new forms, and (2) sources of decreasing diversity, such as competitive exclusion of forms. In other words, an ecology of organizations seeks to understand how social conditions affect the rates at which new organizations and new organizational forms arise, the rates at which organizations change forms, and the rates at which organizations and forms die out. In addition to focusing on the effects of social, economic, and political systems on these rates, an ecology of organizations also emphasizes the dynamics that take place *within* organizational populations.

Questions about the diversity of organizations in society might seem to have only academic interest. In fact, these issues bear directly on important social issues. Perhaps the most important is the capacity of a society to respond to uncertain future changes. Organizational diversity within any realm of activity, such as medical care, microelectronics production, or scientific research, constitutes a repository of alternative solutions to the problem of producing sets of collective outcomes. These solutions are embedded in organizational structures and strategies.

The key aspects of these solutions are usually subtle and complicated. In a large organization, no individual understands the full range of activities and their interrelations that constitute the organizational solution. Moreover, the subtle aspects of the structure, such as decision-making styles and organizational culture, defy attempts at formal engineering specification, as the voluminous literature on the disjunction between formal and informal structures suggests. For these reasons, it will often prove very difficult to resurrect any form of organization once it has ceased to operate. Therefore, reductions in organizational diversity imply losses of organized information about how to produce in certain environments.

A stock of alternative forms has value for a society whenever the future is uncertain. A society that relies on a few organizational forms may thrive for a time; but once the environment changes, such a society faces serious problems until existing organizations are reshaped or new organizational forms are created. Reorganization is costly and may not work at all because it threatens the interests of powerful coalitions within organizations. Relying on new organizations is problematic because such organizations are fragile. Therefore, the time it takes to adapt to the new conditions may be very long. A system with greater organizational diversity has a higher probability of having in hand some form that does a reasonably satisfactory job of dealing with the changed environmental conditions. Adaptation in such a system means reallocating resources from one type of existing organization to another, either by command or by market mechanisms, rather than trying to identify and create appropriate organizational forms.

The claim that diversity of organizational forms is a useful hedge against uncertain future environmental changes is a classic evolutionary argument. For example, it parallels an argument that has been made against going overboard with the so-called green revolution in agriculture. The spread of single strains of crops implies a great reduction in genetic diversity, which may prove problematic if new kinds of pests arise to which the "miracle" crops are vulnerable. The stock of existing solutions would decline.

Organizational diversity affects society in another way. Since careers are played out in organizations, the distribution of opportunities for individual achievement depends on the distribution of organizational forms. When diversity is high, individuals with different backgrounds, tastes, and skills are more likely to find organizational affiliations that match their own qualities and interests. For example, the fact that most industries in the United States contain many small businesses allows ethnic and immigrant communities to create ethnic enclaves within which to develop protected career paths (Wilson and Portes 1980). The presence of such ethnic niches in the economy, one kind of organizational diversity, has apparently proved crucial to the economic success of at least some ethnic communities.

Hannan (1988a) suggests that the diversity of careers in a society is proportional to the diversity of organizations offering employment. The diversity of possible career lines seems likely to have consequences for the level of inequality. When few kinds of careers are possible, a few characteristics are likely to be favored; individuals with these characteristics do well but others do not. As the diversity of possible careers increases, the likelihood that a few characteristics will dominate the processes leading to success declines. That is, increases in the diversity of organizations lead to increases in the diversity of careers, which in turn decreases inequality.

Diversity is also sometimes valued in its own right. Consider the case of the daily press. It is widely agreed in this country that diversity of editorial opinion is a social good and should not be sacrificed to economies of business concentration in the industry. Similar views pertain to the world of schooling, higher education, research laboratories, and all sorts of organizations whose outputs are largely symbolic or cultural.

How do social, economic, and political environments affect organizational diversity? Explaining variations in diversity has much in common with any effort to explain variability in the world of organizations. However, ecological perspectives emphasize the fact that much of the observed variability of organizations comes in a relatively small number of packages, which we call *organizational forms* (see Chapter 3). Thus explaining variations in diversity means explaining both the variation within forms and the variations between forms.

Almost all attempts to answer questions about the effects of social environments on organizational diversity focus on the controlling role of uncertainty. Stable and certain environments almost surely generate low levels of diversity. The main theoretical questions concern the manner in which environmental uncertainty affects diversity. The theoretical and empirical work reported here addresses the effects of environmental variability on organizational diversity from several points of view.

To this point we have discussed organizational dynamics with reference to processes of social change. We think that a population ecology perspective offers novel insights about the nature of organizational change and the role of organizations in broad processes of social change. There are other reasons for developing population ecology theories of organizations, however.

An obvious motivation for developing an ecology of organizations is an interest in the causes of the vital events: organizational foundings and failures. No one would argue that such events are rare; and few would claim that they are random. Yet organizational theory has little to say about when such events happen, and why.

Another motivation flows from a concern with building links between organization theory and social history. Research at the population level leads naturally to a concern with history because the study of population dynamics frequently requires analysis over long periods of time. The life expectancy of the kind of organization under study pushes the researcher to define a time frame for the study that will be long enough to capture variability in rates of founding and failure. The challenge posed by the historical context is separating replicable processes from idiosyncratic events. In later chapters we will show how quantitative analysis can be applied to the study of social processes operating over long periods of time—that is, to social history.

There is a second link between the study of organizational populations and historical research. Ecological research requires an understanding of the institutional contexts of organizational populations. Such information can come from interviewing those familiar with the organizations in question; it can come from the available historiography; and it can be gleaned from the popular press. Whatever the source, good research on the dynamics of organizational populations, which may be highly quantitative, relies on qualitative studies for realistic specification of models and useful research designs.

Finally, ecological studies of organizational populations offer potentially useful links to other branches of social science inquiry. Consider the case of organizational theory and economics. Since Cyert and March's *A Behavioral Theory of the Firm* (1963), few organizational researchers have even tried to develop organizational theory in a manner that would inform microeconomics. It seems obvious that issues of ownership concentration which preoccupy economists interested in industrial organization are population-level phenomena. If it is true that perfectly competitive markets operate differently from oligopolistic markets and monopolies, the processes by which large numbers of buyers and sellers disappear and only a few survivors persist constitute common ground between economists and organizational researchers. The relationship among efficiency, market competition, and the survival of various kinds of firms could hardly be more central to the concerns of microeconomists.

Perspectives on Organizational Change

Although organizational processes figure prominently in social change, most macrosociological theory and research make little reference to systematic research on organizations. In Chapter 2 we argue that this situation reflects the partial intellectual isolation of the field of organizational sociology from the rest of the discipline during the 1960s and 1970s. Organizational sociologists made considerable progress during this period in developing methods for analyzing variations in organizational structures and, to some extent, in developing theories to account for these variations. However, the field became preoccupied with a narrow set of *static* concerns focused mainly on the interrelations of various aspects of formal structure (and with the effects of size and technology on these characteristics). Progress in addressing these narrow issues was achieved at the expense of a retreat from concern with classic problems of the relations of organizations to society and the effects of organizations on social change and levels of inequality.

But during the later 1970s organizational sociology began to return to its roots in political sociology and more generally in macrosociology. Research has shifted from a narrow concern with internal arrangements to the fundamental questions asked earlier by Marx, Weber, Michels, and other pioneering theorists. Theory and research on organizations are once again studying (1) how social and historical transformation has affected the world of organizations, and (2) what role organizational diversity and change play in creating and shaping social change. Contributions have come from diverse directions but nonetheless suggest some common ground for debate. Recent work in population ecology has specified how social changes affect forms of organization as well as how competition shapes the diversity of forms (Hannan and Freeman 1977, 1984, 1987; Carroll 1987, 1988). Institutionalists have developed linkages between broad social norms, especially norms of formal rationality, and organizational arrangements (Meyer and Scott 1983). Recent Marxist work has noted that organizations have become key arenas in struggles for control over the labor process and that organizational structure reflects the character of this struggle (Burawoy 1979; Gordon, Edwards, and Reich 1982).

These and other important strands of organizational theory and research disagree about the processes shaping the world of organizations. The contemporary literature contains at least three broad points of view on organizational change. Each speaks to questions concerning organizational diversity and social change.

Selection Theories

The ecological theories developed in this book hold that most of the variability in the core structures of organizations comes about through the creation of new organizations and organizational forms and the demise of old ones. These perspectives argue that existing organizations, especially the largest and most powerful, rarely change strategy and structure quickly enough to keep up with the demands of uncertain, changing environments. They emphasize that major innovations in organizational strategy and structure occur early in the life histories of individual organizations and of organizational populations.

Adaptation Theories

A second view, which might be called adaptation theory, proposes that organizational variability reflects designed changes in the strategy and structure of individual organizations in response to environmental changes, threats, and opportunities. The numerous variants of this perspective differ widely on other dimensions. Contingency theories emphasize structural changes that match organizational structures to combinations of technologies and environments (Thompson 1967; Lawrence and Lorsch 1967). Resource dependence theories emphasize structural changes that neutralize sources of environmental uncertainty (Pfeffer and Salancik 1978). An institutional version of this perspective holds that organizational structures adapt rationally to prevailing normatively endorsed modes of organizing (Meyer and Scott 1983). Marxist theories of organization typically assert that organizational structures are rational solutions for capitalist owners to the problem of maintaining control over the labor process (Burawoy 1979).

All adaptation theories agree that the largest, oldest, and most powerful organizations have superior capacities for adapting to environmental circumstances. Size and power enable organizations to create specialized units to deal with emerging environmental problems. More important, these characteristics convey a capacity to intercede in the environment and to forestall or direct change.

Random Transformation Theories

The third broad perspective, which might be called random transformation theory, claims that organizations change their structures mainly in response to endogenous processes but that such changes are only loosely coupled with the desires of organizational leaders and with the demands and threats of environments (March and Olsen 1976). This view emphasizes the ubiquity of organizational change and the fact that it is usually random with respect to both the goals of the organization and the demands of the environment.

Progress in explaining organizational diversity and change requires understanding both the nature of organizational change and the degree to which it can be planned and controlled. In this book we concentrate mainly on the first issue: does most of the observed variability in organizational features reflect changes in existing organizations, whether planned or not, or does it reflect changes in populations, with relatively inert organizations replacing one another? In other words, does change in major features of organizations over time reflect mainly adaptation or selection and replacement?

There is a subtle relation between adaptation and selection that depends crucially on the choice of level of analysis. Adaptive learning for individuals usually consists of selection among behavioral responses. Adaptation for a population involves selection among members. More generally, processes involving selection can usually be recast at a higher level of analysis as adaptation processes. However, once the unit of analysis is chosen there is no ambiguity in distinguishing selection from adaptation.

The Demography and Ecology of Organizations

Ecological analysis is appropriate when organizations are subject to strong inertial pressures and face changeable, uncertain environments. Under these conditions there are strong parallels between processes of change in organizational populations and in biotic populations. In such cases it may be useful to eschew the typical social-scientific preoccupation with single organizations and their environments (and the associated predilection to reason anthropomorphically about organizations) and instead concentrate on analyzing selection and replacement in *populations* of organizations. As we try to demonstrate, such a shift in focus opens new and interesting questions.

The population ecology perspective concentrates on the sources of variability and homogeneity of organizational forms. It considers the rise of new organizational forms and the demise or transformation of existing ones. In doing so, it pays considerable attention to population dynamics, especially the processes of competition among diverse organizations for limited resources such as membership, capital, and legitimacy.

A general treatment of the dynamics of the relations between organizations and environments involves analysis at several levels of complexity.

The first level, which concerns the *demography of organizations*,[1] considers variations in vital rates for organizational populations: founding rates, merger rates, and disbanding rates. It considers variations in these rates both over time and between populations and seeks to identify basic regularities in such rates. It also tries to relate variations in the rates to patterns of change in environments. Surprisingly, organizational researchers have devoted little attention to the demography of organizational populations. Thus there is little well-established theory and research on which to base more complicated models of organizational ecology. For this reason we devote considerable attention to establishing demographic baseline models on which to ground ecological and evolutionary models.

The second level, which concerns the *population ecology of organizations*, attempts to link vital rates between populations. Instead of considering each organizational population as an autonomous unit facing its environment, population ecology models describe how founding rates and mortality rates are affected by the presence and density of other populations of organizations. In other words, this kind of analysis tries to accommodate the view that the environments of organizations are not purely exogenous but are comprised of other organizational populations. Thus, population ecology addresses the *interactive* character of organizational change.

A pattern of ecological dynamics can arise for several reasons. Consider the case of differentials in selection, the balance of foundings and mortality. The growth and decline of populations may reflect the strategic responses of managers and leaders to changing environmental conditions. They may also reflect imitation of successful organizations, or the spread of organizational fads from schools of management or professional societies. Alternatively, the patterns of changing numbers might reflect differences in survival chances (or growth rates) of structurally inert organizational forms facing changing environments. Whether a given pattern of selection reflects planned adaptation, social imitation, or organizational competition for scarce resources is a sociologically interesting question.

The third level concerns the *community ecology of organizations*. A community of organizations is a set of interacting populations. Some analysts refer to such communities as organizational fields (Warren 1967) or as societal sectors (Meyer and Scott 1983). A typical community of organizations in industrial settings is composed of populations of firms, populations

1. We refer here to the demography of organizational populations rather than to the demography of the flow of members through a set of ranks in an organization—the sense in which Stinchcombe et al. (1968) and Pfeffer (1983) use the term.

of labor unions, and populations of regulatory agencies. Community ecology investigates the evolution of patterns of community structure. These patterns are usually represented in the pattern of links among constituent populations. That is, community ecology considers how the links between and among populations affect the likelihood of persistence of the community as a whole.

Although we work at all three levels, this book devotes the most attention to demographic and population ecological processes. This emphasis reflects our belief that development of a community ecology of organizations presumes knowledge of the other two ecological processes.

Population Thinking

The unit of observation in the studies we report is the individual organization. We follow the life histories of individual members of organizational populations, studying events such as founding, disbanding, and merger. The formal statistical analyses applied to such histories may look little different from analyses designed to test propositions at the level of the individual organization. In what sense do the analyses address questions stated at the *population* level?

Consider the case of organizational mortality, which plays a prominent role in ecological research. Social scientists want to understand determinants of organizational longevity for various practical and theoretical reasons (see the review by Carroll 1984). To this end, they collect life histories on samples (or whole populations) of organizations and estimate the effects of various covariates on disbanding rates. They tend to find, for example, that age has a powerful effect on disbanding rates for many kinds of organizations. The reasons advanced to explain this fact typically adduce explanations at the level of the individual organization, such as collective learning or development of trust within work teams (Stinchcombe 1965).

Recent analyses of mortality processes from a population ecology perspective also specify dependence on age and use many of the standard covariates. Does the structure of these analyses imply that the unit of analysis is really the individual organization? Admittedly population ecologists seek to understand demographic regularities in the rates at which vital events occur to organizations. Yet our interest does not lie in explaining organizational mortality per se. Rather we want to understand the dynamics of organizational diversity, how social changes affect the mix of organizations in society and vice versa. Analyses of mortality patterns in populations provide only one ingredient for an explanation of the dynamics of diversity. Information about mortality patterns must be combined with similar information about other vital rates in order to make valid inferences about diversity.

Diversity of forms is a property of a population or a community of organizations. In seeking to explain the dynamics of diversity, population ecologists develop propositions about processes holding at the population level. It is in this sense that the population is the unit of analysis.

Explanation of organizational variability and change with reference to selection processes is confusing to some because it seems to turn the usual logic of causal analysis on its head. Causal analysis at the organizational level examines whether the presence (or level) of some organizational characteristic (such as size) affects the likelihood that some other characteristic (or level) of another variable (such as structural differentiation) will occur. Selection analysis explores whether the prevalence of organizational characteristics and their joint distributions are governed by their links to rates of foundings, disbandings, mergers, and changes in forms. In other words, selection analysis asks whether these vital rates control the relation between the distribution of attributes at one time and that at a later time.

In the simplest case, an organizational characteristic may affect one or more of the rates. Such variables are treated in the statistical analysis as the causal factors affecting the rates. Yet at the same time they are *outcomes* to be explained—the fact that an organizational characteristic affects the rates explains variations in the prevalence of that characteristic. Ecologists are generally less interested in mortality processes per se than in their implications for distributions of organizational characteristics.

Reference to selection processes can also explain the prevalence of characteristics that do not affect vital rates directly but are associated with characteristics that do. Consider Stinchcombe's (1965) observation that organizational forms tend to incorporate and retain packages of characteristics that are common when the form emerges. Presumably only some elements in the package affect the vital rates. Analysts attempting to uncover static causal relations among the elements in the package may be badly misled if they do not realize that the items covary because they are linked in a selection process. If Stinchcombe is right, the covariation of organizational characteristics may often reflect the vagaries of selection processes rather than causal relations among the variables themselves. That is, a set of structural characteristics may covary today only because they happened to be associated at an earlier time with a characteristic that

confers strong survival advantages. In this sense, selection analysis can be a useful supplement for—and sometimes corrective to—static causal explanations at the level of individual organizations.

Evolution of Organizational Forms

The view that selection processes govern the dynamics of organizational diversity shades naturally into a Darwinian evolutionary position. Such a position claims that long-run changes in organizational diversity reflect the accumulated effects of short-run differences in net mortality rates of populations facing limited resource environments. Moving from a population ecology of organizations to a theory of organizational evolution involves an extra step, linking long-term patterns of change to short-run variations or even to current cross-sectional patterns. In other words, it involves specifying how the various short-run processes combine to produce change in organizational characteristics over long periods of time.

Before discussing the possible advantages of developing evolutionary theories of organizations, it is necessary to clarify the meanings of evolution and evolutionary theory in this context. The term "evolution" is used in at least two ways in the biological sciences. Sewell Wright (1968, p. 1), one of the three great founders of population genetics, states one meaning as follows: "[Evolution] is not used to indicate all kinds of change . . . There is ceaseless change on the surface of the ocean, but this is not an evolutionary process. Evolution always involves to some extent the opposite idea of persistence. It always refers, in short, to processes of cumulative change." The term is also used frequently to refer to almost any kind of transformation, cumulative or not. The geneticist Richard Lewontin (1974, p. 6), who has written widely on the logical structure of evolutionary arguments, uses this broader conception, claiming that an evolutionary perspective "mean[s] that we are interested in the change of state of some universe in time. Whether we look at the evolution of societies, languages, species, geological features or stars, there is a formal representation that is common to all." The formal representation consists of laws of transformation that tell how to predict the later state of a system from knowledge of earlier states. Note that this definition excludes neither cyclical change nor random motion from the scope of evolutionary change. If evolutionary change is given this broad denotation, there can be little debate about the value of evolutionary analysis in organizational research. In this sense evolutionary analysis just means analysis of change. Even the narrower definition of evolution as cumulative change raises few problems in organizational applications since most researchers agree that change in organizational populations is cumulative. The fact that evolutionary analysis is seen as so problematic in the kind of studies we consider must reflect some additional meanings and connotations of the term "evolutionary theory."

In the specific context of Darwinism, evolutionary theory means at least three things. The founders of the so-called Modern Synthesis (of Darwinian evolutionary theory and Mendelian population genetics) often applied a very limited meaning to the term. They held that Darwin argued convincingly the *fact* of evolution and provided a compelling theoretical explanation—natural selection—for the fact (see, for example, Huxley 1944). In this interpretation, evolution refers to a set of empirical assertions about historical patterns of change in the biotic world. Natural selection provides a set of rules that link earlier and later distributions. In this sense, evolutionary theory is theory that tries to explain these empirical facts.

Darwin's work also contained a theoretical claim about the timelessness of the underlying processes. Theodosius Dobzhansky (1951, pp. 7–8), who played a key role in forming the Modern Synthesis from the side of population genetics, summarizes the Darwinian position by claiming that the theory of evolution by natural selection posits that "(1) the beings now living have descended from different beings which have lived in the past; (2) the discontinuous variations observed at the present time . . . have arisen gradually . . . (3) all these changes have arisen from causes which now continue to be in operation and which therefore can be studied experimentally." In this way, the program of evolutionary biology combines factual assertions about the origins and change of biotic forms with theoretical claims about the nature of the process. Thus a second definition of evolutionary theory is as a research program combining these factual statements and a particular view on the nature of change.

Finally, evolution is sometimes equated with natural selection. But natural selection is not the only rule of biotic change. In fact, R. A. Fisher (1930, p. 1) felt compelled to begin his *Genetical Theory of Natural Selection* with the statement, "Natural selection is not Evolution." Natural selection is a process by which evolutionary change comes about, but it is only one such process. Evolutionary change in biotic populations also comes about through random genetic events such as genetic drift and founder effects. Thus organic evolution is broader than natural selection.

Nonetheless, when biologists assert that they are developing evolutionary theories (as when population ecology became infused with evolutionary theory during the 1960s), they often mean to signal that they are invoking specific transmission processes, usually Mendelian inheritance under random mating, and a natural selection process. The transmission mechanism accounts for the continuity or cumulative character of the process.[2]

Natural selection, as it is actually used in evolutionary population biology, serves mainly as an *optimization process*. In fact, the reasoning that underlies much evolutionary biology often strikes social scientists as strongly reminiscent of neoclassical economics. Evolutionary population biologists wish to provide a theoretical explanation for observed cross-sectional patterns in terms of some underlying mechanism. They invoke natural selection as an optimizing principle that selects one, or perhaps a few, outcomes from the broad range of outcomes that might be consistent with the genetic transmission mechanism. The work of sociobiologists depends heavily on such optimization procedures. (See Oster and Wilson 1978 for a penetrating discussion of the limitations of such analysis for population biology.) Thus a third possible definition of evolutionary theory is a theory of change that depends on the maximization of fitness under some specified transmission mechanism, such as Mendelian inheritance. Fitness means the rate at which genotypes produce copies of themselves across generations. Because of the simplicity of the transmission mechanism in the biotic case, fitness for any population defined in terms of phenotypes can be defined as the net mortality rate: the ratio of birth rates to death rates.

In which of these meanings is our work evolutionary? With regard to the first meaning of the term—evolution as a factual statement about chains of descent—we do describe organizational change as evolutionary. In particular, we reject the view that the diversity of organizational structures at any time reflects only recent adaptations of these organizations in favor of the view that diversity reflects a long history of foundings and disbandings of organizations with fairly unchanging structures. In this narrow sense, our accounts are decidedly Darwinian.

We also accept the broad theoretical claim of the Darwinian evolutionary program. We argue that current qualitative differences between forms and the historical succession of forms can be explained by the same principles or processes. In particular, we think that the *processes* of change are general. Insofar as these processes are involved, organizational change has a timeless, ahistorical quality that permits analysts to work either forward or backward in time, to conduct both retrospective and prospective studies

2. It rarely gives any precise information about the details of the process since change in observable characters occurs at the phenotypic level, and the links between phenotypic characters and genes are all but unknown for most kinds of phenomena, especially so-called quantitative characters. See Roughgarden (1979).

in seeking to understand the processes that govern organizational diversity.[3]

Our views on the third aspect of evolutionary argument, that natural selection is an optimization process and that cross-sectional patterns can be explained as the outcomes of such a process, are more complicated. In fact we do think that selection in organizational populations is systematic, that various kinds of organizations differ in their survival chances, and that selection capitalizes on such differences. To argue otherwise implies that there is no disciplined way to relate environmental events to changes in organizational populations. However, we are not comfortable simply invoking optimization arguments. These arguments depend on an equilibrium assumption, the assumption that the selection processes have worked themselves out. We think that this assumption is rarely plausible for populations of organizations in societies exposed to continuing social changes.[4] Instead of trying to explain patterns in cross sections using optimization arguments, we look directly at dynamics. That is, we examine the structure of selection processes directly. It is only when we try to draw broader sociological implications from patterns of selection that we approach this optimizing style of reasoning.

To summarize the argument to this point, our work approximates a Malthusian–Darwinian position on the nature of change in organizational populations over time. We think that the current diversity of organizational forms reflects the cumulative effect of a long history of variation and selection, including the consequences of founding processes, mortality processes, and merger processes. We also think that organizational selection processes have general properties that hold across historical periods.

However, we do not have anything resembling a fully developed evolutionary theory of organizational change. Although we have learned a good deal about selection processes, we still know very little about the other side of the evolutionary process, the structures of inheritance and transmission. Sociology does not have a simple, well-understood transmission process analogous to Mendelian genetics. It is clear that transmission processes in the organizational world are much more complex than those in

3. As we argue in subsequent chapters, these claims are meaningful only when the analyst has properly defined organizational forms and the characteristics of relevant environments. That is, we argue that both the definitions of forms and of the properties of environments may be historically specific. In this sense, evolutionary analysis of change in organizational populations combines ahistorical and historical elements.

4. A variety of reasons for doubting the utility of equilibrium assumptions in the study of social processes are discussed by Tuma and Hannan (1984, chap. 1).

the biotic world. Processes of transmission of cultural information are not unitary (see Cavalli-Sforza and Feldman 1981; Boyd and Richardson 1985). Social and cultural information passes in many different directions among generations, and it is not nearly as invariant across transmissions as genetic information. It is not possible to specify a simple transmission mechanism by which the ability to construct organizations of a given type is passed along among individuals and social groups. Thus our evolutionary treatment of organizational change is partial at best; it attends mainly to selection in organizational populations.

So far we have emphasized the effects of selection on diversity. Darwinian theory tries to do more than explain variations in biotic diversity. The second major concern of Darwinian theories of evolution by natural selection is *adaptation*, the processes by which biotic forms come to be finely tuned to their environments. Darwin sought a naturalistic explanation for the apparent perfection of so much biotic adaptation, which had been invoked for centuries as a prime proof of the existence of divine intervention in speciation. Part of the genius of Darwin's theory concerns the way in which it links diversity and adaptation: the Malthusian notion of struggle for finite resources implies that selection operates on existing diversity to provide continually better solutions to problems of biotic adaptation.

The portion of Darwin's theoretical structure pertaining to adaptation has been the most troublesome when the ideas are applied to social science problems. It has been tempting for evolutionists to assume that the forms of life that exist or persist in a system are well adapted simply by virtue of their persistence. But such arguments affirm the consequent in Darwin's argument. Selection processes can only work on available diversity; if no good designs are tried, selection cannot cause good designs to proliferate. As Lewontin (1978, p. 222) put it, "The relation between adaptation and natural selection does not go both ways. Whereas greater relative adaptation leads to natural selection, natural selection does not necessarily lead to greater adaptation." Just as adaptation is relative, so too is fitness. If a set of forms facing a particular environment differ in the efficiency with which they can extract resources, prey on other forms, resist predation, or spin off copies of themselves, natural selection processes favor such forms. Such processes lead to numerical domination of the relatively more fit forms over time if the environment does not change. However, an observable population may be very far from ideal in the sense of adaptation, either because good designs have not yet been exposed to selection or because the environment keeps changing faster than the set of organizations can change. Therefore, it is extremely important to avoid the panglossian assumption that selection processes somehow magically produce high levels of adaptation.

One of the chief objections to the use of Darwinian theories in the organizational world turns on the limited nature of the adaptation process. This objection concerns the limited role that *conscious* adaptation plays in neo-Darwinian theories. Most organizational theorists assume that change is Lamarckian, that major changes in the forms of organizations come about through learning and imitation. Many kinds of organizations commit resources to learning; organizations often seek to copy the forms of their more successful competitors. In a rough sense, organizations make copies of themselves either by setting up new organizations, by losing or expelling personnel with the requisite knowledge to copy the form, or by invoking imitation. Nelson and Winter (1982, p. 11) in describing their theory of evolutionary change in organizational populations note that: "Our theory is unabashedly Lamarckian: it contemplates both the 'inheritance' of acquired characteristics and the timely appearance of variation under the stimulus of adversity."

The line of theory we develop builds on the assumption that change in core features of organizational populations is more Darwinian than Lamarckian. It argues that inertial pressures prevent most organizations from radically changing strategies and structures. Only the most concrete features of technique can be easily copied and inserted into ongoing organizations. Moreover, there are density-dependent constraints on adaptation by individual organizations: although it may be in the interests of the leaders of many organizations to adopt a certain strategy, the carrying capacity for organizations with that strategy is often quite limited. Only a few can succeed in exploiting such a strategy, and those in the vanguard (and perhaps those who follow the vanguard closely) have decided advantages.

Even when actors strive to cope with their environments, action may be random with respect to adaptation as long as the environments are highly uncertain or the connections between means and ends are not well understood. It is the *match* between action and environmental outcomes that must be random on the average for selection models to apply. In a world of high uncertainty, adaptive efforts by individuals may turn out to be essentially random with respect to future value.

The realism of Darwinian mechanisms for explaining change in organizational populations also turns on the degree to which change in organizational structures can be controlled. Suppose that leaders of organizations learn to anticipate the future and adapt organizational strategies accordingly. Suppose further that organizations passively act out the intentions of their leaders. Then organizational adaptations would be largely nonrandom with respect to future states of the environment; the Lamarckian image applies.

A growing number of organizational theorists and researchers argue that much organizational change is largely uncontrolled and that the consequences of designed structural changes are difficult to anticipate. If this is so, organizations staffed by rational planners may behave essentially randomly with respect to adaptation. In other words, organizational outcomes are often decoupled from individual intentions. Therefore, it is not enough to ask whether individual humans learn and plan rationally for an uncertain future. One must ask whether organizations as collective actors display the same capacities.

The applicability of Darwinian arguments to changes in organizational populations thus depends partly on the tightness of coupling between individual intentions and organizational outcomes. At least two well-known situations generate weak relations between intentions and outcomes: diversity of interest among members and uncertainty about means-ends connections. When members of an organization have diverse interests, organizational outcomes depend heavily on internal politics, on the balance of power among the constituencies. When such an organization faces an external problem, which action will be taken, if any, depends as much on the coalition structure of the organization as on the contributions of alternative actions to organizational survival or growth. In such situations outcomes cannot easily be matched rationally to changing environments. When the connections between means and ends are uncertain, carefully designed adaptations may have completely unexpected consequences. Moreover, short-run consequences may often differ greatly from long-run consequences. In such cases, it does not seem realistic to assume a high degree of congruence between designs and outcomes.

Thus it may be useful in analyzing patterns of long-term change in organizational forms to employ models that incorporate Darwinian mechanisms rather than Lamarckian ones. The facts that members of organizations plan rationally for change and that organizations often develop structures designed to plan and implement change do not necessarily undercut the value of this view. As long as organizations are political coalitions and environmental change tends to be highly uncertain, the Darwinian theories we propose may clarify the relationships between organizational diversity and environmental change.

Dynamic and Comparative Analysis

We think that research on organizational diversity must attend to dynamics and must analyze the entire range of variation within types of organizations. The remainder of this chapter summarizes these themes and previews the approach that we use in empirical analyses reported in Part III.

Dynamics

The diversity of organizations in society depends on both the *number* of organizational forms and the *distribution* of organizations over forms. The diversity of a collection of organizations in a society can increase either because new forms are created or adopted or because the distribution of organizations over forms becomes more uniform. Social forces can affect diversity either by affecting the number of forms in use or by affecting the relative abundances of the various forms. The two dimensions of diversity are related at the extreme: when the number of organizations with a certain form is zero, the form does not exist in the system. However, ecological processes may differ in strength as they affect the number of forms and the relative abundances of forms. Thus it is useful to keep these two dimensions of diversity conceptually and analytically distinct.

Because organizational diversity has these two dimensions, analysis of the dynamics of diversity must consider a number of basic processes. First, there is the process of creating new organizational forms, including both inventing forms and borrowing forms from other systems. This process can be analyzed with reference to the establishment of abstract designs such as the rational-legal bureaucracy (Weber 1968) or the multidivisional form (Chandler 1977). It can also be analyzed with reference to more concrete, institutionalized forms such as the newspaper wire service or the comprehensive high school (Tyack 1974).

Second, there is the growth of numbers of organizations within existing forms. Interesting examples include the spread of colleges in the United States with the expanding frontier in the nineteenth century (Tewksbury 1932) and the proliferation of specific types of manufacturing firms such as semiconductor producers.

Third, some organizations adapt their core features, that is, they change from one organizational form to another. A classic example is the wholesale switch of single-gender colleges to the two-gender form during the late 1960s and 1970s. Similar changes are frequently reported in the industrial world (see Miles 1982, for example).

Fourth, there is the demise of organizations within populations. There are two quite different processes by which organizations cease to exist as corporate actors: disbanding and merger. Examples of disbanding are routine business failures (Wedervang 1965), closings of public institutions like prisons and mental hospitals, and the withering away of protest movements (Gamson 1975). Examples of merger include cases in which manufacturing firms purchase suppliers and distributors (see Chandler 1977; Williamson 1975) and the amalgamation of political parties.

Finally, there is the disappearance of entire organizational forms, which occurs when the number of organizations using the form reaches zero. Historically interesting examples in the United States include the demise of proprietary medical schools, utopian labor unions (Commons et al. 1927), and the party press (Schudson 1978).

Given our theoretical objectives, should we emphasize the creation of new forms and the demise of old ones, or rather the growth and decline of established sets of forms? In our empirical research we attempt to collect information on all the relevant processes. However, our theoretical work has made the most progress in pursuing the narrower questions of variations in the components of net mortality, the equivalent in organization theory of population ecology. Although we discuss the environmental factors affecting the rate at which new forms are created, this analysis is speculative.

Our approach emphasizes dynamics, the detailed processes of change in organizational populations. Almost all empirical work and most theoretical work on organizations deal with statics, with the relationships between variables in systems assumed to be at rest. Static analysis is appropriate when the systems under study are almost always in or near equilibrium. Such conditions are likely to obtain when environments are certain or stable or when the speed of adjustment of the systems is rapid relative to the rate of environmental change (Tuma and Hannan 1984). We think that both of these conditions are unlikely to hold for most kinds of organizations.

We argue that organizational selection processes favor organizations with relatively inert structures, organizations that cannot change strategy and structure as quickly as their environments can change. If inertial pressures on organizational structures are indeed strong, it is highly unlikely that a great deal can be learned from static analysis. Instead one must study the actual time paths of change in organizational populations, looking in detail at the rates at which organizations enter and leave populations and the rates at which structures are changed in response to environmental threats and opportunities.

We have followed such a strategy. The chapters in Part II outline the research designs we used to trace patterns of change over time in organizational populations and our approach to estimating causal effects using the data produced by our research designs.

Comparative Analysis

Most writing and research on organizations concentrate on the largest and most successful ones of each type. There are a number of reasons for this emphasis. One motivation for studying the largest organizations is a concern with politics in the conventional sense. The biggest and most successful organizations presumably have the strongest impacts on the larger social structure. Given limited time and resources, one might expect to learn more about the impact of organizations on society by studying the ''Fortune 500'' than by studying more representative samples of firms.

A second motivation is practical: more information is usually available on the largest and most successful organizations. It is very difficult to gather information systematically on organizations with brief lifetimes. A third motivation is normative. Some analysts, especially those who want to promulgate a certain organizational form, want to direct attention to the most successful instances of the form as models for others. For example, Peters and Waterman (1982) draw conclusions about appropriate ways to organize from intense study of 62 of America's most successful firms. Likewise, Kanter (1983) draws lessons about success in a changing technical environment from cases on a few of the largest and most solvent firms in the country. Thus organizational analysts, researchers, and prophets are drawn to the study of the biggest and longest-lived organizations.

Although it may seem reasonable to concentrate effort on the current winners, this is almost always a mistake if one wants to learn about the processes that create success and failure. The problem is that all key comparisons—between winners and losers—are *implicit*. Winners may have a certain structural feature; but how does one know that the losers did not have it as well? This is an instance of a very general methodological problem called *sampling on the dependent variable* or *sample selection bias* (see, for example, Heckman 1979; Berk 1983). The general result is that choosing a sample on the basis of values of the dependent variable causes estimates of causal effects to be biased. Thus restricting a study of profitability to the most profitable firms distorts inferences about the conditions producing success; it biases estimates of the effects of all independent variables on the rate of profit. Similarly, it is a mistake to make inferences about risk of business failure from studies of long-lived organizations.

The popularized literature on organizations typically glorifies one form of organization as best. Recent examples include Ouchi's (1981) "theory Z" and Kanter's (1983) "organic" organization. From an ecological perspective, the search for the one best organizational form is misguided. Whether a given form is superior to another depends upon the structure of the relevant environments. Just because some form has been successful in one country or in one industry at some time does not mean that it would be useful the next year under other conditions. In fact, ecological-evolutionary theory suggests that uncertain, volatile environments will support diverse organizational forms and that the apparent winners will fluctuate from time to time as conditions change. A potential benefit of a fully developed ecology of organizations would be the setting of limits on the claims that a given structure is best.

Our research designs make an effort to avoid sample selection bias. We chose to study populations of organizations for which it was possible to collect life histories on both large and long-lived and small and short-lived organizations. The use of such data to estimate parameters of dynamic models is a distinguishing characteristic of the empirical work reported in Part III.

2 | Theoretical Background

This chapter describes the relationship between organizational ecology and other approaches to organizational research. It begins by describing the development of organizational research and its isolation from other branches of sociology. This is useful background because much contemporary theory and research on organizations, including our own, can be seen as efforts to reduce that isolation. The second part of the chapter discusses points of agreement and disagreement between an ecological theory of organizations and other contemporary approaches. The main points of disagreement concern levels of analysis and mechanisms of change. As we discussed in the previous chapter, our ecological approach emphasizes selection and replacement at the population level. The alternative contemporary approaches emphasize adaptation by existing organizations. The third part of the chapter discusses controversies that have arisen over efforts to introduce population thinking and selection logic into the sociology of organizations. The final section discusses similar controversies concerning applications of ecological theory to questions of business strategy.

Organization Theory and Sociology: Missing Connections

The sociology of organizations began with the study of bureaucracy in government, political parties, and labor unions. The hallmark of the classic tradition of organizational analysis in sociology is the assumption that the rise of bureaucratic organization was crucial in shaping modern societies. As Scott (1987, pp. 4–5) put it: "The two great German sociologists, Max Weber and Robert Michels, were among the first to insist that the central political issue for all modern societies was no longer what type of economic structure prevailed—whether capitalist, socialist, or communist—but the increasing dominance of public bureaucracy over the ostensible political leaders." These themes did not affect American sociology of organizations until shortly after World War II. In the meantime, social science research on organizations consisted mainly of research on management[1] and concrete studies of particular kinds of organizations, such as prisons, schools, and armies, which emphasized the peculiarities of each type rather than generic organizational processes.

The major revival of interest in generic organizational processes began mainly at Columbia University, among colleagues and students of Robert K. Merton (see, for example, Merton et al. 1952), and at the Carnegie Institute of Technology, now Carnegie–Mellon University, among colleagues and students of Herbert A. Simon and James G. March (see Scott 1987). Merton and his students emphasized the impact of bureaucracy, both public and private, on its participants, clients, and the broader community. The organizational theorists at Carnegie (Simon 1957; March and Simon 1958; Cyert and March 1963) developed general theories of decision-making within organizations. Both research groups emphasized connections with mainstream work in the social sciences, including sociology, political science, and economics.

During the 1960s the theoretical purview of organizational theory and research expanded considerably, but, paradoxically, the subject began to become isolated from the mainstream in sociology (and other social sciences). The main thrust of this period was a consideration of the processes by which organizations adapt to changing and uncertain environments. Perrow (1961, 1967) and Thompson (1967) explored how organizations adjust to demands imposed by variations and uncertainties in technical and environmental circumstances, drawing heavily on the theories of the Columbia and Carnegie-Mellon schools. Burns and Stalker (1961) argued that bureaucratic or "mechanistic" systems of production tend to break down in the face of complex and changing technologies and tend to be replaced with more fluid "organic" systems of production.[2] Lawrence and Lorsch

1. The most influential developments in this period were Taylor's (1911) scientific management and the human relations approach of Roethlisberger and Dickson (1939), Mayo (1945), and others (see Mouzelis 1968).
2. It is instructive to note that Burns and Stalker found only one instance of an organic system in a situation in which this should have been the appropriate form of organization. Their book is essentially an analysis of why organizations that *ought* to change to organic systems fail to do so, even when there is high agreement among their managers that they should move in that direction.

(1967) developed a perspective they called contingency theory. According to this view, environmental uncertainty pulls organizations in different directions at once as different parts of the organization seek to adjust to their own subenvironments. Such differentiated adaptation creates problems of integration, which in turn lead to the development of new structures. Hage and Aiken (1970) noted similar responses by social service organizations facing uncertainty from changes in programs or from the operation of joint programs with other organizations. The Aston group (see, for example, Pugh et al. 1969), following Woodward (1965), noted that the variability and uncertainty in the flow of work have effects on organizational structure that are similar to those of environmental uncertainties.

These analysts and many others developed the imagery of a set of organizations that frequently fine tune structures in order to adjust to the constraints arising from complex technologies and variable, uncertain environments. The dominant view was that complex, changing technologies and complex relationships with other organizations produce uncertainties that cause rigid, bureaucratic structures to break down and to be replaced with more flexible structures. However, this body of work sought to explain the match between structure and environment as the consequence of adaptive change on the part of existing organizations. The most basic premise of this work is that organizations adjust their strategies and structures to match the contingencies of the flow of work and of the external environment.

For the most part, this stream of work views volatility, complexity, and uncertainty as the causes of organizational change. Organizations are not regarded as passive actors, but the actions of their managers are seen as largely reactive. Yet some leading branches of organizational theory in this period emphasize the proactive behavior of organizations. The most notable example is resource dependence theory, which explains organizational structure as the result of the strategic actions taken by managers to reduce dependence on other organizations that provide key resources (Pfeffer and Salancik 1978). This approach views organizational structure as depending more on the outcomes of power struggles and political contests within and between organizations than on considerations of efficiency. However, like the other adaptation theories, resource dependence theory assumes that major structural features of organizations reflect adaptive changes by existing organizations to changing sets of dependencies.

These intellectual developments established organizational research as a specialty not only in departments of sociology but in various professional schools. However, there was a price. Organizational theory and research lost much of their relevance for research on social organization and change. Organizational theorists in the 1960s and 1970s simply failed to make explicit the links between organizational processes and general processes of social organization and change. Consider, for example, the developments during the same period in the study of social stratification. The dominant status attainment approach treated individuals as facing a generalized occupational structure that did not seem to include the firms that hire, promote, and fire people and pay them wages (Blau and Duncan 1967; Duncan, Featherman, and Duncan 1972). The failure to rely on organizational mechanisms is striking, because one of the founders of the status attainment approach was Peter Blau. The point is not that researchers in the status attainment tradition were parochial but that organization theory had become largely irrelevant to broader sociological concerns.

A related reason for the growing isolation of organizational theory and research was their static quality. Earlier work, especially that of the Columbia school, was based on historical case studies or field research, whereas later research tended to use surveys of samples of organizations. Studying samples of organizations over time requires so much effort and so many resources that cross-sectional research became the norm. And cross-sectional analysis requires an assumption of aggregate equilibrium that is dubious in most settings.

Just as organizational research drifted into this static posture, theories of social organization began to emphasize dynamic issues. For example, analyses of economic and social change (Wallerstein 1974), social movements and collective violence (Tilly 1978), and revolt (Paige 1975) all addressed fundamental issues of change.[3] Each of these studies emphasized the generation of social power through organization, and none relied explicitly on the literature on organizations. Organization theory and research had become divorced from theories of social change, political power, and the state.

A third source of isolation was a common reliance on anthropomorphic imagery. To cite a prominent example, organizations were said to *enact* their environments: "When an organization wants to see things, it usually positions itself so that in seeing things it is also seen" (Weick 1979, p. 168). Organizations, like people, supposedly create their environments by imposing order on information about the environment. The imagery of enactment suggests that the environment is in the eye of the beholder, an organi-

---

3. Tuma and Hannan (1984, chap. 1) discuss these issues in detail.

zational dream. If organizations are understood to relate to social, economic, and political changes in such a surreal way, they can hardly shape the broader processes.

A fourth cause of the trend toward isolation was the growing importance that organization theory attributed to managers. The 1970s saw a sharp change from the older tradition of Barnard (1938), Selznick (1957), and others who viewed business strategy, defined as an organization's domain and its characteristic ways of serving that domain, as more likely to be shaped at the bottom of organizations than at the top. According to this earlier perspective, successful leaders cultivate and systematize ideas developed within the organization instead of imposing strategies. But during the 1960s and 1970s, many leading analysts began to view organizations as merely the tools used by managers in taking strategic action to advance their interests.

When organizational structures are depicted as simple tools, organizations become passive bystanders in the processes of social change. Leaders, interest groups, and social classes that control organizations take action using organizations as tools; but the organizational milieu plays no important role in shaping either the goals or the collective actions. If all that the sociology of organizations has to offer is a set of managerial theories, then theorists intent on explaining social, political, or economic change can safely ignore the role of organization. This seems to be exactly what happened in the 1970s.

With the rise of a managerial emphasis, the role given to unplanned and unconscious actions in organizational theory diminished. Informal organization and latent functions became peripheral ideas. Research on organizations and business strategy is particularly noteworthy in its depiction of organizations as consciously designed for the pursuit of explicit ends; these studies tend to view strategy as the willful choice of top managers (Child 1972). Consider, for example, Miles's (1982) study of the adaptive behavior of the "Big Six" tobacco companies to the threat posed by the growing knowledge that smoking causes cancer. The Big Six reacted by diversifying into other industries. Miles takes this example as evidence that our approach is misguided, that radical changes in strategy are common and that inertial forces are weak.

But Miles studied only large, successful organizations, and he appears to have been misled by sample selection bias. For example, he failed to note that the tobacco business was extremely volatile over the period of his study. According to Standard and Poor's (*Poor's Register* 1956, 1966, 1976, 1986), of the 78 companies in the U.S. tobacco business in 1956, 49 had left the industry by 1986, which is consistent with Miles's account of adaptive adjustment. However, only 12 of the 49 continued operations in other business lines; the remaining 37 firms, nearly half of the original number, had disappeared by 1986.[4] So adapting to environmental threat by diversifying to include business in other industries has apparently been a rather rare phenomenon in the industry that Miles proposes as an exemplar of adaptation.[5]

Another body of literature with a similar rationalist flavor is the closed-system structuralism of the early 1970s. This research program sought to find general laws of organization by concentrating on the relationship between size and structural differentiation (Blau and Schoenherr 1971; Meyer 1972). But this search for general theory seems to have taken the action out of organizations; they do not seem to *do* much of anything except grow and differentiate. So this work also gave short shrift to the implications of organizations for broader sociological concerns.

The fifth source of isolation was the failure of organization theory to take inertial forces into account. Structures that adapt swiftly and effortlessly are unlikely to shape processes of historical change. Another way of putting this is that if organizations are the building blocks of modern societies, as we asserted in the previous chapter, inertia is what gives them this quality. If organizations are plastic, then only the intentions of organizational elites matter. In other words, failure to acknowledge the strength of inertial forces and conceiving of organizations as simple tools are two sides of the same coin.

Comparison of Contemporary Approaches

As we discussed in Chapter 1, our prescription for remaking the connections between organizational theory and general theories of social organization is to take inertial forces seriously. Doing so raises doubts that organizations are flexible, simple tools. It also suggests that many of the most

---

4. We think that this legitimacy crisis, if there was one, applied to all tobacco products; and the Big Six manufactured other tobacco products besides cigarettes. If one confines attention to cigarette producers similar results obtain, albeit with smaller numbers. But because Standard and Poor's did not report cigarette manufacture as a separate category in 1956, the period covered by this comparison is also shorter.

5. It is also debatable whether diversification into other lines of business, when it is conducted by adding corporate divisions, is an *organizational* change at all. Miles provides very little evidence that the tobacco companies changed their mode of organizing in any fundamental sense.

interesting processes of change in the world of organizations occur at the population level.

At roughly the same time that we proposed a population ecology of organizations as a radical alternative to the prevailing theories of organizations (Hannan and Freeman 1974), several other groups of scholars adopted other radical alternatives. One reaction took a Marxist direction. While most researchers were exploring the implications of functionalist statics for organizations, these theorists stressed dialectics (Benson 1977). Struggles for dominance replace adaptation to environmental uncertainties as processes generating organizational change. This work clearly reached out to social scientists whose interests were not confined to organizations. Industrial sociology was resurrected as the sociology of work. Braverman (1974), Burawoy (1979), Edwards (1979), and others updated Marxist ideas of class relations and the organization of production. The core idea is that managers of capitalist enterprises choose technologies and organizational structures that minimize their dependence on the skills of workers rather than those that maximize efficiency of output (see also Clegg 1979; Clawson 1980).

Although this approach differs greatly from the mainstream theory of the 1960s and 1970s in emphasizing power and dominance rather than efficiency, it does not reject managerialism. Indeed, this line of work views managers (and the owners they represent) as having nearly unlimited power to shape organizations. Organizations are still viewed as simple tools. Only the motivations and the processes used to shape organizational behavior are changed in this approach.

A quite different response to the overemphasis of the role of efficiency considerations in shaping structure revitalized the institutional perspective of the Columbia school. Neo-institutional theory, such as that developed by Meyer and Rowan (1977) and by Meyer and Scott (1983), explains organizational structure as a response to normative prescriptions. Organizations, especially those whose outputs are difficult to measure directly, are constrained to follow such prescriptions, at least at a surface level, in order to acquire legitimacy. According to the neo-institutionalists, these normative prescriptions often have little relationship to considerations of technical efficiency. Instead of striving for efficiency, organizations seek institutional isomorphism with prevailing normative standards about appropriate structures. Structures serve a ceremonial purpose, signaling the competence and worth of the organization as a social actor.

Many versions of neo-institutional theory take pains to distance this approach from population ecology theory by insisting that institutional adaptation typically takes the form of adaptation by existing organizations (DiMaggio and Powell 1983). But there is no fundamental inconsistency between the two approaches, a point we discuss at length in subsequent chapters. Institutional processes can and often do work at the population level. New forms of organization can be created by changes in the institutional fabric of the broader society. DiMaggio (1983) shows that changing patterns of federal support created the basis for arts councils, a new coordinating body at the local level. And when conditions such as the patterns of federal funding are constant across a class of organizations, homogeneity of structure in the population of those organizations will increase. But it is not central to this kind of argument whether individual organizations change to fit this prescription or whether new organizations are created to meet the new circumstances.

At roughly the same time, then, several new perspectives were developed in reaction to the organizational theory of the 1970s. Ecological, neo-Marxian, and neo-institutional theory all emphasize links between organizations and macro-sociological processes. All deny the primacy of the logic of efficiency as a rationale for explaining organizational variability. However, the three approaches as commonly stated differ in terms of level of analysis and mechanism of change.

Controversies and Misunderstandings

The use of models based on selection processes in organizational research raises several difficult problems. The following chapters discuss a number of problems concerning the specification of organizational forms, the proper units of analysis, the shifting nature of organizational boundaries, and so forth. But these are not the problems that come to mind first when social scientists think of selection theories. Many social scientists object to the use of selection arguments because they misunderstand the principles of modern evolutionary and ecological theory. In large measure these objections refer to older, vulgarized Darwinian arguments and thus are mainly red herrings. But there are also serious scholarly controversies over the use of such models. This section discusses the leading set of controversies and misunderstandings.

Social Darwinism

Evolutionary theories in the social sciences acquired a well-earned bad name at the turn of the century. Darwin's theory of evolution by natural selection was invoked to justify inequality and unequal advantage under industrial capitalism. This point of view, called Social Darwinism, invoked Spencer's imagery, adopted by Darwin, of the survival of the fittest to argue that individuals who managed to rise to the top of the hierarchy of domination and privilege did so because they were most "fit." The most blatant error in this analogical reasoning is the equation of fitness (expected reproductive success) with social virtue. Moreover, as we pointed out in the previous chapter, this form of argument errs by affirming the consequent. Nothing in the structure of evolutionary arguments supports the assertion that the forms that proliferate are well adapted in an engineering sense. In no sense does the use of a selection logic imply that this is the best of all possible worlds or that organizations that have thrived in some period are somehow deserving of their success. Selection models insist on the importance of randomness in success.

It should be clear in what follows that our theories and empirical studies do not share a Social Darwinist perspective. Moreover, we do not find it either useful or sensible to think of much organizational change as progress. Although there appears to have been an overall historical trend toward increased organizational diversity, there is no reason for assuming that this trend is irreversible. That is, we are not convinced that change in populations of organizations reflects a unilinear evolutionary process of the sort described by sociocultural evolutionists following Spencer or by historical materialists following Marx.

Hyperefficiency

There is a long tradition in economics of assuming, often tacitly, that selection processes applying to firms in competitive markets shape the behavior of firms. This view, made most explicit by Milton Friedman (1953), recognizes that not all firms behave according to the principles of rational choice when, for example, they make production decisions or set pricing policies. However, Friedman argued, it is useful to describe firms as though they do behave as rational optimizers because selection processes systematically favor firms that do so. Those that fail to optimize will disappear either because they will be unable to compete or because they will be attractive takeover targets for managers who recognize that higher profits could be generated under more rational policies. In other words, the selection processes operating are assumed to favor *efficiency* and are assumed to be sufficiently strong that the populations in existence contain mostly efficient organizations.

The view that selection processes in markets are so strong that analysts can ignore departures from rationality and optimality has been severely criticized. Perhaps the most sustained and sophisticated attack has been mounted by Nelson and Winter (1982), who argue that selection in populations of firms does not lead unambiguously to the results usually assumed by economic theories of the firm. Yet even Nelson and Winter continue to assume that selection favors efficient organizations.

We are not convinced that selection in organizational populations invariably favors efficient producers. We think that selection processes are multidimensional and that efficiency in production and marketing, defined broadly, is only one of the relevant dimensions. In many circumstances, political ties are more important to survival than efficiency. Moreover, the most efficient producers in any cohort of new organizations are presumably the most attractive targets for takeovers. There is much anecdotal evidence that the entrepreneurs who have founded firms in recent years often plan to sell out within several years as well. The distinctive competence and efficiency of small firms is apparently often lost when they are folded into older, larger firms; thus the takeover processes may systematically eliminate efficiency, leaving only the least efficient producers (still capable of staying in business) in any cohort as freestanding organizations. For these and other reasons discussed in later chapters, we think it is unwise to assume that selection processes in organizational populations strongly favor efficiency. In this sense, we depart strongly from the economic tradition.

Gradualism

Darwinian analysis has had until recently a decided tendency toward gradualism. This tendency is captured in the conventional opposition of evolutionary and revolutionary change: evolutionary change is seen to be gradual and continuous, while revolutionary change is seen to be sharp and episodic. Does the use of an ecological or evolutionary perspective commit a social scientist to a gradualist position on change?

Darwin emphasized gradual and continual change for good reasons: he sought to replace biblical accounts of the creation of species with a naturalistic alternative. Naturally he wished to sharpen the differences between his theory and creationist accounts, which held that all biotic life was created in a brief period. Consequently Darwin rejected all saltational views on biotic evolution. His antisaltationalism became deeply embedded in the core of modern evolutionary theory.

Recently Darwin's gradualism has come under attack by a new generation of paleontologists. Their attack rests mainly on the recent accumulation of good geologic evidence on rates of speciation. In *The Origin of the Species*, Darwin argued that the inability to find fossil evidence of various intermediary forms (like "missing links") was due to the gaps in the geologic record, and that a more intensive search would eventually uncover such evidence. However, the situation now seems to be exactly the opposite. As the quality of samples of cores from the ocean floors has improved, it appears that most speciation has taken place in periods that are quite short on a geological time scale. That is, evolutionary change does not appear to be gradual and continuous in even the best-documented cases. It appears to be episodic, with sharp divergence in character in brief geologic periods. Using this evidence, Gould and Eldridge (1977), Stanley (1979), and others have argued that evolutionary change takes the form of punctuated equilibria, in which most of evolutionary history shows little change (approximating an equilibrium) except for brief periods or punctuations in which there is rapid speciation and great increases in diversity. They argue further that the punctuations are due to combinations of environmental circumstances that open new niches into which new forms of life can radiate.

It should be emphasized that the proponents of punctuated equilibrium do not reject the core of the Darwinian theory and research program. They accept all of the standard arguments and adapt them to fit situations in which evolutionary change has a decidedly revolutionary character.

The notion of punctuated equilibria seems highly appropriate for the study of social change, including organizational change. In fact, Stinchcombe's (1965, pp. 168–169) widely cited argument that organizations retain traces of the sociopolitical conditions of the time of their founding makes an explicitly punctuationalist claim: "Organizational types generally originate rapidly in a relatively short historical period, to grow and change slowly after that period." Both the theories and the empirical research we report here are at least broadly consistent with such a punctuationalist position.[6]

6. This position differs from that attributed to population ecology or organizations by Astley (1985). One does not have to resort to a community level of analysis to explain the rise of new forms and the populations of organizations, as we show in Chapter 3. Furthermore, there is nothing inherently graduational about population analysis. There is nothing inherently punctuational about community-level analysis either.

The Question of Size

Many commentaries on the ecological perspective view it as particularly well suited for the study of small organizations and, by implication, less well suited for the study of big ones (see, for example, Aldrich and Pfeffer 1976; Aldrich 1979; Perrow 1986; Scott 1987). We do not agree with this assessment, as our research shows. Our empirical studies contain data on very small organizations and very big ones. For example, our study of national labor unions includes unions with as few as one hundred members and others whose membership is nearly two million.[7]

As we explained in our early statement of our approach, time spans must be lengthened to analyze the ecology of large and powerful organizations (Hannan and Freeman 1977). This point seems elementary, but it has not been widely understood. For example, little would be learned by studying the population of multinational oil firms over a period of one or two arbitrary months. Interesting analysis of such a population undoubtedly requires information on events occurring over several decades, including the possibly brief period in which the industry took shape and basic organizational forms were worked out.

Determinism

If it is true that organizations experience strong inertial pressures and that much of the variability in structures reflects differential rates of founding and failure of organizational forms, how much difference does any individual make? Organizations are composed of social relationships among persons, who have their own ambitions, desires, and fears. To a great degree, sociological analysis downplays the consequences of idiosyncratic variation in these characteristics. The contribution of sociological analysis is to explain how influences that transcend individuals constrain individual choice and how organizational structure shapes the patterns of incentives and constraints for members. To say that each organization is best understood as the extension of the will of a key actor is to ignore both the complexity of organizational influence systems and the patterned environmental and technical limits on choice.

---

7. "Big" and "small" are relative terms in such discussions. A small oil company is much bigger than a big restaurant. So population studies of oil companies are studies of big organizations, even when the smaller variants are analyzed.

Of course individual actions do matter for organizations, but they matter more to the subunits in which these individuals work than to the organization as a whole. And they matter more to that organization than they do to the population of organizations. From the perspective of explaining variability in the organizational world, the motivations and preferences of particular actors probably do not matter very much.

Debates about the importance of particular individuals or of managers generally in shaping the world of organizations frequently bog down in discussions of the role of free will and determinism in social behavior (Burrell and Morgan 1979; Astley and Van de Ven 1983). Part of the confusion is that determinism is mistakenly contrasted with voluntarism rather than with probabilism. Determinism in this sense characterizes *any* sociological theory of organizations, not just ecological theory. To the degree that social structure constrains choice, its effects are deterministic.

Yet our models and analyses are not deterministic. Despite the claims of our critics to the contrary, the models presented and estimated in subsequent chapters are formally *probabilistic*. The dependent variables are transition rates, defined as the limit of a conditional probability of a certain kind of change. In no sense do we think that the history of organizational populations is preordained to unfold in fixed ways. Quite the opposite: the ecological approach treats processes of change as contingent but also as random.

Managerial Implications and Applications

What of the manager? There is no escaping the antiheroic implications of population ecology. A retrospective analysis of any industry, market, or form of organizing can identify individuals whose actions appear with hindsight to have stood out from those of their peers. The myths that develop around these people are magnified and romanticized by undisciplined retrospective analysis. We do not know how to answer whether the person makes the times, or whether the times make the person.

An example helps to make this point. In analyzing the invention and spread of modern business organization and the rise of the managerial class, Alfred Chandler (1977) examines wholesale jobbing and steel-making in detail. Initially, no single firm stands out as the pioneer in wholesaling. No one individual is singled out as the catalyst of change from traditional to modern organizational forms; indeed, no individual receives more than a few lines of discussion. Chandler's analysis of change in this industry is structural. As railroads and telegraph lines spread across the nation, centrally organized distribution became feasible. Increasing volume of business, large scale of inventories, and geographic dispersion of the market gave great advantage to firms with formal and precise organization, which depended on the employment of middle managers.

In the case of steel-making, however, a different picture emerges. Andrew Carnegie stood out as an innovator and skillful manager. He followed the trend toward designing plants to fit the new technology. However, it was in cost accounting and managerial controls that Carnegie was most innovative. He made good use of the technical capacity for combining formerly separate manufacturing processes in a single plant, while minimizing transaction costs with efficient management. Carnegie used the techniques that characterized his times. He did not create them but adapted them successfully to his ends. Yet even in analyzing this case in which a single individual played a dominant role, Chandler does not assign causal primacy to individual achievement. He makes it clear that a set of technical, legal, and social changes drove the development of new modes of organizing.

Ecological analysis reformulates issues of innovation at the population level. Put loosely, such analysis tries to estimate the odds of success for any particular organizational or strategic variation, including the survival of its carriers and the rate at which these strategic variations are adopted by other organizations. If the odds of survival run against organizations with a particular variant, this does not mean that an organization choosing that variant is doomed. But it does mean that managerial skills matter a great deal in such circumstances. If there is a time when managerial acumen does not matter, it is when the dice are loaded so heavily in favor of the organizational variant in question that it could hardly fail.

At least four factors limit the capacities of managers to reshape existing organizations. The first is the organization's form, which includes characteristics of the control system, the norms guiding behavior, and incentives used. The existing form constrains the choices available for any organization member, including managers. The second factor limiting the ability of individual actors to bring about adaptive change is scarcity of resources. Scarcity makes adaptive change difficult to manage. The pattern of competition within and between populations limits choice. That is, competitive pressures magnify the effects of other factors. Finally, all the limitations on rationality described by contemporary decision theorists apply (see, for example, Kahneman, Slovic, and Tversky 1982). Whether attempts at adaptive, managerially guided reorganization succeed in reshaping organizations depends on the circumstances. Attempting to analyze adaptations by individual organizations presupposes that the constraints just discussed are well understood. We think it is hard to achieve such understanding without considering processes at the population level.

But just because there are strong constraints does not mean that strategic choice is irrelevant to processes of change in organizations. Hrebiniak and Joyce (1985) argue in favor of considering jointly individual choice, particularly strategic choice, and external constraint in explaining the adaptation of individual organizations. But, as we pointed out previously (Hannan and Freeman 1977, p. 929), the difference between adaptation and selection processes depends on levels of analysis. Selection at the level of organizational populations may be adaptation at the level of federations of organizations. Trade associations provide a useful example (Aldrich and Staber 1988). They are created to organize the firms in an industry so as to boost the fortunes of these firms at a societal level. The Semiconductor Industry Association (SIA) was founded for exactly these reasons. The U.S. producers selling their product on the open market anticipated competition from Japanese producers that were part of large, diversified corporations. The Japanese firms had different ways of organizing, lower costs of capital, protection from external competition in their home markets, and trivial antitrust constraints. Each of these features provided competitive advantages over the American specialists. The SIA was formed in large measure to push for revision of governmental policies threatening to make the American forms of organization nonviable. So the SIA represents an industry-level attempt to adapt.[8]

Why do organizational analysts cling so tenaciously to explanations of organizational variability that feature individual actors? This question would take a book of its own to answer. However, we can suggest that scholars develop explanations based on their own experience and on readily available evidence. Data pertaining to entire populations of organizations have rarely been available, much less used to test predictions about adaptive behavior of individual organizations. Organizational research is almost always conducted on units selected from samples of opportunity, often of the largest and most visible firms; such data are also usually cross-sections that cannot support systematic analysis of sources of change (Freeman 1978, 1986a).

We suspect that the tenacity of explanation at the single-organization level also persists partly because it is easier to empathize with single cases

8. The failure of this attempt is manifested in the high rates of bankruptcy and acquisition of organizations in the population.

than with populations; thus one can pique the interest of an audience more readily with the story of Elsa the lion "born free" than by telling the story of lions in general and how the changing ecosystem of the African plains makes survival for any one of them in the next time period less and less likely.

We think that the desire for such empathic understanding underlies Perrow's complaints about our treatment of the environment (1986, pp. 242–243). He asks whether an allusion to the workings of a nonspecific environment would provide a satisfactory explanation to a steel worker who has just been laid off. Would not this worker prefer Perrow's detailed argument? But if Perrow had taken the trouble to construct an ecological argument, he might have found that it did not differ greatly from his, as far as his goes. Stripped of its polemics, his explanation of a high level of unemployment in the steel industry includes: (1) worldwide overproduction of steel; (2) failure of large American steel manufacturers to adopt new technologies; (3) ability of large firms to coerce favorable treatment from government; (4) the effects of favorable government treatment on independence of workers (and, implicitly, their labor unions). Each of these elements could be translated into hypotheses that could be tested at the *population* level, given data on the populations of firms in this and other industries. But Perrow's explanation is an ad hoc attempt to explain the actions of one class of organizations, large steel manufacturers. His analysis ignores the persistence and recent expansion of smaller specialist steel manufacturers.

Population ecology analysis can in principle explain the changing mix of sizes of firms in this industry. And this issue has real consequences for steelworkers and others. Wage rates tend to be lower in the smaller firms, as does representation in the United Steel Workers Union. The changing mix of firms in the steel industry also affects the cities and regions in which the industry has been concentrated. Levels of pollution have declined in cities such as Pittsburgh and Buffalo since steel production is more geographically dispersed than it used to be. And the managers of large steel manufacturers are less able to coerce the rest of society than they once were. Indeed, Perrow's query suggests that ecological analysis would provide considerable insight into the changing fortunes of steelworkers and their families.

If individual managers do not matter much in accounting for variability in organizational properties, and if the theory is stochastic at the population level, than what does population ecology have to say about understanding organizations in order to make them "work better"? The answer is that population studies provide a context for analyses of individual organizations and for drawing normative implications about management, technical or market strategy, or, indeed, organizational sabotage.

Generalizations about the effects of environmental variations on rates of growth and decline of organizational populations serve as statements about probabilities for individual organizations. What could be more germane to business strategy than to identify the circumstances under which business firms dissolve or are acquired? What better warning signal could a manager have than knowledge that new firms employing a particular strategy or organizational device are failing at unusually high rates? Patterns of life events in the population provide a context for gauging the success of managerial actions. Knowledge of population processes can serve as an alternative to conventional profit-and-loss accounting exercises with all their measurement problems (Freeman and Boeker 1984).

Many of the issues and controversies discussed in this chapter are currently far from resolution. To some degree, the confusions that have characterized debate about organizational ecology reflect the absence of a fully articulated statement of the ecological approach. To a perhaps greater degree, they reflect the paucity of empirical knowledge about processes of change in organizational populations. The rest of this book tries to fill these gaps.

3 | Boundaries of Forms and Populations

The actors in our scheme are *populations of organizations*. Our strategy of theory and research depends on several assumptions about such populations. The first assumption is that populations can be defined in such a way that they have a unitary character, which means that the members of the populations have a common standing with respect to the processes of interest. The most salient kind of unitary character for our concerns is *common dependence on the material and social environment*. A population of organizations has a unitary character in this sense if its members are affected similarly by changes in the environment, including other populations. So ecological analyses of organizations assume that populations can be identified in such a way that member organizations exhibit very similar environmental dependencies. This is equivalent to assuming that discontinuities in the world of organizations exist and can be identified.

Given the criterion of common environmental dependence, it might seem tempting to define populations post hoc, using information on the effects of observed environmental changes on the growth rate of populations defined in various ways. We do not do this because we want to make falsifiable predictions about the effects of populations on growth rates of other populations. This requires that populations be identified a priori using information on characteristics of the organizations or on the location of social boundaries prior to collecting and evaluating evidence about outcomes. So the second assumption is that populations of organizations can be identified in a meaningful way on the basis of information about structures of organizations and social boundaries. Failure to distinguish meaningful populations will almost certainly invalidate attempts to establish general processes in empirical research. The case that meaningful populations can be identified is most secure when the world of organizations is discontinuous and there is reason to think that classifications used in empirical analysis reflect the discontinuities.

Conventional cognitive maps of the social world, as reflected in language, do make numerous sharp distinctions among organizational forms. We routinely distinguish hospitals, prisons, political parties, universities, stock exchanges, coal mines, and fast-food chains. Within each category, further distinctions are also made routinely. Social scientists also use conventional classifications in designing research. For example, recent studies use observations on collections of voluntary organizations (McPherson 1983), museums (DiMaggio 1983), social service agencies (Singh, House, and Tucker 1986), and hospitals (Scott et al. 1978). The fact that much research is organized around conventional distinctions among forms suggests that sociologists assume implicitly that these distinctions reflect fundamental differences.

Not all research on organizations uses conventional classifications; much research builds on more abstract conceptions of form. For example, much recent work on industries and labor markets argues that both firms and labor markets can be partitioned usefully into a core and a periphery. Dual economy and dual labor market theories argue that forms of organization and of labor control differ between core and periphery, that the seeming diversity of industrial organization and career paths can be reduced to two main forms. The best-known statements of this perspective argue strongly that the industrial world is discontinuous (Averitt 1968; Gordon, Edwards, and Reich 1982).

Just because ordinary people and social scientists use a few types or forms, either concrete or abstract, in making maps of the organizational world does not mean that this world is really discontinuous. Perhaps these distinctions refer to arbitrary cuts in continuous joint distributions of organizational characteristics. This situation may be similar to the case in which an essentially continuous income distribution is cut more or less arbitrarily into categories such as rich versus poor.

These are questions of realism versus nominalism. Do the sets of forms identified and studied by current macro theorists reflect real or nominal sociological distinctions? Consider the example of dualism. Proponents of dualist theory in naming the approach directed attention to a presumed discontinuity in the organizational base of modern capitalist economies. Beginning with Averitt (1968), dualists have argued that the core and periphery are distinguished by (1) the complexity and scale of organizational arrangements, and (2) the degree of market dominance. The core form has

large scale, vertical integration, extensive markets, intense bureaucratization, and institutionalized labor relations. Firms in the core can also use
their market power to exploit firms in the periphery. Baron and Bielby
(1984, p. 456) note the connection between dualist notions and general
concerns with defining organizational forms: "Averitt differentiates center
from periphery firms in terms of organizational goals and strategies, procedures for structuring work, and definitions of economic, political, and
normative boundaries, the same criteria ecologists use to demarcate
forms."

Does the distinction between core and periphery correspond to a discontinuity in the organization of production? Establishing such a discontinuity
means showing that continuous distributions of firm size, degree of bureaucratization, and dominance over workers have not been cut arbitrarily
in two. Work in the dual-economy tradition has rarely made systematic
arguments on this matter and has instead relied mainly on assumption.[1]

Numerous critics have shown that the dimensions supposed to characterize the core form do not covary strongly (Wallace and Kalleberg 1982;
Kaufman, Hodson, and Fligstein 1981). Recent analysis, using data on
establishments rather than industrial aggregates, finds "little evidence of
discrete sectors of economic activity" (Baron and Bielby 1984, p. 471).
These and other recent studies of the joint distribution of organizational
characteristics, market power, and worker outcomes fail to reveal discontinuities. Critics conclude either that the dualist distinction is misleading or
that it is a possibly useful but mainly nominalist distinction.

The debate about dualism is characteristic of other debates about forms.
An initial set of forms is proposed as exemplifying some assumed discontinuity and as perhaps also reflecting a specified social process. Close
empirical examination reveals that the presumed discontinuity does not
appear unambiguously, if at all, in available data. Theorists then typically
either argue that the distinction is helpful anyway or refine the classification scheme by adding intermediate or hybrid forms. Work on dualism
seems to be following the latter path, with theorists such as Gordon,
Edwards, and Reich (1982) introducing a kind of semiperiphery. We argue
in this chapter that such debates are more productive when the argument
focuses on the dynamics of boundaries around forms.

---

1. As Hodson and Kaufman (1982) point out, Marxian notions of accumulation and
exploitation have been invoked by Averitt and others to explain why the modern economy should tend toward a dual structure. Such processes may turn a small initial advantage into large qualitative differences, producing the presumed discontinuity.

Approaches to Defining Forms

We have already noted that an organizational form gives unitary character to a population of organizations. But what does this mean concretely? A number of answers to this question have been given in the population-ecology literature.

Organizational Genetics

One set of answers looks for an analogue to the genetic structure that reproduces biotic forms. When viewed abstractly, such genetic mechanisms can be thought of as blueprints in the spirit of Monod (1971): the structure of DNA molecules contains a set of instructions for building biotic structures. We have suggested (Hannan and Freeman 1977) that organizational forms be defined analogously, as instructions for building organizations and for conducting collective action.

The blueprint imagery refers to qualitative patterns—a blueprint codes specific, discrete instructions. It has the advantage of allowing variations in structures produced from the same blueprint, because the relation between blueprint and final structure depends on the cultural conceptions and training of those who implement it, the quality of tools and resources at hand, and the nature of environmental shocks during the period of assembly. So this conception of form recognizes the possibility that populations with different forms may overlap in terms of observable characteristics. That is, modest overlap of quantitative characteristics is consistent with qualitative differences between underlying blueprints.

This approach has the strong disadvantage that blueprints for organizations are not observable, making this conception of form far from concrete. Earlier (Hannan and Freeman 1977) we proposed that blueprints could be inferred from formal structure, patterns of activity, and forms of authority. But these observable features of populations often overlap considerably, as in the case of the core and peripheral forms discussed earlier. In the absence of strong theory it is hard to locate the underlying invariance; and no strong theory exists for this problem.

Taxonomy Based on Organizational Genetics

A related proposal for identifying forms makes a stronger appeal to the analogue to population genetics and makes a strong claim for the priority of taxonomy over explanation (McKelvey 1982; McKelvey and Aldrich

1983). It treats the problem of classifying organizational forms as analogous to classifying biotic species and tries to find the analogue to the individual gene. For example, McKelvey (1982) argues that bits of productive knowledge, which he calls "comps," serve as a useful analogue. Tracing flows of comps between organizations specifies family trees and allows classification of forms based on considerations of organizational genetics.

We have serious doubts about the utility of an organizational genetics approach to the problem of classification. First, there is the question of whether comps exist as individual properties disembodied from organizational context. In particular, can they be transferred unchanged from one organization to another? Even the simpler biotic case involves strong nonlinearities; structure depends on combinations of genes in a highly nonadditive way. The best example of this kind of process concerns the so-called regulator gene that controls the timing of developmental events. Small differences in timing have enormous consequences for structure.

The routines that coordinate elementary production in organizations are analogous to regulator genes. Even when the competencies of individual members are standardized across organizations, as in the case of certain crafts and professions, the coordinating routines tend to be highly specific to organizational forms and to particular organizations.[2] It would be very difficult to discern the differences between, say, public and private universities by simply recording a list of the competencies held by members of the two kinds of organizations. The difference in form would seem to lie elsewhere.

Second, the process of transmission of structure is not unitary for organizations as it is for biotic species. In the biotic case, virtually all of the information governing structure is passed from parent to offspring in the single event of reproduction. The genetic material possessed by an individual is essentially constant over the lifetime except for mutations in cell reproduction. In the case of organizations, there are two important differences. Transmission is not unitary; information comes from diverse sources, which means that there is no clear-cut parent. In addition, the flow of information about building structure never ceases for an organization because members come and go continually over its lifetime. These

---

2. Nelson and Winter (1982), who think of organizations as being constructed from routines held in organizational memory, take care to point out that organizational structure cannot be reduced to the routines held in the memories of individual members.

differences greatly complicate the prospect of building an evolutionary taxonomy of organizations.

We also wonder whether definition of forms based on organizational genetics is necessary for organizational ecology. The usual presumption is that a Darwinian theory of organizations cannot be built until Linnaean classifications have been constructed. But it is far from obvious that this was true even in the case of Darwin and Linnaeus. Darwin relied less on a complete set of species classifications than on his own naturalistic observations, both the well-known studies in the Galapagos and his lifelong studies of barnacles. In fact, if history had worked out differently and Darwin had known and used Mendel's theory of particulate inheritance, the conventional wisdom would no doubt say that Darwinian theory could not have been built without an understanding of these genetic mechanisms.

Darwin built a successful theory of evolution using the wrong theory of genetics—a theory of blending inheritance—and an inaccurate set of species classifications. The connection between creating useful theories of change and correct classification is a loose one. In fact, what matters is that classifications accurately reflect discontinuities in nature. All that mattered for Darwin is that he understood the main distinctions among species of finches and among species of barnacles. This is not to say that organizational taxonomy, based on organizational genetics or on other principles, is irrelevant to developing theories and empirical research on organizational ecology and evolution; rather, the success of the former is not a precondition of the success of the latter.

Duality of Niche and Form

An alternative approach tries to identify forms in terms of the niche structure of populations.[3] The niche of a population consists of combinations of resource abundances and constraints in which members can arise and persist. There is a fundamental duality here: niches define forms and forms define niches. Niche structure can be summarized by a fitness function, which is a rule relating levels of environmental conditions to growth rates of the population. So a reasonable idea is to infer differences between forms from empirical fitness functions. That is, we might use empirical estimates of fitness functions to decide whether a claimed distinction be-

3. The concept of niche is developed more fully in the next chapter. The duality that is the subject here makes it difficult to discuss form without discussing niche and vice versa.

tween a pair of similar populations reflects some fundamental difference in form. Unfortunately, fitness functions are not directly observable and are costly to estimate; thus a great deal of research is required just to define forms in this way.

This strategy of using the duality of niches and forms to define the latter can be approximated by defining populations in terms of a set of core properties. For example, we suggested earlier that four properties—stated goals, forms of authority, core technology, and marketing strategy—provide a useful basis for classifying organizations into forms because an organization's initial configuration on these dimensions commits it to a set of environmental dependencies and to a long-term strategy (Hannan and Freeman 1984).

As we discuss at length in Chapters 5 and 6, a fitness function implies a *carrying capacity*. Thus propositions about fitness functions can be restated as propositions about carrying capacities. In particular, the structure of the niche can be defined in terms of effects of environmental conditions on carrying capacities. In this sense, two populations can be said to be distinct if their carrying capacities are affected differently by the same environmental conditions or by different sets of environmental conditions.

McPherson (1983) used the dependence of carrying capacities on environmental conditions to analyze the niche structure of a set of voluntary associations. Using data on memberships in a list of conventionally defined kinds of associations such as labor unions, sports associations, and youth-serving associations, he measured niches in terms of concentration of membership in a space defined in terms of attributes of potential members, including age, occupation, sex, and education. Competition between pairs of kinds of associations for members is measured as the degree of overlap of these niches. Assuming aggregate equilibrium, McPherson used these estimates to solve the Lotka-Volterra competition equations[4] for the fundamental carrying capacity (the carrying capacity in the absence of competitors) of each form of organization. Finally, he showed that inserting estimates of intrinsic carrying capacities into the model gives a reasonably good fit to observed population sizes which, under the assumption of equilibrium, equal the realized carrying capacities. McPherson notes that this result confirms the validity of the typology of associations used in his analysis.

---

4. These equations are discussed in Chapter 5.

Structural Equivalence

DiMaggio (1986) points out that our definition of forms is "based firmly in the logic of structural equivalence." The notion of structural equivalence, developed mainly by Harrison White and his collaborators (White 1963; Lorrain and White 1971), has become most familiar in the formal structure and operational procedures of blockmodeling (White, Breiger, and Boorman 1976). A blockmodel is a hypothesis about a set of ties among some population of actors. Suppose that each tie is represented in the population as a square matrix whose entries tell whether the tie exists between the indicated pair of actors. Arrange each matrix so as to create blocks (that is, sets of actors) for whom the tie does not exist; these are the so-called zero-blocks. Consider the set of all the relevant matrices. A blockmodel is a hypothesis that some single partition of the population will reproduce the zero-blocks for all of the tie-matrices. The set of actors identified as members of the same block are said to stand in a structurally equivalent position with respect to the ties examined and the boundaries specified for the population.

A number of algorithms exist for developing blockmodel images of data on ties. DiMaggio (1986, p. 360) argues that these procedures provide a natural way to implement our conception of forms: "The power of the population ecology perspective may, in certain circumstances, be enhanced by returning to an operational definition of niche and form as mutually defined by observable patterns of relations among sets of actors." The idea is to obtain data on flows of resources among organizations and to use blockmodeling procedures to identify structurally equivalent sets of organizations. Such sets are then considered to be populations having a common organizational form and occupying the same niche.

This proposal has the advantage of directing attention to patterns of dependence on environments including other organizational populations. We wonder, however, whether this approach can provide temporally stable classifications of forms. It seems likely that small changes in ties in a network, resulting perhaps from the demise of one of the earlier organizations, will cause numerical clustering or blockmodeling procedures to yield quite different block structures.[5] That is, it is likely that such a procedure is sensitive to relatively small perturbations in the observable data. If so, this approach will have difficulty identifying *enduring* bases of unit character of

---

5. Obviously the relations used to classify organizations into blocks may be associated with founding processes and mortality processes.

populations. However, it remains to be seen whether this approach offers advantages that offset this likely disadvantage.

The various approaches reviewed in this section diverge in considering internal attributes of organizations versus external dependencies as bases for classification. However, they converge in focusing on the content of the organization structures or the character of external relations. The implicit underlying idea is that content and relations define the boundaries around populations. That is, boundaries should be drawn in organizational space to produce uniformity within populations in terms of observable attributes and relations.

A Focus on Boundaries

In the remainder of this chapter we argue that approaches emphasizing content and pairwise relations should be supplemented by others that emphasize the dynamics of boundaries in organizational space. To motivate this alternative perspective, it is instructive to consider a seemingly quite different problem. Social life in many societies is channeled by boundaries that partition populations into ethnic groups. Such boundaries persist in physical and social space despite large-scale movement of individuals across the boundaries. How is the persistence of ethnic boundaries to be explained? One approach, which parallels those sketched in the previous section, looks to differences in sociocultural *content* of ethnic populations, suspecting that content shapes interaction and creates social boundaries. However, close inspection reveals that content often varies greatly within stable ethnic populations both at one point in time and over time. Moreover, distributions of sociocultural attributes of sharply distinguished ethnic groups often overlap considerably while the social boundaries often remain strong.

Fredrik Barth (1956, 1969) proposed a brilliant solution to the seeming paradox of variable cultural content within ethnic groups and shifting membership, on the one hand, and stable, strong ethnic boundaries, on the other. He turned the problem on its head, treating the boundaries as the primary social phenomena and the cultural content as the by-product of the boundaries. The problem then becomes the identification and explanation of the social processes that create and sustain ethnic boundaries. This shift in perspective from attribute-based reasoning to explicit consideration of ethnic boundaries has stimulated much productive research (see the review by Olzak 1983).

We suggest a parallel shift toward boundary-based reasoning in identifying and classifying organizational forms.[6] The main idea is to locate the boundaries and the processes that sustain them as a first step in identifying the structure and dynamics of the niche (Hannan 1979). Instead of beginning with problems of classification, this approach begins with the question: Where do organizational forms come from?

The key issues in considering boundaries around forms pertain to segregating processes and blending processes. Continuity in the world of organizations depends on the relative strength of these opposing processes and, in some cases, on the initial conditions. If segregating processes dominate, discontinuities are sharp and distinctions among forms reflect real qualitative differences. If blending processes dominate, distinctions among forms are more arbitrary.

Some of the characteristics of organizations cited in conceptions of forms based on dependencies seemingly play a role in creating and maintaining boundaries between populations. We think that technologies and the transaction costs involved in implementing them in particular social environments play such a role. But most of the discussion in this section directs attention to factors that have not been given much weight in previous treatments: social networks, collective action by members of organizational populations, and institutional processes.

A broad class of *technological factors* apparently creates differences between forms, at least at the plant level. Much research has shown that certain forms of technical production are inconsistent with certain kinds of control structures and other features of structure. Classic statements of this view have been made by Burns and Stalker (1961), Woodward (1965), and Thompson (1967). Stinchcombe (1983) provides a detailed analysis of the technical constraints shaping manufacturing, construction, farming, and commercial industries.

The case of the semiconductor industry is instructive. It is widely taken for granted that the set of firms producing semiconductor devices constitutes an industry. Undoubtedly the fact that most such firms have located in the Santa Clara Valley, now dubbed Silicon Valley, has heightened the imagery of a bounded industry with a distinctive technology, distinctive organizational forms, and closed networks of mobility. But is this industry really so sharply differentiated from the broader electronics industry?

---

6. This proposal does not assume that ethnic dynamics and organizational dynamics are similar. Rather we think that Barth's approach is a good one for analyzing *all* kinds of social processes.

The distinction between semiconductor producers and other electronics manufacturers seems to be based on real differences in technology. As Brittain and Freeman (1980) noted, the dominant producers of vacuum tubes failed miserably in trying to produce semiconductor devices. This failure apparently stemmed from discontinuities between technologies for producing the two types of devices. Successful producers of vacuum tubes used standardized methods of production with tight managerial controls to drive production costs down in the face of a stable, well-known technology. Production of semiconductor devices, initially more an art form than a standardized technique, involved high levels of uncertainty and rapid technical change. The organizational structures and management styles appropriate for producing vacuum tubes could not accommodate the arrangement of work demanded by the new products. Engineers with specialized knowledge of semiconductor design and fabrication eventually left the giant electronic firms and joined or started specialized semiconductor producers using different organizational forms.

A more general formulation of this argument points to qualitative differences in *transaction costs*. Williamson (1975, 1985) has argued that technological differences per se are less important in determining organizational forms than are considerations of transaction costs. Technology surely affects the costs of production and of completing transactions; but so too do problems of control, scheduling, supervision, and enforcement of contracts. Efforts to minimize the costs of completing certain transactions typically result in bundling sets of transactions together within the same corporate actor. What Williamson calls the "efficient boundaries" of the organization are those that bundle transactions so as to minimize transaction costs. When transaction-cost considerations lead to distinctive and persistent bundling of sets of transactions, organizational forms will tend to diverge. Selection of forms of organizations employing efficient boundaries or rational adaptation by reshaping boundaries of existing organizations creates discontinuities among populations of organizations engaged in different kinds of transactions.

Closure of social networks also creates and maintains differences between populations giving rise to distinct forms. For example, when organizations hire each other's employees, they develop a high degree of inbreeding with respect to the elements of structure coded in individual memory and routines. Inbred populations tend to diverge from general populations of organizations. Idiosyncratic language and culture develop and diffuse through the closed population, sharpening the differences between insiders and outsiders. Because idiosyncratic language and culture tend to become markers of competence, inbreeding feeds on itself. Populations separated in such networks tend to become different social worlds.

Successful collective action on behalf of a population also creates boundaries.[7] When, for example, collections of firms create industry associations, they sometimes produce a sense of collective identity and of distinctiveness. Moreover, collective action often stimulates passage of laws and creation of other institutional rules that reinforce a proto-boundary around the population. The pharmaceutical industry, for example, has used this strategy successfully (Hirsch 1975). The existence of these monopolies creates discontinuities in the world of manufacturing organizations.

Perhaps the most important segregating mechanisms arise from two kinds of *institutional* processes. One kind is purely structural: a social actor (using a specific organizational form) is institutionalized to the extent that other powerful actors in the system endorse its claims in disputes (Stinchcombe 1968). In this sense, labor unions became institutionalized in the United States only after passage of the Wagner Act in 1935, which held that organizations using a specified labor union form had special standing in making certain claims. That is, the state became committed to intervening in certain ways to support workers' claims if they used this organizational form but no other.

The case of labor unions illustrates an important point: The events that institutionalize a boundary around an organizational population at the same time often codify the features of the form. Both the consequence of becoming institutionalized and the accompanying process of codification strengthen boundaries around forms.

Institutionalization conveys powerful advantages. Because institutionalized actors can call upon other powerful actors for aid in resisting raids on their resources, institutionalization lowers mortality rates. Unless this tendency is offset by a founding process that blurs boundaries, such a process produces a world of organizations with clear discontinuities and defended boundaries. That is, selection in favor of institutionalized forms intensifies the boundaries around the forms that emerge from the selection process.

A second institutional process pertains to the taken-for-granted character of certain forms (Meyer and Scott 1983; Zucker 1983). A form is institutionalized in this sense when no question arises in the minds of actors that

---

7. Although the issues go beyond the scope of this chapter, it is worth pointing out that the likelihood of successful collective action undoubtedly depends on forms of social networks and technological and transaction-cost considerations.

a certain form is the natural way to effect some kind of collective action. In this sense, the labor union form became institutionalized long before the Wagner Act, which was enacted several decades after workers had stopped debating whether labor unions were the natural vehicle for collective action for improving conditions of work. The capacity to mobilize members and other resources to begin unions, firms, and other kinds of organizations increases greatly when controllers of resources take the question of organizational form for granted. Not having to defend choice of form saves time and other organizing resources. As a consequence, attempts at creating copies of legitimated forms should be more common, and the success rate of such attempts should be relatively high.

Both kinds of institutional processes operate on any source of initial diversity, transforming arbitrary differences into differences with real social consequences. In this sense, nominal classifications become real classifications. They become real in their consequences when they serve as bases for successful collective action, when powerful actors use them in defining rights and access to resources, and when members of the general population use them in organizing their social worlds. Thus the clarity of a set of boundaries is not a permanent property of a set of classifications. Rather, the realism of distinction among forms depends on the degree of institutionalization that has occurred.

It is important not to overstate the strength of segregating mechanisms. Blending processes work to erode boundaries among populations. Organizational foundings provide occasions at which forms and routines can be both consciously and unintentionally varied from orthodoxy. Much entrepreneurial activity involves conscious attempts to revise forms and routines to take advantage of changing opportunities and constraints or to avoid defects in orthodox designs. As Freeman (1986b) notes, ongoing organizations are the training grounds for entrepreneurs and often provide negative lessons about organizing. For example, according to the lore of Silicon Valley, some of the early entrepreneurs in the industry consciously set out to create the opposite of the authoritarian control systems used in Shockley Semiconductor Laboratories, the founding firm in the industry. When efforts to implement novel forms succeed, they can result in a blurring of the boundaries among a set of forms or in the rise of a distinctly different form. Even if the innovations result eventually in a new boundary, the transition period is characterized by blurring of prior boundaries.

Planned variations in design are not the only sources of new diversity. Attempts at replication in a particular context often involve subtle, unplanned changes in routines or procedures. Such unintended changes occur frequently in attempts at translating forms between sociocultural contexts because cultural differences in interpreting the template create unexpected and unplanned differences in structure.

Copying mistakes also occur routinely in ongoing organizations. Structure is rarely copied exactly from week to week or from year to year in the same organization. Processes of unintended change can blur boundaries between forms as organizations diverge from common standards. In such cases the blending mechanism, which might be called *random drift*, reflects the cumulation of a large number of unintended changes in procedures or routines within existing organizations. Even when each change is small, the cumulative impact of random drift on structure can be substantial over long periods. Becker (1982) provides a useful example of such drift as a source of change in the conventions sustaining institutions of an art world.

Whether drift blurs boundaries depends on its magnitude and trend. Its impact on structure also depends on organizational size: drift is unlikely to cause major changes in large organizations. However, the presence, accuracy, and speed of mechanisms for monitoring unintended changes in procedures also affect the impact of drift. Small organizations may be better able to monitor and correct unintended changes.

An important source of random drift is turnover in personnel, both movement of individuals across jobs and recruitment of new members. Granted, the functioning of organizations depends less on the exact identity of its members than is the case for other social units such as families and dynasties, as Weber (1968) pointed out in discussing bureaucracy. Nonetheless, turnover in personnel does affect the functioning of organizations. Indeed, high turnover is often cited as an explanation for business failure (Carroll 1983). Much detailed operational information is stored in the memories of participants. Thus the magnitude of drift depends on the rate of movement among positions, the rate of recruitment, and the heterogeneity among members both within and between cohorts of recruits.

Another blending process involves *recombination* of existing routines and structures into new packages. Organizations seek to adapt to changing technical and institutional environments by copying routines and structures, what DiMaggio and Powell (1983) call mimetic isomorphism. Unconstrained copying can erode boundaries among forms if not opposed by strong segregating processes.

Because inertial forces are strong and the liabilities of initiating new routines and forms are high, organizations often change structures by merging with other organizations or by acquiring them. For example, the boundary between craft and industrial unions became increasingly blurred in the early decades of this century as unions organizing single crafts merged in response to technical changes that eroded craft distinctions. These merged unions often retained the craft principle of organizing by work role rather than industrial location but incorporated increasingly diverse kinds of workers.

Joint ventures provide another opportunity for recombining existing structures in ways that blur boundaries between forms. For example, the current joint ventures between Japanese and American automakers and French and American elite wineries may result in organizational forms that combine elements of the heretofore sharply different forms.

A final blending process is *deinstitutionalization*. Dramatic examples of this process occur when legal or other rules maintaining boundaries between populations with similar structures are relaxed. Consider, for example, the boundary between banks and other financial institutions such as so-called thrift institutions (savings and loan associations, mutual savings banks, and credit unions) and stock brokerages. The Bank Holding Act of 1956 restricted bank holding companies to activities "closely related" to banking and charged the Board of Governors of the Federal Reserve Bank with policing this restriction. Thrift institutions were permitted to pay higher interest rates on passbook savings accounts but were prohibited from offering checking accounts and credit cards. However, in 1981 thrift institutions were granted the right to offer "negotiated order of withdrawal" accounts, which the consumer cannot distinguish from checking accounts. This single event weakened the boundary considerably, and it has become increasingly blurred as other regulations have been relaxed.

At the same time, the boundary between banks and stock brokerages began to crumble. The *Wall Street Journal* (July 1, 1983, p. 7) noted that "the comptroller [of the currency] has used a loophole in the Bank Holding Act to let some manufacturing and securities companies acquire banks. Because banks acquired this way have charters that don't quite meet the definition of a bank in the law—and thus escape Fed regulation—they have won the confusing appellation, 'nonbank banks.' " Bank holding companies retaliated by entering joint ventures with discount stock brokerages to offer brokerage services in bank offices. It is unclear that the boundary between these two populations will persist without legislative or judicial intervention.

Deinstitutionalization also occurs when rules defining a boundary are widely broken. Such a case has occurred in the organization of athletics. At one time the boundary between professional and amateur sports organizations was unambiguous. It was policed by college sports federations, the

International Olympic Committee, and other agencies. However, state funding of athletics in many countries and the provision of college scholarships, under-the-table payments, and product endorsements to "amateur" athletes in the United States have created confusion and a welter of conflicting rules about amateurism. It is now very difficult to distinguish amateur and professional sports organizations.

It is easy to think of situations where blending processes dominate and others where segregating processes dominate. But it is probably not helpful to think of the two kinds of processes as stages in an evolutionary process, in the style of Aldrich (1979). Evolutionary change in the world of organizations is a stochastic process that consists of subprocesses involving the creation of forms, foundings of organizations, dissolution of organizations, and various other events. There is no fixed sequence; each of the subprocesses can occur at any time and at the same time. We have sketched an *editing process* operating on a continuous supply of new diversity. At any moment, new organizational forms are being created. But much potential diversity is edited out. Organizations attempt to filter out mistakes in copying procedures. Key actors in the environment often resist attempts at building novel kinds of organizations. But when a new form does establish a foothold, the whole game sometimes changes quickly. If a new form conveys real advantages in mobilizing resources or producing collective products, institutional arrangements can change quickly to accommodate it. Thus, long-term evolution in organizational populations tends to be punctuational: long periods of relatively minor change are punctuated with brief periods of very rapid alteration in forms and boundaries. Understanding boundary dynamics means learning how social conditions affect the strength and precision of the editing process.

Most issues in ecological analysis depend on *relative* rates of change. If the boundaries between forms shift quickly relative to rates of environmental change, the distinctions between forms are little more than an analytical convenience. But if the boundaries change slowly, the forms reflect real discontinuities. So in addition to answering the question of where organizational forms come from, organizational theorists and researchers need to pay attention to the relative speeds of segregating and blending processes.

Boundary Dynamics and Diversity

Segregating and blending processes have immediate implications for organizational diversity, a main concern of ecological theories. When segregating processes dominate, institutional and other constraints create holes in the social structure in the sense that some feasible kinds of organizations do not exist because of these constraints. Thus it appears that (1) strong segregating processes limit diversity, and (2) elimination of boundaries necessarily increases diversity of forms. There are surely historically important cases in which this was so. As Marx and others insisted, the destruction of feudal constraints on production organization (especially constraints on reallocation of land and labor) was essential to the emergence of capitalism and the accompanying proliferation of forms. Stinchcombe (1965) provides a broad account of the importance of institutional and resource constraints on the creation of new kinds of organizations. His main conclusion reinforces and clarifies the Marxian notion that old social structures, with their institutional and infrastructural constraints, must be broken for new organizational diversity to arise.

We think that the relationship between segregating processes and diversity is more complicated than has been noted previously. The existence of holes in the social structure may actually increase organizational diversity. Consider processes of competitive exclusion, the tendency for one population to eliminate all others that depend on exactly the same set of resources. The existence of strong boundaries presumably localizes competitive struggles. That is, in a discontinuous world, competition processes operate strongly within boundaries and less strongly across boundaries. Although competitive exclusion may occur within some or all bounded sectors, it is unlikely that a single organizational form can outcompete rival forms in many sectors. Yet the relaxation of a constraint creating a boundary often unleashes a competitive struggle between populations that either did not compete before or competed only weakly. An example is the case of deregulation of banking mentioned earlier. Elimination of legal and institutional constraints may decrease organizational diversity in the financial sector, as one form comes to dominate the previously segmented activities of banking and stock brokerage.

When organizational forms can be copied, the absence of institutional barriers may permit a single form to dominate many sectors. However, if there are strong boundaries, imitation will be localized; it will occur mainly within the boundaries. Again, a relaxation of boundaries can lead to lowered diversity in such circumstances.

The two arguments implying that elimination of boundaries, with the constraints that sustain them, may lower diversity are instances of a general proposition. We have argued, by analogy to general ecological principles, that the diversity of organizational forms is proportional to the diversity of resources and constraints (Hannan and Freeman 1977).

In the terms of this proposition, there is no disagreement between the views described earlier in the chapter. The social changes and revolutions that broke the constraints of feudalism greatly increased the diversity of productive resources available to build organizations. Reduction of constraints was apparently more than balanced by increased variety of resources. The central question in exploring the effects of discontinuities on diversity in the organizational world is whether the creation or elimination of a boundary increases or decreases the number of distinct resources and constraints. For any concrete historical case, answering this question demands close analysis of the boundaries and the processes underlying them. The perspective sketched in the previous section does not answer such questions, but it does provide a framework for addressing them.

Implications for Research

We have suggested that the boundaries around organizational forms change over time in response to segregating and blending processes. An important ingredient in the research agenda of organizational ecology is to understand these boundary dynamics. Another ingredient is to understand the dynamics of interaction of populations given some set of boundaries. For this latter purpose, researchers must define a set of forms that are stable over the period of study.

Implementing this strategy in empirical research is often uncomplicated. As indicated earlier, "native" classifications abound in the social world, and data frequently come bundled in categories that fit useful definitions of organizational form. The organization of such available data usually is derived from some conventional wisdom based on the ideas of participants and industry analysts, legal conventions, and existing organizational practices. For example, until the trucking industry was deregulated in the 1980s the Interstate Commerce Commission (ICC) defined an elaborate set of organizational forms in the motor freight industry through its enforcement of the Interstate Commerce Act. This complex set of categories begins with the distinction between common and contract carriers: the former offer to transport goods for the public at large, while the latter contract with a specific shipper to carry a specific load. Significantly, no terminal transshipments are required for contract carriers because the service is "dock-to-dock"; consequently the capital and managerial requirements are lower for contract carriers. Common carriers follow specified routes and charge according to specified tariffs. "Such carriers are regulated in the areas of entry, rates, mergers and acquisitions, securities issuance, public reporting, and minimum service quality" (Chow 1978, p. 14).

The ICC licensed 17 different categories of commodity carriers (to carry bulk goods of specific type) and "general freight" common carriers. Among the latter operating intercity routes, three classes are distinguished by size: Class I, small, independent truckers; Class II, an intermediate size class; and Class III, the corporate trucking companies. Because reporting requirements increase with size class, the level of bureaucratization almost certainly varies by class. Firms in the largest size class are also more likely to sell stock to the public (thereby exposing them to a different environment), and they are more likely to be organized by the Teamsters Union.

Because the ICC regulated most of these kinds of carriers and enforced reporting requirements, huge amounts of data exist that have been grouped by form. The distinctions used by the ICC had real significance for the operators of the firms and the recipients of their services. As the description given above suggests, the forms distinguished by the ICC depend on somewhat different sets of resources. They also differ in internal structure and in the patterns of links they maintain with other organizations, such as client firms and unions. Therefore, this set of distinctions seems promising as a provisional set of forms of trucking firms in any study that covers the years of regulation (Wyckoff and Maister 1977).

In contrast to using the conventional wisdom, a second approach involves deduction from a theory. The theory may permit predictions of specific features of specific structures or processual differences that are readily observable. This amounts to building typologies such as those advanced by Blau and Scott (1962) and Etzioni (1961). The utility of any such typology depends critically on the theorist's insight in choosing a set of dimensions for organizing the categories of the typology.

Finally, operational definitions of organizational forms can be developed with a numerical clustering method: the use of multivariate statistical procedures to reduce large amount of data to types (McKelvey 1975). This approach is most likely to be useful when the researcher thinks that survival implications accompany subtle and complicated differences among organizations, differences that are not commonly understood and, therefore, are not reflected in the common wisdom of those actively involved in the organizations.

We have relied on the conventional wisdom of participants and observers. However, we have not always used the conventionally defined forms directly in analysis; rather we have usually arrayed the forms along some analytic continuum and focused on variations along the continuum. For example, consider our analysis of restaurants, the details of which are reported in Chapter 12. We began by using conventional distinctions among forms of restaurants, often self-designations in advertising in the *Yellow Pages*. We came up with 33 forms, including such items as pizzerias, doughnut shops, steak houses, hotel restaurants, and a wide variety of ethnic specializations. We could have analyzed the demography and ecology of each of these 33 forms. But we were less interested in the precise forms than in underlying differences in specialism with respect to segments of the market. We reasoned that Japanese restaurants and doughnut shops, though very different in many ways, both restrict themselves to providing a very narrow range of the full spectrum of restaurant products and services. Likewise, a hotel dining room and a roadside diner also differ considerably but use a common strategy of offering a broad array of products and services. Because we were interested in the evolutionary dynamics of specialism versus generalism, we classified the 33 forms into specialist and generalist types and conducted our analyses of the dynamics of niche width using this distinction.

Some critics have questioned whether collapsing forms along analytic distinctions such as that between specialism and generalism is warranted (Carroll 1984; Astley 1985). Since our ultimate objective is to understand the forces that shape the dynamics of abstract properties of organizational forms, we do not think that our strategy has been misguided. However, the critics are at least partly right in faulting a tendency in our earlier research to elide the difference between forms and some abstract characterization of the strategies and structures associated with the forms. It is important to retain the distinction between forms as concrete entities whose boundaries are created and retained by technological factors, collective action, and institutional processes, and higher-order abstractions characterizing one or another dimension of a set of forms.

We have tried to make clear in this chapter that the definition of forms is a complicated business. Success in developing an ecology of organizations depends critically on careful attention to the issues discussed here. We think that a dynamic conception, one that treats the processes that create and erode boundaries among forms, has potential for resolving some of the complexities of classification of forms. It has the decided advantage of potentially transforming issues of definition into researchable questions. However, we have not yet pursued this approach in detail. Instead, we have concentrated on empirical analysis of populations in which definitions of forms and boundaries around populations are largely noncontroversial. We think that beginning with the simplest cases makes sense in early efforts to build a program of theory and research. If this program continues to develop, however, the issues treated in this chapter will eventually need much more attention than they have received.

4 | Structural Inertia and Organizational Change

Even if stable forms and populations can be identified, the application of ecological models to organizations is complicated by the possibility that individual organizations can change their strategies and structures. Unlike the biotic case, in which membership in a population is encoded in inert genetic material, individual organizations can and sometimes do make radical transformations in strategy and structure. If organizations can make fundamental changes quickly and routinely, it is hard to claim that the populations have strong unitary character. Common environmental dependence of members is transitory in such a situation. No partition of organizations into populations provides stable dimensions for the space within which organizational evolution occurs. Unless the dimensions can be anchored, we cannot explain change over time.

So another core assumption of the population ecology of organizations is that the characteristics locating individual organizations in a population rarely change rapidly relative to the processes of interest. We assume that individual organizations are characterized by *relative* inertia in structure and in the other characteristics that define membership in a population. But we do not assume that individual organizations never change form. Rather, we assume that such changes are infrequent and cannot be timed precisely to coincide with shocks that favor a particular (destination) population.

How strong are inertial forces on those elements of organizational structure that define forms? This question is substantively interesting in its own right. It is also strategically important, because the claim that adaptation theories of organizational change should be supplemented by population ecology theories depends partly on these inertial forces being strong.

Organizational changes of some kinds occur frequently; organizations sometimes even manage to make radical changes in the strategies and structures defining forms. Nevertheless, we hold that selection processes tend to favor organizations whose core structures are difficult to change quickly. That is, we claim that high levels of structural inertia in organizational populations can be explained as an *outcome* of an ecological-evolutionary process. In addition to deriving structural inertia as a consequence of a selection process, this chapter explores some of the details of inertial forces on organizational structure. It considers how inertial forces vary with the life cycle, organizational size, and complexity, and suggests some specific forms for these dependencies.

Our earliest formulation of an ecological theory of organizational change pointed to a variety of constraints on structural change in organizations (Hannan and Freeman 1977, p. 957): "for wide classes of organizations there are very strong inertial pressures on structure arising from both internal arrangements (for example, internal politics) and from the environment (for example, public legitimation of organizational activity). To claim otherwise is to ignore the most obvious feature of organizational life."

A minimal list of the constraints arising from internal considerations follows. First, an organization's investments in plant, equipment, and specialized personnel constitute assets that are not easily transferable to other tasks and functions. The ways in which sunk costs constrain adaptation are obvious. Second, organizational decision makers also face constraints on the information they receive. Research on flows of information in organizations reveals that leaders fail to receive anything close to full information on activities within the organization and in the relevant environment. In his influential essay on the information economics of organization, Arrow (1974, p. 49) suggests that "the combination of uncertainty, indivisibility, and capital intensity associated with information channels and their use imply (a) that the actual structure and behavior of an organization may depend heavily upon random events, in other words on history, and (b) the very pursuit of efficiency may lead to rigidity and unresponsiveness to further change." Third, internal politics contribute to inertia. Altering structures upsets political equilibria. When resources controlled by an organization are fixed, structural change requires reallocating resources among subunits; so at least some subunits are likely to resist any proposed reorganization. If resistance is strong, it can block change completely. Even weak resistance can greatly slow processes of change.

The benefits of reorganization are likely to be general. They are usually designed to benefit the organization as a whole. They are also likely to take a considerable time to be realized. Any negative political response will generate short-run political costs that may be high enough that decision-makers will forgo the planned reorganization. Recent research on decision-making shows that individuals tend to give greater weight to potential losses in making decisions than to equally likely potential gains (Kahneman, Slovic, and Tversky 1982). That is, the disutility of a loss of a given magnitude is greater than the utility associated with a gain of the same magnitude. This suggests that leaders and members in subunits facing losses from a change will tend to oppose it more strenuously than those who stand to gain will push the reorganization. Such a process generates strong inertial tendencies.

Finally, organizational histories generate constraints on fundamental change. Once standards of procedure and the allocation of tasks and authority have become the subject of normative agreement, the costs of change increase greatly. Normative agreements constrain adaptation in at least two ways. First, they provide legitimate justifications beyond self-interest for those who wish to oppose reorganization. We presume that such principled opposition to change has a great chance of success either in preventing change or at least in slowing it. Moreover, normative agreements also preclude serious consideration of many responses to threats and opportunities in the environment. For example, few research universities seriously consider adapting to declining enrollments by eliminating undergraduate teaching; entertaining this option challenges central organizational norms.

The external pressures toward inertia seem to be at least as strong as the internal ones for typical organizations. They include at least the following three factors. First, legal and fiscal barriers to entry and exit from markets are numerous. Discussions of industrial organization typically emphasize barriers to entry such as state-licensed monopoly positions. Barriers to exit may also be important sources of inertia. There appear to be numerous cases in which political and legal decisions prevent firms from abandoning certain activities. For example, the state of California has rejected numerous requests that the Union Pacific railroad be allowed to end its passenger service and specialize completely in freight. All such constraints on entry and exit limit the breadth of adaptation possibilities.

Second, internal constraints on the availability of information are paralleled by external constraints. Acquiring information about relevant environments is costly, especially in turbulent situations where the information is most essential. In addition, personnel tend to specialize in using certain information channels even when other, perhaps newer, channels would provide superior information. This is another kind of sunk cost, an accumulation of specific human capital (Arrow 1974). Such specialization limits the range of information about the environment that an organization can obtain and process, thus reducing the possibilities of adaptive change.

Third, the environment also imposes legitimacy constraints. Legitimacy constitutes an asset in sustaining flows of resources from the environment. When adaptive change violates legitimacy claims, organizations incur costs. Entertaining the possibility of eliminating undergraduate instruction in a research university might create internal legitimacy battles. Surely it would pose huge problems of legitimacy with alumni, foundations, state legislatures, and so forth. The likelihood that adaptation will compromise legitimacy serves as a strong brake on fundamental change.

Our view that organizations rarely change their fundamental structural features departs from the mainstream of oranizational theory and research. Consider the contrast with March's (1982, p. 563) summary of his review of research on organizational change: "Organizations are continually changing, routinely, easily, and responsively, but change within organizations cannot be arbitrarily controlled . . . What most reports on implementation indicate . . . is not that organizations are rigid and inflexible, but that they are impressively imaginative."

There are two issues here: (1) the frequency and speed of organizational change, and (2) the degree to which it can be planned and controlled. In this book we concentrate mainly on the the first issue: does most of the observed variability in organizational features reflect changes in existing organizations, whether planned or not, or does it reflect changes in populations, with relatively inert organizations replacing each other? In other words, does change in major features of organizations over time reflect mainly adaptation or selection and replacement?

The selection and adaptation perspectives are so different that it is hard to believe they are talking about the same things. Scott (1987, p. 202), in contrasting the most visible instance of each approach, claims that they are not: "The population ecology perspective seems to us to be particularly useful in focusing on the core features of organizations, explaining the life chances of smaller and more numerous organizations, and accounting for changes in organizational forms over longer periods. By contrast the resource dependency approach emphasizes the more peripheral features of organizations, is better applied to larger and more powerful organizations, and stresses changes occurring over shorter periods." This contrast provides a useful point of departure for an attempt to clarify the conditions under which the two perspectives apply.

Structural Inertia

The existing literature usually stresses the capacity of organizations to learn about and adapt to uncertain, changing environments. We think this emphasis is misplaced. The most important issues about the applicability of evolutionary-ecological theories to organizations concern the *timing* of changes.

Learning and adjusting structure enhance the chance of survival only if the speed of response is commensurate with the temporal patterns of relevant environments. Indeed, the worst of all possible worlds is to change structure continually only to find each time upon reorganization that the environment has already shifted to some new configuration that demands yet a different structure. Learning and structural inertia must be considered in a dynamic context. Do organizations learn about their environments and change strategies and structures as quickly as their environments change? If the answer is negative, replacement or selection arguments are potentially applicable.

Three things must be known in order to answer questions about the applicability of selection theories to populations of organizations. The first issue is the temporal pattern of changes in key environments. Are typical changes small or large, regular or irregular, rapid or slow? The second issue is the speed of learning mechanisms. How long does it take to obtain, process, and evaluate information on key environments? The third issue is the responsiveness of the structure to designed changes. How quickly can an organization be reorganized?

Claiming that organizational structures are subject to strong inertial forces is not the same as claiming that organizations never change. Rather, it means that organizations respond relatively slowly to the occurrence of threats and opportunities in their environments. Therefore, structural inertia must be defined in relative and dynamic terms. It refers to comparisons of the typical rates of change of the processes identified in the previous paragraph. In particular, structures of organizations have high inertia when the speed of reorganization is much lower than the rate at which environmental conditions change. Thus the concept of inertia, like fitness, refers to a correspondence between the behavioral capabilities of a class of organizations and their environments.

Our definition of structural inertia implies that a particular class of organizations might have high inertia in the context of one environment but not in another. For example, the speed of technical change in the semiconductor industry has been very high over the past twenty years. Firms that would be considered remarkably flexible in other industries have not been able to reorganize quickly enough to keep up with changing technologies.

An important threat to extant organizations is the creation of organizations designed specifically to take advantage of some new set of opportunities. When the cost of building an organization is low and the expected time from initiation to full production is short, this kind of threat is intense unless there are legal barriers to the entry of new organizations. If existing organizations cannot change their strategies and structures more quickly than entrepreneurs can begin new organizations, new competitors can establish footholds. Other things being equal, the faster the speed with which new organizations can be built, the greater is the relative inertia of a set of existing structures.

Even such a successful firm as IBM moves ponderously to take advantage of new opportunities. Granted, IBM eventually moved into the market for minicomputers and microcomputers and may come to dominate them. Still, the protracted period of assessing those markets, waiting for technologies to stabilize, and reorganizing production and marketing operations created the opportunity for new firms to become established. As a consequence, the structure of the computer industry is almost certainly different from the way it would have been had IBM been willing and able to move quickly. The point is that IBM did change its strategy somewhat, but this change took long enough that new firms using different strategies and structures were able to flourish, as in the case of the makers of clones of IBM microcomputers.

Organizations are special corporate actors. Like other corporate actors, they are structures for accomplishing collective action as well as repositories of corporate resources. Unlike other collective actors, organizations receive public legitimation and social support as agents for accomplishing specific and limited goals. Although individual members often manipulate organizations to serve private goals, and organizations operate in ways that diverge from their public goals, the basis on which organizations initially mobilize resources and gain support from society is their *claim* to accomplish some specific set of ends such as making a profit, treating the sick, or producing basic scientific research.

Creating an organization means mobilizing several kinds of scarce resources. Organization builders accumulate capital, commitment of potential members, entrepreneurial skills, and legitimacy (see Stinchcombe

1965). Once such resources have been invested in building an organizational structure, they are difficult to recover. Although one can sell the physical assets of a disbanded organization and sometimes its name, most resources used to build it are lost when it is dissolved. Not only are the costs of starting an organization nontrivial, but organizations consume resources in maintaining and reproducing their structures rather than in performing collective action. Just as in the case of biotic creatures, there is a substantial metabolic overhead relative to the amount of work performed. Thus the creation of a permanent organization as a solution to a problem of collective action is costly compared to other alternatives.

Why do individuals and other social actors agree to commit scarce resources to such expensive solutions to problems of collective action? A number of answers to this question have been put forth (see Scott 1987, pp. 143–159, for an insightful review). The new institutional economics argues that organizations arise to fill the gaps created by market failure (Arrow 1974). Williamson's (1975, 1985) influential analysis proposes that organizations are more efficient than markets in situations in which economic transactions must be completed in the face of opportunism, uncertainty, and small-numbers bargaining. Although sociologists tend to deny that organizations arise mainly in response to market failures, they tend to agree that organizations have special efficiency properties, emphasizing their efficiency and effectiveness for coordinating complex tasks (Blau and Scott 1962; Thompson 1967).

Although these efficiency arguments are plausible, it is not obvious that they are correct. Many detailed accounts of organizational processes raise serious doubts that organizations minimize the costs of completing many kinds of transactions. Indeed, there appears to be a strong tendency for organizations to become ends in themselves and to accumulate personnel and an elaborate structure far beyond the technical demands of work. Moreover, many organizations perform very simple tasks that involve low levels of coordination. In contrast, collections of skilled workers collaborating in ad hoc groups can often complete quite complex tasks. From the perspective of the performance of a *single* complex collective action, it is not obvious that a permanent organization has any technical advantage.

We emphasize different competencies. The first of these is *reliability*. Organizations have unusual capacities to produce collective products of a given quality repeatedly. In a world of uncertainty, potential members, investors, and clients may value reliability of performance more than efficiency. That is, rational actors may be willing to pay a high price for the certainty that a given product or service of a certain minimum quality will be available when it is needed. Reliability depends on the *variance* of performance, including its timeliness, rather than its average level.

Organizations have higher levels of reliability than ad hoc collectives in two senses: one cross-sectional and the other temporal. Cross-sectional reliability means that an outcome chosen at random from a population of organizations will have a lower variance than one chosen at random from a population of other kinds of producers. Temporal reliability means that variability over time in the quality, including timing of delivery, of an outcome is lower for those produced by organizations than for those produced by ad hoc groups. Overall, we argue that the distinctive competence of organizations lies in the capacity to generate collective actions with relatively small variance in quality.

Organizations have a second property that gives them an advantage in the modern world: *accountability*. The spread of general norms of rationality (Weber 1968) and a variety of internal and external contingencies demand that organizations be able to account rationally for their actions. They must be able to document how resources have been used and to reconstruct the sequences of organizational decisions, rules, and actions that produced particular outcomes. This does not necessarily mean that organizations must tell the truth to their members and to the public about how resources were used or how some debacle came about; what matters is that organizations produce internally consistent accounts indicating that appropriate rules and procedures existed to produce rational allocations of resources and appropriate organizational actions.

Norms of procedural rationality are pervasive in the modern world. Structural organizational legitimacy, in the sense of high probability that powerful collective actors will endorse an organization's actions (Stinchcombe 1968), depends on ostensible conformity to these norms. Coleman (1974) has argued that corporate actors favor other corporate actors over individuals. We add that corporate actors especially favor other corporate actors that give signals of procedural rationality and accountability.

Testing for accountability is especially intense during organization building, the process of initial resource mobilization. Potential members want assurance that their investments of time and commitment will not be wasted. When membership involves an employment relation, potential members often want guarantees that careers within the organization are managed in some rational way. Potential investors or supporters also assess accountability. In fact, the profession of public accountancy arose in the United States in response to the desires of British investors in American railroads for assurances that their investments were being managed in appropriate ways (Chandler 1977). Demands for accounting rationality in this narrow sense are both widespread and intense in modern societies. For example, the federal government will not allocate research grants or contracts to organizations that have not passed a federal audit, meaning that they have given evidence of possessing the appropriate rules and procedures for accounting for the use of federal funds.

Accountability testing is also severe when resources contract. Members and clients who would otherwise be willing to overlook waste typically change their views when budgets and services are being cut. Pressures for accountability are especially intense when (1) organizations produce symbolic or information-loaded products, such as education; (2) substantial risk exists, as in medical care; (3) long-term relations between the organization and its employees or clients are typical; and (4) the organization's purposes are ostensibly political (Weber 1968). Our arguments presumably apply with special force to organizations in these categories. Still, we think that pressures toward accountability are generally strong and getting stronger. The trend toward litigating disputes and pressures for formal equality in modern polities intensify demands for accountability. All organizations seem to be subject to at least moderate levels of accountability testing.

The modern world favors collective actors that can demonstrate or at least reasonably claim a capacity for reliable performance and can account rationally for their actions. So it favors organizations over other kinds of collectives and favors certain kinds of organizations over others, since not all organizations have these properties in equal measure. Selection within organizational populations tends to eliminate organizations with low reliability and accountability. The selection processes work in several ways. Partly they reflect testing by key actors and environments in the organization-building stage; potential members, investors, and other interested parties apply tests of reliability and accountability to proposed new ventures. Such testing continues after founding. Unreliability and failures of accountability at any stage in a subsequent lifetime threaten an organization's ability to maintain commitment of members and clients as well as its ability to acquire additional resources. Thus we assume that selection in populations of organizations in modern societies favors forms with high reliability of performance and high levels of accountability.

When does an organization have the capacity to produce collective outcomes of a certain minimum quality repeatedly? The most important prerequisite is so commonplace that we take it for granted. Reliable performance requires that an organization continually reproduce its structure—it must have very nearly the same structure today that it had yesterday. Among other things, this means that structures of roles, authority, and communication must be reproducible from day to day. In other words, reliability and accountability require that organizational structures be highly reproducible.

A structure can conceivably be reproduced repeatedly by negotiation and conscious decision-making; the members of an organization with such practices might happen to decide each day to recreate the structure that existed the previous day. But this seems unlikely. Reproducibility is far more likely under different conditions. In general, organizations attain reproducibility of structure through processes of institutionalization and by creating highly standardized routines.

The first solution, institutionalization, is a two-edged sword. It greatly lowers the cost of collective action by giving an organization a taken-for-granted character such that members do not continually question organizational purposes, authority relations, and so forth. Reproduction of structure occurs without apparent effort in highly institutionalized structures. The other edge of the sword is inertia: the very factors that make a system reproducible make it resistant to change. In particular, to the extent that an organization comes to be valued for itself, changes in structural arrangements become moral and political rather than technical issues. Attempts at redesigning structures in organizations built on moral commitment are likely to spark bursts of collective opposition premised on moral claims in favor of the status quo. Even if such opposition does not prevail, it delays change considerably.

As a brake on structural change, institutionalization applies both to the organization as a whole and to its subunits. But what about the diversity among sets of differentiated activities within the organization? Some kinds of organizations perform diverse sets of activities, sometimes in parallel and sometimes sequentially. Military organizations provide a striking example; they maintain peacetime and wartime structures. Similarly, labor unions gear up for organizing drives or for waves of strikes and then return to more placid bread-and-butter collective bargaining. Manufacturing firms concentrate sometimes on redesigning products and at other times on marketing an extant set of products. Each phase of organizational activity involves mobilizing different kinds of structures of communication and coordination. In a real sense these kinds of organizations can be said to use different structures in different phases.

Does this mean that these organizations have somehow escaped inertial tendencies? We think not, at least from the perspective of attempts at building theories of organizational change. These organizations have multiple routines; they shift from one routine (or set of routines) to another in a fairly mechanical fashion. We think that organizations have high inertia both in the sets of routines employed and in the set of rules used to switch between routines.

According to Nelson and Winter (1982, p. 96) routines are the "source of continuity in the behavioral patterns of organizations." They are patterns of activity that can be invoked repeatedly by members and subunits. One way of conceiving of routines is as organizational memory; an organization's repertoire of routines is the set of collective actions that it can do from memory. Nelson and Winter emphasize that organizations remember by doing. Like knowledge of elementary algebra or high school Latin, collective knowledge as the basis of organizational routines decays rapidly with disuse. Even occasional use reveals some decay in recall and demonstrates the need to reinvest in learning to keep skills at their former levels. Organizations that have the capacity to use a broad repertoire of routines do so by virtue of large investments in keeping their routines sharp. For example, peacetime armies devote a great deal of their resources to simulating wartime situations for training. Armies that fail to make such an investment experience great difficulty in making the transition to battle readiness.

The fact that organizational routines decay with disuse implies that organizations face the classic dilemma of specialism versus generalism in deciding how many routines to maintain at any fixed level of resources. Generalists—organizations with many routines—are no less inert than specialists in the manner in which they adapt to environmental change in the sense that they still use a limited number of routines. As Nelson and Winter (1982, p. 134) put it: "It is quite inappropriate to conceive of firm behavior in terms of deliberate choice from a broad menu of alternatives that some outside observer considers to be 'available' to the organization. The menu is not broad, it is narrow and idiosyncratic . . . Efforts to understand the functioning of industries and larger systems should come to grips with the fact that highly flexible adaptation to change is not likely to characterize the behavior of individual firms."

We think that it is a reasonable first approximation to think of organizations as possessing relatively fixed repertoires of highly reproducible routines. Then the argument of this chapter can be applied either to the organization as a whole, where the issue is the diversity of the repertoire, or to the individual routine. Thus we argue that the properties that give some organizations reproducibility also make them highly resistant to structural change, whether designed or not. As we noted earlier, this means that some aspects of structure can be changed only slowly and at considerable cost because many resources must be applied to produce structural change. Such structures have a dead weight quality; there are large lags in response to environmental changes and to attempts by decision-makers to implement change. Since lags in response can be longer than typical environmental fluctuations and longer than the attention spans of managers and outside authorities, inertia often blocks structural change completely.

The inertia of reproducible organizations is usually viewed as a pathology. A classic statement of this position is Merton's (1957) essay on the dysfunctions of bureaucracy. High levels of inertia may produce serious mismatches between organizational outcomes and the intentions of members and clients in situations in changing environments. On the other hand, organizations that try to reorganize frequently may produce very little and have slight chances of survival. Here the issue is the cause of structural inertia rather than its consequences. Our argument is that resistance to structural change is a likely by-product of the ability to reproduce a structure with high fidelity: high levels of reproducibility of structure imply strong inertial pressures.

The three assumptions of this section form the core of our argument. Taken together, they imply that selection within populations of organizations in modern societies favors organizations whose structures have high inertia. This argument holds that structural inertia can be a *consequence* of selection rather than a precondition. All that is required is that some organizations in an initial population have high levels of reproducibility with associated high levels of inertia and that selection pressures be reasonably strong. Under such conditions, selection pressures in modern societies favor organizations whose structures are resistant to change, which makes selection arguments all the more applicable.

A Hierarchy of Inertial Forces

So far we have considered organizations as unitary actors, either adapting to their environments or remaining inert. This is simplistic in that it ignores the obvious fact that some parts of organizations change more quickly than others, and that adaptive changes are sometimes not difficult to discern or implement. Universities, for example, constantly change their roster of courses. They do so in an adaptive way, by keeping up with the constantly evolving knowledge in their various fields. Persuading a university faculty to change its mission, for example to abandon liberal arts for the sake of vocational training, is something else again.

Why would the university's mission be so difficult to change? A number of answers come quickly to mind. The mission embodies the university's identity with reference both to the broader society and to its faculty, students, staff, administration, and alumni. The mission also represents one of the bases on which resources are distributed. A change toward a more vocationally oriented mission threatens entrenched interests; professors of classics and other humanistic fields that would have a lesser role in such an institution could be expected to resist such a change. The mission is difficult to change, then, because it represents the heart of the university's organizational identity and underlies the distribution of resources across the organization. In these ways, it can be said to lie at the university's core. The view that organizations have a core that is more difficult to modify than more peripheral parts of its structure is not new. As Parsons (1960, pp. 59–69) pointed out, hierarchies of organizational authority are not continuous; qualitative breaks occur between the technical, managerial, and institutional levels. The technical system is that part of the organization that directly processes the materials used by the organization. The resources used by the technical system to do the organization's basic work are allocated by a broader organizational apparatus, the managerial or administrative system, which also relates those technical activities to the public served. Although each depends on the other, the managerial level stands in a superordinate position: it both controls and services the technical level's operations, while the reverse is less often the case. The third part, the institutional system, links the organization with the broader society. Parsons emphasized its role in legitimating the organization. Boards of trustees and directors are responsible for long-run policy and for the conduct of the organization with regard to its reputed goals. Because the institutional and managerial levels of the organization stand prior to the technical level in controlling the flow of resources, any important change in their operations leads to changes in the details of the operations of the technical system, while the reverse is less often true.

Thompson (1967) adopted these distinctions in arguing that organizations are designed to protect structural units carrying out the core technology from uncertainties emanating from the environment. Thompson, however, drew core-periphery distinctions with reference to the organization's operating technology. Since we think that the importance of technology in determining structure varies greatly across kinds of organizations, we emphasize institutional characteristics more than technical ones. In this way our approach is closer to Parsons than to Thompson.

An argument similar to ours has been advanced by Downs (1967, pp. 167–168) in his use of the metaphor of organizational depth: "Organizations have different structural depths. Our analysis recognizes four 'organizational layers'. The shallowest consists of the specific actions taken by the bureau, the second of the decision-making rules it uses, the third of the institutional structure it uses to make those rules, and the deepest of its general purposes." The layers supposedly differ in characteristic speeds of response. We might add that the different layers are typically oriented to environmental conditions that change at different rates as well.

Earlier (Hannan and Freeman 1984) we suggested defining organizational forms in terms of four core characteristics: stated goals, forms of authority, core technology, and marketing strategy. Although these four properties encompass much of organizational strategy and structure, they do not come close to exhausting the dimensions of structure that interest social scientists. In particular, the list does not include structure in the narrow sense of numbers and sizes of subunits, number of levels in authority structures, span of control, patterns of communication, and so forth. Nor does it contain what Scott (1987) calls peripheral structures, the detailed arrangements by which an organization makes links with its environment and tries to buffer its technical core, for example, by forming interlocking directorates and joint ventures.

We think that organization charts and patterns of specific exchanges with actors in the environment are more plastic than the core set. The former aspects tend to change as organizations grow and decline in size, as technologies change, and as competitive and institutional environments change. They can be transformed because attempts at changing them involve relatively little moral and political opposition within the organization and in the environment, since they do not raise fundamental questions about the nature of the organization. In short, inertial forces on these aspects of structure and on peripheral or buffering activities tend to be weaker than those on core features.

Most organization theories assume that peripheral structures are premised on and adapted to a core structure. Changes in core structures usually require adjustment in the peripheral structures. However, the reverse is not true.[1] If a core structure is subject to strong selection pressure, peripheral structures will also be subject to at least weak indirect selection. In such cases, ecological theory applies at least indirectly to changes in pe-

---

1. Hawley's (1968, 1986) principle of isomorphism makes a similar argument concerning the relation between "key functions" and other organizational structures.

ripheral structures. The tighter the coupling between the core and peripheral structures, the more direct is the applicability of our theory.

Variations in Strength of Inertia

New organizations presumably have lower levels of reproducibility than older ones. As Stinchcombe (1965) pointed out, new organizations typically rely on the cooperation of strangers. Development of trust and smooth working relationships takes time, as does the working out of routines. Initially there is much learning by doing and comparing alternatives. Existing organizations have an advantage over new ones in that it is easier to continue existing routines than to create new ones or borrow old ones (Nelson and Winter 1982, pp. 99–107). Such arguments underlie the commonly observed monotonically declining cost curve at the firm level, the so-called learning curve.

In addition, reliability and accountability of organizational action depend on members' having acquired a range of skills that are specific to the organization, such as knowledge of specialized rules (especially how to cut through "red tape") and tacit understandings about political agreements among departments. Because such skills have little or no value outside the organization, members may be reluctant to invest heavily in acquiring them until an organization has proved itself (Becker 1975). Once an organization survives the initial period of testing by the environment, it makes more sense for members to make investments in organization-specific learning. In this sense, early success breeds the conditions for later success. Thus collective action becomes more reliable and accountable with age simply because of the temporal pattern of investments by members in organization-specific skills. Moreover, the collective returns to investments by members in organization-specific learning may take time to be realized, just as for other forms of human capital. For both of these reasons, the levels of reliability and accountability of organizational action should increase with age, at least initially. Once members have made extensive investments in acquiring organization-specific skills, the cost to them of switching to other organizations rises. Consequently the stake of members in keeping the organization going tends to rise as it ages, and they will presumably make greater efforts in its behalf. Finally, processes of institutionalization also take time. In particular, it takes time for an organization to acquire institutional reality to its members and to become valued in its own right.

Taken together, these assumptions imply that reproducibility of structure increases monotonically with age. Combined with our first derivation, this proposition implies that structural inertia increases monotonically with age, and that organizational mortality rates decrease with age.

The so-called liability-of-newness hypothesis (Stinchcombe 1965) has been well documented empirically, as we show in Part III. Mortality rates appear to decline approximately exponentially as organizations age. One explanation for this finding is that reproducibility rises roughly exponentially with age over the early years of an organization's life.

Processes of external legitimation also take time. Although an organization must have some minimal level of public legitimacy in order to mobilize sufficient resources to begin operations, new organizations and new organizational forms have rather weak claims on public and official support. Nothing legitimates both individual organizations and forms more than longevity. Old organizations tend to develop dense webs of exchange, to affiliate with centers of power, and to acquire an aura of inevitability. External actors may also wait for an initial period of testing to be passed before making investments in exchange relations with new organizations. Thus age dependence in processes of institutionalization in the environment and in developing exchange relationships with relevant sectors of the environment may account for the relationships stated in this section. The argument to this point cannot distinguish between the internal and the external sources of the relationships.

If dampened response to environmental threats and opportunities is the price paid for reliable and accountable collective action, organizations respond on average more slowly than individuals to environmental changes. However, some organizations are little more than extensions of the wills of dominant coalitions or individuals; they have no lives of their own. Such organizations may change strategy and structure in response to environmental changes almost as quickly as the individuals who control them. Change in populations of such organizations may operate as much by transformation as by selection.

Except in exceptional cases, only relatively small organizations fit this description. An organization can be a simple tool of a dominant leader only when the leader does not delegate authority and power through long chains of command. Failure to delegate usually causes problems in large organizations. Indeed, the failure of moderate-sized organizations is often explained as resulting from the unwillingness of a founder-leader to delegate responsibility as the organization grew. (Of course, this is an example of inertia at the level of key actors within the organization.)

One way to conceptualize these issues is to assume that there is a critical size, which may vary by form of organization and also, perhaps, by age, at which failure to delegate power sharply limits viability. In such a threshold model, organizations may be quite responsive below the threshold level of size, while organizations above the threshold tend to have higher inertia. Or the relationship between size and inertia may be roughly continuous. Downs (1967, p. 60) argues that for the case of public bureaus, "the increasing size of the bureau leads to a gradual ossification of its action . . . the spread and flexibility of its operation steadily diminish." Whether there is a threshold as we have suggested or a continuous relationship as Downs believes, it seems clear to us that the level of structural inertia increases with size for each form of organization.

This assumption seems to suggest that selection arguments are more appropriate for large organizations than for small ones, contrary to the widespread opinion discussed in Chapter 2. However, the situation is more complex than this. The likelihood that an organization will adjust structure to changing environmental circumstances depends on two factors: the rate of undertaking structural change and the probability of succeeding in implementing change, given an attempt. The assumption stated above suggests that the first quantity, the rate of attempting change, is higher for small organizations. But what about the second quantity?

It is helpful in answering this question to complicate the model slightly. Fundamental change, that is, change in core aspects of structure, rarely occurs overnight. More commonly, an organization spends some period of time reorganizing, either by design or happenstance. Usually there is a period of time during which existing rules and structures are being dismantled or successfully challenged and new ones are being created to replace them. Similarly, existing links with the environment are cut and new links forged. During such periods, organizations have elements of both old and new structures. The presence of multiple rules and structures greatly complicates organizational action; so too does a shifting set of environmental relations. Such changes increase the likelihood of conflict within an organization as contending parties seek to shape rules to benefit their self-interest.

Fundamental reorganization may sometimes occur gradually and imperceptibly. But sometimes sharp breaks with the past can be discerned, and one can identify the approximate time of onset of the reorganization. One clear example is a declaration of bankruptcy in order to obtain relief from creditors during a period of attempted reorganization. In many other circumstances, organizational leaders announce planned shifts in strategy and structure such as entries into new markets and internal restructuring.

In such cases it may be helpful to introduce a new state into the model: the state of attempting fundamental reorganization. Figure 4.1 depicts the possible transitions in this expanded state space. The parameters associated with each transition, the μ's, are transition rates. In terms of this representation, the assumption given above states that the rate of moving to the state of reorganization decreases with size. But it says nothing about the other rates.

The processes of dismantling one structure and building another make organizational action unstable. Consequently, the variance of quality and timeliness of collective action decline during reorganization. That is, the process of attempting reorganization lowers reliability of performance. This assumption along with the core argument of the chapter implies that attempts at reorganization increase mortality rates.

In the midst of structural reorganization, organizations are highly vulnerable to environmental shocks. Large size presumably enhances the capacity to withstand such shocks. Small organizations have small margins for error because they cannot easily reduce the scope of their operations very much in response to temporary setbacks. Thus organizational mortality rates decrease with size. Indeed, the claim that mortality rates decrease with size is nothing more than a restatement of the idea advanced earlier (Hannan and Freeman 1977) that longer time spans must be used to study replacement in populations of large organizations. We assume that size has qualitatively similar effects on all three mortality rates in Figure 4.1: μ_d, μ_e, and μ_f. Thus small organizations are assumed to be more likely than

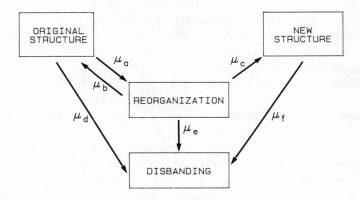

Figure 4.1   Rates of transition between structures

large ones to enter the state of reorganization but are also more likely to exit this state by mortality.

Finally, there is the issue of success at implementing change, the rate of moving from reorganization to new-structure. An organization undertaking reorganization can successfully make the transition to the new state or it can drift back to its original structure, assuming that it does not die. The model in Figure 4.1 contains two rates that pertain to these processes: μ_c, the rate of moving to the new structure, and μ_b, the rate of returning to the old one. The effect of size on these rates is unclear. On the one hand, the greater inertia of large organizations might lower the rate of success at reorganization; on the other hand, success at reorganization might depend on the magnitude of resources applied to the task. Since large organizations typically have more resources than small ones, this line of reasoning suggests that the rate of achieving structural change increases with size.

The relationship between size and the rate of structural change is indeterminate in our theory for two reasons. The first is ignorance about the effects of size on rates of completing structural reorganization, conditional on having attempted it. The second source of indeterminacy is the implication that small organizations are more likely to attempt structural change but are also more likely to suffer mortality in the attempt.

The model in Figure 4.1 may be substantively interesting in its own right, assuming that approximate information on dates of leaving states of reorganization can be obtained, which may not often be the case. This model provides a framework for addressing a variety of questions about inertia and change. It has the advantage of transforming what have been mainly rhetorical questions about the applicability of the ecological perspective into specific research questions. For example, consider again the question of life-cycle variations discussed in the previous section. Recall that we assume that reproducibility increases with age because routines become worked out, role relations stabilize, and so forth. What effect, if any, does structural reorganization have on these processes? Reorganization is sometimes tantamount to creating a new organization. When it involves such fundamental change, work groups are reshuffled bringing strangers into contact; routines are revised; lines of communication are reshaped; and the mix of resources used by the organization is changed. In this situation reorganization robs an organization's history of survival value. That is, reorganization reduces the reliability of performance to that of a new organization. The stability of the previous structure does not contribute to reducing variability with new sets of procedures, role relations, and so forth.

If internal processes are solely responsible for the tendency of organizational mortality rates to decline with age, the mortality rate for an organization that has just entered the state new-structure should be similar to the mortality rate of a completely new organization with that structure (and levels of resources). In this sense, reorganization sets the liability-of-newness clock back toward zero. In other words, structural reorganization produces a liability of newness. If, for example, one assumes that the hazard of mortality has a Gompertz form (discussed in Chapter 8), then the mortality rate has the form:

$$\mu_d(t|t_0) = \alpha' + \beta' \, e^{-\gamma'(t-t_0)},$$

where $\gamma' > 0$. Then for the case of an organization founded at t_0 that switches to this structure at $t_n > t_0$, the mortality rate is given under this scenario by

$$\mu_d(t|t_n) = \alpha' + \beta' \, e^{-\gamma'(t-t_n)}.$$

That is, development over the period (t_0, t_n) has no impact on the organization's mortality rate, other things being equal.

The argument in the preceding paragraphs can be viewed as one way to formalize some long-standing notions about organizational crises. Child and Kieser (1981, p. 48) put the issue as follows: "To some extent, a crisis successfully overcome may represent a new birth, in the sense that changes initiated are sufficiently radical for a new identity to emerge." We suggest that such questions be viewed in terms of shifts in age dependencies in organizational mortality rates.

External processes may also account for the tendency of mortality rates to decline with age. For example, we mentioned the tendency for organizations to acquire legitimacy simply by virtue of longevity as well as the fact that it takes time for organizations to develop enduring exchange relations with key actors in the environment. Some sorts of changes in strategy and structure strain external relations, especially when the changes imply a shift in ostensible goals. But simple structural reorganization, without any apparent change of goals, does not rob an organization's history of its value for public legitimacy and does not necessarily upset exchange relations with the environment. Old organizations can presumably count on their existing exchange partners for support during and following such structural change.

If the liability of newness reflects internal processes, the mortality rate will jump with structural changes. In contrast, if the decline in the mortality rate with age reflects mainly the operation of external processes of legitimacy and exchange, the mortality rate will not jump when structural changes do not imply a change in basic goals. That is, arguments about internal and external processes lead to different predictions about the effect of structural reorganization on the mortality rate. Therefore, the study of such effects may shed light on the relative importance of internal and external processes in accounting for age variation in the mortality rate in various organizational populations.

Finally, there is no reason to suspect that the mortality rate declines with duration in the state of reorganization. On the contrary, as the length of time over which reorganization is attempted increases, the costs (especially the opportunity costs) of reorganization increase. As the fraction of organizational resources devoted to reorganization increases, the capacity of the organization to produce collective products declines along with its capacity to defend itself from internal and external challenges. Hence protracted periods of reorganization disrupt organizational continuity and increase the risk of mortality. That is, the mortality rate of organizations attempting structural change rises with the duration of the reorganization.

This framework can perhaps elucidate another claim in the literature on organizations. March (1982, p. 567), in commenting on research on organizational change, suggests that "organizations facing bad times will follow riskier and riskier strategies, thus simultaneously increasing their chances of survival and reducing their life expectancy. Choices that seek to reverse a decline, for example, may not maximize expected value. As a consequence, for those that do not survive, efforts to survive will have speeded up the process of failure." It is hard to imagine how an action can both increase a survival probability and increase the mortality rate in conventional models for the mortality rate because life expectancy is a monotonically decreasing function of the mortality rate. However, the framework introduced above is consistent with this sort of pattern.

Consider the case in which the mortality rate of organizations in some environment rises precipitously at a certain moment t_1, perhaps as a result of some discontinuous change in the environment. The mortality rate of organizations that retain their structures, μ_d, will gradually decline to an asymptote that is considerably higher than the asymptotic rate in the old environment.

Suppose that some organizations in the population attempt structural change at t_1. Consider two kinds of trajectories of mortality rates by age.

The dashed trajectory in Figure 4.2 depicts the mortality rate of an organization that successfully implements the new structure at t_3. The dotted trajectory pertains to an organization that reverts to the old structure at t_4. In a collection of histories like those in Figure 4.2, one would see that strategic action to promote survival exposes an organization to great risks, thereby "reducing its life expectancy" (in the words of March). But, because the mortality rate declines rapidly with duration in the new structure, a successful transformation eventually leads to a lower mortality rate. So the change may appear to "increase chances of survival." However, it is not clear that structural change necessarily increases unconditional life expectancy; this depends on the various rates. Still, introducing the competing risks of mortality and reorganization allows one to deal systematically with this complicated problem.

We argued earlier that large organizations are less likely than small ones to initiate radical structural change. Does this mean that we think larger organizations have greater inertia, as Downs (1967) and others have

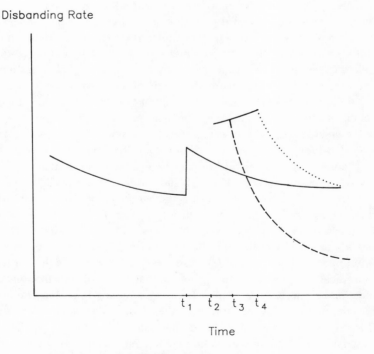

Figure 4.2   Trajectories of mortality rates by age

claimed? If inertia is equated with low absolute rates of initiating structural change, it does. When inertia is viewed in comparative terms, as we argue it should be, the relationship of size to inertia is more complicated than the literature has indicated.

We derived the proposition that organizational mortality rates decline with size. This statement is equivalent to the proposition that time scales of selection processes stretch with size, as we noted earlier. One way to visualize such a relationship is to consider environmental variations as composed of a spectrum of frequencies of varying lengths: hourly, daily, weekly, annually. Small organizations are more sensitive to high-frequency variations than large organizations. For example, short-term variations in the availability of credit may be catastrophic to small businesses but only a minor nuisance to giant firms. To the extent that large organizations can buffer themselves against the effects of high-frequency variations, their viability depends mainly on lower-frequency variations; the latter become the crucial adaptive problem for large organizations. In other words, the temporal dimensions of selection environments vary by size.

We proposed earlier that inertia be defined in terms of speed of adjustment relative to the temporal pattern of key environmental changes. Although small organizations are less ponderous than large ones and can therefore adjust structures more rapidly, the environmental variations to which they are sensitive tend to change with much higher frequency. Therefore, whether the adjustment speeds of small organizations exceed those of large ones compared to the volatility of relevant environments is an open question. One can easily imagine cases in which the reverse is true, in which elephantine organizations face environments that change so slowly that they are relatively less inert than the smallest organizations.

The complexity of organizational arrangements may also affect the strength of inertial forces. Although the term "complexity" is used frequently in the literature to refer to the numbers of subunits or to the relative sizes of subunits, we use the term to refer to patterns of links among subunits. Following Simon (1962), we identify a simple structure with a *hierarchical* set of links, which means that subunits can be clustered within units in the fashion of Chinese boxes, a lattice in technical terms. Hierarchical systems have the property that flows of information, commands, and resources are localized: an adjustment within one unit affects only units within the same branch of the hierarchy. Simon (1962) argued that hierarchical patterns have an evolutionary advantage: "Nature loves hierarchy." Research on population ecology supports Simon's argument. For example, May (1974), Šiljak (1975), and Ladde and Šiljak (1976) show analytically and with simulation experiments that ecological networks are destabilized when links of predation, competition, or symbiosis are introduced. Both the number of links and the complexity of the pattern affect stability.

We think that similar arguments apply to structural change within organizations. When links among subunits of an organization are hierarchical, one unit can change its structure without requiring any adjustment by other units outside its branch. However, when the pattern of links is non-hierarchical, change in one subunit requires adjustment by many more subunits. Such adjustment processes can have cycles; change in one unit can set off reactions in other units, which in turn require adjustment by the unit that initiated the change. Long chains of adjustment may reduce the speed with which organizations can reorganize in response to environmental threats and opportunities.

Although slow response does not necessarily imply a lower rate of attempting structural change, it seems likely that this is the tendency. As we noted earlier, a slow speed of response increases the likelihood that the environment will have changed before an organization can complete a process of reorganization. Knowledge of this fact may dissuade organizational leaders from initiating change and may serve as a powerful objection to proposed change by parties who benefit from the status quo.

Complex systems have slow response times not because they are any slower than simpler systems in detecting environmental threats and opportunities but because the process of adjustment takes longer. In terms of the framework developed in earlier sections, this argument implies that *complexity increases the expected duration of reorganization*. That is, once a complex organization has begun structural change, it will tend to be exposed to a longer period of reorganization than a simpler organization attempting similar changes. Therefore, complexity increases the risk of mortality due to reorganization.

A complete analysis requires consideration of the effects of complexity on rates of initiating change and of its effects on success in implementing change, as we discussed earlier in analyzing the effects of size. We are not yet ready to make any claims about the effects of complexity on these rates. Still, the proposition that complexity protracts reorganization suggests that population ecological analysis might be more appropriate for explaining change in populations of complex organizations than in populations of simple ones because complexity increases inertia by at least one mechanism. This result, like that concerning the effect of size, disagrees with the conventional wisdom.

The goal of this chapter has been to clarify the conditions under which it is reasonable to assume that organizational structures have inertia in the face of environmental turbulence. We have argued that selection pressures in modern societies favor organizations that can reliably produce collective action and can account rationally for their activities. A prerequisite for reliable and accountable performance is the capacity to reproduce a structure with high fidelity. The price paid for high-fidelity reproduction is structural inertia. Thus if selection favors reliable, accountable organizations, it also favors organizations with high levels of inertia. In this sense, inertia can be considered to be a by-product of selection. Our argument on this point may be considered an instance of the more general evolutionary argument that selection tends to favor *stable* systems (Simon 1962).

Of course, the claim that selection favors organizations with high inertia is not a warrant for assuming that most organizations have high inertia. Most organizational populations are replenished more or less continuously by an inflow of new members. Younger organizations tend to have less inertia than older ones, and new organizations are more likely to adopt structures that differ greatly from those that would dominate any steady state of the process subject to selection and closed to new entries.

Organizational selection operates on many dimensions besides reproducibility of structure. If selection pressures on specific features of structure are sufficiently strong, organizations with the characteristics appropriate to the environment are favored even if they have relatively low levels of reproducibility. By the same token, environments in which change is turbulent and uncertain may not constitute a systematic regime of selection; the traits that are favored may shift frequently enough that no clear trend emerges. Such settings may favor organizational forms that can take quick advantage of new opportunities. The capacity to respond quickly to new opportunities presumably competes with the capacity to perform reliably and accountably (see Brittain and Freeman 1980; Freeman 1982). Such dynamics may dilute the importance of reliability and accountability in organizational selection. For all these reasons, it is not sufficient to assume that selection processes favor organizations with high inertia and to proceed as though observed populations contain only such organizations.

5 | Competition and the Niche

We turn now to discussion of how we use general ecological theory to build models of organizational dynamics. As we have indicated, our approach explores the relations between organizations and larger social structures. Most of our questions concern the effects of changes in social environments on the world of organizations. These questions are sometimes stated in terms that imply that social environments are exogenous to processes of organizational change. (Some critics have charged that organizational ecologists incline toward this view; see Perrow, 1986, and Astley and Van de Ven, 1983, for example.) Does it make sense to assume that changes in social environments are somehow *given* and that they affect the world of organizations without being affected in turn? Making such an assumption misses a crucial duality: the social environment of individual organizations and populations of organizations consists mainly of other organizations.

A typical organization's social environment includes many kinds of organizations. There are the states that claim jurisdiction over an organization's activities, schools that prepare cohorts of potential recruits, firms that supply technical, material, and symbolic inputs, organizations that produce similar products and services, and those that purchase or use the products and services. Change in the environment of one organizational population usually means changes in the composition or activities of other organizational populations. If a particular social change alters the composition and activities of a focal population, these changes in turn reconstitute the larger social structure.

Recognizing the duality between major aspects of social structure and the composition and action of the organizations in society suggests a better

way to state our orienting questions. Understanding the causes and consequences of large-scale change requires analysis of the dynamics of the
world of organizations. It is difficult to understand these dynamics from
analysis of any single organization. Similarly, it is difficult to do so from
analysis of a single population of organizations, because the dynamics of
populations are usually linked (and each is environment to the other). So
we develop a theoretical approach that places attention squarely on *interactions within and between populations of organizations*.

As we noted in previous chapters, we found useful precedents in what is
sometimes called neoclassical population ecology. Classical bioecology
took its inspiration from Darwin, especially his notions about natural selection and the complex "web of life." But bioecology, with its emphasis
on naturalistic description, became isolated from the mainstream as evolutionary theory developed power from the synthesis of genetics and Darwinian evolution. However, starting in the 1960s a group of theorists led by
G. Evelyn Hutchinson and Robert MacArthur reinfused explicit evolutionary mechanisms into population and community ecology. These so-called
neoclassical theories try to explain patterns reported by naturalists as the
outcomes of population-genetic processes and of competition within and
between populations.

Modern population ecology concentrates on *numerical* aspects of population interactions. Analysis of the processes that constrain fluctuations in
sizes of populations and in the number of populations illuminates fundamental ecological processes. Hutchinson's (1959) famous essay "Homage
to Santa Rosalia" bears the subtitle "Why Are There So Many Kinds of
Animals?" The essay makes it clear that the subtitle poses a surprisingly
deep question. Explaining the seemingly simple numerical features of ecology raises virtually all the pressing theoretical issues in bioecology.

We use a similar strategy, concentrating on numerical features of the
world of organizations. In our earliest statements of the approach (Hannan
and Freeman 1974, 1977), we paraphrased Hutchinson: Why are there so
many kinds of organizations? This is a natural and important question for
sociology because individual organizations can in principle grow without
limit (Blau and Scott 1962). Under what conditions will one or a few
organizations expand to take on many activities in society? When will the
growth of organizations be constrained so that none grow really large and
many kinds proliferate? We suggested that the social science literature did
not have good answers to these questions and that trying to answer them
would shed new light on the dynamics of the organizational world.

Our focus on numerical aspects of the ecology of organizations leads naturally to an interest in diversity. The question of whether the number of kinds of organizations is growing or declining has immediate implications for the diversity of organizational actors in the society, as we discussed in Chapter 1. Therefore, we often formulate theoretical issues in terms of the processes that shape the diversity of organizations in society.

The Principle of Isomorphism

Until fairly recently, the sociological literature lacked explicit treatments of the causes of organizational diversity. The absence of theory and research on this issue is doubtless a result of the strong concentration of interest at the level of the *individual* organization. But recent theory on the organizational level does contain an implicit proposition about the causes of diversity. Most theory and research at the organizational level assume that organizations adjust structure to ensure the continued flow of critical resources. From an adaptationist perspective, organizations take on different structures only when crucial resources come in diverse streams. If key resources are few or if there are many that can be exploited with a few strategies and are also controlled by a few agents, there is no "need" for diversity. As the diversity of the resource base increases, the diversity in a set of adapting organizations increases.

An assumption of this kind lies at the core of sociological human ecology. Amos Hawley (1968), the main architect of the neoclassical perspective in human ecology, proposed a principle of isomorphism: "Units subjected to the same environmental conditions or to environmental conditions as mediated through a given key unit, acquire a similar form of organization. They must submit to standard terms of communication and to standard procedures in consequence of which they develop similar internal arrangements within limits imposed by their respective sizes." This principle implies that organizational diversity in a social system depends on the diversity of agents that control the flow of key resources into the system.

We noted earlier that Hawley's principle, like other adaptationist theories, does not apply when organizational resource environments are heterogeneous (Hannan and Freeman 1977). But most organizations obtain resources from many other organizations. They may obtain trained personnel from educational organizations and apprenticeship programs of labor unions, financial capital from banks and venture capital firms, material inputs from firms in different industries and perhaps in different countries, and licenses from federal, state, and local agencies. Moreover, change in the activities of agents who control key resources is often uncertain. For example, the policies of governmental agencies often change quickly when regimes change or when high courts issue rulings. In either case, the resource environment of each organization is heterogeneous, either at a point in time or over time or both. Heterogeneous environments pose complicated problems of adaptation.

According to the recent literature, organizations facing inconsistent demands from different environments try to create specialized structures to deal with each one. This view reflects the long-standing tradition in organization theory of emphasizing the tendency for organizations to develop differentiated substructures for performing specialized functions.

Leading institutional theorists such as Meyer and Scott (1983) suggest that organizations in the institutional sector deal with inconsistent demands from the environment by a strategy called loose coupling. According to Meyer and Scott, these organizations adapt to each environmental demand symbolically, by creating a substructure that deals or pretends to deal with the problem. But the activities of these peripheral structures are kept "loosely coupled" with the activities of the core of the organization. In other words, the activities of the peripheral units are not allowed to interfere with the real work of the organization. Organizations that use the strategy of ritual conformity only appear to be isomorphic to several environments that pose inconsistent demands; that is, they are symbolically or institutionally isomorphic to the environment.

The strategy of institutional isomorphism solves the problem of adapting to heterogenous environments with the organizational equivalent of smoke and mirrors. Such solutions appear unlikely to work—that is, to satisfy the diverse actors in the environment—for long periods, especially when competition for resources intensifies. When resources shrink, as they have for public education in recent years, actors who control key resources may investigate the tightness of coupling and may demand measurement of the quality and quantity of outputs. In fact, the Meyer-Scott scenario reads like a description of one possible outcome of environmental heterogeneity for organizations like public schools. The larger environment fluctuates between two conditions. When resources are abundant, inconsistencies among the various demands placed on these organizations are "solved" by creating special pools of resources for each problem and encouraging the target organizations to create specialized programs for each demand. When resources are scarce, public organizations are required to justify programs and document the links between claims and practices. The strategy of institutional isomorphism may be a good one when resources are rising; but it may not be so good when resources decline.

Perhaps some organizations can adapt to heterogeneous environments by multiplying peripheral structures and by weakening the link between public claims and actual practice. But this strategy handles only *cross-sectional* heterogeneity, variability among segments of the environment at a point in time. Once *temporal* heterogeneity is considered, the meaning of isomorphism as applied to heterogeneous environments is once again unclear. When environments shift over time, does isomorphism mean switching structures every time the environment changes? Or does it mean retaining a large number of peripheral structures at all times?

A general approach, one that deals symmetrically with cross-sectional and temporal heterogeneity in environments, seems needed. Extending the principle of isomorphism to apply to heterogeneous environments requires specification of the underlying dynamic processes. The dynamic processes of greatest interest to us are *competition* and *legitimation*. We think that a conceptualization based on niche theory allows specification of these processes in a sociologically interesting way that also provides a fresh view of issues of isomorphism. This approach allows us to develop propositions about change in the structure of populations of organizations that (1) face cross-sectionally and temporally heterogeneous environments, and (2) compete with other organizations, both within the population and in other populations, for limited resources.

The Niche

The main point of contact between existing organization theory and modern ecological theory is the concept of the niche. The concept provides a useful general way to express how environmental variations and competition affect the growth rates of populations. The imagery of the niche expresses the *role* of a population (or species) in a community, a population's "way of earning a living." Elton (1927, pp. 63–64), the most important pioneer in niche analysis in bioecology, put it this way: "It is . . . convenient to have some term to describe the status of an animal in its community, to indicate what it is *doing* and not merely what it looks like, and the term is 'niche' . . . When an ecologist says 'there goes a badger' he should include in his thoughts some definite idea of the animal's place in the community to which it belongs, just as if he had said 'there goes the vicar.'"

Although Elton's metaphor proved useful in naturalistic studies, it was not sufficiently precise for theoretical development. Modern niche theories began with Hutchinson's (1957) abstract geometric definition (see also Hutchinson 1978). He defined the niche as the set of environmental conditions within which a population can reproduce itself. That is, the niche is the set of conditions in which the population's growth rate is non-negative. Because growth rates usually respond to numerous environmental dimensions, the relevant environment consists of an N-dimensional space with each dimension telling the level of some relevant environmental condition, such as average rainfall or average diurnal temperature fluctuation. Each point in this space corresponds to a particular state of the N-dimensional environment. Hutchinson defined the *fundamental niche* of a population as the hypervolume formed by the set of points for which the population's growth rate (fitness) is non-negative. In other words, the fundamental niche consists of the set of all environmental conditions in which the population can grow or at least sustain its numbers. It is called the fundamental niche because it refers to the physiological capacities of the members of the population.

The analogue for populations of organizations is straightforward. Classical theorists, notably Marx and Weber, paid much attention to the social, economic, and political conditions required to sustain particular organizational forms, such as a capitalist business enterprise or a rational-legal bureaucracy. They suggested, for example, that the environmental dimensions that affect the growth of populations of rational-legal bureaucracies include the fraction of exchanges that are monetized, the availability of literate employees, and stability in flows of resources to the state. Taking the various dimensions together defines an N-dimensional social environment. The niche of rational-legal bureaucracy (or of any other organizational form) consists of the set of social arrangements in which this population can grow or at least not decline.

Specifying the niche of an organizational form requires intensive analysis of its natural history. Learning about the social, economic, and political conditions required to sustain a form of organization requires study of the details of the organizational form and the functioning of organizations that embody it. In fact, the concept of the fundamental niche of a form provides a felicitous device for incorporating institutional knowledge about kinds of organizations into systematic theory about population dynamics and evolution. It fits well with the actual practice of social scientists and others who provide detailed accounts of the functioning of various kinds of organizations.

A fundamental niche characterizes growth rates of isolated populations. The next step in the development of niche theory adds the effects of *interactions* among populations. From an ecological perspective, two or more populations interact if the presence of one affects the growth rate of the other(s). These effects may be either positive or negative. The term "competition" is often restricted to the case in which the negative effect is mutual, that is, to situations in which the presence of each population lowers the growth rate of the other. The predator-prey (or host-parasite) case has one negative and one positive link. The case in which both links are positive is called commensalism (or sometimes symbiosis).

We consider organizational instances of each of these kinds of situations in the chapters that follow. Many of the situations we analyze involve two populations competing for the same limited resources. For example, we contrast the life chances of populations of specialist and generalist restaurant firms competing for the business of the same set of consumers. We also find examples of a predator-prey pattern; we show, for example, that the growth of the population of craft unions stimulated the founding rate of industrial unions, but that the subsequent spread of industrial unionism depressed the founding rate of craft unionism. There are many obvious examples of commensalism in the organizational world. The creation of a new industrial form such as the semiconductor industry creates conditions for the establishment and growth of a set of related industries, such as the firms that produce the boards on which chips are placed.

When populations interact, the expansion of one population changes the niche of the others. If two populations compete, the presence of the competitor reduces the set of environments in which a population can sustain itself. Hutchinson called this restricted set of environments the *realized niche*. Two populations compete if and only if their fundamental niches intersect. The assumed equivalence of niche overlap and competition has played a crucial role in allowing ecologists to relate naturalistic observations on realized niches to dynamic models of population growth and expansion. We think that it can play a similarly central role in empirical and theoretical analysis of organizational dynamics. In order to make the potential connections clear, we first review classical theories of population growth and interaction and then discuss theories of niche width.

Classical Competition Theory

The development of competition theory in population bioecology was influenced strongly by Gause's (1934) experiments on the coexistence of closely related species of beetles in controlled environments. He found that mixing two populations in the laboratory invariably caused one population to disappear. Gause summarized his findings by proposing a general ecological law. His *principle of competitive exclusion* holds that two species that occupy essentially the same fundamental niche cannot coexist in equilibrium.

Subsequent research has ruled out competitive exclusion as a general principle. For example, it turns out to be simple to produce coexistence of closely related species in the laboratory: one makes the environment more complex, creating subenvironments in which the inferior competitor can find refuge or may possess an adaptive advantage. Nonetheless, this "principle" has proved useful in directing attention to the crucial role of niche overlap in competition processes. It has also stimulated the application of general models of population dynamics to concrete ecological processes.

In order to make the foregoing discussion concrete, we consider the simple case of one environmental dimension, where niche intersection takes the form of simple overlap. Following Levins (1968), we use a graphic representation in which the adaptive capacity of each population is summarized by a fitness function which relates growth rates (fitness) to levels of the environmental condition. A fitness function tells the speed of growth of populations of various phenotypes bearing levels of a trait, y, in a particular environment. The fitness function tells which level of y is optimal in the sense of providing maximum population growth rates as well as how sharply departures from the optimum are penalized in terms of reduced growth.

In an organizational example, y might be the proportion of revenues that firms spend on research and development, and the environmental dimension might be the speed of technical change in the industry. During an era in which an industry's technology is developing rapidly, high expenditures on research and development produce high growth rates for the firms, as well as high profits. Such firms attract imitators, and high research and development firms become more numerous. When technological change slows and new discoveries come farther apart, heavy expenditures on research and development produce lower payoffs, and imitation of technical pioneers is less likely. So the fitness of firms displaying high values of y is lower at low rates of technical change.

Figure 5.1 shows hypothetical fitness functions for three populations. In this example population B competes with both A and C, but A and C do not compete with each other. However, the overlap of the niches of A and B is considerable, while the overlap of B and C is slight. What happens in the regions of overlap? Do populations A and B coexist, sharing the resources? Does one exclude the other? Although these questions have not been raised in the context of organization theory, they are not new questions. Since these issues have been investigated for some time in the con-

FITNESS

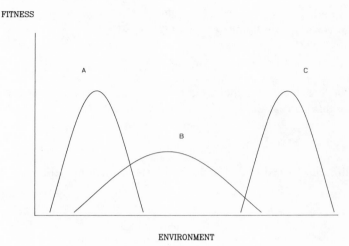

ENVIRONMENT

Figure 5.1 Hypothetical fitness functions

text of other disciplines, notably population biology, it makes sense to try to build on existing theory and models.

Alfred Lotka (1925) and Vito Volterra (1927) independently proposed models of population dynamics that incorporate effects of competition between populations. They began with models that imply that population growth of isolated populations has an S-shaped growth path. They assumed that the growth rate of an isolated population is given by the product of a growth rate and the current size of the population:

(5.1) $$\frac{dN}{dt} = \rho_N N,$$

where N denotes the size of the population. The growth rate, ρ_N, is defined as the difference between the birth and the death rates of the population:

$$\rho_N = \lambda_N - \mu_N.$$

Suppose that birth and death rates are constant, that is, that they do not vary with the size of the population. Then the model in (5.1) implies exponential growth. But such growth processes are not realistic in finite environments, as Malthus insisted. The growth model can be made more realistic by assuming that birth and death rates vary with density (the size of the population). Lotka and Volterra assumed that the birth rate falls approximately linearly with the size of the population:

$$\lambda_N = a_0 - a_1 N, \qquad a_1 > 0$$

and that the death rate increases approximately linearly with population size (assuming that the resources available are finite):

$$\mu_N = b_0 + b_1 N.$$

Substituting the last two equations into the growth model (5.1) gives

(5.2) $$\frac{dN}{dt} = \pi_1 N - \pi_2 N^2,$$

with $\pi_1 = a_0 - b_0 > 0$ and $\pi_2 = a_1 + b_1 > 0$. This is the model of logistic population growth. It holds that the population grows almost exponentially at low values of N, but that competition for fixed resources eventually drives the growth rate toward zero.

Note that (5.2) and the restrictions on the signs of coefficients imply a steady state for the population. Setting equation (5.2) equal to zero shows steady states at $N = 0$ and $N = \pi_1/\pi_2$. The non-zero steady state of the population is usually called the *carrying capacity* of the environment for the population in question. It has traditionally been denoted by K in bio-ecology.

The logistic model of population growth can be expressed in terms of the carrying capacity:

(5.3) $$\frac{dN}{dt} = rN \left(\frac{K - N}{K} \right).$$

The coefficient $r = a_0 - b_0$ is called the *intrinsic growth rate*. It tells the speed with which the population grows in the absence of resource constraints. That is, when the population size is small compared to the carrying capacity, the growth rate essentially equals r. When the population size equals the carrying capacity, the growth rate is zero. If population size exceeds the carrying capacity (perhaps because some shock has reduced the carrying capacity), the growth rate is negative.

The parameterization in equation (5.3) provides a substantively appealing way to introduce competition. Two populations compete if the size of each population lowers the carrying capacity for the other. The Lotka-Volterra (LV) model of competitive interactions, which plays a prominent role in much contemporary population bioecology, assumes that the effect of the density of the competitor on the realized carrying capacity is *linear*. In the case of two competing populations, the model is

(5.4a) $$\frac{dN_1}{dt} = r_1 N_1 \left(\frac{K_1 - \alpha_{12} N_2 - N_1}{K_1} \right),$$

(5.4b) $$\frac{dN_2}{dt} = r_2 N_2 \left(\frac{K_2 - \alpha_{21} N_1 - N_2}{K_2} \right).$$

Comparing (5.4a) and (5.4b) with (5.3) shows that the presence of the competitor reduces the carrying capacity for the first population from K_1 to $K_1 - \alpha_{12} N_2$. The so-called *competition coefficients*, α_{12} and α_{21}, tell how the carrying capacity for each population declines with the density of the competitor. This model decomposes the growth rate for each population into the effects of three components: (1) r_i, the intrinsic properties of the form that affect its speed of growth in the absence of resource limitations and competition; (2) K_i, limits on growth that reflect generalized conditions of resource availability; and (3) α_{ij}, competition with specific populations (where the coefficient indicating the effect of intrapopulation competition, α_{ii}, has been scaled to unity).

Even though the LV model builds on simple notions of density-dependence in birth and death rates and of the effects of competitive interactions, the system of equations in (5.4) does not have a known solution. Therefore, analysis of questions of coexistence of competing populations, that is, whether models like (5.3) have stable steady states with non-zero sizes of both populations, relies on study of the qualitative behavior of the system of differential equations (see, for example, Wilson and Bossert 1971). The general result is that coexistence requires that the effects of density on mortality rates within populations must be stronger than the competitive effects between populations.

This is easy to see in the case of two competing populations. Setting equations (5.4a) and (5.4b) equal to zero and solving for the non-zero equilibrium values of N_1 and N_2 shows that stable coexistence requires that

$$\frac{1}{\alpha_{21}} < \frac{K_2}{K_1} < \alpha_{12}.$$

Therefore, very similar populations (that is, populations whose competition coefficients are very near unity) can coexist only under a precise K_2/K_1 ratio. Any shock to the system that alters either carrying capacity is likely to drive the system away from the special conditions that support coexistence. Since this is an unstable equilibrium, the system will not tend to restore itself to the condition of coexistence.

Analysis of LV systems provides a way to assess Gause's principle. If two populations occupy essentially the same niche, both competition coefficients are close to unity, because addition of a member of the competing population has almost the same dampening effect on population growth as addition of a member of the population in question. Coexistence of competing species is extremely unstable when competition coefficients are close to unity. This does not mean that the principle of competitive exclusion follows logically from the LV model; but it suggests that his principle does describe accurately the instability of coexistence of populations that occupy the same niche.

The general (I-dimensional) LV system has the form:

$$\frac{dN_i}{dt} = r_i N_i \left[K_i - \sum_{i=1}^{I} \frac{\alpha_{ij} N_j}{K_i} \right], \qquad \alpha_{ii} = -1.$$

The matrix of competition coefficients, sometimes called the community matrix, governs stability. Although this matrix is not generally symmetric because the competition coefficients for pairs of populations are not equal, it does equal the product of a symmetric matrix of overlaps and a diagonal matrix whose entries indicate the total resource use of a population (Roughgarden 1979). The equilibrium point of this dynamic system satisfies

$$\sum_{i=1}^{I} \alpha_{ij} N_j = K_j.$$

If one or more of N_j are zero or negative, it follows that not all I populations can coexist in a stable equilibrium, and competitive exclusion occurs. If the vector of the sizes of the populations is strictly positive, the stability of the coexistence of all I populations depends on the properties of the community matrix.

Stable coexistence requires that the matrix of competition coefficients has a non-zero determinant. Levin (1970) proved that, in the context of populations whose growth depends on resources and constraints, this requirement means that at least *I* distinct resources and constraints are needed to support the stable coexistence of *I* populations. Thus the number of coexisting populations is constrained by the number of resources and constraints. Earlier (Hannan and Freeman 1977) we suggested that this qualitative result could be applied in organizational analysis. We proposed that the diversity of a community of organizations, that is, the number of coexisting organizational populations, increases when new resources and constraints are added to social systems and declines when resources and constraints are eliminated.

Even though LV models do not have explicit solutions, they can still be estimated with data. Interestingly, the first attempt we have seen to do so with nonexperimental data is Carroll's (1981) analysis of growth and decline in populations of organizations (see also Tuma and Hannan 1984, chaps. 11 and 14). By estimating an exact-discrete approximation to the LV model, Carroll was able to estimate competition coefficients directly from data. Recently Brittain and Wholey (1988) have used Carroll's approach to estimate competition coefficients among subdivisions of the American semiconductor manufacturing industry.

Niche Overlap and Competition

Competition, unlike conflict, is difficult to observe directly because it is often indirect. Therefore, empirically-minded analysts look for ways to study competition indirectly. One way is to exploit the relationship between niche overlap and competition that is implied by classical competition theory. This is the tack that population biologists have taken. They typically do not use the LV model or its relatives to estimate α's from nonexperimental data. Instead they rely on the close relationship between competition theory and niche theory to obtain indirect estimates of competition from overlap of niches defined in terms of observed utilization of resources. The profile of utilization of a population is a summary of its concentration on various levels of a continuous resource or on categories of a discrete resource. We denote the utilization function of population i by $u_i(z)$. That is, $u_i(z)$ indicates the intensity with which a population uses the resource in question at level z. An example in organizational ecology is the size of a particular kind of transaction, such as a contract for construction. Such contracts vary from those involving hundreds of dollars for small household repairs to some involving billions of dollars for constructing dams or highways. Different populations of contractors apparently specialize in making bids in different portions of the range, with local general contractors at the lower end and multinational corporate contractors at the other.

Suppose that two populations of firms, i and j, use the same general resource base but with differing profiles of utilization. Following MacArthur (1972), we define the competition coefficient for this case as:

$$\alpha_{ij} = \frac{\int u_i(z)u_j(z) \, dz}{\int u_i^2(z) \, dz}.$$

This expression tells the probability that a member of population i will encounter a member of population j at a particular resource position averaged over all resource positions divided by the probability that it will encounter a member of its own population at each position. Thus the competition coefficient tells the probability of inter-population interaction in resource acquisition relative to intra-population interaction.

When the resource has a discrete distribution, the corresponding measure of the competition coefficient is equivalent to an index well known to sociologists: Bell's (1954) p^* index of segregation (see also Lieberson 1969). The p^* index was devised to measure the probability of contacts between racial or ethnic populations over neighborhoods or census districts. Olzak (in press) has generalized this index to measure occupational competition between ethnic groups. This analysis treats occupations as resources and compares the utilization of these resources for different ethnic groups as the way to measure competition. A similar approach for measuring niche overlap appears to have considerable merit in organizational research.

A population's *niche width* is the variance of its resource utilization:

$$w_i = \int (z - \bar{z})^2 u_i(z) \, dz.$$

So, for example, a set of construction firms that bids only on contracts for renovations of residential housing has a low variance of utilization of the resource base in terms of size of contract; they have a narrow niche. A population of firms that bids on those projects as well as on many other types has a broad niche.

Some resources have discrete distributions, for example the set of industries over which labor unions can organize. For such cases, niche position is defined as the discrete distribution of utilization over the categories, and niche width is defined as an index of dissimilarity. Population biologists typically use Shannon's information (entropy) measure:

$$w_i = - \sum_{r=1}^{R} u_r \log u_r.$$

These measures generalize naturally to multiple dimensions for both continuous and discrete resources.

We use this approach in measuring niche width. For example, we measure the niche width of semiconductor manufacturing firms in terms of the fraction of the industry's mix of products that a firm produces. (Since we do not have complete data on the proportion of each firm's value of sales for each product, we cannot compute an entropy measure of diversity for firms.) Similarly, we characterize a labor union by the number of occupational and industrial categories that it claims to organize.

It is worth emphasizing that the niche of any population is multidimensional. Niche width can be defined with respect to each dimension of the niche. A particular unit (or population) may have a broad niche with respect to one dimension and a narrow niche with respect to another. For example, a union may organize broadly in terms of occupations but narrowly with respect to industries, as when classic industrial unions try to organize all trades in one or a few industries. On the other hand, many classic craft unions organized a single trade across many industries that employ the trade. Which dimensions of the niche to emphasize in any analysis is an important substantive question.

What are the advantages and disadvantages to a population of organizations of having a narrow niche? Attempting to answer this question exposes fundamental issues in organizational ecology; it raises a jack-of-all-trades problem that is central to the analysis of organizations but has so far been given little attention. This is the obvious tradeoff between tolerance of widely varying conditions and capacity for high performance in any particular situation. Organizations just cannot do all kinds of activities superbly. Investment in the capacity to perform one kind of action efficiently and reliably means less investment in other capacities, since resources and the time of members are finite. Moreover, as we have already discussed, maintaining the capacity to do many kinds of activities consumes a great many resources and thereby implies reduced efficiencies and reliability in performing at least some kinds of activities. So organizations and their designers face a classic problem: should they seek to become jacks-of-all-trades (and masters of none), or should they concentrate on developing one or a few capacities?

Although this question has not been pursued seriously by organization theorists, it has been the focus of much attention in population biology. Again we suggest that it would be useful to try to build on these efforts rather than trying to reinvent the wheel. In particular, we have found Levins' (1968) theory of niche width to be a useful point of departure in answering questions about specialism versus generalism in populations of organizations (Hannan and Freeman 1977; Freeman and Hannan 1983).

Some of the efficiency resulting from specialism derives from lower requirements for maintaining excess capacity. Given some uncertainty about the environment, most organizations maintain some excess capacity to ensure reliability of performance when conditions change. In rapidly changing environments, the definition of excess capacity changes frequently. What is fully employed today may be excess tomorrow, and what is excess today may be crucial tomorrow. Because generalists hold some capacity in reserve and specialists commit most of their resources to a few tactics for dealing with the environment, specialist organizations will appear to be leaner than generalists, to have less organizational "slack." So in a sense niche theories ask whether organizational slack provides an evolutionary advantage.

Niche width theories address both temporal and spatial variations in environments. They typically focus on two features of temporal and spatial distributions. The first is the level of environmental *variability*, the variance of a spatial or temporal series about its mean; the second is the pattern of variation or *grain*. Grain refers to the pattern of mixing of different types of outcomes in the spatial or temporal distribution. Think of a spatial distribution as being composed of small patches of different types. When the patches are well mixed, large runs of one type are rare. Such a distribution is said to be fine-grained. Alternatively, when the patches are not well mixed, large runs of one type can occur. Such a distribution is said to be coarse-grained.

In the case of a temporal series, the variability of a series can be represented by combinations of waves with different frequencies. When high-frequency variations dominate, the series has fine grain. When low-frequency variations comprise much of the variance in the series, it has coarse grain. Except for the extreme case of complete stability (for which grain is undefined), variability and grain can vary independently. In our analysis of mortality in the semiconductor industry we characterized the industrial environments of firms in terms of the variability in aggregate sales in the industry for the product categories they produced and in terms of lengths of cycles in the time series of aggregate sales. We treated series with mainly short (high-frequency) cycles as fined-grained, and those with longer (low-frequency) cycles as coarse-grained.

Consider how environmental variations affect growth rates (fitness) by examining the simple case of environments that fluctuate between two kinds of patches either spatially or temporally. Figure 5.2 displays hypothetical fitness functions for two cases. In the top panel, the fitness functions for the two kinds of patches overlap considerably, meaning that the two kinds of patches impose similar adaptation demands. In the bottom panel, the overlap is small, meaning that the two kinds of patches pose very different adaptive demands—high fitness in one environment precludes high fitness in the other.

Now consider many different kinds of populations with differing levels of fitness in the two kinds of patches. Levins represented fitness sets with curves like those in Figure 5.3, whose axes represent fitness in the two kinds of patches. Each population, with a fixed pair of fitness values in the two patches, is a point in the fitness set. The boundaries of the fitness sets are the points of maximum fitness. In the top panel, which represents the fitness sets for the curves in the top part of Figure 5.2, the fitness set is convex along its upper right boundary. That is, all straight lines connecting points in the fitness set fall within the set. The case of dissimilar patches, the bottom panel of Figure 5.3, produces a concave fitness set.

Levins introduced a graphic method for finding optimal strategies, assuming a principle of allocation that makes strategic analysis interesting: each population has a constant sum of fitness that may be allocated across strategies for playing the evolutionary game. This method involves using so-called adaptive functions, which tell how selection processes weight fitness in two kinds of patches. In the case of fine grain, actors encounter the environment in small patches.[1] Fine-grained environments are experienced as an average of the various types of patches. Levins reasoned that selection in fine-grained environments weights fitness in the two kinds of patches additively (see also Roughgarden 1979, p. 269). This reasoning

1. Since a given patch will be large for some kinds of forms and small for others, patch size must be defined relatively. A patch is small for a population if typical durations are short relative to life expectancy of individual members of the population.

FITNESS

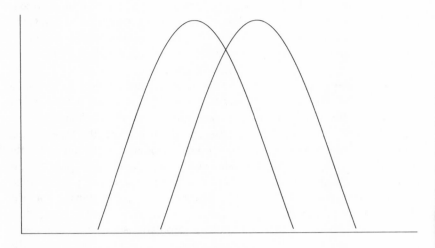

ENVIRONMENT

FITNESS

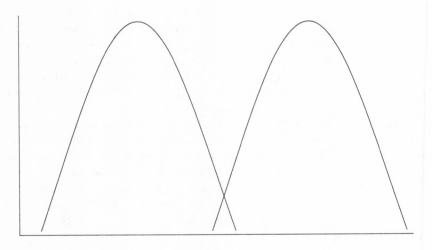

ENVIRONMENT

Figure 5.2   Fitness functions. (*top*) Similar environments; (*bottom*) dissimilar environments

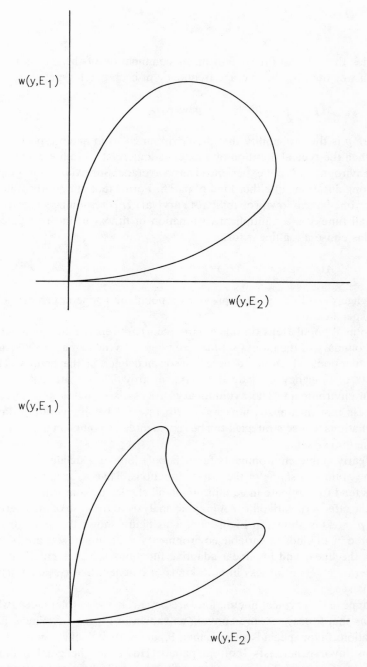

Figure 5.3 Fitness sets. (*top*) Similar environments; (*bottom*) dissimilar environments

implies that overall fitness is a linear combination of the fitness in each patch weighted by the average frequency of each patch type:

$$A(f) = pw(E_1) + (1 - p)w(E_2),$$

where p is the probability that the environment is in patch type 1.

When the typical duration of a patch is long relative to life expectancy, the environment is not experienced as an average. Survival requires enduring long durations of either kind of patch. Forms that are poorly suited to either one have a low probability of survival. This reasoning suggests that overall fitness is a multiplicative function of fitness in the two patches. Levins chose a log-linear form:

$$A(c) = w(E_1)^p \, w(E_2)^{1-p}.$$

Roughgarden (1979, p. 269) provides a population-genetic justification of this specification.

Optimal populations (in this environment) are represented by points on the boundary of the fitness set that are tangent to the highest-valued adaptive function, which are denoted by dashed lines in the figures. These points of tangency indicate the maximal growth rates attainable in the given environment. The evolutionary process is modeled as a selection process that maximizes fitness (growth rates). That is, evolution favors populations whose strategies can be represented as points on the boundary of the fitness sets.

Clearly stable environments favor populations of specialists regardless of the grain and shape of the fitness functions. That is, specialist populations tend to dominate in equilibrium in all stable environments. But what are the effects of variability? A graphic analysis of the case of high variability ($p \approx .5$) is shown in Figure 5.4. This figure shows that generalism is favored in all kinds of variable environments when fitness sets are convex. Both the linear and log-linear adaptive functions select populations with moderate levels of fitness in both kinds of patches, that is, generalists in this case.

Suppose that typical fluctuations are large relative to tolerances, which means that fitness sets are convex, as shown in Figure 5.5. Fine-grained variations favor specialists (top panel, Figure 5.5), but coarse-grained variations favor generalists (bottom panel). However, the combination of coarse-grain variability and concave fitness sets favors populations consisting of mixtures of specialists. Populations that contain mixtures of

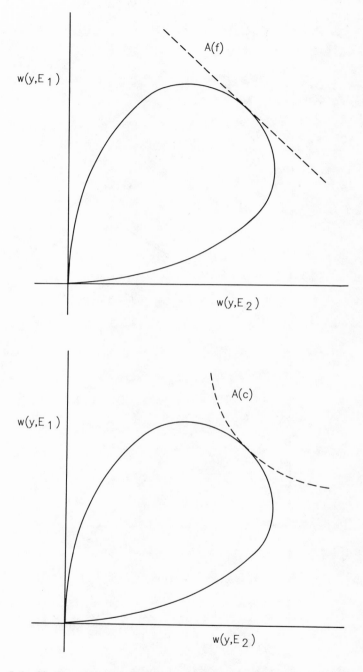

Figure 5.4 Similar environments. (*top*) Optimal strategy with fine grain; (*bottom*) optimal strategy with coarse grain

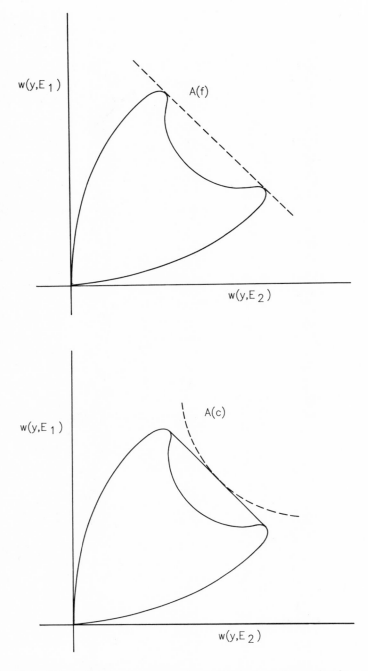

Figure 5.5 Dissimilar environments. (*top*) Optimal strategy with fine grain; (*bottom*) optimal strategy with coarse grain

specialists are called *polymorphs*. The fitness of polymorphic populations is bounded by the straight line on the upper right boundary of the fitness set in the bottom panel of Figure 5.5. Note that selection favors polymorphic populations over generalists when both are present; otherwise it favors generalists over specialists.

Earlier (Hannan and Freeman 1977) we discussed an organizational analogue to polymorphism. Organizations may federate in such a way that supraorganizations consisting of heterogeneous collections of specialist organizations pool resources. When the environment is uncertain and coarse-grained and it is costly to establish and dismantle subunits, the costs of maintaining the unwieldy structure imposed by federation may be more than offset by the fact that at least a portion of the amalgamated organization will do well no matter what the state of the environment.

Such a holding company (or H-form) pattern seems to characterize modern universities. Enrollments, research support, yields on invested endowments, and levels of public funding fluctuate over time for most universities. Some of these fluctuations follow predictable cycles; others do not. What is the optimal adaptation to such fluctuations? One possibility is to reallocate funds internally among subunits so that currently favored units expand and others contract. In the extreme, universities might create schools and departments when there is external support for them and close them down when the support dwindles. However, it is extremely expensive to build up and dismantle academic units; this is costly not only in material terms but also in the energies consumed by political conflict. It also takes time to build new academic units, and it is doubtful whether most universities can do so quickly enough to keep pace with fads and fashions. Consequently, universities tend to "tax" subunits with bountiful environments to subsidize less fortunate subunits. It is common, for example, for universities to allocate faculty positions according to some fixed master plan, undersupporting departments in rapidly growing fields and maintaining excess faculty in others. This partial explanation of the unwieldy structures that encompass liberal arts departments, professional schools, extension services, and research laboratories is at least as persuasive as explanations that emphasize intellectual interdependence among units and use of shared resources.

Consider another application of niche width theory. Stinchcombe (1959) pointed out that construction firms do not fit the common bureaucratic model of organization. Instead of relying on bureaucratically organized administrative staffs to coordinate work, they employ high-wage skilled craftsmen. They implicitly leave the coordination of most work to craftsmen, who follow a set of blueprints. These firms also delegate selection, training, and allocation of workers to the craft construction unions. Stinch-combe argued that this is an expensive set of solutions. Considerably higher wages are paid than would be the case if construction firms created a fine-grained, "deskilled" division of labor with bureaucratic labor con-trols. It may also be expensive in the sense that the firms can exercise little control over the detailed flow of the work. What explains the continued reliance of construction firms on this apparently expensive solution?

Stinchcombe suggested that the answer to this question lies in consider-ing the consequences of large seasonal fluctuations in construction work. Administrative staffs constitute an overhead cost that remains relatively constant over the year. Under a craft system, levels of employment of production workers can easily be shifted up or down with the level of demand. When coordination is relegated to the craft workers and their union, construction firms avoid keeping employees on the payroll during the slack winter season. Stinchcombe claims that the savings obtained more than offset the additional costs of hiring skilled craftsmen during the high-demand seasons.

In ecological terms, the demand environment is coarse-grained. In addi-tion, the high and low seasons place very different demands on construc-tion firms, resulting in a concave fitness function. Craft-administered hous-ing construction firms are probably quite inefficient when demand is at its peak and when the kind of building is standardized. If such conditions persisted, the craft-form population of construction firms would face stiff competition from a more bureaucratic form. For instance, in regions where housing construction is less seasonal, the construction business ought be more bureaucratically organized and to rely less on unionized skilled craftsmen by this argument. This does seem to be the case.

Another variation in demand follows business cycles and interest rates. Although seasonal fluctuations are regular, it is more difficult to predict interest rates, quality of labor relations, and costs of materials. Variations of this sort should favor generalist forms (including polymorphic forms) over specialized ones, because such environments have coarse-grained variability and the fitness sets are concave. For this reason, we think that craft-administered construction organizations tend to be general contrac-tors who not only build houses but engage in other kinds of construction as well, such as shopping plazas and office buildings.

We have adapted Levins' theory to develop parametric models of the effects of variability and grain on the mortality of populations of specialist and generalist organizations. We discuss our version of niche width theory in Chapter 12, where we implement the models empirically.

Glenn Carroll (1985) has developed a slightly different model of the dynamics of organizational niche width. He suggests that the life chances of specialist and generalist organizations depend on the level of concentration in the environment. Imagine a geographically dispersed market whose center has high, concentrated demand and whose periphery consists of pockets of heterogeneous demand. When there are few organizations, each attempts to exploit the center of the market. As the number of organizations grows, the largest, most powerful generalists typically push other organizations from the center. If generalists are numerous, some of them will be forced to exploit more peripheral segments of the market. Carroll assumes that their size and power allow them to outcompete specialists in the periphery. So the life chances of specialists deteriorate when the number of generalists in the market increases.

If, however, one or a few generalists come to dominate and push the other generalists completely out of the market, the opportunity arises for specialists to thrive in the periphery. Thus concentration in a market has opposite effects on the life chances of specialists and generalists. As a market (or more generally an organizational community) concentrates, the mortality rates of generalists rise and those of specialists fall.

Carroll specified this model in terms of the Makeham model of age dependence, which is discussed in Chapter 8. His model of the mortality rates (μ) of specialist and generalist organizations has the form:

$$\mu_s = \alpha_s + \exp(\beta_{0s} + \beta_{1s} C(u)) \cdot \exp(\gamma_s \mu),$$

$$\mu_g = \alpha_g + \exp(\beta_{0g} + \beta_{1g} C(u)) \cdot \exp(\gamma_g \mu),$$

where μ_s and μ_g denote the mortality rates of specialists and generalists respectively, u is an organization's age, and C is a measure of the concentration of the market. Concentration is measured as the inequality of the distribution of consumers and advertisers over newspapers in the local market (using Gini indices). The predictions from Carroll's model of niche width are

$$\beta_{1s} < 0 \quad \text{and} \quad \beta_{1g} > 0.$$

Analysis of mortality rates in populations of local newspaper firms supports this argument (Carroll 1985).

We have emphasized selection on the basis of niche width for two reasons. First, we think that variations in degree of specialism are an obvious and important feature of the contemporary world of organizations. The existence of large variations makes it easy to apply the theories and models to the social world. The likely importance of variations in specialism to the life chances of organizations suggests that trying to answer issues about the niche and niche width of organizations raises fundamental issues about the causes of organizational diversity. The second reason for concentrating on niche width is to emphasize a core idea in the program of evolutionary ecology, that is, the relationship between niches defined in terms of observable patterns of resource utilization and underlying processes of growth and competition. The next chapter builds on this notion in developing parametric models of the dynamics of organizational populations.

6 | Modeling the Dynamics of Organizational Populations

In this chapter we take the concepts and arguments of previous chapters and build concrete models for the dynamics of organizational populations. Since our empirical research in subsequent chapters deals explicitly with these models, this chapter serves as a bridge between the general theoretical perspective and the empirical research.

The previous chapter introduced the idea of a carrying capacity in terms of the Lotka-Volterra (LV) model of competitive interactions in population growth. We have found the general approach that underlies the LV model, though not always the models themselves, to be useful in framing questions about organizational ecology. Particularly useful is the three-way decomposition of population growth rates into components involving (1) intrinsic speed of expansion, (2) general environmental limits on growth or carrying capacities, and (3) specific competition within and between populations. We now discuss each component in the context of models for organizational change.

Variations in Intrinsic Growth Rates

We begin with variation among organizational populations in intrinsic growth rates, that is, the rates of growth in the absence of any resource or competitive constraint. One advantage of the ecological perspective is that it directs attention to the possible importance of such variations in the social world. Although the fact and its implications have not received much if any attention, organizational forms appear to differ greatly in intrinsic speed of expansion. In this section we review a bioecological theory of life history strategies and then consider parallel issues in organizational ecology.

Life History Strategies

MacArthur and Levins (1964) proposed that evolution shapes adaptive strategies in part by affecting the investment made in each reproductive attempt. An opportunist strategy leads to many reproductive events with fixed energy and material resources spread thinly over attempts. Because the investment in each reproductive event is quite small, the life chances of each offspring are poor. However, populations using this strategy grow rapidly under favorable conditions. So this strategy maximizes the intrinsic growth rate, the speed of growth in an open environment. Because the parameter that indexes an intrinsic growth rate is conventionally denoted by *r* in ecological models, this type of life history strategy is called an *r-strategy*.

The polar opposite strategy makes a small number of reproductive events and invests much energy and time in each one. Individual offspring have relatively good life chances under this strategy. As a result, populations using such strategies can expand even in the face of dense competitive pressure. That is, they can expand even when most competing populations are close to their carrying capacities and demand on resources is high. Because carrying capacities are typically denoted by *K* in ecological models, the strategy of maximizing the ability to expand even in the face of dense competition is called a *K-strategy*.

Like the distinction between specialist and generalist strategies discussed in the previous chapter, these polar life history strategies represent different positions on a classical evolutionary tradeoff. For the *r*-strategy, fast growth rates provide the capacity to exploit new and ephemeral opportunities quickly, but at the expense of the capacity to withstand dense competition. For the *K*-strategy, extensive investment in each reproductive attempt provides the ability to withstand competitive pressure, but at the expense of lowering greatly the speed with which new opportunities can be exploited.

Selection among populations using different life history strategies depends on the volatility of the environment. Environments that change slowly and regularly favor *K*-strategists. Environments whose variations are rapid and uncertain favor *r*-strategists. That is, *r*-strategies are favored only when the high death rate (low life expectancy) characteristic of entities using such strategies can be more than balanced by high birth rates.

Analysts of business strategy have identified strategies that parallel those just discussed: *first mover* strategies and *efficient production* strategies. First mover or first to market strategists rely on the capacity to move quickly into markets opened by technical change or other social changes (Williamson 1975). Efficient producers rely on stringent managerial controls and efficient organization to enter markets opened by first movers and to outcompete the first movers by driving costs and prices down.

Business analysts have treated these strategies as properties of individual firms. They tend to think of first movers as firms that have developed a capacity to identify new opportunities and to change structures and procedures quickly to take advantage of them. But many first movers do not appear to have such flexible strategies. Rather, they develop the specialized capacity to move quickly in a small number of directions within a particular technological or industrial context. For example, in the semiconductor industry, new entrants have commonly begun by investing heavily in a narrow capacity for research and development. They have also tended to delay acquiring manufacturing capacities.[1] Such firms begin when an entrepreneur raises capital to fund a specialized team of designers. Since teams of designers can be assembled much more quickly than an efficient manufacturing organization and plant, initial entrants into new markets are likely to be mainly firms specializing in design and product development. Such firms often eventually develop their own manufacturing operations, but they tend to add production capacity in stages rather than by building a plant with scale efficiencies at the outset. Often they contract with larger established firms for production, or they have their products manufactured by specialists in production, the so-called silicon foundries.

New branches of technology are often populated initially by new firms using first mover strategies. Some new entrants achieve very high growth rates for some time, as is typical for successful r-strategists. Firms that specialize in efficient production are slower to move into new markets and new branches of the technology. But once they do move, they tend to compete successfully against the first movers and thus seize the market. One would expect death rates among r-strategists to rise relative to those of K-strategists as the market and technology develop, and this does seem to have been the case in the semiconductor industry.

This example conveys some of the advantages of conceptualizing the dynamics of organizational populations in terms of life history strategies. One advantage is that this approach emphasizes the interplay of the life histories of industries and populations with the life histories of the organi-

1. See Brittain and Freeman (1980) for an extended discussion of these ideas.

zations that comprise those industries and populations. As industries pass through stages of high and low technical and social change, the relative abundances of subpopulations relying on first mover strategies and efficient production strategies change systematically. Changes in relative abundances affect the life chances of organizations with each strategy.

This approach also provides a clear illustration of the logic of population analysis. Populations of r-strategist organizations flourish under conditions of rapid technical and social change not because the member organizations have the capacity for flexible response to widely varying conditions; rather they flourish because the speed with which they can be constructed allows a founding rate that is high enough to offset high mortality rates. Indeed, individual mortality rates of r-strategists are typically much higher than those of individual K-strategists at every stage in the development of an industry. And even though organizational r-strategists may populate many diverse environments, this does not mean that the same set of flexible firms moves freely from one environment to the other as conditions change.

Variations in Speed of Founding

Forms of organization differ in their intrinsic growth rates, their rates of growth in the absence of resource constraints, because they vary greatly in characteristic uses of personnel, resources, and legitimacy. Some kinds of organizations have superb efficiency and high legitimacy. Once founded, such organizations have long expected lifetimes and often come to dominate their sectors. But such organizations are difficult to create. They use considerable capital and skilled staff, which are typically in short supply. Their rates of founding are also sensitive to turbulence in the environment because the complicated routines that convey high efficiency take longer to learn and stabilize. These organizations are, therefore, particularly vulnerable to early environmental difficulties. As a result, rates of initiation and rates of successful completion of organizing attempts are typically low for these kinds of organizations. One consequence is that such organizations are relatively rare. Some imagined or planned "best" organizational forms may never appear. On the other hand, some kinds of organizations, which may seem trivial to analysts who delight in complex structures, persist in large numbers even though individually they have poor life chances because of scanty resources and low legitimacy. Understanding these differences in abundance requires analyzing differences among forms in ease and speed of founding.

As we discussed in Chapter 4, Simon (1962) argued that evolution favors structures composed of stable subassemblies arranged in a simple hierarchy. Disruption caused by environmental turbulence is more likely to destroy uncompleted structures than structures that have been fully developed. Structures built of subassemblies that can be completed rapidly, therefore, minimize exposure to high risk of destruction.

Forms differ greatly in structural complexity even at founding. Some are formed like Simon's simple hierarchies, with commands and flows of information running along simple chains. Others, like so-called matrix organizations, have overlapping controls and cross-cutting flows. Organizations with complex structures have more complex dynamics than do those with simple hierarchical structures. It presumably takes much longer to complete a complex structure than a hierarchy, as Simon argued. Other things being equal, a hierarchical organization will be up and running faster than a nonhierarchy.

Not all kinds of organizations, however, can rely on simple hierarchies to carry out their programs of activity. Social movement organizations can, and often do, have a simple, hierarchical cell structure. General hospitals do not, because professional and bureaucratic authority are located in different parts of the hospital structure. Such organizations necessarily have cross-cutting, and often partially competing, control structures. More generally, choice of organization strategy partly constrains the range of feasible initial simplicity.

Small organizations can obviously be built faster than big ones, just as houses can be built faster than skyscrapers. A store-front church can be established overnight, but it takes years to build a nuclear power plant. Organizations using forms that require a large scale to carry out routine activities, therefore, have long gestation periods.

Some kinds of organizations, like retail stores, operate in market contexts with only minimal levels of institutional control. Others, like hospitals and public utilities, face heavy public regulation. Two dimensions of institutional control and regulation seem relevant to ease and speed of starting: concentration of external control and degree of licensing. When control is focused and concentrated, the maximum speed of organization building depends on the speed of decision-making by the relevant agency. When control is dispersed, especially when lines of authority overlap, authorization for new ventures, especially for new organizational forms, can take a very long time. The general proposition is that extensive and dispersed external controls lengthen the gestation period for new organizations.

The spread of knowledge about how any kind of organization works also affects the ease and speed with which new organizations of the type can be built (Stinchcombe 1965). One way in which knowledge of how to build an organization can be widely disseminated is through codification. Franchised restaurants, for example, spread rapidly because they use a standard, codified form. Reliance on such a codified form makes it easier to convince lenders that the organization can actually be built and run profitably. It also simplifies the tasks of hiring and training employees and writing contracts with suppliers. In short, franchises are based on formulas for organizing that are codified organizational forms.

Simplicity, scale, regulation, and requirements for specialized knowledge about building and operating an organization affect the speed with which resources can be mobilized to create it. Factors that lengthen periods of organization building depress growth rates of the population by lowering founding rates. We think that this effect occurs in three main ways.

First, long periods of gestation increase the costs of organizing. Entrepreneurs and potential participants face high opportunity costs because their resources and time do not yield any payoffs during the building period. It takes large and fairly certain gains from organizing to induce people to invest in long-run projects, and many proposed organizations promise quite uncertain returns. Second, lengthy periods of start-up intensify selection pressure. New organizations face a strong liability of newness. The mortality rates of organizations are presumably even higher in the start-up period, before they actually begin operations. Third, the longer the wait from attempted initiation to full functioning, the greater is the difficulty in fine-tuning organizational strategy and structure to opportunities and constraints in the environment. Ability to forecast the future declines with the length of the forecast period, probably at least exponentially. Slow-to-build organizations must forecast environments over much longer periods than quick-assembly organizations. This tendency accentuates the risk of investing in efforts to create slow-to-build organizations.

These arguments imply that variations in intrinsic growth rates affect organizational evolution. Organizational populations are replenished with new entrants, many of which are likely to be simple and small. Even if large size and complex strategy and structure convey strong survival advantages, organizational communities seldom contain only or even mainly populations of large, complex organizations. That is, populations whose forms allow high founding rates tend to persist even when individual organizations in these populations have short life expectancies.

Populations of easy-to-build organizations can reasonably be described as *r*-strategists. As we pointed out earlier, such forms characteristically require small initial resources and can be built rapidly. Thus populations of quick-assembly organizations have high intrinsic growth rates and can take advantage of ephemeral resources. At the same time, individual members of such populations have short life expectancies because of their small size and lack of dominance. Our proposition that easy-to-build organizations proliferate in modern society amounts to an argument that the character of environmental variations in such societies favors *r*-strategists, or more precisely that *r*-strategist populations do not face overwhelmingly strong selection pressure.

Effects of Environments on Carrying Capacities

The notion of a carrying capacity for a population of organizations summarizes the dependence of the growth rate of the population on numerous dimensions of the social and economic environment. We have found that sociologists tend to assume that use of the notion of carrying capacity implies that a society has some fixed or intrinsic capacity to support organizations of a particular type. But this is not so. Because the notion of carrying capacity summarizes the effects of social and economic conditions that usually vary over time, the carrying capacity of an organizational population also varies over time. In a dynamic context, we can think of a carrying capacity as a "moving target" toward which a population adjusts.

Analysis of the effects of social and material environments on carrying capacities provides points of contact between organizational ecology and much other sociological work on organization-environment relations. Indeed, we borrow freely from other research traditions in specifying how carrying capacities depend on classes of environmental conditions.

Institutional Rules

Creating an organization means mobilizing people and resources for specific purposes. Differences in social and political arrangements affect components of the mobilization process. First, there is the matter of specialized purposes. The notion that individuals and collections of individuals have autonomous interests is a relatively modern invention. John Meyer and his collaborators have emphasized the importance of the rise of modern institutional structures as a source of rational organization building (Meyer and Rowan 1977; Meyer and Scott 1983). These structures are "rationalized and impersonal prescriptions that identify various social purposes as technical ones and specify in a rulelike way the appropriate means to pursue these technical purposes rationally'' (Meyer and Rowan 1977, pp. 343–344). The existence of such modern views makes the job of constructing organizations easier; the existence of rational organizations gives greater force to the rational myths.

A major implication of this argument is that variations in the strength of institutional rules endorsing rational organization as the appropriate vehicle for attaining collective goals affect the ease of founding organizations. In particular, in the historical periods in which the social forces reflecting rationalistic views gained ascendancy, one would expect to find enormous waves of organization building, as in the Progressive era in the United States (see Chandler 1977 for discussion of the case of modern industrial administration).

Institutionalization of forms has obvious implications for mortality processes, as we noted earlier. Two main proposals have been offered about the nature of these effects. Meyer and Scott (1983) suggest that the world of organizations has been split into two sectors, a competitive sector in which survival depends on efficiency and an institutional sector in which survival depends on isomorphism to institutionally approved ways of organizing. If they are correct, the life chances of organizations in the institutional sector depend critically on the capacity to institute practices demonstrating symbolically that the organization conforms to prevailing norms. If these norms prescribe a narrow range of structures, they presumably rule out large classes of organizational forms. So changes in institutional rules will adversely affect the life chances of populations that cannot quickly display a new face to the institutional world.

DiMaggio and Powell (1983) make a similar argument but locate it in a time domain. They suggest that organizational populations have characteristic life histories with youthful periods in which efficiency properties shape selection and a mature period in which institutional isomorphism governs survival. Like Meyer and Scott, they give the impression that conformity to institutional pressures is easy and inexpensive since it involves only symbolic activities loosely tied to work within the organization. This assumption leads them to claim that mature populations do not face selection pressures.

Unlike most organization theorists, we do not see any contradiction between institutional processes and selection processes. In fact, we claim that the two generally apply to all kinds of organizations and in all sectors and tend to reinforce each other.

Availability of Resources

Institutionalization of rational organization or of particular organizational forms affects the likelihood that *organizational* solutions to collective-action problems will be tried. But whether a concrete organization will be built depends on the availability of resources, both human and material (Weber 1968; Eisenstadt 1958). There are two issues here: (1) the levels of resources that could potentially be mobilized, and (2) the degree to which these resources are fixed to other social units. Under norms of rationality, the founding rate of new organizations rises when the levels of resources rise and/or when a changing balance of power among contending groups frees resources from previous uses. The classic examples of the first process are population growth and economic development; the classic example of the second process is social revolution (Stinchcombe 1965). Such revolutions have been especially important historically in affecting organization building because they break legal and institutional constraints on the uses of resources.

Expansion of the resource base can affect both the founding rate and the diversity of new ventures. Durkheim's theory about the causes of the division of labor in society is one version of an argument relating the size of the resource base to organizational diversity. According to Durkheim (1893/1933, p. 266), "If work becomes divided more as societies become more voluminous and denser, it is not because external circumstances are more varied, but because the struggle for existence is more acute." He developed the imagery of a set of isolated communities whose economic enterprises have expanded to the limits of the local markets and local competitive interactions. When these isolated communities are brought into close contact with one another by changes in the costs of communication and transportation, a competitive struggle ensues: "There is always a considerable number of enterprises which have not reached their limits and which have, consequently, power to go further. Since there is a free field for them, they seek necessarily to spread and fill it. If they meet similar enterprises which offer resistance, the second hold back the first . . . But if some of them present some inferiority, they will necessarily have to yield ground heretofore occupied by them, but in which they cannot be maintained under the new conditions of conflict. They no longer have any alternative but to disappear or transform, and this transformation must necessarily end in a new specialization . . . Although the preceding examples are drawn particularly from economic life, this explanation applies to all social functions indiscriminately" (Durkheim 1893/1933, pp. 268–270). To the extent that new specializations come about by the creation of new enterprises, this argument implies that increased levels of interaction, which Durkheim called "moral density," increase both the disbanding rate and the founding rate (see also Hawley 1950).

The second major process that affects organizational diversity concerns social revolutions, which reshape class structures and political structures, and other political crises. Social revolutions and political crisis almost invariably change the mix of organizations in society. Breaking the hegemony of ruling groups means destroying the organizations with which they ruled and extracted economic value. Solving political crises usually means constructing new organizations either to repress dissent or to incorporate contending groups into the polity. Social revolutions normally involve both the large-scale destruction of existing organizations and the creation of new ones. In contrast, institutional response to political and social crises usually involves the addition of new organizations and new organizational forms without the destruction of much existing organization. For example, the incorporation of organized labor into the American polity during the 1930s involved the creation of numerous state and local agencies designed to enforce the newly won rights of unions. Subsequent attempts by conservative governments to roll back New Deal concessions to labor unions often involved attempts to eliminate agencies. Similar reactions followed War on Poverty program development.

Periods of political crises and social revolution seem to be peak times for building new forms of organizations. Yet there is a strong current in organization theory that makes an opposite prediction. Weber (1968) argued that rational-legal bureaucracies are politically neutral tools of such efficiency that they are nearly indestructible. New elites have no need to destroy existing bureaus and create new ones to change policies; doing so incurs needless costs when existing bureaus can be smoothly changed. Kaufman (1976) claims to have shown that Weber is right—that the disbanding rate of government bureaus is so low that they are nearly immortal.

If the Weberian argument were correct, changes in control over the state should not affect the demography of bureaus. But if bureaus, like other organizations, develop agendas of their own and become subject to strong inertial pressures, it may be very difficult to reshape their policies and practices. Changes in top management may mean little to the actual functioning of established bureaus. Therefore, elites intent on fundamental transformation will be inclined to close some bureaus and create new ones.

In fact, more careful analysis of the life chances of bureaus of the federal government shows that their life expectancies do not differ substantially from those of large business firms (Nystrom and Starbuck 1981). Moreover, at least some periods of intensive political transformation, such as the New Deal and the War on Poverty, involve the creation of many new kinds of organizations. So for these various reasons, the rate of organization building will rise during periods of political crisis and transformation.

Social changes that destroy monopolies of social units over resources can either increase or decrease diversity. Sometimes the victorious social forces create new organizational forms that coexist with and perhaps compete with existing organizations. For example, the creation of a secular public school system in France after the revolution increased diversity in the educational sector because parochial schools persisted. On the other hand, the Soviet revolution apparently destroyed most prerevolutionary forms of organization and replaced them with new ones. The set of forms changed, but the level of diversity probably declined. This means that the rate of destroying existing forms exceeded the rate of creating new ones. Presumably only a unified elite can effect such change. Dispersed power within the rising social groups is likely to result in the creation of many special-purpose organizational forms, each tailored to the distinctive agendas of the various factions.

Periods of social crisis and political transformation play an important role in affecting the *timing* of waves of organization building. These periods transform broad and cumulative social and economic change into bursts of organizational activity. Although the events surrounding the crisis may do little more than signal fundamental changes in the power balance among contending groups, the response to the crisis may profoundly affect the world of organizations. If organizations are imprinted with the milieu of their founding periods, then the timing of social and political crises with their attendant waves of organization building dictates the distribution of imprinted structures. In this way processes of political transformation filter the effects of broad economic, demographic, and social change for the world of organizations.

Strategic Organizations

Some kinds of organizational innovations have multiplier effects on the rates of founding of other kinds of organizations and organizational forms. For example, the creation of banks and stock markets had such effects in the world of commerce. The chances of mobilizing the resources necessary to initiate a large venture improve dramatically with the creation of a stock market. A stock market lowers the time it takes to learn whether holders of capital are interested in participating in some joint venture, and it also increases the size of the potential pool of capital available. By jointly lowering the costs of search and increasing the size of possible combinations, this organizational innovation speeds the founding process. Once the stock market has been created, both the founding rate and the diversity of new ventures should increase.

In the case of the semiconductor industry, venture capital firms have supposedly played a similar role. These firms specialize in creating consortia of private investors to back small, risky, high-technology ventures. Like the stock market, they reduce the costs of searching for capital and increase the size of the pool of capital available to scientist-entrepreneurs.

Technical innovation has also played a key role in the creation of new organizations and especially new forms of organizations. We have already mentioned that the organizational forms used by the established vacuum tube producers were unsuitable for exploiting the new semiconductor technology. Other recent examples of technologically driven organization building are in biotechnology, which depends on new knowledge of recombinant DNA biochemistry, and in the overnight delivery business, which depends critically on extensive computer networks and scheduling algorithms. Each wave of technical innovation produces new sets of opportunities. Sometimes these new opportunities are exploited by members of existing organizational forms. Quite often, however, only new organizational strategies and structures can meet the demands of efficiently producing, servicing, and marketing the new products and services that arise from application of the new techniques.

In analysis of particular organizational populations, attention must be paid to the flow of specific technical innovations. But, for purposes of characterizing the broad features of the dynamics, it is interesting to focus on organizational innovations that affect the creation and dissemination of new technology. Two kinds of organizations have played a central role in these processes: research and development laboratories and research universities. We have already mentioned the role these organizations played in the establishment of the semiconductor industry. The initial technical breakthrough was made at a research and development lab, Bell Laboratories, where three scientists won a Nobel prize for inventing the transistor. A research university, Stanford University, trained several scientist-entrepreneurs and was an important source of technical support for many of the Silicon Valley high-technology firms. Stanford, along with other universities in the area, provided a labor pool of highly trained technical specialists who helped local firms develop. The result was a concentration of electronics firms in the Stanford area, often called Silicon Valley. The information flow from universities to private firms is asserted by some as a major mechanism of support (Gibson 1970; Cooper 1972). The location of various high-technology firms close to major research universities underscores the importance of these organizations in creating organizational diversity.[2]

Discussion of environmental processes has thus far concentrated on the effects of *levels* of institutionalization or of various resources. Ecological theory directs attention as well to the effects of variation in relevant environments, as we discussed in the context of niche width in the previous chapter. This issue is examined in detail in Chapter 12.

Conceptualizing the Size of Populations

We have now developed an image of a set of interacting populations whose numbers are constrained by the speed of founding of new organizations and by social and material processes that set (time-varying) carrying capacities. The last step in model building considers the effects of interactions within and between populations on the growth and decline of numbers in each population. Given a fixed intrinsic growth rate and a set of time-varying factors that determine a carrying capacity, we want to learn how vital rates depend on the density of each population. Before considering specific models of density dependence, we discuss alternative ways to conceptualize the size of an organizational population.

Population bioecology takes for granted that the relevant state space of the process of population growth counts the *number of members in the population*. For example, studies of predator-prey interactions sometimes analyze counts of rabbits and counts of foxes. In the biotic context, it is reasonable to assume that each rabbit exerts roughly the same demand on

---

2. At least one researcher questions the strength of such ties (Oakey 1984). Regular contacts with universities as mechanisms for acquiring technical information are, according to this study, rare. However, this study was based only on high-technology firms with fewer than 200 employees. We believe that the sample was ill-suited for such inferences. Only small high-technology firms were studied, but they were not necessarily young. When 23.3 percent of the U.S. sample report important contacts with other organizations as sources of technical information, the conclusion is that this is a surprisingly small number. This sounds like a high level of contact to us. The study says nothing at all about universities as sources of trained personnel, nor does it discuss their relationships with the entrepreneurs.

the resource environment. Likewise, one fox is pretty much like another. The density of rabbit and fox populations relative to some environmental condition is well expressed by the simple counts of numbers in each population, perhaps adjusting for age and sex distributions.

We often follow a similar strategy of modeling the dynamics of counts of organizations in competing populations. For example, we analyze the effects of the number of craft unions and the number of industrial unions on the rates of founding and mortality in each population. However, the sociological case is more complicated than the biotic one because populations of organizations sometimes exhibit considerable diversity in size among members. For example, some specialist craft unions that we studied had as few as one hundred members; other generalist industrial unions had close to two million members. The addition of a small union may have quite different consequences for existing unions than does the addition of a huge one.

It may be useful to measure the size of an organizational population in terms of the aggregate size of all of its constituent organizations. Continuing with the example of labor unions, virtually all published research on growth and decline in the population of labor unions takes aggregate membership of all unions in the country as the dimension of interest. Sociologists, economists, and labor historians have analyzed fluctuations in the total number of union members in the society or, more commonly, fluctuations in the fraction of the labor force that union members comprise. From this perspective, issues concerning carrying capacities focus on the availability of members and on legal and social constraints on the process of enlisting members. Such research, even when it does not employ the notion of a carrying capacity, recognizes that changes in the social composition of the labor force affect the number of members that could be mobilized by the population of unions at a particular moment. Changes in the industrial composition of the economy and in laws regulating conditions of collective bargaining also affect potential membership in labor unions. From this perspective, the study of unions as organizations is made an ingredient of the study of the labor movement.

We favor the other side of this issue. Although the dynamics of aggregate membership involve interesting social processes, understanding such dynamics is not the only way—or even the best way—to analyze change in the world of labor unions. We think that the *number* of unions in a society is an interesting sociological variable in its own right. A society in which, say, all union members belong to a single union has a quite different structure from one in which the same number of members are organized into a thousand unions. For one thing, the average and maximum size of unions differ greatly in the two cases; and size is associated with a great many dimensions of internal structure. For another, the totality of collective actions by unions will obviously be more diverse in the second case than in the first.

Our theoretical program attempts to explain variations in organizational diversity in society. Diversity is affected both by the numbers of organizations and organizational forms and by the distribution of resources and members among them. A society with one huge organization of a certain type has a quite different social structure from that of a society with many smaller organizations of the same type even though the aggregate size, in terms of members or resources, may be the same.

In essence, these are issues of *concentration*, which lie at the center of any attempt to understand the structure of dominance and control in society. Analyzing the causes of concentration requires understanding the processes that affect variations in numbers of organizations and organizational forms as well as processes that affect the distributions of members and resources among them. We focus on rates of founding, disbanding, and merger because these rates control fluctuations in numbers of organizations and organizational forms. So it makes sense to ask how these rates depend on the numbers themselves.

We based our research designs on a strategic bet that there are regularities in the processes that constrain growth and decline in numbers of various kinds of organizations and that analysis of such regularities can illuminate basic processes of organizational ecology.

Carrying Capacities and Density Dependence

In developing the LV model in the previous chapter, we noted that carrying capacities are simple functions of parameters expressing density dependence in rates of birth and death. The existence of a finite carrying capacity depends on the assumption that the birth rate falls with density and that the mortality rate rises with density. Density serves as a surrogate for the difficult-to-observe features of the material and social environment that affect the rates, particularly competition and legitimacy. Now we consider organizational applications of such models.

Founding Rates

We think that density affects founding rates through several processes. Knowledge about organizational strategies and structures is often available only to "insiders," that is, to those already participating in such organizations. This is commonly the case when organizational functioning is shielded from public observation and when essential features of the organizational form have not been codified. In such situations, existing organizations are the only training grounds for knowledgeable organization builders. The number of foundings in such populations depends on the number of jobs in existing organizations that give the requisite training (Brittain and Freeman 1980). When the number of such organizations is small, the founding rate is depressed as a result of the absence of potential organization builders. Marrett (1980) argues that high density increases the founding rate by widening and strengthening the networks that connect individuals with the inclination and skills to succeed in creating a certain kind of organization.

Institutional processes also link density and founding rates. If institutionalization means that certain forms attain a taken-for-granted character, then simple prevalence of a form tends to give it legitimacy. When numbers are small, those who attempt to create a form must fight for legitimacy; they must argue both for the special purposes of a proposed organization and for the design of the form. Once many instances of the form exist, the need for elaborate justifications diminishes. Reducing the need for such justifications reduces the cost of organizing. Other things being equal, legitimation of a form increases the founding rate of populations using that form. If, as we argue here, legitimacy increases with prevalence of the form in society, then legitimation processes produce a *positive* relationship between density and founding rates.

By contrast, competition within and between populations induces a *negative* relationship between density and founding rates. Given a set of environmental conditions that set a carrying capacity, the more abundant the competitors, the smaller will be the potential gains from founding an organization at a given level of demand for products and services. Fewer resources are available, and markets are packed tightly in densely populated environments. For these reasons, collectives with the knowledge and skills to build organizations are less likely to make attempts in densely populated environments. Capital markets and other macro structures often reinforce this effect. For example, investors may be reluctant to participate in new ventures in dense markets. Likewise, professional associations often try to restrict entry when density is high.

In general terms, high density implies strong competitive interactions within populations dependent on limited resources for organizing (when levels of such resources have been controlled). As density grows relative to the current level of the carrying capacity, supplies of potential organizers, members, patrons, and resources become exhausted. Moreover, existing organizations respond to increasing competitive pressures by opposing attempts at creating still more organizations. For both of these reasons, the founding rate declines as the number of organizations in the population increases.

Use of a simple model of the process helps convey the main point of our argument (see Hannan 1986b). To keep the exposition simple, assume that legitimacy (L) and competition (C) are the only relevant factors. That is, assume that we have already adjusted for the changing environmental conditions that affect carrying capacities. We propose that the founding rate at time t, $\lambda(t)$, is proportional to the legitimacy of the population and inversely proportional to the level of competition within the population:

$$(6.1) \qquad \lambda(t) = a(t) \cdot \frac{L_t}{C_t}.$$

In addition, we think that it is often useful to assume that levels of legitimation and competition are functions of density (N):

$$(6.2) \qquad L_t = f(N_t) \quad \text{and} \quad C_t = g(N_t).$$

The crucial modeling questions concern the forms of these relationships. Unfortunately, institutional and ecological theories have not addressed these issues. Our understanding of the process is that both of the relationships in (6.2) are nonlinear.

Consider the dependence of legitimacy of an organizational form on the number of copies of the form in existence. From the perspective of legitimacy as taken-for-grantedness, it seems clear that extreme rarity of a form poses serious problems of legitimacy. If almost no instances of a form exist, how can it be taken as the natural way to achieve some collective end? On the other hand, once a form becomes common, it seems unlikely that increases in numbers will have a great effect on its institutional standing. Therefore, we assume that legitimacy is sensitive to variations in density in the lower range but that there is something like a ceiling effect on the relationship, that is, that density increases legitimacy at a *decreasing* rate:

$$\frac{dL}{dN} > 0 \quad \text{and} \quad \frac{d^2L}{dN^2} < 0.$$

In the case of competition, variations in the upper range have more impact on founding rates than variations in the lower range. When numbers are few, addition of an organization to the population increases the frequency and strength of competitive interactions slightly at most. But when density is high, the addition of an organization strongly increases competition. So we assume that density increases competition at an *increasing* rate:

$$\frac{dC}{dN} > 0 \quad \text{and} \quad \frac{d^2C}{dN^2} > 0.$$

Moreover, we propose that the legitimacy process dominates when N is small but that the competition process dominates when N is large. That is, the effect of density on the founding rate is *non-monotonic*. This is the core idea of the modeling effort.

The next step in moving toward empirical research is to build a model using particular functional forms. We use simple functional forms that are consistent with these assumptions and with the restriction that a transition rate must be non-negative. In the case of legitimacy, we propose that legitimacy increases with density according to a power law:

(6.3) $L_t = f(N_t) = \alpha N_t^\beta, \quad \alpha > 0, \quad 0 < \beta < 1.$

As long as the inequalities on parameters are met, the level of legitimacy increases with density but at a decreasing rate. In the case of the level of competition, we assume an exponential relation between competition and the square of density:

(6.4) $C_t = \gamma\, e^{\delta N_t^2}, \quad \gamma > 0, \quad \delta > 0.$

As long as both parameters are positive, the level of competition increases at an increasing rate as required.

Inserting equations (6.3) and (6.4) into equation (6.1), the simplified model of the founding rate, yields the basic parametric model:

(6.5) $\lambda(t) = \phi(t) N_t^\beta\, e^{-\delta N_t^2},$

where $\phi(t) = a(t)\alpha/\gamma$. As we noted earlier, we chose this model because its qualitative behavior agrees with the theory. In particular, it implies that there is a non-monotonic relationship between density and the founding rate. To see this, note that

$$\frac{d\lambda(t)}{dN} = \phi(t) N_t^{\beta-1}\, e^{-\delta N_t^2}(\beta - 2\delta N_t^2).$$

There is a point of inflection (a maximum) at

$$(6.6) \qquad N^* = \sqrt{\frac{\beta}{2\delta}}.$$

The founding rate rises as density increases until N reaches the level indicated in (6.6); from that point on, the founding rate falls with increasing density.

In empirical testing the key issue is whether this non-monotonic model represents an improvement over a simpler model with only monotone dependence on density. A secondary but still interesting issue is whether the point of inflection falls within the observed range of density. So in estimating models with this form, we check first to see that the estimated parameters have the predicted signs and second whether the implied behavior of the process over the range of density is non-monotonic. If the founding rate rises initially and then falls with increasing density, the process implies the existence of a carrying capacity for the population.[3] So it is important in evaluating this theoretical approach to learn whether founding rates vary with density and, if they do, whether the dependence is non-monotonic.

This model of density dependence in founding rates is more complicated than the corresponding assumption in the LV model. As we explained in the previous chapter, the LV model is built on the assumption of *linear* density dependence in vital rates, whereas our model implies non-monotonic dependence on density. This added complexity reflects the greater complexity of organizational ecology.

Next we consider how density affects organizational mortality. Because we suspect that density affects the two main components of the mortality rate differently, so we consider the rate of disbanding and the rate of merger separately.

Disbanding Rates

We assume that the processes by which density affects founding rates also apply to disbanding rates, with some modifications. The modifications follow from the observation that founding rates pertain to attempts and the absence of attempts at creating organizations while disbanding rates per-

---

3. More precisely, the rate approaches zero asymptotically, as a result of the assumption of an exponential function in (6.4).

tain to existing organizations. Disbanding rates presumably depend on properties of individual organizations such as age and size as well as on population characteristics such as density. But founding rates depend only on population characteristics, since a founding that does not occur cannot be associated with an organization's characteristics.

Some of the processes by which density affects disbanding rates operate mainly at low densities and others at higher densities. At low densities, the growth of populations of organizations is constrained by the novelty and rarity of the form. The fact that there are few organizations in the population presumably makes it difficult to convince key actors such as banks and government agencies to transfer material and symbolic resources to organizations in the population. It may likewise be difficult to convince talented people to join such organizations and to remain in them.

Earlier we suggested that rarity of an organizational form undermines its legitimacy. Most organization theorists assume that legitimacy decreases disbanding rates (Meyer and Rowan 1977). Thus, increasing density will lower disbanding rates by increasing the legitimacy of the form and of populations using the form. Low density also hampers attempts at coordinated political action to protect and defend claims of the population or of some of its members. Increases in numbers alleviate these problems. Growth in numbers of organizations gives force to claims of institutional standing and also provides economies of scale in political and legal action. That is, increases in numbers lower the disbanding rate.

At high density, competitive interactions intensify. Growth in numbers increases the likelihood and intensity of both *direct* competition between pairs of organizations and *diffuse* competition among all or many of them. Individual organizations can easily avoid direct competition for members and other scarce resources when there are few organizations in the system. As the number of potential competitors grows, however, avoidance becomes more difficult.

For example, labor unions have competed for the services of skilled organizers and dedicated staff, political support and influence, attention from the news media, and so forth. In the late nineteenth and early twentieth centuries, such competition was often virulent. Sometimes it involved direct rivalry, as when two or more unions seeking to organize the same workers competed for support of and membership in a national federation, such as the AFL and CIO. More often the competition was diffuse—it had more the character of congestion than rivalry. As the number of unions grew large, more of the resources used to build and sustain unions were claimed by unions that could defend themselves against raids. Such diffuse competition lowers the life chances of new unions and also affects the life chances of existing unions. In other words, when density is already high, further growth increases disbanding rates, after controlling for the environmental conditions that affect carrying capacities.

We assume that the disbanding rate at age u, which we denote by $\mu(u)$, is proportional to the level of competition and inversely proportional to the legitimacy of the organizational form at the time that the organization reaches age u:

$$\mu(u) = b(u) \cdot \frac{C_u}{L_u}.$$

As in the case of the founding rate, we assume that competition increases with density at an increasing rate but that legitimacy increases with density at a decreasing rate.

There is no obvious reason for not using the parametric assumptions regarding the dependence of legitimacy and competition on density that we used for the founding process. However, it is unlikely that the parameters of each part of the process are identical for the two rates. So we merely repeat the assumed relationships using a different set of parameters to acknowledge possible differences between the processes:

$$L = \nu N^\kappa \qquad \text{and} \qquad C = \zeta \, e^{\lambda N^2}.$$

With these assumptions the model for the disbanding rate is

$$(6.7) \qquad \mu(u) = \psi(u) N_u^{-\kappa} \exp(\lambda N_u^2),$$

where $\psi(u) = \zeta \, b(u)/\nu$. What matters are the functional form and signs of the parameters. Again the crucial qualitative feature of the model is that the effect of density on disbanding rates is non-monotonic. The model implies that the disbanding rate falls with increasing density up to the carrying capacity and then rises with increasing density. (Note again the departure from the LV assumption of linear density dependence.)

We have found it difficult to obtain convergent estimates of the model in (6.7) using some of the data described in the next chapter. Therefore, we shifted to an alternative specification whose parameters have essentially the same qualitative interpretation:

$$(6.8) \qquad \mu(u) = \psi(u) \exp(-\theta_1 N_u + \theta_2 N_u^2).$$

Differentiating the rate with respect to density, we have

$$\frac{d\mu(u)}{dN_u} = \mu(u) \cdot (-\theta_1 + 2\theta_2 N_u).$$

Again the model implies a point of inflection (a minimum), which this time is given by

$$(6.9) \qquad N^* = \frac{\theta_1}{2\theta_2}.$$

Below this level of density the rate declines with increasing density; above this level the rate increases with increasing density.

It is worth noting that the argument pertaining to low founding rates and high disbanding rates at low densities mixes two kinds of processes. The first kind of process involves what we might call a strong form of low-density dependence. In this case, the fact of low density implies low founding rates and high disbanding rates at any age of the population. Examples of processes of this type are those that emphasize the role of existing organizations as training grounds for potential organization builders and those that call attention to the importance of numbers in collective actions to defend the interests of the organizations in the population. The second kind of process involves a weak form of density dependence in the sense that density stands as a surrogate for processes that unfold over the history of a population. The prime example of this type is the argument that organizational forms acquire a taken-for-granted status as their numbers grow large.

The distinction between the two kinds of density-dependence processes becomes important in those cases where density crashes after an organizational form and population have acquired institutional standing. Consider the examples of the populations of wineries and breweries in the United States after Prohibition (Delacroix and Solt 1988) or the population of newspapers in Argentina after the protracted repression of the Rosas' dictatorship (Delacroix and Carroll 1983). Does low density in such situations imply low founding rates and high disbanding rates net of the level of demand for the products and services provided by the population? It seems to us that the strong-form processes hold but that the weak-form processes may not. Whether a population of organizations facing these circumstances has low legitimacy may depend on the length of the period of low density. At the repeal of Prohibition many individuals still possessed skills in brewing and wine making, and the organizational forms were still widely known to potential investors and consumers. But what if Prohibition had lasted for several generations? We have not yet seen an analysis of an organizational population that answers this question.

These questions do not arise in our empirical studies because the density of the populations we studied grew monotonically over much of the history of the industries and then declined moderately. So we do not observe the combination of low density far from the initiation of the population.

Merger Rates

We also explore the effects of density on rates of merger among organizations in a population. However, we do not have any a priori model of the process. Merger is a more complicated kind of event than disbanding. Among other things, organizations merge both when they are failing and when they are succeeding. That is, some mergers are last-gasp attempts to avoid collapse of an organization; others are attempts to incorporate successful technologies and organizational forms, as when established giant firms acquire newer, innovative firms.

The semiconductor industry provides many examples of mergers in which firms outside the industry that are seeking access to technology acquire independent semiconductor companies. Examples are General Electric's acquisition of Intersil and Honeywell's acquisition of Synertek. It makes little sense to buy a badly run company if this is the motivation. Other mergers reflect the low valuation of merger targets—firms that are faring poorly can often be acquired cheaply. So the merger rate depends on organizational outcomes in a very complicated way.

We suspect that the merger rate also depends on density in a complicated way. In particular, merger rates may be affected by competition and legitimation processes that parallel those discussed for disbanding rates. But there is an additional consideration: as density increases, the number of potential partners for merger increases. Since availability of potential partners seems likely to increase the rate, the merger rate is likely to increase with increasing density in the lower range. But we suggested earlier that the disbanding rate decreases with increasing density in this range. Because of this complexity, we have not developed a model of the merger process.

Competition among Populations

The various processes responsible for density-dependence within populations have strong parallels in processes occurring between populations.

Just as the addition of an organization to a population affects the founding and disbanding rates in that population, the addition of an organization to a competing population may also affect those rates. These are both forms of density-dependence. The only distinction is whether the effect occurs within a population or across the boundary between populations.

In conceptualizing interactions among organizational populations, we retain the classic sociological distinction between competition and conflict. As Durkheim and Simmel insisted, conflict is a social relation that requires interaction between the parties. Parties to a conflict take each other into account. Competition, by contrast, is often indirect. The growth of one population of organizations may depress the growth of another even though the members of the two populations never interact directly. In fact, the members of the populations may not even be aware that they stand in a competitive relation if they compete indirectly for resources. In one classic form of competitive situation, the undominated market of many buyers and sellers, no actor needs to know the identity of its competitors.

Our analyses rely on competition between populations for limited material and social resources for building and sustaining organizations. We do not assume anything like a fully competitive market. Our theories hold even when the number of competitors is sufficiently small that the actions of one competitor can change the terms of trade significantly. In these circumstances, competition often causes conflict. There is no reason for us to assume the absence of conflict. In fact, we think that the usual state of affairs is for intense, localized competition to turn into conflict. However, we do not assume the existence of conflict as a precondition for our arguments.

We investigate whether the density of other populations affects the founding and disbanding rates of a target population. If such a link exists and the density of population B decreases the founding rate and/or increases the disbanding rate of population A, we infer that population A competes with B. If, in turn, the density of A depresses the founding rate and/or raises the disbanding rate of B, we have an example of classic reciprocal competition. But if the density of A raises the founding rate or depresses the disbanding rate of B, the interaction has the predator-prey form. Several other cases are possible, including symbiosis, in which the density of each population increases the founding rates and/or decreases the disbanding rates of the other.

Although there may be particular cases in which the legitimation of one population depends on the *size* of some other population, it seems unlikely that this is the case generally. However, whenever two populations seek to exploit the same limited resources, the density of each affects the strength of competitive interactions, as we noted earlier in discussing the LV model. Therefore, in developing a multi-population model, we specify only competitive effects between populations. It seems likely, as Lotka and Volterra assumed for the biotic case, that the strength of competitive interactions increases monotonically with density. So assume that the strength of competitive pressures on the first population is *monotonic*:

$$C_{12} = g(N_1, N_2),$$

with

$$\frac{dg}{dN_1} > 0, \qquad \frac{d^2g}{dN_1^2} > 0,$$

and

$$\frac{dg}{dN_2} > 0, \qquad \frac{d^2g}{dN_2^2} > 0, \qquad \frac{d^2g}{dN_1 N_2} > 0.$$

A simple parametric model consistent with these assumptions (and with the constraint that transition rates must be non-negative) is

$$C_{12} = \exp(\beta_1 N_1^2 + \beta_2 N_{2t}).$$

This assumption, when combined with the assumption made earlier about legitimacy, implies the following form of density-dependence in the founding rate:

(6.10) $\lambda(t) = \phi(t) N_{1t}^{\alpha} \exp(-\beta_1 N_{1t}^2 + \beta_2 N_{2t}).$

The cross-effect of density (β_2) captures the effect of *inter-population competition*. Whenever the two populations use the same resources, the cross-effect is negative for both populations. We also add such cross-effects into models for mortality in the same way.

Rate Dependence and Diversity Dependence

Delacroix and Carroll (1983) argue that the founding rate for a particular kind of organization depends on the flow of recent foundings (the crude founding rate) rather than on density per se. They found that founding rates in populations of newspaper firms have cycles and that the cyclic behavior can be fitted well by a quadratic function of foundings in the prior period. The number of foundings in one period affects the number of foundings in the succeeding period, but this effect diminishes with the magnitude of the prior founding rate. Delacroix and Carroll suggest that this pattern is consistent with an imitative process in which potential entrepreneurs use a high founding rate as a signal that opportunities are favorable but also respond to saturation of the market.

Parallel arguments pertain to mortality processes. High numbers of disbandings, for example, may make it difficult for members of a population to convince those who control resources in the environment to continue flows of essential resources. It may also encourage the foes of the population to conduct an intense offensive against it. We explore these issues in Part III with respect to disbandings (and mergers) by including counts of recent disbandings (and mergers) in models like equation (6.7).

In Chapter 1 we suggested that the gains from creating new kinds of organizations are greatest when diversity is low (see also Hannan 1988a). When only a few kinds of organizations operate in a market or sector, at least some potential demand for goods and services is either unfilled or met only partially. On the other hand, when diversity is high, markets tend to be packed tightly with few unexploited resources or opportunities. Rational organization-builders respond to these differences; they are more likely to take the risk of beginning an organization when diversity is low.

A possible countertendency must be noted. When diversity is low, a few organizations or a few organizational forms can more easily dominate a sphere of activity. If these few organizations have high market power, they may be able to prevent other organizations from getting started. For example, they may pressure banks and suppliers to deny credit to new ventures. (If this intervention occurs early in the process of organization building it will imply low founding rates; otherwise it means high disbanding rates at early ages.) Just as important, the dominant organizational forms in low-density sectors are likely to become institutionalized as the "natural" organizational forms for the activity in question. When the prevailing organizational forms are highly institutionalized, it may be difficult to mobilize support for heterodox organizational solutions. Moreover, when diversity is low there are few models of organization with which to experiment and try recombinations. Such a situation yields high returns to deviance but low rates of attempting deviance.

Nielsen (1986) found an instance of negative diversity-dependence in studying the spread of a new organizational form: Flemish separatist political parties in Belgium in the post–World War II period. The new challenging party gained votes most rapidly in those electoral districts (cantons) with the lowest levels of prior political diversity. Electoral districts in which one party had dominated were less tightly packed electoral markets than those in which two or three parties had reasonably large shares of the vote. Although this analysis considered the spread of an organizational form over social space, electoral success in a local district presumably requires the creation of a local political organization. In this sense, Nielsen's findings bear on the issue under discussion. The rate at which these new kinds of local political organizations can be created is highest in political environments with low diversity but with laws allowing free electoral competition.

Dynamics of Selection

As we have noted in previous chapters, evolutionary selection refers to processes of differential replacement in populations. A characteristic conveys a selective advantage if it increases the likelihood that actors with the characteristic will be represented in future populations. In the biotic case, where lifetimes are reasonably tightly controlled by genes and structural characteristics are passed from parent to offspring, selection processes can be identified with differences in net reproductive value of populations with differing characteristics. A characteristic can contribute to net reproductive value because actors with the characteristic are more likely to survive to a reproductive age, are more likely to engage in reproductive attempts, or are more likely to produce viable offspring. One can either treat these components of reproductive success separately or combine them into an overall measure of fitness (expected number of offspring in the next generation of reproducing actors), depending on the analytic purposes.

Organizational ecology and evolution are more complicated than comparable processes in bioecology for several reasons. We have already mentioned the fact that forms of organization are not coded in inert genetic material. Individual organizations can and sometimes do change their forms. In addition, information about building structure does not pass from parent to offspring. There is often no clear-cut parallel to a parent. Moreover, there is no reason why individual organizations cannot live forever. This means that an organization can contribute to future generations *directly*, by persisting. Many generations of formal religious organizations have included the same subpopulation: for instance, the Roman Catholic Church and its constituent orders.

Because of these complexities, we do not attempt to combine the various dimensions of organizational selection processes into a single index such as net reproductive value. Instead we concentrate on the various rates that comprise the process: founding rates, merger rates, disbanding rates, and rates of structural change. Our theoretical and empirical work concentrates on the effects of environments and competition within and between populations on these rates.

In addition to concentrating on the component rates rather than on fitness, we also deal with *local dynamics* of change in organizational ecology rather than with the equilibria implied by certain selection processes. Population-ecology theory in biology usually tries to characterize the equilibria implied by a selection process and sometimes also tries to treat the global dynamics of the system. Our goals here are more modest. Because we knew little about the local dynamics of organizational ecology (for example, how changes in density affect founding rates) when we began, we did not set out to characterize the long-run implications of the local changes we study. We think it is complicated enough to model local dynamics in ways that can be studied empirically. We leave to later research the task of putting together the pieces and drawing implications about global properties of processes of evolution and change in the world.

The remainder of this book seeks to implement the main ideas of this chapter empirically. In Part II we describe our research designs and data and introduce the models and estimators that we use; in Part III we report our findings.

II | *Methods*

7 | Designs of Empirical Studies

The theoretical developments discussed in Part I have numerous empirical implications. We have explored several of them using data on national labor unions, semiconductor manufacturing firms, newspaper publishing companies, and restaurants. The two chapters in Part II provide essential background for the reports of the empirical studies in Part III. This chapter outlines the research designs we used in these studies.[1] Our treatment is quite detailed because interpretation of the analyses in subsequent chapters depends heavily on these designs.

Defining Events

We collected information about the life histories of all (or most) members of the organizational populations under study. In concrete terms, this means obtaining information on the timing of a series of vital events. Because organizations differ from other social actors such as individuals, a number of special issues arise in defining these vital events.

Starting Events

The first step is deciding when an organization begins. It is common in the literature on organizations to view the process of starting an organization as a set of stages (Van de Ven 1980), often assumed to be analogous to human birth and early development (Miles and Randolph 1980). We doubt

---

1. We discuss the design of the more specialized study of restaurants in Chapter 12.

that it is helpful to build on this analogy. The process of beginning an organization is a distinctive social activity which differs in important ways from biotic birth and development. Under close scrutiny, the founding process can be seen to consist of a set of subprocesses, including:

1. *Initiation*: A group gathers and declares its intention to organize.
2. *Resource mobilization*: Funding is sought, space is purchased, leased, or allocated, equipment is purchased or leased, and so forth.
3. *Legal establishment*: Papers of incorporation are filed, a charter is issued, or a legislative mandate is passed.
4. *Social organization*: Employees are hired, members join, social roles are worked out, norms are developed and authority relationships established.
5. *Operational start-up*: The organization begins to function as products are shipped, services are provided, and/or information is processed.

We suspect that the dynamics of these subprocesses vary in important and systematic ways among organizational forms, and we doubt that there is a universal sequence of subprocesses. Formal announcement of an intention to organize may occur before or after resources have been gathered or allocated. Government agencies are often mandated by a legislature long before anyone has declared the intention to organize. Legal establishment of an organization often occurs before the founding group solicits venture capital or approaches others about their interest in joining. So the resource-gathering process may precede initiation or legal establishment, or it may follow.

Aside from their temporal ordering, these subprocesses may proceed at varying paces, and these are likely to differ by form. The start-up of manufacturing operations in the semiconductor industry, for example, is a lengthy process involving purchasing or leasing space and equipment, hiring operational employees, acquiring raw materials and the licenses necessary to transport and use them, and so forth. Voluntary social service organizations often require lengthy periods to acquire a legal charter and to recruit and organize members. But they begin providing services relatively quickly once these other hurdles have been crossed (Singh, Tucker, and House 1986).

The literature on organizational foundings has seldom clearly distinguished among these phases, much less specified the differences in the causal structures affecting them. It would be interesting to analyze the various components of an organizational founding rate separately. For example, we would like to know whether founding rates for certain forms are low because there are few attempts at founding such organizations, or because many attempts are made and most fail to produce a functioning organization. Unfortunately, it is difficult to bound the universe of attempts at making organizations with existing data. Therefore, we confine ourselves at present to studying variations in rates of starting, as indicated by the appearance of functioning organizations. Our empirical materials differ in how they define time of starting. For labor unions, it is the date of a national convention that writes a charter for a new union or the date on which a merger between unions is ratified at national conventions. For semiconductor manufacturing firms, the starting date is the date of entry into the production and sale of semiconductor devices. For newspaper publishers and restaurants, it is the date of start of business (publishing newspapers or serving meals).

Ending Events

Similar issues arise in the case of organizational mortality. Deciding on the time of ending for an organization is complicated by "lingering death." Some organizations lose members and capital and virtually cease operations, but retain a corporate identity. Though such organizations eventually disappear as corporate entities, legal disbanding may come long after operations cease. (Of course similar problems now arise in defining human mortality, since modern technology has greatly expanded the capacity to maintain vital functions on life support devices even after so-called brain death.) Given our focus, we define mortality in strictly *organizational* terms. An organization ends when it ceases to carry out routine actions that sustain its structure, maintain flows of resources, and secure the allegiance of members. For example, in our view a labor union that still has a charter and a national office but no labor contracts, no organizers, and no active locals has ended as a union. Likewise, a manufacturing firm that retains a corporate name but does not rent or own space, employ workers, or maintain contracts has ended as a manufacturing firm.

Subprocesses in the mortality process include:

1. *Formal dissolution*: Some formal decision is made to end an organization. In the case of firms, this step often involves a declaration of bankruptcy. Bankruptcy may be followed by closure and sale of as-

sets. But even if these do not occur, the restructured organization that emerges from bankruptcy with the same name usually has a radically different mode of organizing.

2. *Resource contraction*: Organizations, especially those tied to an area or to a technology, often experience a period of protracted decline in resources prior to failure.

3. *Loss of participation*: Employees are laid off or quit, members resign, board members resign, regular customers and suppliers withdraw.

4. *Disorganization*: The structure dissolves as people's behavior no longer fits customary organizational roles, deviant behavior abounds, and coercive power replaces authority. This is the common pattern observed in military units defeated in battle.

5. *Cessation of operations*: The organization no longer makes its products, provides its services, or processes information. Whatever it claims to be doing is no longer done.

As in the case of starting events, these subprocesses may occur in characteristically different orders and at different speeds for different organizational forms. For manufacturing firms loss of resources usually presages bankruptcy, but cessation of operations may lag far behind. When operations do cease, however, employees are laid off and disorganization occurs very quickly. Military organizations, in contrast, often retain resources and legal mandates but cease operations upon defeat in battle. Loss of participation may occur more gradually; some soldiers may maintain their identity with the army long after it ceases to function. During World War II Japan took the island of Guam and lost it two years later. An American soldier continued to behave as a member of the U.S. Army while hiding in the interim. Not to be outdone, some Japanese soldiers continued to behave as soldiers long after the war was over. A soldier of the Imperial Japanese Army was found on Guam in 1972, twenty-eight years after the island was retaken by the United States. He had known for twenty years that the war was over but is supposed to have explained that "we Japanese soldiers were told to prefer death to the disgrace of getting captured." (*Newsweek* 1972).

There are at least four generic kinds of organizational mortality: disbanding, absorption by another organization, merger, and radical change of form. In the first, the structure of the organization disintegrates, and it either breaks into subunits or its members withdraw participation completely. Because of the possibility of lingering death, there may be some arbitrariness in defining the time of disbanding. Whether this is a serious problem in research depends on the typical durations in the state of lingering disbanding relative to the life expectancy of organizations in the population. It is unlikely to be a serious problem in the study of populations of long-lived organizations. Moreover, the length of time spent in lingering death is undoubtedly affected by the opportunity costs of maintaining the organization. Organizations with high capital requirements (for example, hospitals, auto manufacturers) are unlikely to remain legally alive while not producing because their capital assets have resale value. Moreover, organizations run by individual founders may persist longer than more public organizations (such as publicly traded firms) because the founder has a stake in retaining the corporate identity of the failing organization in the hope of resurrecting it.

The cases of absorption and merger raise the most difficult conceptual issues. Does an organization end when it enters a merger? We consider three underlying features of organizations in answering this question. First, we consider the structure of the organization, particularly its governance structure. When leaders of the merged organization are replaced or clearly subordinated to the leaders of the organization with which it merges, there is reason to assume that its autonomy of action has disappeared, and it may make sense to view this as an ending. More generally, our interest is in organizational forms: if the structure of the organization changes radically as it merges, so that it no longer manifests the form in evidence before the merger, this is counted as an ending.

A second basis for making such decisions is the pattern of resource utilization of the organization before and after the merger. Since we view the niche as a characteristic of the form, we can sometimes observe changes in the use of resources when we cannot tell much about the internal structure of the organization. Thus a hospital operated as a local charity, when sold to a for-profit corporation, may change its patient base to exclude those not covered by health insurance. Such a merger can probably be safely viewed as a terminal event even though internal data on the operation of the hospital are not known.

Finally, we can rely on the way the organization represents itself to the outside world. Name changes and publicity generated by the organization often signal important life events such as endings. This basis for making a decision about how to treat a merger is likely to be more useful when the organization relies on such outward signals in acquiring resources. For example, retail firms invest heavily in establishing a presence in their markets, which they abandon reluctantly. When such firms are purchased by other organizations, customers are not likely to know it unless the new owner intends a dramatic change, one that we would probably treat as a change in form. Thus retail customers are rarely aware of the sale of a company such as Hertz or Avis in the automobile rental business. Each has been independent, and has been bought and sold repeatedly; but their names have not been changed when these events have occurred. In contrast, when the Federal Deposit Insurance Corporation takes over an insured bank and sells it to another bank, the name is usually changed eventually and the acquired bank is folded into the organization of the new owner. The change of name signals the end of the acquired organization, as it is meant to do. Insolvency is not the sort of "good will" that any organization can carry on its books as an asset.

We use these features of organizations in different ways in the studies reported in subsequent chapters. Emphasis of one over the others depends on the kind of organization under study and on the researcher's understanding of the form of organization. It also depends on the availability of pertinent data. We consider merger again when we discuss the empirical studies later in this chapter and in subsequent chapters.

Discussion of the issue of merger is often sidetracked by consideration of an issue that we think is extraneous. Disbandings are often thought to be bad outcomes. But mergers are often good for some of the people involved. For example, individual labor unions have increased their social power by making mergers. Many entrepreneurs reportedly establish firms with the intention of selling out within a few years if the venture is successful. If some mergers are good and organizational disbandings are bad, how can organizations that merge be said to "die"? Are not mergers intended and disbandings not only unintended but avoided?

Ecological analysis is unconcerned with intentions. Instead, as we have already pointed out, it asks which of the many feasible forms of organization actually arise and persist. From an ecological viewpoint, it does not matter if the reason for the disappearance of a form of organization is that each organization in the population has been absorbed by organizations with different forms or that each has disbanded. In each case the social structure has changed—a distinctive form of social action has been lost. However, the absorption/merger and disbanding processes may operate quite differently. We show some of the differences in our analysis of unions.

As we discussed at length earlier in the book, we classify organizations by form. Although we think that changes in form by individual organizations are relatively infrequent, we have tried to record the timing of all such changes. So, for example, we note the time at which a union abandons the craft form in favor of the industrial form. Such changes do not mark the end of an organization as a distinctive corporate actor, but they do mark the end of an implementation of a certain organizing strategy. We discuss this issue further in describing the research designs we used and the populations we studied.

National Labor Unions

It may seem ironic that we studied unions at a time when labor historians have largely abandoned the subject, preferring to study noninstitutionalized forms of labor action (see Gutman 1976, for example). The American labor movement has lost its momentum. In each year since 1957, the fraction of the civilian labor force affiliated with labor unions has declined. The history of the union movement in the United States is now being rewritten as a history of failure—the history of a movement that has fallen victim to its own limited earlier success.

This state of affairs does not, however, diminish the value of the roughly 150-year history of this movement as a source of data about organizational ecology. It may be true that national labor unions in the United States adapted narrowly to peculiar economic and social conditions that are disappearing and may not be repeated. In particular, the fact that labor unions can almost never organize across national boundaries (except in the case of the United States and Canada) while capital and capitalist production move freely across such boundaries is a notable problem of fit for the union movement. The current form of union organization may be an evolutionary dead end. Evolutionary biologists and paleontologists continue to be fascinated with dinosaurs and the evolutionary situation they typify; perhaps we can profit from the study of what may become sociological dinosaurs.

Analyzing the ecology of labor unions allows us to deal with two common criticisms discussed in Chapter 2: that organizational ecology cannot deal effectively with large and powerful organizations, and that it cannot deal with "non-market" organizations. Some unions have grown large and powerful; the largest unions have had more than a million members. Individually and collectively, labor unions have had a major impact on American politics and on industrial structure. So it is hard to argue that they have been especially small and powerless organizations. At the same time, unions are not profit-seeking participants in markets as conventionally defined. So analysis of the dynamics of populations of unions should help to clarify the boundaries of application for organizational ecology.

Another advantage is a tactical one. As we have noted, much organizational research is limited by the fact that all but the largest and longest-lived organizations are ignored. We have already noted the importance of studying the full range of variation on these dimensions. In the case of national labor unions, the record contains information on numerous small unions with short lifetimes (often less than a year). The richness of the record reflects the adversary and often radical nature of many new unions. The formation of national labor unions, no matter how small, has apparently seldom escaped notice and mention in the press. In addition, labor historians and the older schools of institutional economists (especially the Wisconsin school under John R. Commons) have made a sustained effort to reconstruct the historical record, painting a broad picture of the evolution of unions and pointing to many of the relevant primary sources. For these reasons, the study of national labor unions can avoid the problem of bias resulting from endogenous sampling (sampling on the dependent variables, size and longevity).

The available data are also rich in the time dimension: the record extends back 150 years. Since the length of the period is long relative to founding rates and disbanding rates of individual unions, components of selection processes can be studied directly.

Diversity of Forms

Collective action directed at affecting levels of compensation, conditions of work, control over jobs, and other more fundamental changes in the organization of work has taken many forms. Sometimes it consisted of bursts of spontaneous collective action by workers and their families. Some episodes of collective action were directed narrowly at employers at the work site, as in strikes and boycotts. Other episodes were directed at other corporate actors such as legislative and judicial bodies, as in general strikes and political demonstrations.

At various times each kind of collective action by workers became embodied in permanent formal organizations. Organizations of workers that are directed at controlling the work relation are usually called labor unions. Those taking on broader political agenda are usually called worker political movements or political parties. The distinctions between these more or less organized forms of collective action are sometimes blurred in historical reality. Strikes sometimes begot unions; unions sometimes transformed themselves into political movements; political parties sometimes created unions, demonstrations, and strikes. Although analyzing the ecology of the full diversity of forms of worker collective action would be a fascinating study, we did not have sufficient resources to attempt this. Instead, we decided to study only national labor unions for the reasons mentioned earlier.

A labor union is defined here as a permanent organization of workers with the ostensible goal of affecting the conditions of work by threatening the collective withholding of labor. The restriction to an organization that is intended to be permanent distinguishes a union from a prolonged strike or boycott. The restriction to the goal of affecting conditions of work distinguishes a union from broader political movements of workers (such as socialist parties) and from utopian movements (such as Owenite community movements of the 1870s). The restriction to the device of threatening to withhold labor distinguishes a union from employee associations (such as company-sponsored unions), mutual-benefit or benevolent associations of workers, and organizations of workers that try to affect working conditions by other means (such as terrorist organizations).

We studied only *national* labor unions, those that organized in more than one state. However, we note briefly the other kinds of union organization that have existed in this country. The point of this overview is to show that there has been considerable diversity of form in the union movement in the United States and that much of this diversity occurs *within* the category of national unions.

The most obvious dimension of diversity among American labor unions is *scope of organizing*. Unions have varied widely in the breadth of types of workers (crafts and occupations) and types of industries they tried to organize. The forms defined on this dimension can be described as follows.

Single-craft, single-city unions. The first permanent labor organizations in the United States, called trade societies, organized journeymen in a single craft in a single city. The first was apparently the Federal Society of Journeymen Cordwainers, founded in Philadelphia in 1794. The trade society form was dominant until the Panic of 1837, which destroyed most unions.

Multicraft, single-city unions. Next federations of trade societies within cities were formed. The first, the Mechanics Union of Trade Associations, established in Philadelphia in 1827, initially included carpenters, painters, bricklayers, and glaziers. The New York Trades' Society included 52 crafts by 1836 (before being wiped out by the results of the Panic in the next year).

National craft unions. The period just before the Panic of 1837 saw the creation of national unions of craftsmen. Apparently the first was the

Society of Cordwainers, founded in 1836 by a convention of representatives of trade societies of cordwainers (shoemakers) from 16 cities. In the same year, the Society of Journeymen House Carpenters and the National Typographic Society were also begun. Mittleman (1927, pp. 452–453) reports that national unions of comb makers and of hand loom weavers were also created in 1836.

Multicraft unions. As industrialization increased in scope, it became apparent that many craft unions had organized too narrowly. A number of mergers took place in the late nineteenth century among unions whose members had a relatively high degree of shared fate by virtue of working at the same site (meaning that a strike by one union would stop work for the others), working with substitutable processes or materials (for example, painters and wallpaperers), or working along a vertical flow of work (for example, warehousemen and stevedores). For instance, the Bricklayers' International Union (1865–1985) absorbed the Stonemasons' Union in 1883.

More commonly, multicraft unions were created by expansion of the jurisdiction of a union, with no formal merger. The most spectacular example is the United Brotherhood of Carpenters. The UBC began with its membership consisting only of carpenters and joiners. In 1901 it expanded its jurisdiction to cover "all that's made of wood," later extended to "or that was ever made of wood." Using this jurisdictional claim, the UBC eventually organized millwrights, pile drivers, bridge, deck, and wharf carpenters, underpinners, timbermen, boat builders, caulkers, cabinet makers, millmen, floor layers, shinglers, insulators, acoustic and drywall applicators, house movers, loggers, lumber and sawmill workers, furniture workers, casket and coffin makers, and others.

National industrial unions in a single industry. Craft unionism did not always match well with the changing nature of industrial organization in later periods. Semiskilled and unskilled workers played an increasingly important role as technical innovations replaced some kinds of skilled workers, the scale of enterprise grew, and technical change kept reshuffling the roster of identifiable jobs. What came to be known as industrial unionism used a different organizing principle. Instead of defining its jurisdiction in terms of a set of crafts or occupations, an industrial union attempted to organize all production workers in a set of industries, regardless of job title or skill level.

The first unambiguous industrial union in the United States was the American Miners' Association (1861–1867), which attempted to organize all workers "in and around the mines." The Knights of St. Crispin (1867–

1878), which tried to organize all workers in the shoe industry, became the first really large union, with membership estimated at half a million.

Multiple-industry industrial unions. Some industrial unions organized workers in more than one (broadly defined) industry. The most interesting example is the Industrial Workers of the World (1905–1921). The IWW began as a mixed syndicalist political movement and labor organization. However, it directed most of its attention to organizing semiskilled and unskilled workers in mills, agriculture, mining, and lumbering. It had its greatest success in the textile industry (following its support of the famous strike in Lynn, Massachusetts), in the timber industry of the Pacific Northwest, and among tenant farmers and sharecroppers in the Southwest. For a brief period the IWW mobilized thousands of workers in a truly radical union movement. The IWW was crushed by the state for its radical politics during the First World War and had ceased to operate as a national union by 1921.

This brief sketch of the evolution of labor union forms suggests that the composition of the population of labor unions has changed markedly over time. But there is no simple trend toward increasing breadth at the level of the national union, as is often asserted (see Brooks, 1937, for example). Many of the most successful nationals have retained a narrow craft orientation. In at least one well-known case, that of the International Typographical Union (1850–1985), the direction at the organization level was toward more narrow organization. The ITU, though initially dominated by compositors, included all of the crafts in the printing trade as well as journalists. However, each of the other crafts eventually split off and began independent unions, making the ITU a single-craft union.

We think that the dynamics of diversity in union populations have been more contingent than a simple trend hypothesis implies. Unions merged and then dissolved mergers; they admitted new classes of members and then expelled them; they lost whole classes of members as production processes became obsolete. More important to our perspective, the life chances of narrow craft and broad industrial unions seem to have depended on the nature of the industrial and political environments.

Research Design

We have tried to collect information about every national labor union that has existed, however briefly, in the United States. The first step was to compile the lists of names (with starting dates) contained in reports published in various years that claimed exhaustive coverage of the population of unions. We found listings for the following years:

1887 (New Jersey Bureau of Labor Statistics 1898)
1893 (Finance 1894)
1901 (Industrial Commission Report, vol. 17, 1901)
1926 (U.S. Bureau of Labor Statistics 1926)
1936 (Stewart 1936)
1944 (Peterson 1944)
1956 (National Industrial Conference Board 1956)
1962 (Troy 1965)
1975 (Fink 1977)
1985 (Gifford 1985)

These publications, supplemented by annual reports of the Department of Labor from 1932 through 1985, yielded an initial master list of unions. We extended the master list by consulting standard histories of the labor movement, which were especially useful for the period 1830–1870. We relied mainly on reports in Commons et al. (1927), Foner (1947), and Fink (1977).

Each union on the master list was given an identification number, and a file was begun. As the search for information progressed, we found that records of the existence of marginal and short-lived unions which had been ignored previously were sometimes noted in historical accounts of unions on the master list. Each newly identified union was added to the master list, and the process was repeated. We eventually identified 633 unions on which some usable data could be coded.[2] Although there is no way to tell exactly what fraction of all national unions this number represents, we believe that we have identified most members of the population.

In collecting data on individual unions, we relied heavily on published histories of unions, of the union movement, and of industries. When it was feasible, we also used union periodicals and proceedings. We did not try to code data from general newspapers because the relevant events occurred in many cities over a long time period.

---

2. In about fifty cases we found mentions either that a union had been created at a certain time with no further information about it or that a union had existed at a certain date with no other information. We have not included these fragmentary records in our analyses.

Unit of Observation

A national labor union stands midway in a hierarchy of organizational forms. In almost all cases, it is composed of local unions. In some ways national unions are federations of locals. At the same time, many national unions are embedded in federations of nationals, such as the American Federation of Labor (AFL) and the Congress of Industrial Organizations (CIO). Each level is a meaningful actor for some kinds of processes.

One way of conceptualizing the relationship between nationals and locals is to think of the national as a *population* of local unions. From this perspective, the fate of a national reflects the dynamics of the population of locals. In particular, the demise of a national would be equivalent to the extinction of a population. This reasoning makes it appropriate to apply population logic to the histories of *individual* national unions.

The main problem with this approach is that national unions frequently disappear through merger with other nationals. Although merger requires approval of the majority of the membership, it is an event that pertains to the national per se. This kind of event cannot be reduced to events at the level of the locals. Therefore, we consider individual national unions to be the appropriate units of observation, acknowledging that their subunits, the locals, are partially autonomous.

Records of Vital Events

Each observation begins with a *starting time* and a *starting event*:

1. *Founding*: A national union is formed by the joint decision of several locals or by some unorganized group of workers; of the 633 unions, 479 (76%) began with a founding.
2. *Secession*: A union is formed by a faction that secedes from a national union—for example, the National Woolsorters' and Graders Union (1909–1912) was created by a split in the United Textile Workers; 95 unions (15%) began this way, including 7 that had previously been independent unions.
3. *Merger*: Two or more unions merge to form a new national union—for example, the Fur Workers' International Union (1913–1939) merged with the National Leather Workers' Association (1933–1939) to form the International Fur Workers and Leather Workers' Union (1939–1955); 55 unions (9%) began with mergers.

4. *Transformation*: An employee association adopts the goal of collective bargaining and becomes classified as a labor union (for example, the National Education Association announced that it would engage in collective bargaining in 1947); 4 unions were created in this way.

The record for each union also includes an *ending date* and an *ending event*. The main complication in evaluating ending events concerns mergers. We have characterized each merger as one of three types for each partner: (1) the organization is absorbed without changing the strategy and structure of the dominant party to the merger; (2) the organization absorbs another; and (3) the organization merges with one or more roughly "equal-status" partners and a new organization results. We use information on name changes, distributions of executive positions, and the sizes of the partners to make these distinctions.

Thus we distinguished four ways in which a union record might end:

1. *Right-censoring*: The data record ends before the union has ended—the data are censored on the right (for example, the Coopers' International Union, founded in 1890, was still in existence when our coding ended in 1985); of the 633 unions, 160 (25%) were right-censored.
2. *Disbanding*: A union is dissolved (for example, the National Forge of the United Sons of Vulcan, formed in 1862, disbanded in 1876). A total of 203 (32%) unions disbanded. However, 12 of these events occurred on the same day to members of the Trade Union Unity League at the order of the Comintern. Since these were obviously not independent events, we exclude these 12 unions in our analysis of disbandings. Therefore, the effective count of disbandings is 191.
3. *Absorption*: A union is absorbed by merger to a dominant union (for example, the Tunnel and Subway Constructors' Union, founded in 1910, was folded into the International Laborers' Union in 1929); 140 (22%) unions were absorbed in mergers.
4. *Equal-status merger*: A union merges with one or more "equal-status partners," in which case the records for all partners end and a new record begins—a type 3 starting event (for example, the Oil Workers' International Union, founded in 1937, merged with the Union of Gas, Coke, and Chemical Workers of America, founded in 1943, to form the Oil, Chemical, and Atomic Workers of America in 1955); 130 (21%) unions ended in such mergers.

Range of Occupations Organized

We have attempted to code each union's initial organizing strategy together with the dates of all subsequent major changes and the new strategies adopted. In order to do so reliably for a broad range of unions over a long period, we defined organizing strategies in simple and relatively conventional ways.[3] Labor historians appear to agree that specialism in terms of the *range* of jobs and occupations to be organized is the key distinguishing element among different kinds of unions. Thus we paid most attention to coding variation on this dimension, using the following categories:

1. *Single narrow occupation*: The union organizes only members of one narrowly defined craft or occupation, usually skilled.
2. *Composite occupation*: A union organizes members of several crafts or jobs which involve some differentiated skills and training but which share a common set of skills, training, and experience.
3. *Several occupations*: A union organizes two or more separate work roles. Often these work roles are skilled crafts or occupations distinguished by training, experience, and sometimes credentials. Although there may be common skills (for example, the ability to read blueprints), the variations in training and work tasks are more salient than the commonalities.
4. *All production occupations*: A union organizes all of the production workers at the work site.

We simplified this coding scheme in the analyses reported in later chapters by collapsing the first three into one "craft union" category. We call the other category an "industrial union."

Skill Levels

Unions also specialized on the skill dimension. Some unions organized a narrow range of skills; others organized mixes of skills. Although no single

---

3. We also tried to code a number of aspects of internal structure, such as the degree to which decisions about strikes and other key issues were centralized in the national headquarters, the homogeneity of locals in multicraft unions, and the racial, ethnic, and gender composition of the union. However, we found that such information was rarely available before 1930 except for a few famous and well-studied unions, and we abandoned the attempt at coding it.

skill hierarchy applies across the entire work force, each industrial sector recognizes some crude skill hierarchy. As we pointed out earlier, many unions were begun mainly by skilled craft workers. The question of admitting less skilled workers usually generated intense political conflict within unions. Changes in the mix of skill levels provide a potentially interesting case of adaptive change. As technical changes made narrow craft organizations increasingly unfit, the gains from broadening the mix of skills increased. Yet doing so threatened the privileged position of skilled workers. Struggles for political control within the union sometimes threatened its existence as much or more than continuing with an obsolete craft form. We can learn about both the rates of such adaptive changes and their consequences for survival chances by coding event histories of changes in skill levels.

We do not pretend that we can code skill-level composition uniformly across industries. The distinctions among skill levels that unions have made and that labor economists and sociologists recognize are at least partly specific to the history of each industry. Industries that began earlier are more likely to contain clearly defined crafts and skill hierarchies than more recent industries. Moreover, skill levels imputed to positions change over time. A review of census classifications over the period from 1890 to 1920 shows that many jobs once considered skilled became less skilled (that is, semiskilled) when the production process became mechanized. This was the case for cigarmakers, chainmakers, tool makers, and others. The semiskilled category is especially problematic. In many ways it has been used as a residual category for cases about which it was hard to decide whether the skills needed for the job required much training. Therefore, it includes such jobs as sailor, brakeman, meatcutter, weaver, sawyer, and welder.

Instead of trying to code absolute distinctions between skill levels, we identified times at which unions widened or narrowed the mix of skills represented. This always meant organizing some new class of workers or dropping some class of workers who were considered to have a different skill level. In particular, we did not try to code changes over time in the skill levels of the same class of workers. For example, when cigarmaking was demoted in census classifications to a semiskilled job, we did not record a change for cigarmakers' unions on skill composition. Thus our measure of changes in skill composition refers to changes in the *kinds* of workers a union tried to organize rather than to changes in the real skills possessed by its members or to changes in the processes of production.

Our histories of changes in skill composition record a union's initial position: which skill levels it organized, and the dates of all subsequent changes with the new mix. The basic coding categories include:

1. *Professional workers*: Examples include the American Federation of Physicians and Dentists (1973–1985) and the White Rats Actors Union (1900–1919).
2. *Proprietors, managers, and officials*: For example, the National League of District Postmasters (1894–1976) organized managers and the Journeymen Barbers, Hairdressers, and Cosmetologists (1887–1984) represented proprietors.
3. *Clerks and kindred workers*: Examples are the Insurance Workers of America (1950–1959) and the United National Association of Post Office Clerks (1899–1961).
4. *Skilled workers*: Examples of unions of skilled workers are the Journeymen Tailors' National Trades Union (1865–1876), the Diamond Workers' Protective League (1902–1955), and the Brotherhood of Commercial Telegraphers (1898–1900).
5. *Semiskilled workers*: Examples include the Seafarers' Union (1891–1985) and the International Ladies Garment Workers' Union (1900–1985).
6. *Unskilled workers*: Examples are the United Farm Workers' Union (1962–1985) and the Brotherhood of Railroad Freighthandlers (1901–1915).

There has been considerable diversity in coverage of skill levels by American unions. The commonest strategy was to organize only skilled workers ($N = 155$). Yet 149 unions organized unskilled and semiskilled workers. We simplified the conventional census classifications to provide a binary variable, which we call LOWSKILL. It receives a value of one if all of the workers organized by the union are in occupations classified as "semiskilled" or "unskilled"; otherwise its value is zero.

Affiliations

We also collected data on the dates of affiliation with federations. Of course, the main federations over the recent period have been the AFL and the CIO. Other affiliations that show up in our data are the Knights of Labor, the (officially Communist) Trade Union Unity League, the IWW, and the Alliance for Labor.

In addition to these event histories, we collected whatever data were available on membership. Such data are available after 1930 but are scanty before then for all but AFL unions. We can, however, obtain information about membership size around the time of founding for 519 unions.

Finally, we collected diverse information about the environments facing unions. We discuss these data in Chapters 9 and 11 in the context of presenting analyses of ecological processes.

Semiconductor Merchant Producers

Our second major empirical study concerns the population of firms that manufactured and sold semiconductor electronics devices in the United States between 1946 and 1984. The term "semiconductor" refers to the electrical properties of the materials from which microelectronic devices are made. Silicon is the most commonly used semiconducting material. Slices of silicon crystals are coated with other materials that have varying conducting and insulating properties. There are two major categories of products based on this structure. Discrete devices include transistors, diodes, and rectifiers. Integrated circuits, the newer branch of the technology and the one with the largest market, includes analogue devices (used heavily in telecommunications) and logic, microprocessor, and memory devices. These products are themselves components in larger electronic systems of all sizes, such as computers, consumer electronic products, communications switching and transmission equipment, and weapons.

The integral role of semiconductors in other advanced technologies makes the study of this industry interesting for policy reasons. Our interest concerns the ecological dynamics of the industry, including the effects of the environments within which the population operates. The relevant environments are the markets for semiconductor products and the technology itself.

We study only the firms participating in the *merchant* market, firms that sell semiconductor products to other firms. This restriction excludes some of the largest semiconductor manufacturers in the world, those that sell only to other branches of the same company and not on the open market. This is often called *captive production.* An example is IBM, which is probably the largest semiconductor producer in the world. In 1979, it was estimated that 30 percent of the world's semiconductors were produced by captives (Wilson, Ashton, and Egan 1980). Large corporations design and manufacture their own semiconductor components in order to capture the profits generated by the high value added by manufacture, to ensure a supply of these crucial components, and to ensure that research and development are devoted to applications having the highest payoff for the development of their products. In such cases, the capital allocation, research and development, and production scheduling of the semiconductor division are all subordinated to the requirements of other corporate divisions. Further, the larger corporation buffers the semiconductor division from much of the uncertainty stemming from the market and provides a cushion that lowers the uncertainty generated by change in the technology. Specialization, with appropriate planned lead times for development, protects captive producers against the vagaries of having to design semiconductor devices representing the state of the art. For example, a firm that produces a microprocessor to be used in its own industrial process control system might settle for one that is not the fastest microprocessor available if it performs certain specialized functions better than a generic device available on the merchant market.

Merchant and captive producers are, therefore, quite different kinds of organizations, and there is good reason to expect them to exhibit different life-event dynamics. Rates of entry and exit for captive producers should be functions of the fortunes of their parent companies. Merchant market producers, even those owned by bigger corporations, are likely to be affected more directly by demand for semiconductors. Uncertainty stemming from the technology should affect them more directly as well, because unforeseen changes in technology will be underwritten by the parent and the divisions using semiconductor output.

Data are available on merchant market producers, as we describe below. For captive producers, however, data are difficult to find. When the captives start and cease operations, which products they manufacture, and how they are organized are facts not usually reported and often treated as trade secrets. Consequently, captive producers are extremely difficult to study. So for both practical and theoretical reasons, we confine ourselves to merchant market producers.

Our analysis of the population of semiconductor firms is confined to American firms and operations. One reason for this limitation is availability of data: information on the existence of the firms and on the products they produce is available for the American market but not for the rest of the world. Furthermore, foreign producers operate in quite different financial and regulatory environments. They are included in our study only when they have a subsidiary in the United States.

Semiconductor markets are famous for two qualities: an exponential pattern of growth in sales and a magnified business cycle. Although other semiconductor devices predated transistors, the transistor was the product that began the trend toward miniaturization in electronics. When the transistor was invented in 1947, germanium was used. Germanium transistors could not tolerate the variations in temperature and humidity that most applications would require, and consequently the market for transistors in the early years was confined to specialized products such as hearing aids. The introduction of silicon transistors in 1954 had two important consequences. The first was great expansion in the variety of applications, resulting from better tolerance of fluctuations in temperature and humidity. Second, batch manufacturing techniques were more easily applied to silicon. Batch production not only increased the efficiency of manufacture, it also lowered the risk. Before the development of the most important production process, the planar process, product design was linked to production equipment design. Obsolescence in product design required replacement of production equipment, at great cost.

As the technology advanced, the market expanded. Although prices fell both in absolute terms for a particular product and in cost per function performed, total sales grew at a breathtaking rate. But the business cycle in the semiconductor industry exaggerates the cycle in the economy at large. As indicated earlier, semiconductor devices are generally expensive components of broader systems. As a result of the rapid pace of technological change in the industry, products become obsolete quickly. Consequently, holding large inventories of semiconductor components is both expensive and risky for the system manufacturer; by the time they are needed, alternative designs may be more desirable. When the economy goes into recession, buyers of semiconductor devices look for ways to reduce expenditures and cut their orders for semiconductors. But in order to shrink bloated inventories, they cut orders by a greater percentage than the decline in their own orders. When orders for systems pick up, the process works in reverse. Semiconductors are often in short supply, and when orders for systems begin to grow, a shortage in these critical components can stifle recovery. So customers rebuild inventory, increasing orders by amounts greater than the expansion of orders for systems. Thus the market for semiconductors is characterized by erratic change in the context of long-term exponential growth.

A similar pattern of change characterizes the technology itself because uncertainties stemming from technical change exacerbate the market uncertainties just described. The long-run trend in this technology is toward increasing miniaturization and functional capability. Over time, semiconductor devices have become increasingly complex and able to perform more complicated combinations of functions, to the point that single chips now include all of the capabilities of a computer. In 1965 Gordon Moore, the president of Intel, asserted that the functional density of integrated circuits would double every year. Moore's Law, as this prediction is called, was remarkably accurate. Technical change involves secular trends, not just inventions occurring randomly in time. Those who follow the technology closely often know what the next major innovation will do. The question is when it will occur, which firm will introduce it first, and what the details will be. So the technology changes in such a way that the functional capabilities of semiconductor devices increase exponentially with time but erratically as well.

The pattern of change in the technology exacerbates the change in the market because extensive research and development requires organizational structures that are costly to assemble and disassemble. When cash flow shrinks during slack markets, cutbacks in development threaten a firm's return to prosperity later. Falling behind in such a rapidly developing technology guarantees failure. So the pressures from market cycles run counter to the pressures from changing technology.

These dual patterns of change in technology and market create opportunities for entrepreneurs (Brittain and Freeman 1980). They also create risks because the time periods required to perform various organization-building tasks do not map perfectly onto periods in which resources are available. The dramatically expanding market offers promises of rewards that compensate for taking those risks. Hence the semiconductor business has been a highly volatile one, and it constitutes a particularly interesting laboratory for population studies of organizations.

Unit of Analysis

We argued earlier in this chapter that beginning and ending processes are actually composed of subprocesses that occur at varying speeds and in varying orders across organizational forms. One must choose to focus attention on one or the other of these processes as the basis for deciding when life events of interest have occurred. For one kind of organization it may be the legal existence, with filing papers of incorporation and filing under Chapter 13 of the Bankruptcy Act defining the important life events. For another, it may be the start and end of operations. This is the subprocess of interest here because marketing semiconductor products defines the existence of the organization as a semiconductor manufacturer. Initiation procedures, such as seeking the participation of potential founding team members, or resource-gathering activities such as seeking venture capital, are often carried out for companies that never actually are formed. The development of an organization with a division of labor and authority relations is difficult to observe for organizations such as these by methods other than direct observation. Direct observation would confine the number of observations in such a way as to vitiate population-level analysis. Consequently, it seems to make sense to record the time when an organization begins to produce and sell semiconductor devices as the beginning of the organization. Nevertheless, to avoid confusion we refer to "entries" and "exits" in the remainder of this book when discussing semiconductor firms rather than to "foundings" and "disbandings."

The unit of analysis for the semiconductor study is the part of the organization producing and selling semiconductor devices. It may be a privately held firm, a complete corporation, or a set of corporate divisions. The time of starting for semiconductor manufacturers is defined by market participation. Manufacturing organizations may be bought out by other corporations, but we treat them as intact so long as they market products under their own name. We treat companies that stop making and selling semiconductor devices as ending, even though they may not go through bankruptcy. Employees may come to work and produce other things, and this would be a serious problem were it not for the rather demanding requirements for manufacturing semiconductor devices. One does not blithely acquire the necessary equipment, train the operators, design the products, and commence manufacturing. An organization abandoning all of this to take up some other line of business almost necessarily undergoes a transformation of such magnitude that it would make little sense to call it the same organization even if its name remains the same or its legal ownership is unchanged.

Sources of Data

Our key source of information on semiconductor manufacturing companies is the *Electronics Buyer's Guide*. This is a standard industry source book for purchasing agents and others interested in buying commodity electronic devices, including semiconductor devices. We obtained copies of this source for each year from 1946 to 1984 and coded a three-dimensional data array: firms by devices by years. This produced 6,856 observations of firms in various years. The entry date was defined as the year of entry of each firm in the *Guide*. There were 1,197 entries. The terminal date was the last year the firm appeared. When a firm was absent for more than one year and then reappeared, it was assumed that a new firm had begun, even if it had the same name as a firm that disappeared. A firm that appeared in only one year but then disappeared for several years was coded as starting at the beginning of the extended string. The single observation was dropped because we assume that the listing in the *Guide* was in error. There were 302 semiconductor firms still in existence in 1984. Not counting these right-censored cases, there were 895 exits from the industry, our operational definition of mortality for semiconductor firms.

Some large corporations operate multiple divisions that produce and sell semiconductor devices. Sometimes product lines and their production facilities are shifted from one division to another. General Electric, for example, began selling standardized semiconductor products through a sales office in 1965, and GE stopped reporting the names of the corporate divisions actually producing those devices. So GE's Rectifier Components, Receiving Tubes, and Semiconductor Products divisions all disappeared from the *Guide* in 1964. Obviously, one would not want to treat these events as exits from the industry. So we aggregated divisional data to the corporate level. The starting date for the organization is then the first year when any of its divisions markets a semiconductor device. In the case of GE this is 1951, when it appeared in the *Guide* selling discrete devices through its Apparatus Sales division. The exit date attached to any particular firm is the first year in which none of the divisions is still in the semiconductor business. When another company absorbs a free-standing semiconductor firm, a judgment has to be made. If the newly acquired division operates as a subsidiary and maintains its own name, then we do not aggregate the division into the parent company's observation. However, we treat it as an ending event because the independent company becomes a subsidiary of a bigger firm. Thus when Schlumberger acquired Fairchild, we did not backdate Schlumberger's observation to the year Fairchild entered the business. On the other hand, if a company gets into the business by acquiring the assets of an existing company but does not sell products under the old company's name, we use the date when it starts selling semiconductors under its own name as the date it entered.

The *Guide* listed 85 separate product categories over the 39-year period. Since the purpose of the *Guide* is to indicate sources of supply, data on the size, organization, and financial performance of firms are not included. We used industry sources, principally data provided by the market research firm Dataquest, to measure the volume of sales in various product families.

We were able to obtain worldwide and North American sales data for nine aggregate families from Dataquest, and from other sources for the earliest years. These families are as follows:

A. *Discrete Semiconductor Components*
  1. Diodes and rectifiers
  2. Transistors and thyristors
B. *Integrated Circuits*
  3. Digital integrated circuits
  4. Analog/linear integrated circuits
  5. Signal converting integrated circuits
C. *Custom and Semi-Custom Devices*
  6. Custom integrated circuits
  7. Hybrid circuits
D. *Optoelectronic Devices*
  8. Light-emitting devices
  9. Photo-sensitive devices

In the case of the appearance of new products in the *Guide*, a decision was made to include them within one of the existing product families, or to add to the list of product families. We then matched the sales data to firms so that we could measure characteristics of the markets in which they did business with the dates of their entry or exit.

Lack of Precision on Dates

The data just described tell the year in which a firm appeared in the market, the last year in which it was observed, and the years in which various products were sold. We do not know the month or day during the year on which these events occurred. Large numbers of ties in the time spell between entry and exit result. We dealt with this in a number of ways, as we describe in the chapters in Part III.

Organizational Forms

One can view the history of the American semiconductor industry as a contest among organizational forms. Some of the first entrants were specialized entrepreneurial ventures; others were established manufacturers of integrated electrical equipment. American Telephone and Telegraph licensed its transistor invention at least partly because antitrust proceedings against it led to a promise not to develop the commercial possibilities. Giants such as RCA and General Electric as well as small companies such as the oil exploration equipment manufacturer Texas Instruments sent engineers to the meetings that laid the groundwork for licensing the technology.

Initially the specialists flourished while the integrated giants backed off. The giants seemed unable to cope with the uncertainties that such an immature technology imposed. In the 1980s foreign firms, especially those from Japan and Korea, made great progress in penetrating the world market, particularly in the mass manufacture of the memory chips so essential to the computer industry. These foreign firms were almost all integrated manufacturers and were active in many of the same industries as were the American giants previously forced to surrender technological leadership in semiconductors. Companies like RCA and Westinghouse had made initial efforts in the industry but lost out competitively to companies like Texas Instruments and Fairchild Semiconductor in the 1960s. The very diversity of the larger companies made it difficult to tolerate the uncertainty of a rapidly changing technology with distant and vague profit potential (Brittain and Freeman 1980). Our data do permit us to examine whether or not the semiconductor firm under study is a division of a larger organization. When it is, we call it a subsidiary; when it is not, we call it independent. The variable SUBSIDIARY assumes a value of one when the firm in question is a subsidiary and zero when it is independent.

In general, we believe subsidiaries are better protected from life-threatening disruption stemming from resource scarcity or temporal variations in resources. Because they are parts of bigger corporations that are usually less driven by technology than semiconductor firms, we expect subsidiaries to be more bureaucratic. Fortunately, we have detailed data on a subsample of semiconductor firms which we can use to describe the difference between these two forms in more detail.

In 1984, we conducted interviews in 47 of the 56 merchant market semiconductor firms in the area south of San Francisco commonly called Silicon Valley. We gathered data on the structures, business strategies, technologies, and histories of these firms. The respondent was usually the chief executive, but sometimes a subordinate was interviewed. For the larger firms, multiple interviews were conducted with managers responsible for such areas as research and development and manufacturing. The data we collected are summarized in Table 7.1.

Table 7.1.   Characteristics of subsidiary and independent semiconductor firms in Silicon Valley, 1984

	Subsidiary firms				Independent firms			
Variable	Mean	Standard deviation	Median	N	Mean	Standard deviation	Median	N
Year founded	80.3	4.7	—	20	74.2	7.5	—	26
Number of employees	—	—	94	20	—	—	300	27
Sales in 1983 (thousands)	—	—	2,000	15	—	—	7,733.5	24
% sales to top 5 customers	37.3	24.0	—	20	25.8	21.6	—	27
% sales of commodity chips	—	—	9	20	—	—	30	27
% sales second sourcing	—	—	12	20	—	—	9	27
% wafer fabrication done in house	43.0	49.0	—	20	71.5	44.3	—	27

	Subsidiary firms		Independent firms	
Variable	Percent	N	Percent	N
Have an organization chart	85.2	23	65.0	13
Have a functional structure	26.9	7	5.0	1
Have a profit-sharing plan	29.6	8	10.0	2
Have a personnel manual	64.0	16	50.0	10
Have written job descriptions for all positions	68.0	17	45.0	9
Market worldwide	81.5	22	60.0	12

Our purpose here is descriptive; we test no hypotheses. Therefore, Table 7.1 does not report tests of significance. We define a subsidiary here as a firm for which, according to our data, more than 50 percent of the equity is held by some parent corporation. Obviously, retrospective data cannot be used to test theories about organizational mortality, and even such descriptive exercises as this must be interpreted with caution because the population in 1984 is a population of survivors.

Some of the variables reported in Table 7.1 are continuously distributed, while others are categorical. Some of the continuously distributed variables are highly skewed. When the absolute value of skewness is greater than 1 for both subsamples being compared, we report medians rather than means. When the size of the combined subsamples is less than 47, there are missing values in the data.

The youth of both kinds of firms is striking; but the subsidiaries are slightly younger than the independents. This should not be too surprising given that we predict a liability of newness in the exiting rate of semiconductor firms, and one of the major ways of exiting is to be acquired by a bigger firm.

There are also size differences between the two forms. The independents are approximately three times larger as measured by either sales or number of employees. Again, the smallness of the average firm is striking. The largest of them has sales of well over a billion dollars per year, but the averages are less than ten million dollars.

The subsidiaries sell to a somewhat more concentrated market, and they devote fewer of their efforts to the production and sales of commodity chips. A common business strategy for new firms is serving as a second source of devices invented by other firms. This turned out not to be any more prevalent among the independents than among the subsidiaries; in fact, it is slightly less common among the independents.

The independents do more of their own wafer fabrication than do the subsidiaries. Integrated circuits are made from disks of silicon. Each disk, or wafer, has hundreds of devices on it at the end of the process. After testing, these are cut from the wafer chip by chip. Wafer fabrication is the heart of the manufacturing process and involves the most expensive equipment. We should note that the unit of observation here is the firm or establishment in Silicon Valley. If the same parent has other subsidiaries located elsewhere, wafer fabrication may be located there. It is not necessarily true that the corporations of which the subsidiaries are a part are less likely to do their own wafer fabrication. Indeed, we would be surprised if this were so.

A number of categorical variables seem to support our belief that the subsidiaries are likely to be more bureaucratic than the independents. They are more likely to have produced an organization chart, to have a functional structure, to have a formal profit-sharing plan, and to have written a personnel manual. They also use written job descriptions more often than the independents.

Finally, the independents are more likely to market locally or regionally, whereas the subsidiaries are more likely to market on a worldwide basis. This reflects the greater financial muscle of the latter and allows them to spread out the risks of local booms and busts.

A second difference in form is the level of *specialization*. Some manufacturers attempt to produce the full variety of semiconductors existing as of the time in question, while others have chosen to work only within one or two branches of the industry. Specialization allows scale within narrow niches. It suggests risks, however, since the vagaries of a rapidly developing technology may compound business risk with technology risk.

Technical Change and Industry Characteristics

Our interest in the ecology of semiconductor firms centers on the patterns of change in the technology and changes in the market. We rely on two sources of information on change in the technology. First, we examine dates of introduction of various technical innovations. In particular, we examine difference in foundings and failure rates over periods of time:

1. *P1 (Early)*: We begin the study of semiconductor firms with the year 1946. For the first few years production was confined to various discrete devices such as metallic rectifiers that preceded the invention of the transistor. The period ends in 1959.
2. *P2 (Middle)*: The middle period begins in 1960 with the introduction of the integrated circuit. In the next year, 1961, the planar process was introduced. In fact, the early 1960s were a very rich period for technical innovation in this industry; oxide masking, diffusion and epitaxial techniques, and planar techniques were all introduced and broadly disseminated (Tilton 1971, pp. 66–67). The period ends in 1969.
3. *P3 (Recent)*: The 1970s saw a surge of developments that made relatively inexpensive computing a reality. In 1970 the first dynamic random access memory chip was introduced by Intel and Advanced Memory Systems. The following year the microprocessor was introduced by Intel. So the third period begins in 1970 and continues to 1984.

It is obvious that one could define a period for every year, since both large and small innovations have come almost continuously. Also, of course, the innovations do not diffuse instantly. The dates are, therefore, only approximations.

Our data on markets come from industry sources such as the Semiconductor Industry Association's annual reports, as well as various reports supplied by the market research firm, Dataquest. We used these sources to develop the list of product groups presented earlier. We note the date of introduction of the various products in the *Electronics Buyer's Guide* and the speed with which firms enter new product markets to measure their innovativeness. We check our dates against various industry sources, including those produced by the Semiconductor Industry Association as well as reports such as those by Tilton (1971), Braun and MacDonald (1978), and Wilson, Ashton, and Egan (1980).

Finally, we refer to a variety of government reports to deflate data on sales using the Consumer Price Index, the Industrial Producer Price Index (Bureau of Labor Statistics), and the interest rate for Triple A Rated Corporate Bonds (Federal Reserve Bulletin). Variables from these reports were coded as yearly time series. They are, then, constant across firms in a given year.

Newspaper Publishers in San Francisco

The most fruitful empirical studies of organizational ecology to date have used data on populations of firms producing newspapers. Studies by Carroll and Delacroix (1982) and Delacroix and Carroll (1983) analyzed data on such populations in Argentina and Ireland in the nineteenth and twentieth centuries. Carroll (1987) analyzed populations over similarly long periods in seven SMSAs in the United States, and Amburgey, Lehisalo, and Kelly (1988) have conducted similar research on the Finnish population. Although these studies have treated age dependence, rate dependence, niche width, and a variety of other ecological processes, they have not yet considered processes of density dependence, which play a central role in our scheme. Therefore, we collaborated with Glenn Carroll in reanalyzing his data on the population of newspapers in the San Francisco Bay area. What follows is a brief sketch of Carroll's research design (full details can be found in Carroll 1987).

The first task was to develop a definition of a newspaper that makes sense for the full historical period. This means distinguishing early newspapers from newsletters, pamphlets, and corantos and later newspapers from journals and magazines. Carroll defines a newspaper as a periodical printed by mechanical means, which appeals to those with common literacy, whose contents consist of timely information, and whose publication is directed to a geographically delimited market of consumers and advertisers.

The unit of observation is a newspaper publishing firm. The initiation of a firm is defined in terms of the beginning of publication. The ending of a firm consists of disbanding, absorption by another firm, or equal-status merger that produces a new firm. These three events are considered jointly as mortality. In the case where a publisher produced more than one newspaper, the earliest and last dates of its publishing operations mark the beginning and end of its history.

Ecological analysis of newspaper publishing firms is attractive because good data on even small and short-lived firms are available over long historical periods. The availability of such data reflects the fact that newspaper publication leaves dated material products of direct interest to historians who have catalogued their publishing histories. In addition, publications directed at advertisers have been published yearly for almost the entire history of the industry in the United States. Records on the histories of newspaper publishing firms were collected from the following archival sources: Gregory (1937) for the period 1821–1869, Rowell (various years) for the period 1869–1880, and Ayer (various years) for the period 1881–1980. In the case of the San Francisco Bay Area, these histories were supplemented by records from special studies by Daggett (1939) and Wheeler (1973).

The San Francisco Bay area (San Francisco, Oakland, and San Jose) is by far the largest of the SMSAs included in Carroll's study. It contains enough variation in density and vital rates to sustain an analysis of the effects of density on such rates. The earliest newspapers in this area began in the 1840s. Over the ensuing 140 years, 2,168 publishing firms have produced newspapers in this area.

Comparison of Data Sets

The labor union, semiconductor, and newspaper data sets cover their respective organizational populations over their full histories. However, the histories of unions and newspapers are a good deal longer than the 39 years for the semiconductor industry. The result is more observations over time in the union and newspaper studies. On the other hand, many variables that one might want to employ in the study of unions and newspapers are simply unavailable for the first decades of their existence.

An important difference between the three kinds of organizations is the more obvious specification of resource bases for semiconductor and newspaper companies. The linkages between market and technology and the life chances of semiconductor and newspaper firms are simply more apparent than are comparable linkages for national labor unions. Unions organize workers, but they can persist for long periods of time with few members and relatively little money. The difficulty of identifying resource bases of unions with confidence is in part a function of their changing nature over time. Over the history of the American labor movement, unions changed from social movements to organizations. With this change came shifts in the resources they used and the factors generating waves of foundings and disappearances. Semiconductor companies and newspaper publishing firms have changed primarily in the corporate context. As capital requirements rose with sophistication in production technology and the efficient scale of the minimal production unit increased, the vagaries of the capital markets became more significant. In the case of semiconductor manufacturing firms, operating as a free-standing merchant market specialist became problematic as financial might and marketing acumen came to rival technical excellence as factors dominating the life chances of semiconductor firms. In the case of newspaper publishers, the rise to dominance of national publishing companies (''chains'') has had a dramatic impact on the shape of the industry.

These differences are useful in this study because we want to learn whether the processes we have identified are general ones. Despite the differences among the forms, we have been able to code the histories of all organizations in the three populations using the same basic scheme. The next chapter describes how we analyze these organizational histories.

8 | Models and Methods of Analysis

This chapter explains how we analyze the life histories of organizations and test ecological hypotheses. Our objective in empirical analysis is two-fold: we want to develop models that provide a realistic description of organizational dynamics, and we want to test a variety of hypotheses drawn from our demographic and ecological theories.

The previous chapter, which described our research designs, noted several features of our data: (1) events can and do occur at any time or age; (2) there are multiple kinds of events, such as disbanding and merger; and (3) some histories end before organizations cease functioning—that is, portions of some histories are unobserved. Each of these characteristics must be accommodated in developing realistic models of organizational dynamics.

The first feature favors use of continuous-time models. There is no fixed time interval in any of the processes we study. Since we also assume that the occurrence and timing of mergers, changes of forms, and dissolutions are affected by a large number of factors other than those we emphasize, stochastic models are needed to describe these histories. Therefore, following the sociological modeling tradition begun by Coleman (1964), we assume that the organizational histories that we study are realizations of *continuous-time, discrete-state stochastic processes*.

A stochastic process can be described using a number of parameters (or functions of the processes) such as transition rates, transition probabilities, waiting times, and so forth. We concentrate on *transition rates*. That is, we test ecological hypotheses by expressing transition rates as functions of observed characteristics of organizations and environments, unobserved heterogeneity, and various measures of time such as age and historical ·time.

This chapter explains the advantages of analyzing effects on transition rates and describes the causal models and methods of analysis that we use. It also shows how event-history data can be used to estimate causal parameters and to test ecological hypotheses when data are censored (the third characteristic mentioned above). Thus the chapter summarizes the modeling and estimation strategies that form the basis of the empirical analyses reported in Part III. More detailed discussions of most of the matters touched on here and advantages of the approach can be found in Tuma and Hannan (1984). Excellent technical references are Kalbfleisch and Prentice (1980) and Cox and Oakes (1984).

Describing Organizational Histories

An event-history (or sample-path) observation plan records information on *all* changes in state within some observation period. Let $Y(t)$ denote the random variable indicating an organizations's position at time t, and let $y(t)$ denote a particular realization of this random variable. The set of all distinct values that $Y(t)$ can take is called the state space of Y, whose size we denote by Ψ. We concentrate on qualitative variables that have a countable number of states. The states in our analyses usually consist of a set of forms and a set of ending events such as merger and disbanding.

The state entered at the nth event is denoted by the random variable Y_n. The period of time between successive events is called an *episode* or *spell*. The nth episode refers to the period between the $(n - 1)$th and nth events. The length of time from event $n - 1$ until event n is called the *waiting time* to the nth event. We often refer to the waiting time until an event as the *duration* in a state. In the case of the first spell, the waiting time in a state is also the age of the organization at the time of the first change of state.

When data on $Y(t)$ are lacking for the beginning of the history, the data are said to be left-censored; when data are lacking for the end of the history, they are said to be right-censored. Event-history data available to organizational researchers are almost always censored on the right (that is, we do not know what will happen in the future). Often they are censored on the left as well. Censoring presents special problems in analyzing event-history data. Right-censoring turns out to be a manageable problem given assumptions that are usually plausible. Left-censoring is far more difficult to handle. Because our designs usually avoid problems of left-censoring, we focus here on analysis of event histories that are censored on the right but not on the left.

Survivor Function

The first step in analyzing a set of histories is to summarize them in a compact way. One useful summary is the survivor function. This function tells the probability that the event of interest does not occur before time t:

$$G_j(t) \equiv \Pr\{T_j \geq t\},$$

where T_j is a random variable that denotes the waiting time in state j.

In our empirical analyses, more than one event can occur: organizations change form more than once, they absorb other organizations repeatedly, they are absorbed and then re-emerge, and so forth. Since the timing of events can depend on previous history, the survivor function should be expressed as a function of previous history in any general treatment. We suppress this dependence to avoid cluttering the notation. This does not mean that we believe previous history is unimportant; in the chapters that follow, we explore dependence on history when it seems substantively important. We usually do so by including indicators of previous history as covariates in our models.

The standard approach to summarizing event-history data uses Kaplan and Meier's (1958) product-limit estimator, a nonparametric maximum-likelihood estimator of the survivor function. Since we are typically interested in the logarithm of the survivor function (for reasons discussed in this section), we rely instead on an estimator of the latter.

Hazard Function

The hazard function tells the rate at which transitions *from* a state occur. It is the limiting probability of "failing" (that is, leaving a state, at time t, given that failure has not occurred before t). The hazard function for the nth event is defined in terms of the corresponding survivor function:

$$h_j(t) \equiv \lim_{\Delta t \downarrow 0} \frac{G_j(t) - G_j(t + \Delta t)}{G_j(t) \, \Delta t} = -\frac{d \log G_j(t)}{dt}.$$

Solving this differential equation (with initial condition $G_j(0) = 1$) gives the *integrated hazard function*:

$$(8.1) \qquad H_j(t) \equiv -\log G_j(t) = \int_0^t h_j(s) \, ds.$$

The relationship in (8.1) plays an important role in estimating hazard functions from empirical data. It shows that the hazard function of a process defines the survivor function, and vice versa.

The integrated hazard function has direct substantive significance. For instance, estimates of this function tell whether hazard functions are constant. When the hazard is indeed constant across sample members and over time for each sample member, the integral in (8.1) is a linear function of the waiting time, that is, $H_j(t) = h_j t$. This means that a plot of an integrated hazard function against duration (or age in the case of first spells) will be approximately linear if the hazard is constant in the population. Thus departures from linearity in such plots are indications that the hazard varies among organizations (there is population heterogeneity), varies over time for an individual organization (there is time dependence), or both.

According to (8.1), a hazard function can be estimated from a plot of the logarithm of an estimated survivor function versus time. The estimated hazard function at any time t is the slope of $H_j(t)$. So any graphic or analytic technique for evaluating this function's slope is a possible method for estimating the hazard function. The logarithm of the Kaplan-Meier estimator can be used as an estimator of the cumulative hazard function. Since the logarithm is a monotonic transformation and the large-sample properties of maximum likelihood (ML) are preserved under monotonic transformations, this estimator of the cumulative hazard function has good asymptotic properties. However, because of the nonlinearity of the transformation, this estimator of the cumulative hazard function is biased in small samples.

Aalen (1978) has used martingale theory to derive a better estimator.[1] His nonparametric estimator of the cumulative hazard function is

$$\hat{H}_j(t) = \sum_{t_{(i)} < t} \frac{1}{I - (i) - c(t_{(i)})},$$

where I is the number of cases at risk initially, $t_{(i)}$ is the time of the ith event, (i) is the count (order) of the event at $t_{(i)}$, and $c(t_{(i)})$ is the number of cases lost to right-censoring by $t_{(i)}$. This estimator is unbiased, consistent, and asymptotically normal. Its variance is

$$\text{Var } \hat{H}_j(t) = \sum_{t_{(i)} < t} \frac{1}{[I - (i) - c(t_{(i)})]^2}.$$

1. His estimator generalizes one proposed earlier by Nelson (1972).

This estimator forms the basis of a powerful approach to nonparametric estimation of the cumulative hazard function.

Conditional Survivor Function

The notion of a survivor function can be generalized to apply to the case of organizational demography and ecology in which several destinations are possible, the case of competing risks. If Ψ different destinations (risks) are possible, each organization can be thought of as having Ψ unobserved or latent waiting times, one for each destination. Let these latent random variables be denoted by T_{jk}^*. The conditional survivor function for a particular destination is defined in terms of the corresponding latent waiting time:

$$G_{jk}(t) = \Pr\{T_{jk}^* > t\}.$$

If no event has occurred by some t, this means that $T_{jk}^* > t$ for all k. Unless we note otherwise, we assume that the Ψ processes are *independent*. Notice that

$$(8.2) \qquad G_j(t) = \prod_{k=1}^{\Psi} G_{jk}(t),$$

when the competing risks are independent.

Instantaneous Transition Rates

The hazard rate for a particular state tells the speed with which that state is vacated. When only one destination is possible, knowledge of the rate of leaving suffices to describe the process. However, as we noted earlier, organizational ecology usually considers processes in which multiple destinations are possible. For example, organizations can leave a population by disbanding, by merging with another, or by changing form. In such cases, we need to know both the rate at which some state is vacated and the relative odds of moving to the various destinations. A standard way to consider these kinds of issues is in terms of the instantaneous transition rate.

A transition rate is the limit of an ordinary discrete-time transition probability:

$$r_{jk}(t) \equiv \lim_{\Delta t \downarrow 0} \frac{\Pr\{Y(t + \Delta t) = k \mid Y(t) = j\}}{\Delta t}$$

Because the hazard is the rate of leaving a state irrespective of destination,

(8.3) $\displaystyle\sum_{k=1}^{\Psi} r_{jk}(t) = h_j(t).$

That is, the rate of leaving state j (that is, of entering any state k) is identical to the hazard function for state j.

The relationship between the transition rate and the survivor function is important in estimation. Equations (8.1) and (8.3) imply that

$$G_j(t) = \prod_{k=1}^{\Psi} \exp\left[-\int_0^t r_{jk}(s)\, ds\right].$$

When the competing risks are independent so that (8.2) holds, this last statement implies that

$$G_{jk}(t) = \exp\left[-\int_0^t r_{jk}(s)\, ds\right],$$

which provides a definition for a generalization of the hazard to the case of multiple destinations, which is called the *integrated transition rate*:

(8.4) $\displaystyle R_{jk}(t) \equiv -\log G_{jk}(t) = \int_0^t r_{jk}(s)\, ds.$

The relationship between the integrated hazard and the instantaneous transition rate can be seen by differentiating (8.4):

$$r_{jk}(t) = -\frac{d \log G_{jk}(t)}{dt}.$$

So the slope of $R_{jk}(t)$ at time t gives an estimate of the corresponding transition rate. Aalen's estimator is readily extended to provide an estimator of $R_{jk}(t)$, the cumulative transition *rate*. Because the term "cumulative hazard" is often used to apply both to hazards of leaving a state and transition rates to particular states, we sometimes refer to R_{jk} as a cumulative hazard.

Transition rates cannot be observed directly. They can be estimated, however, using estimates of $R(t)$ and the relationship in (8.4). Later in this chapter we discuss how this is actually done. But first we turn to issues concerning causal models for organizational transition rates. Henceforth we suppress the subscript *jk* in order to simplify the notation. With this simpler notation, *r* refers to a rate of transition between two unspecified states. The context tells the particular states involved.

Models for Transition Rates

A major goal in our research is to explore the effects of population heterogeneity on transition rates. This means analyzing how measured characteristics of organizations, populations, and environments affect rates of initiation, merger, and dissolution.

The Exponential Model

The baseline for comparison is the model of a constant rate:

$$r(t) = \lambda,$$

which implies that

$$G(t) = e^{-\lambda t}.$$

Because the constant-rate model implies an exponential distribution of durations, it is commonly referred to as the *exponential model*. Alternatively, we can express the constant rate (or exponential) model as a "regression model" for the log of the waiting time (age or duration, depending on the context):

$$\log T = -\alpha + W,$$

where $\alpha = -\log \lambda$ and the disturbance, W, has an extreme value distribution. That is,

$$(8.5) \qquad f(W) = \exp(w - e^w), \qquad -\infty < w < \infty$$

(see Johnson and Kotz 1970, chap. 2.1). Since failure times are not always observed because of censoring, procedures must be developed to estimate such regressions from censored data, as we discuss in the last section of this chapter.

In considering the effects of covariates, the most important question confronting analysts is substantive: how are transition rates and explanatory variables related? The theories presented in Part I do not provide guidance about the exact functional forms of organizational processes. Therefore, we choose simple, tractable functional forms that agree qualitatively with the substantive arguments. We use a variety of models that specify log-linear relationships between transition rates and explanatory variables:

$$(8.6) \qquad r = e^{\beta' x},$$

assuming for the moment that the vector of covariates, x, does not vary over time.

In terms of the regression model for the log of duration (or age), this model implies that

$$(8.7) \qquad \log T = -\beta' x + W,$$

where the disturbance term, W, again has an extreme value distribution. Note that the signs of the effects have been reversed (that is, multiplied by -1) in (8.7) because a variable that increases the hazard decreases the expected time to failure or exit.

We often estimate models that specify more complicated dependence of rates on covariates than in (8.6). All that is required for the class of models we are considering is that the model be log-linear in *parameters*. Restricting models to ones that are log-linear in parameters is not very confining. In particular, we rely heavily on quadratic relationships between density in a population and founding and disbanding rates as a way to analyze intra-population competition.

Since we use the log-linear specification repeatedly, it is worth discussing interpretation of its parameters. The situation is simplest for covariates that are dummy variables. Consider the effect of X_1. Under the log-linear specification, the model can be written as

$$r = r^*(e^{\beta_1})^{X_1},$$

where r^* is the rate given by all of the other covariates. That is, $r^* = \exp(\beta_0 + \beta_2 X_2 + \cdots + \beta_N X_N)$. When the dummy variable X_1 equals zero, the rate is just r^*. When the dummy variable equals unity, the rate is r^* multiplied by $\exp(\beta_1)$. Thus the antilog of the coefficient of a dummy variable tells the ratio of the rate for those whose value on the dummy variable is unity to those whose value is zero. Put differently, it is the *multiplier* that must be applied to the rate for those with the value of zero on the covariate to obtain the rate for those with the value of unity. For example, in analyzing the disbanding rates of labor unions, we use a covariate that equals one in years of economic depression and zero otherwise. The estimated effect of this variable is approximately 0.30. Since $\exp(0.30) \approx 1.35$, this finding means that economic depressions increased the disbanding rate by a factor of 1.35. In other words, they increased the rate by 35 percent.

When the covariate is metric, the coefficient β_n gives the effect of a marginal change in X_n on the logarithm of the rate. When such effects have substantive importance, we describe them using plots and numerical calculations.

Because transition rates, like any other instantaneous quantity, cannot be observed directly, it may be hard to think substantively about such relationships. However, there is a simple relationship that often proves helpful in interpretation. When transition rates are independent of time, the expected duration in a state j equals the inverse of the hazard function:

$$E[T \mid x_i] = \frac{1}{h}.$$

For instance, we find that the hazard of mortality from all causes for national labor unions created by a merger of existing unions equals 0.027. With this hazard, the expected lifetime of a union has been 37.3 years.

Because distributions of durations tend to be positively skewed, calculations of expected durations are usually dominated by extreme values. Therefore it is often useful to summarize the implications of a transition rate in another way, using the concept of half-life. The half-life of a stochastic process is the expected duration (or age) at which half of the units of risk of leaving a state will have left, that is, $G(t) = .5$. For example, if the hazard of leaving a state does not vary over time, using (8.1) and setting $G(t) = .5$ gives

$$.5 = \exp\left(-\int_{t_0}^{t} h \, ds\right) = \exp(-ht),$$

or

$$\frac{.69}{\hat{h}} = \hat{t},$$

since $\log(.5) \approx -0.69$. For example, the half-life of labor unions implied by the constant rate of 0.027 is 25.6 years. Notice that the half-life implied by this hazard is substantially smaller than the expected lifetime (37.3 versus 25.6 years). This difference reflects the fact that extreme values play a less powerful role in determining half-lives.

Changing Covariates

To this point we have treated the covariates as fixed over time. However, the environmental factors and competitive relations that shape population dynamics are rarely stable. The simplest way of allowing the levels of covariates to change over time is to generalize the model in (8.6) to include effects of preselected periods, denoted by p:

$$(8.8) \qquad r_p(t \mid x_p) = e^{\beta'_p x_p}, \qquad p = 1, \ldots, P.$$

In the simplest case, we constrain the effect parameters to be constant over periods but update the values of the covariates at the beginning of each period:

$$r_p = e^{\beta' x_p}.$$

We usually chose the periods to coincide with calender years because the values of covariates are often supplied as yearly time series. So we assume that the covariates are step functions in time, that they are constant within years and change values at the start of each year.[2]

   Time dependence in rates of organizational change is relevant to a number of core theoretical issues in organizational demography and ecology, as we pointed out in Part I. Models in which the hazard or rate depends on a set of covariates but not on time imply that the distribution of times of events is exponential. Because of the memory-less property of the expo-

---

2. When our models are specified in terms of duration (t), the value of x_p is defined as the level in the calender year t in which the organization attained duration t.

nential distribution, this model implies that the distribution of event times does not depend on the length of time since the previous event.

We now want to consider models in which the hazard *does* depend on the time since the previous event, that is, on duration. The Gompertz model (and its extension the Makeham model) have formed the basis of most previous research on age dependence in organizational mortality (Carroll 1983; Freeman, Carroll, and Hannan 1983; Singh, House, and Tucker 1986). This model assumes that the rate is an exponential function of the waiting time:

(8.9) $r(t) = \lambda e^{-\gamma t}.$

Of course, this model assumes that time dependence is monotonic. When γ is positive, as in the case of organizational mortality, the rate declines from λ to zero. Since it is unreasonable to assume that very old organizations escape the risk of mortality completely, organizational researchers have used a variation of the Gompertz model called the Makeham model, which introduces a non-zero asymptote:

$$r(t) = \omega + \lambda e^{-\gamma t}.$$

Although this slight change makes analysis much more complicated (because the model is no longer a member of the exponential family and is also not a proportional-hazards model), the qualitative behavior of the model in the crucial early portion of the waiting time distribution is essentially the same as that of the Gompertz model.

Note that the logarithm of the rate of the Gompertz model is a linear function of the waiting time. We use this fact in evaluating the fit of the Gompertz model.

The Weibull Model

The second model of time dependence that we use, the Weibull model, holds that the rate is a power function of the waiting time:

(8.10) $r(t) = \rho\lambda(\lambda t)^{\rho-1}.$

The rate is a monotone-decreasing function of duration (or age) if $\rho < 1$, a monotone-increasing function of duration for $\rho > 1$, and it equals the exponential when $\rho = 1$. We use the last relationship to construct likelihood ratio tests of Weibull models against the null hypothesis of an exponential model.

The fit of a Weibull model can also be evaluated by considering plots of empirical log-hazards against age or duration. Whereas the Gompertz model implies that the log-hazard is a linear function of duration (or age), the Weibull model implies that it is a linear function of the *logarithm* of duration (or age).

According to the Weibull model, the integrated hazard of a Weibull process is a power function of the waiting time:

(8.11) $\log H(t) = \rho(\log T + \log \lambda)$.

So another way to evaluate the fit of the Weibull model is with plots of the logarithm of the estimated integrated hazard against the waiting time (age or duration, depending on the context).

We generalize the Weibull model to include the effects of measured covariates, using the assumption:

$$r(t|x_i) = \rho(\lambda t)^{\rho-1} e^{\beta' x}.$$

So the baseline Weibull hazard is multiplied ("accelerated") by the effects of the vector of covariates according to this generalization. In terms of a regression model for the logarithm of the waiting time, this generalization of the Weibull model implies that

(8.12) $\log T = -\beta^{*'} x + \sigma W$,

where $\sigma = \rho^{-1}$ and $\beta^* = -\beta\sigma$ (see Kalbfleisch and Prentice 1980, pp. 31–32). Note again that the signs of the effects of covariates have been reversed from their effects on the rate.

A Gamma Model

Although we have tried to measure the most important determinants of the various rates studied, we surely have not measured all of them. Suppose that a transition rate such as an organizational disbanding rate varies within a population, but we assume mistakenly that the rate is a constant (conditional on a set of measured covariates). What difference does this error make? The substantively most important implication is that ignoring unobserved variation in transition rates produces spurious time dependence in estimated transition rates. So we explore whether apparent time dependence in rates might plausibly reflect the operation of unobservables rather than genuine time dependence in the rates at the level of the individual organization.

We use a parametric approach. That is, we specify a particular parametric distribution for the effects of the unobservables. We assume a gamma distribution for the disturbances. Because it is so flexible, the gamma distribution is used commonly in contexts like the ones we are considering. Of the various tractable nonnegative probability distributions, it is perhaps the most flexible. Depending on the values of its parameters, a gamma distribution can range from a highly skewed J–shape to a nearly symmetric unimodal shape.

So we introduce a gamma-distributed disturbance into the regression model for the logarithm of the waiting time. That is, we specify that

$$\log T = \alpha + W,$$

and that the density of the disturbance, W, equals

$$(8.13) \qquad f(W) = \frac{\exp(kw - e^w)}{\Gamma(k)}$$

The implied transition rate is

$$(8.14) \qquad r(t) = \frac{\lambda(\lambda t)^{k-1} \, e^{-\lambda t} \Gamma(k)^{-1}}{1 - \Gamma_k(\lambda t)},$$

where $\Gamma_k(\lambda t)$ is an incomplete gamma integral. Notice that the presence of this form of unobserved heterogeneity produces duration dependence or age dependence in the transition rate. The rate is a monotonic-increasing function of duration or age if $k > 1$ and a decreasing function of duration or age if $k < 1$. This model has as a special case the exponential ($k = 1$), which means that there is negligible unobserved heterogeneity. We use this fact to construct a likelihood ratio test of the gamma model against the exponential.

A Generalized Gamma Model

It turns out to be useful in our substantive work to use a model proposed by Stacy (1962) that generalizes the gamma model (see also Kalbfleisch and

Prentice 1980, p. 227). This model is most easily specified in terms of the regression model of the logarithm of the waiting time:

$$(8.15) \qquad \log T = -\beta'\mathbf{x} + \sigma W,$$

where $\sigma = \rho^{-1}$ and W has the density given by (8.13). This model has as special cases the exponential ($\sigma = 1, k = 1$), the Weibull ($k = 1, \sigma \neq 1$), and the gamma ($\sigma = 1, k \neq 1$). So we estimate this generalized model by maximum likelihood and conduct likelihood ratio tests to see whether the generalized model including the gamma-distributed disturbance improves the fit significantly compared to the Weibull model with covariates and a gamma model with covariates.

Log-logistic Model

There are suggestions from previous research that hazards of mortality for organizations may be *non-monotonic* functions of age. Carroll and Huo (1988) report that hazards of mortality for local unions of the Knights of Labor rose over the first two years before beginning the expected decline with aging. Langton (1984) reports a similar pattern for unions in the service sector. Singh, House, and Tucker (1986) have reported a similar pattern for mortality rates of voluntary social service agencies in Toronto. Given these findings, we have also explored the fit of two widely used parametric models of age dependence that imply non-monotonic relationships between hazards and duration or age: the log-logistic and the log-normal models. Because the two typically had equally good fits to our data and have similar interpretations, we concentrated on the log-logistic model, which has the nice property that it can imply either monotonic or non-monotonic duration dependence or age dependence, depending on the value of its scale parameter. The log-logistic model for the rate holds that

$$(8.16) \qquad r(t) = \frac{\lambda\rho(\lambda t)^{\rho-1}}{1 + (\lambda t)^{\rho}}.$$

The numerator of this expression is the same as the Weibull model. The log-logistic is a monotone-decreasing function of duration or age if $\rho \leq 1$. It is a non-monotonic function of duration or age, increasing and then decreasing with duration or aging, if $\rho > 1$. In terms of the regression model for the logarithm of the waiting time, the log-logistic model is

$$\log T = -\beta'\mathbf{x} + \sigma W,$$

where W has the logistic density

(8.17) $f(W) = \dfrac{e^w}{(1 + e^w)^2}$,

and $\sigma = \rho^{-1}$.

Counting Process Models

In developing stochastic process models of organizational foundings, the conceptual unit of analysis is obviously not the individual organization whose appearance is observed. Rather, the unit of analysis, the unit in which the foundings take place, is the population. Detailed information on foundings tells the times at which increments to the population take place. The data structure for analyzing foundings differs somewhat from the case for mortality analysis, in which the previous history of the individual organization can be taken into account. There is no previous history for a new organization. Thus, the range of relevant covariates in the analysis of founding rates includes only properties of the environment and of the population.

The situation is actually more complicated than just described. If one wishes to study the appearance of a new population, then the population cannot be the unit of analysis. In such cases, the larger environment or social system is the relevant unit within which founding processes occur. Thus we can follow two approaches in empirical analysis: (1) treat the social environment as the unit and analyze the timing of first and subsequent foundings of each type of organization; and (2) condition on the appearance of the first organization of a type and analyze the timing of subsequent foundings within the population (see also Amburgey 1986). The first approach, which we call system-level analysis, is the natural one for addressing questions pertaining to the rise of new kinds of variability. The second, which we call population analysis, is the natural one for analyzing effects of composition of the population of founding rates.

For both kinds of analysis the state space of the stochastic process is the set of non-negative integers that count the number of foundings. The cumulative number of foundings observed by historical time t, denoted by B_t, is assumed to be a nondecreasing stochastic process that possesses the property of regularity (no more than one founding in any instant).

One of the things that differs for these two forms of analysis is the nature of the time index of the stochastic process. In population analysis, which conditions on the time of the first founding, the starting time of the process is nonarbitrary; the duration until the "first" event (which is really the founding of the second organization) has direct substantive interpretation. But how do we assign a starting time of the process in the case of system-level analysis? For example, at what point does the United States become meaningfully "at risk" of giving rise to the first national labor union? Any answer to this question seems at least partly arbitrary. Luckily, the situation is not always so complicated. For example, in the case of semiconductor manufacturers (or any other kind of firm whose form is defined in terms of a particular product or process), it is meaningful to assume that the invention of the technology for producing semiconductors begins the process. The length of time from invention (or perhaps licensing) of the product or process until the first founding of an organization specialized to using it is a substantively meaningful quantity.

The subsequent discussion assumes that the start of the process is known and is not arbitrary. This means that we assume that the time scale has substantive meaning at all points. In discussing particular analyses in later chapters we consider cases in which this assumption is not appropriate.

The founding process we have been discussing is an instance of a widely studied class of processes known as *arrival processes*. Such processes count the number of arrivals to some state, such as events of radioactive decay, arrivals to a waiting line, cell divisions, and births. The natural baseline model for arrival processes is the *Poisson process*. This process assumes that the rate of arrival is independent of the history of previous arrivals (including the time of the last arrival) and of the current state of the system. Among other things, this assumption implies that the arrival rate for the second event does not differ from that of the third event or of subsequent events. That is, the *order* of the event does not affect the arrival rate. If the rate at which new organizations arrive in the population (or environment) follows a Poisson process, then the founding rate is a time-independent constant. That is, the rate of arriving at state $b + 1$ at time t is

$$\lambda_b(t) = \lim_{\Delta t \downarrow 0} \frac{\Pr\{B(t + \Delta t) - B(t) = 1 \,|\, B(t) = b\}}{\Delta t} = \lambda$$

under the assumptions of a Poisson process. In other words, the rate does not vary over time or with other factors.

Our theoretical arguments suggest that the Poisson model is too simple

for the founding process. We build models that incorporate time dependence and the effects of explicit causal factors into empirical models of
founding rates. In general, we use the same strategies outlined in the
previous section for introducing the effects of covariates and time dependence into the rate of the counting process. That is, we use models of the
form:

$$\lambda_b(t\,|\,\mathbf{x}_t) = e^{\beta'\mathbf{x}_t}$$

in order to explore the effects of measured covariates on the rate in a
model in which the baseline distribution of event times is exponential.
Then we compare the fit of Weibull and generalized gamma models, as
discussed earlier.

Because our data on foundings and entries come in two forms (mixtures
of exact dates and approximate dates for unions and only yearly counts for
semiconductor manufacturing firms), we actually analyze generalized
Poisson models in two ways. In one, we treat the dates of founding as
exact and use the durations between foundings to estimate rates and effects of covariates on rates by maximum likelihood and partial likelihood
(see the following section). In the second, we treat the data as yearly
counts resulting from a Poisson process and use methods of "Poisson
regression." That is, we estimate the parameters of models of the form:

$$(8.18\text{a}) \qquad \Pr(B = b_t) = \frac{e^{-\lambda}\lambda^{b_t}}{b_t!},$$

$$(8.18\text{b}) \qquad \lambda = e^{\beta'\mathbf{x}_t},$$

where b_t is the number of events (foundings) that occur in year t.

Estimation and Testing

Our empirical analysis is done with maximum likelihood (ML) and partial
likelihood (PL) estimation. This section gives a brief overview of how
these two kinds of estimation strategies are used with event-history data.

Maximum Likelihood

The likelihood function $\mathcal{L}$ is defined as the joint probability (or joint probability density) of sample observations. When observations on different
sample members are statistically independent, the likelihood equals the

product of the contribution of each sample member i (assuming random sampling):

$$\mathscr{L} = \prod_{i=1}^{I} \mathscr{L}_i.$$

An estimate of the lower bound of the variance–covariance matrix of $\boldsymbol{\phi}$, a vector of parameters estimated by ML, is given by

$$\left[\frac{\partial^2 \log \mathscr{L}}{\partial \boldsymbol{\phi}^2} \right]^{-1}.$$

The diagonal elements of this matrix provide asymptotic estimates of variances of parameters. We use this information to test hypotheses about single parameters. In all tables, we report estimated asymptotic standard errors in parentheses below point estimates of the parameters.

We also report the logarithms of the maximized likelihoods. These numbers can be used to compute likelihood ratio tests on sets of parameters. In the typical tables we report, the models to the left are nested within some of those to the right in the table. Usually the left-most columns in the tables report estimates of simple models that exclude the effects of some of the covariates; the effects of these covariates are then included in the more complex models in columns on the right-hand side of the tables. The likelihood ratio test statistic is defined as

$$\lambda = \frac{\max \mathscr{L}_0}{\max \mathscr{L}_1},$$

where $\mathscr{L}_0$ and $\mathscr{L}_1$ denote the likelihoods of the null model (with, say, k constraints imposed) and the alternative model that relaxes the constraints, respectively. With suitably large samples, $-2 \log \lambda$ is distributed as χ^2 with k degrees of freedom. So -2 times the difference of the log-likelihoods of the pair of hierarchical models in our tables has approximately a χ^2 distribution under the null hypothesis (that the k constraints hold in the population). We refer often to such tests in discussing our findings.

When the dates of events are known, we use PROC LIFEREG (SAS Institute 1985) to obtain ML estimates of the parameters of regression models of the form:

$$\log T = -\boldsymbol{\beta}'\mathbf{x} + \sigma W,$$

as discussed earlier, by maximum likelihood. Letting $f(W)$ and $G(W)$ denote the probability density function and the survivor function of the random variable W, the log-likelihood can be written, following Kalbfleisch and Prentice (1980), as

$$(8.19) \quad \mathscr{L} = \sum_{i}^{N} d_i \log \left[f(w_i)/\sigma \right] + (1 - d_i) \log \left[G(w_i) \right],$$

where d_i is an indicator variable that equals unity if the observation is uncensored and equals zero if it is censored. The program LIFEREG maximizes this log-likelihood using one of several assumptions about the distribution of W. In the case of the exponential model, W is assumed to have the extreme-value distribution and σ is constrained to equal unity. For the Weibull model, the distributional assumption is the same but the scale parameter is unconstrained. In the case of the gamma model, W is assumed to have a gamma distribution with parameter k, and the scale parameter, σ, is constrained to equal unity. In the generalized gamma model the latter constraint is relaxed. Finally, in the case of the log-logistic model, W is assumed to have a logistic distribution.

In reporting estimates of these models, we report $\hat{\boldsymbol{\beta}}$ rather than $-\hat{\boldsymbol{\beta}}$; that is, we report the negative of the vector of the regression coefficients. We do so because we are interested in the effects of the covariates on the rates rather than on the expected waiting times. In the case of the Weibull and generalized gamma models, the negative of the vector of regression coefficients actually estimates $\boldsymbol{\beta}^* = \boldsymbol{\beta}\sigma$, as we pointed out earlier. So the estimates we report should be divided by $\hat{\sigma}$ to estimate $\boldsymbol{\beta}$.

As we have noted repeatedly, $\sigma = \rho^{-1}$ in all models for which this parameter is defined. We report estimates of σ in the tables of findings; these are labeled the "scale parameters." ML estimates of ρ are found by forming $\hat{\sigma}^{-1}$. The tables also report a "shape parameter" for models that use the gamma distribution. The shape parameter equals $1/k^2$ in the conventions of PROC LIFEREG.

When the dates are known only to the year, we use ML to estimate parameters of Poisson regression models; that is, we calculate ML estimates of the vector of regression coefficients, $\boldsymbol{\beta}$, in (8.18b) and their asymptotic standard errors. We use LIMDEP (Greene 1986) to perform these calculations. Since these models are a special case of log-linear models for counted data, we report G^2 as a measure of fit. Let b_t denote the count of events in year t and $\hat{b}_t$ the fitted count under a particular model.

Then

$$G^2 = \sum_t b_t \log \left(\frac{b_t}{\hat{b}_t} \right).$$

In comparisons of nested models, the difference in G^2's is distributed approximately as χ^2 under the null hypothesis that the k constraints embodied in the simpler model hold.

Partial Likelihood

Cox's (1972, 1975) method of partial likelihood is useful when transition rates vary in some unknown way over time but the variations are the same for organizations at risk of the event. This method applies only to models of *proportional hazards* (or *rates*):

(8.20) $r(t) = q(t)\phi(\mathbf{x}_t)$

Both the exponential and Weibull models fall in this class. The first component on the right-hand side of (8.20) is an unknown, (possibly) time-dependent nuisance function $q(t)$, which affects the rate of every member of the population in the same way. The second component, $\phi(\mathbf{x}_t)$, is a function of a vector of (possibly time-varying) observed causal variables $\mathbf{x}_t$, and possibly also of time t.

Although the PL approach to event-history analysis does not require specification of $q(t)$, it *does* require parametric assumptions about the dependence of $\phi(\cdot)$ on the observed variables $\mathbf{x}_t$. The simplest model we use holds that

(8.21) $r(t) = q(t) \, e^{\beta' \mathbf{x}_t}.$

The parameters in (8.21) cannot be estimated by ML because the specific form of $q(t)$ is unspecified, which means that a parametric expression cannot be written for the survivor function, a key component of the full likelihood. However, PL estimators can be used.

The PL estimator is formed as follows. The data are first arranged in the order in which events occur in the sample, assuming for simplicity that only one sample member has an event at any moment. So, for example, $t_{(1)}$ denotes the time (duration) of the first event that is observed in the sample, while $\mathbf{x}_{(1)}$ denotes the value of the vector of explanatory variables for the sample member that has the first event, and so forth. Usually the times of events are observed for only some subset I^* of the sample, $I^* \leq I$. The remaining $I^c = I - I^*$ cases are right-censored. No events occur within the period during which they are observed. Let the collection of cases still at risk of experiencing the event at duration (or age) t_i, the *risk set*, be denoted by $R(t_{(i)})$. The PL for the whole sample is the product of I^* such terms:

$$(8.22) \qquad {}_p\mathscr{L} = \prod_{i=1}^{I^*} \frac{\exp(\boldsymbol{\beta}'\mathbf{x}_{i,t_i})}{\sum_{v \in R(t_{(i)})} \exp(\boldsymbol{\beta}'\mathbf{x}_{v,t_i})}.$$

The PL estimate of $\boldsymbol{\beta}$ in (8.21) is obtained by finding the value that maximizes ${}_p\mathscr{L}$ in (8.22); one treats the PL as though it were a full likelihood. Cox (1975) claimed that the PL estimators of $\boldsymbol{\beta}$ are consistent; Efron (1977) proved that under fairly general conditions the PL estimators are efficient (see also Cox and Oakes 1984). Tsiatis (1981) proved that the PL estimators are consistent.[3]

This concludes our review of the models and methods used to estimate effects of theoretically relevant covariates on the transition rates of organizations. We turn now to the empirical studies that implement these methods.

3. We use the program PHGLM written by Harrell and distributed by SAS Institute (1986) as well as the program PL2 in BMDP.

III | *Empirical Findings*

9 | The Population Ecology of Founding and Entry

We now turn to concrete analyses of how social structure affects the ecology of populations of three dissimilar kinds of organizations. As we pointed out in Part I, organizational diversity depends on several rates: the rate of founding and entry into a population, the rate of change in strategy and structure, and the rate of failure or mortality. A broad social change can shape organizational diversity by affecting any one of these rates.

We have argued that organizations are subject to inertial forces resulting from both internal and external arrangements. If so, the dynamics of diversity depend mainly on the rate at which new and diverse organizations are created and the rate at which organizations of various types disappear. The formation of new kinds of organizations is central to the process of increasing diversity in the world of organizations. If the rates of founding and fundamental structural change became zero, organizational diversity could only decline over time as various forms of organizations lost competitive struggles. Thus the founding rate of organizations constrains the dynamics of diversity and the speed of organizational evolution. In this chapter we report empirical analyses of the ecology of rates of founding of labor unions and newspaper firms and rates of entry of manufacturing firms into the semiconductor industry. We concentrate on the role of density, the flow of recent foundings, and environmental variations in shaping these rates.

Core Questions

In Part I we argued that rates of founding and entry in organizational populations are much more complicated than birth rates in biotic populations. In particular, we proposed that organizational founding and entry rates respond to processes of competition and legitimation. According to our model, levels of competition and legitimacy vary with the number of organizations in the population and with environmental conditions. The theory presented in Chapter 6 implies a particular form of non-monotonic density dependence in founding rates. That is, it implies that the founding rate rises initially and then falls with increasing density. This hypothesis is pivotal to our analysis because it implies that entry into populations of organizations does not mimic biotic birth processes, with their monotonic density dependence. Thus it is important to learn whether rates of founding and entry vary with density and whether such dependence has a non-monotonic form. If it does, we can infer that opposing effects of legitimation and competition on founding rates contribute to the apparent stability of numbers in organizational populations.

In Chapter 6 we introduced our model of density dependence in founding rates. This section compares this model with other simpler models of the process that we use as baselines in evaluating goodness of fit. An organizational founding process (at any level of analysis) can usefully be considered an instance of an *arrival process*, one kind of point process. As described in the previous chapter, arrival processes characterize the stochastic behavior of the flow of arrivals to some state, such as events of radioactive decay, arrivals to a waiting line, events of cell division, and births. We denote the cumulative number of foundings (or entries, depending on the application) by time t with the random variable $B(t)$.

The natural baseline model for arrival processes is the Poisson process (discussed in the third section of Chapter 8). Recall that the Poisson process assumes that the rate of arrival is independent of the history of previous arrivals, including the number of previous arrivals and the time of the last arrival. If the rate at which organizations enter a population follows a Poisson process, then the rate of founding or entry is a time-independent constant.

The Poisson process does not seem to be a plausible substantive model. If our theoretical arguments are correct, founding rates vary in response to changes in density and environmental conditions that affect carrying capacities. Therefore, we concentrate on models in which the rate varies in some explicit way with observed covariates. The first part of our modeling effort was devoted to specifying density dependence and environmental effects. We began with the simple and classic *Yule process*[1] often used to

---

1. Karlin and Taylor (1975, pp. 119–123) provide background on this process.

model phenomena for which each element can be assumed to have the same probability of producing a "birth" in a period, such as radioactive decay and growth in bacterial populations. The Yule process assumes that the *per capita* rate of founding or entry is a constant:

(9.1) $\lambda(t) = cN_t,$

where N_t denotes the number of elements in the population at time t. Note that this model assumes that the rate varies with the number of entities in the population rather than with the cumulative number of arrivals. In our applications the number in the population does not usually equal the number of previous arrivals because of mortality—organizations disband, they merge with other organizations, and they undergo radical change leading to exiting the population.

Inspection of data on organizational foundings and entries suggests that the per capita founding rate is not constant. Instead, the rate appears to rise initially and then to slow at higher densities. Therefore, in order to build a plausible baseline model of monotonic density dependence, we relax the assumption of constant per capita rates of founding and entry. We do so by using a *generalized Yule model*:

(9.2) $\lambda(t) = cN_t^\alpha.$

Dividing both sides of equation (9.2) by N_t shows that the per capita rate, $\lambda(t)/N_t$, varies with N_t in this generalization of the Yule model. Depending on the value of α, several kinds of qualitative density dependence are possible. If $\alpha = 1$, this model is identical to a Yule process. If $\alpha > 1$, the rate rises at an increasing rate with density; if $0 < \alpha < 1$, the rate rises at a decreasing rate with density. Finally, if $\alpha < 0$, the rate falls with density.

We begin empirical analysis in the next section with a version of the generalized Yule model in which the constant c is replaced by a log-linear effect of a set of observed environmental covariates and period effects:

(9.3) $\lambda_p(t) = N_t^\alpha \cdot \exp(\pi' \mathbf{x}_t + \phi_p),$

where $\mathbf{x}_t$ represents a vector of environmental conditions measured at time t and ϕ_p are a set of period-specific effects. In this model the founding rate varies in response to density, levels of measured environmental conditions, and shifts between periods chosen to represent qualitative changes in the social structure impinging on the population. Since this appears to be a plausible model of density dependence in rates of founding and entry, we use it as a baseline against which to assess the fit of our non-monotonic model.

Our theory of competitive and institutional processes implies that there is *positive* density dependence at low densities but *negative* density dependence at high densities. Thus we expect the rate to rise with increasing density to some critical level (the carrying capacity) and then to decline with further increases in density, assuming that the appropriate environmental conditions have been controlled. In contrast to the logic of the generalized Yule model, we predict that the effect of density on the rate is *non-monotonic*.

In Chapter 6 we specified our theory in terms of the following model:

$$(9.4a) \qquad \lambda(t) = N_t^\alpha \cdot \exp(\gamma N_t^2),$$

with the prediction,

$$(9.4b) \qquad \alpha > 0, \qquad \gamma < 0.$$

Because of the log-linear form of (9.4a), the founding rate never equals zero in this model. Thus this model cannot imply a carrying capacity in the usual sense that growth rate of the population is zero. Nonetheless, if the parameters have the signs predicted by our theory (expressed in 9.4b), the founding rate begins to fall at some level of density and approaches zero at high densities. If the decline is rapid within the observed range of density, something like a carrying capacity exists. We explore such effects qualitatively in discussing our findings.

But the number of organizations in the population alone does not tell us the strength of competitive processes; we also need to take into account the environmental conditions that control variations in the resources over which competition occurs. Assume that some such conditions can be identified and measured. Then, in parallel with our specification of the generalized Yule model, we assume that the rate of founding or entry rate depends on the level of these environmental conditions and on a set of period-specific effects:

$$(9.5) \qquad \lambda_p(t) = N_t^\alpha \cdot \exp(\gamma N_t^2) \cdot \exp(\pi' \mathbf{x}_t + \phi_p),$$

where $\mathbf{x}_t$ denotes the set of measured environmental characteristics and ϕ_p are a set of period-specific effects, as in (9.3). Of course, the set of relevant environmental variables depends on the population under study and the social/historical context. We discuss the measurement of such environmental variables and the choice of periods in the course of describing each empirical study.

In addition to investigating effects of density and environmental conditions, we also consider rate dependence, the possibility that the founding rate or entry rate in a population depends on the number of recent foundings and entries. Delacroix and Carroll (1983) analyzed rate dependence by estimating a quadratic relationship between prior foundings and the number of foundings in a year. We use a related specification for the effect of prior foundings (B) on the rate:

$$(9.6a) \qquad \lambda_p(t) = N_t^\alpha \cdot \exp(\gamma N_t^2 + \delta_1 B_t + \delta_2 B_t^2) \cdot \exp(\pi' x_t + \phi_p),$$

with the hypothesis that a wave of foundings increases the rate but that a very large number of recent foundings exhausts the supply of unclaimed resources needed to build new organizations. That is, we hypothesize that the effect of recent foundings is also non-monotonic, that

$$(9.6b) \qquad \delta_1 > 0 \quad \text{and} \quad \delta_2 < 0.$$

The last topic we investigate concerns links between populations. We begin with the model in (9.6a) as a representation of the founding process of a population in isolation, that is, when the other population is absent. Then we add two *cross-effects*, the first-order and second-order effect of the density of the second population:

$$(9.7) \qquad \lambda_i(t) = N_{it}^{\alpha_i} \cdot \exp(\gamma_i N_{it}^2 + \delta_{1i} B_{it} + \delta_{2i} B_{it}^2 + \theta_{1i} N_{jt} + \theta_{2i} N_{jt}^2)$$
$$\cdot \exp(\pi_i' x_t),$$

where i and j denote the two populations. In this model the parameters α_i and γ_i tell the effect of "own density" on the rate; the parameters θ_{1i} and θ_{2i} tell the cross-effect, the effect of "other density." The cross-effect of density captures the effect of *interpopulation competition*. When populations compete in attempting to mobilize resources, the cross-effect of density will be negative for both populations. However, it is not obvious to us whether such effects are likely to be monotonic or non-monotonic; therefore, we explore both possibilities.

In developing qualitative implications of these models, we use the fact that their multiplicative structure allows them to be expressed as a product

FOUNDINGS

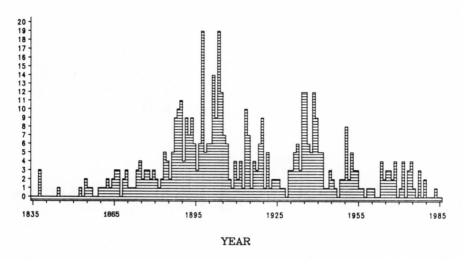

YEAR

Figure 9.1   Labor union foundings by year

of several terms. When focusing on the effects of density, we refer to the *multiplier* of the rate due to the effect of density. For example, equation 9.6a can be written as:

$$\lambda_p(t) = N_t^\alpha \exp(\gamma N_t^2) \cdot \exp(\delta_1 B_t + \delta_2 B_t^2) \cdot \exp(\pi' \mathbf{x}_t + \phi_p).$$

The expression immediately to the right of the equal sign, $N_t^\alpha \exp(\gamma N_t^2)$, tells the effect of density on the rate. In order to calculate the founding rate at any level of density, one evaluates this term for the level of N_t using the estimated parameters and then multiplies the result by the rest of the model. So we call this term that tells the effect of density the *density multiplier*. Similarly, we refer to $\exp(\delta_1 B_t + \delta_2 B_t^2)$ as the *multiplier effect of prior foundings*. In order to learn about the qualitative behavior implied by our estimates, we plot estimated multipliers against density and number of prior foundings or entries.

Founding Rates of Labor Unions

Our study of national labor unions recorded 479 foundings over the 1836–1985 period.[2] Figure 9.1 shows how the events were distributed over time. A surge in foundings began in 1883 and continued until 1906; this was the most important period of building national unions. The peak years were 1897 and 1903, each with 19 foundings. A second brief peak occurred right after World War I, and a broader period of high activity occurred during the 1930s. In broad terms, we seek to learn whether these fluctuations in foundings were related to density, as our theory predicts.

The number of unions in existence (N_t) reflects the cumulative numbers of foundings and ending events (disbandings, mergers, and absorptions). Figure 9.2 shows how the number of unions (density) varied over the period of interest. The number fluctuated near zero until the Civil War era. It rose modestly until about 1881 and then grew explosively until 1905. From that point on, growth in numbers was slower and more erratic until the series reached its peak level of 211 in 1954. The last portion of the series shows consistent but modest contraction in the number of unions. Indeed, the number of unions in existence was stable during a period in which union membership surged and the national polity and economy changed greatly. This pattern suggests that fluctuation in density in this population has more to do with organizational ecological processes within the population of unions rather than with changes in social, economic, and political environments.

A crude way to learn about density dependence in union founding rates is to compare the series on foundings and density in Figures 9.1 and 9.2, respectively. This comparison suggests that the number of foundings has not simply been proportional to the size of the population. The rate was highest during a period in which density was considerably below its maximum (1881–1905); and the number of foundings was quite low in the period of peak density (1940–1960). So the comparison of the two series suggests that the relationship was indeed non-monotonic. We examine whether this conclusion holds under controls for environmental conditions and period effects in the analysis discussed next.

Figure 9.2 also shows the growth in numbers of the two most commonly distinguished forms of union organization: craft and industrial unions. The

2. The analysis of this section is an extension of a previously published analysis (Hannan and Freeman 1987).

NUMBER OF UNIONS

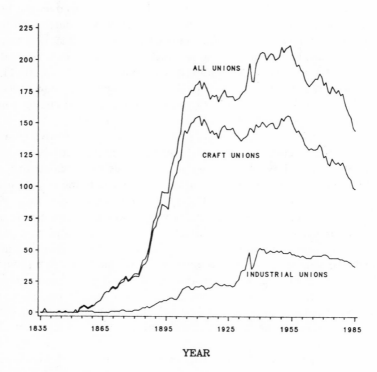

YEAR

Figure 9.2   Density of union forms by year

craft union form has its roots in the guild. It consists of journeymen craftsmen organized collectively for the purpose of controlling conditions of
work, including regulating the flow of new members into the trade and
training new members (apprentices). A key feature of the craft form is that
workers at a work site were typically organized into several different
unions. We classify unions as using the craft form when they define their
target membership in terms of occupations rather than industrial locations.
The craft form, defined this way, has not been restricted to the highest skill
levels; semiskilled and unskilled workers often formed narrowly defined
unions in industries dominated by the craft form of organization (for example, the Union of Hodcarriers and Building Laborers, founded in 1893). As

Figure 9.2 makes clear, most national unions in the United States have had the craft form. Consequently, the growth profile of craft unions closely follows the pattern for the whole population. The number of craft unions reached a peak level of 156 in 1953 and has dropped by about a third since that time.

The industrial form ignores differences among occupations and skill levels. Unions with this form seek to organize all production workers at work sites. The number of industrial unions, always much smaller than the number of craft unions, began to grow gradually in the 1890s and spurted during the 1930s. It reached its peak level of 52 in 1940 and has remained quite stable since that time.

Our research strategy capitalizes on knowledge of the full history of the population of national unions. Inspection of Figure 9.2 makes it clear that little would be learned about the underlying dynamics by considering only the twentieth century. Analysis must include the middle of the nineteenth century in order to capture the growth from low to high density. This means that the set of covariates available for use in analysis is limited to those whose series cover this crucial period. Since most of the commonly used time series on industrial activity, wage levels, strike activity, and so forth begin in 1890, or even 1930, this is a severe restriction.

In fact, only a few measures of environmental conditions are available for most of the 1836–1985 period, as we pointed out in describing the design of the union study in Chapter 7. For this reason, we conducted much of the empirical analysis using period effects. That is, we assumed that the founding rate varied by historical periods but was constant within periods (net of the effects of density and the flow of recent foundings). We tried a number of alternative period definitions and obtained the best results with a five-period model.[3]

This analysis divides the 150-year history as follows. The first period begins in 1836, the start of national unionization, and ends in 1886, the year in which the AFL was founded. The second period begins in 1887 and ends in 1931. The third period begins in 1932 with the New Deal and the Norris–LaGuardia Act of 1932, which limited the power of employers to gain injunctions against striking unions, and the National Industrial Recovery

---

3. In a previously published analysis of these data we used a simpler three-period model (Hannan and Freeman 1987). However, we have since learned that the process can be better understood by making a finer set of distinctions among periods. This change does not affect the main findings regarding density dependence. It does, however, change the pattern of competitive effects between populations.

Act in 1932–1933. The subsequent Wagner Act, passed in 1935, gave substantial legal protection to unions and union organizing campaigns (see Tomlins 1985). This third period ends in 1947, when the Taft–Hartley Act rolled back some of the gains that unions won under the Wagner Act. The fourth period runs from 1948 to 1954. The last period begins in 1955, the year of the merger of the AFL and CIO, and runs to 1985. It is characterized by continuous decline in the fraction of the labor force in unions.

In representing period effects we used an "effect coding." The first period is the (excluded) baseline. The variable called "Period 2" in the tables is coded as one for the years 1887 through 1985 and zero otherwise. "Period 3" is coded as one from 1932 through 1985, and so forth. This coding makes it easy to evaluate the effects of adjacent periods. In the log-linear models we use, the antilog of the effect of "Period 2" is the ratio of the rate in the second period to that in the first; the antilog of the effect of "Period 3" is the ratio of the rate in the third period to that in the second, and so forth.

We also used period effects to deal with the claim that coordinated nationwide offensives by employers damaged the fortunes of unions and depressed the founding rate. Although it is difficult to find agreement on the precise dates of these offensives, it seems clear that the peak periods were 1903–1908, the period of a national "open shop" drive, and 1919–1929, the period of the so-called "American Plan of Employment" campaign, led by the National Association of Manufacturers. We constructed an index that distinguished the years of these employer offensives from other years.

Finally, we also used period effects to deal with the possibility that wartime conditions affected the founding rate of unions. We used periods that distinguished years during the Civil War, the two world wars, the Korean War, and the Vietnam War as well as periods that distinguished only the two world wars, during which unions were given a relatively protected status under wartime production controls.

We explored the effects of several measures of general economic conditions. These include an index that identifies years of economic crisis and depression (1836–1984), taken mainly from Thorp and Mitchell (1926); the real wage of common laborers (1836–1974), as compiled by David and Solar (1977); and a number of indicators coded from *The Historical Statistics of the United States: Colonial Times to 1976* (U.S. Bureau of the Census, 1975): the number of business failures (1857–1984), gross national product per capita (1889–1984), indexes of the value of new building permits (1868–1939), and an index of railroad construction (1830–1925). We also used the number of patents issued for inventions (1830–1984), an index of productivity per man hour in manufacturing (1860–1914), and an index of capital investment (1865–1984) as indicators of rising mechanization of production. In addition, we used data on the flow of immigrants (1836–1984) and year-to-year changes in such flows. None of these measures has any systematic or sizeable effect on the union founding rate when period effects and these measures are included in the model.[4]

We recorded the exact dates of foundings and other events when this information was available. We learned the exact founding date for slightly fewer than half of the cases, and only the year of founding for the rest. With this mixture of data, two strategies for analysis make sense: (1) ignore the information on exact timing and analyze only year-to-year variations in numbers of foundings; or (2) use some scheme for allocating events with missing information on month and day to some date within the known year of founding. In previous publications we used the second strategy (Hannan and Freeman 1987). When the timing within a year was not recorded, we assigned a time using a random number uniformly distributed over the year.[5] Here we report estimates using both approaches. We report the results of partial likelihood (PL) estimators as well as maximum likelihood (ML) estimators of Weibull models, in each case using either the exact observed date or a randomly chosen date within the year of founding. We also report ML estimates of Poisson regressions that use only the yearly counts of foundings.

Both procedures have implications for measuring the density and number of recent foundings. When dates within years are unknown, the ordering of events within the year is also unknown. Therefore, we defined density (N_t) for all spells beginning in a calendar year as the number of unions in existence on January 1 of the year in question.[6] Similarly, we

4. Using a simpler three-period model, our analysis showed that the founding rate was affected by immigration and the real wage of common laborers. Shifting to a five-period model reduces these effects considerably so that they do not differ significantly from zero at the .10 level.
5. It is unlikely that this choice affects qualitative inferences. In order to learn whether our estimates are sensitive to the timing of events within years, we repeated the main analyses with another set of randomized dates within years for those cases in which only the year of founding was known. These estimates agreed very closely with those reported here.
6. Foundings are not the only source of variation in N_t. A total of 191 unions disbanded; 269 were absorbed or entered into mergers during this period. Thus we are not simply relating the founding rate to the cumulative number of prior foundings.

defined the number of foundings in the prior year, B_{t-1}, as the count in the calendar year prior to the year in which the interval begins. Each interval in the same calendar year is assigned the same values of N_t and B_{t-1}, those pertaining to the density at the beginning of the year and the count of foundings in the prior year. Similarly, in the Poisson regressions, counts of foundings in a year, B_t, are regressed on the number of unions in existence at the beginning of the year, N_t, and the number of foundings in the previous year, B_{t-1}.

Results

Our empirical analysis of national labor unions deals with four questions. (1) Does the founding rate depend on density, and, if so, what is the form of the dependence? (2) Does the rate also depend on the number of recent foundings? (3) Do effects of density and recent foundings persist when environmental effects are included in the models? (4) Does competition between forms affect the founding process?

In considering density and prior foundings, we are particularly interested in contrasting monotonic and non-monotonic models. Non-monotonic effects support our claim that the effects of institutionalization are countered by strong competitive processes. Thus comparisons of the two kinds of models provide information about the strength of intrapopulation competition on the founding process and the role of founding processes in stabilizing numbers in the population.

We begin with the two models of density dependence developed at the beginning of the chapter: the generalized Yule model and our non-monotonic model. The main results appear in Table 9.1, which reports estimates for the period from 1836 to 1985 using two different approaches.[7] Columns 1–3 contain PL estimates, which treat the dates as exact, including those that were chosen at random within years. Columns 4–6 report ML estimates of Poisson regressions of the yearly counts of foundings. The models in the two sets, columns 1–3 and 4–6, differ in how they specify the effects of density and recent foundings. The first and fourth columns report estimates of a generalized Yule model (equation 9.1) in which the rate

7. We report levels of significance for two-tailed tests even though we usually make explicit directional predictions. In doing so, we avoid referring constantly to whether such directional predictions were made. In consequence, we use a fairly tolerant minimum significance level, $p < .10$, which corresponds to the more common $p < .05$ for one-tailed tests.

Table 9.1. Estimates of effects of density on the founding rate of national labor unions, 1836–1985

Independent variable	PL estimates			Poisson regression estimates		
	(1)	(2)	(3)	(4)	(5)	(6)
Intercept	—	—	—	.053 (.172)	−.456[a] (.256)	−.528[b] (.252)
log $N(t)$	.179[c] (.062)	.379[c] (.086)	.340[c] (.086)	.235[c] (.060)	.453[c] (.087)	.386[c] (.086)
$N^2(t)/1000$	—	−.044[c] (.007)	−.035[c] (.007)	—	−.050[c] (.006)	−.037[c] (.007)
$B(t)$	—	—	.088[c] (.037)	—	—	.122[c] (.036)
$B^2(t)$	—	—	−.003 (.002)	—	—	−.004[a] (.002)
Period 2 (1886–1985)	.381[a] (.203)	.859[c] (.211)	.567[c] (.229)	.514[b] (.209)	1.03[c] (.211)	.615[c] (.227)
Period 3 (1932–1985)	−.164 (.131)	.491[c] (.169)	.361[b] (.176)	−.170 (.131)	.566[c] (.166)	.379[b] (.173)
Period 4 (1947–1985)	−.234 (.233)	−.032 (.235)	.051 (.237)	−.470[b] (.227)	−.253 (.229)	−.111 (.231)
Period 5 (1955–1985)	−.720[c] (.265)	−1.21[c] (.279)	−1.01[c] (.288)	−.864 (.251)	−1.38[c] (.260)	−1.07[c] (.270)
Number of cases	497	497	497	150	150	150
Log-likelihood	−2,441.14	−2,418.84	−2,413.81	—	—	—
G^2	—	—	—	342.1	278.3	257.4
Degrees of freedom	5	6	8	6	7	9

Note: Figures in parentheses are asymptotic standard errors.
a. $p < .10$.
b. $p < .05$.
c. $p < .01$.

varies among five periods discussed earlier. The estimated effect of density, which is the parameter α in (9.1), is 0.179 with the PL estimator and 0.235 with the Poisson regression estimator. Since both estimates lie between zero and one, these results imply that the founding rate increases at a (rapidly) decreasing rate with increasing density.

The crucial step, according to our argument, is adding the square of density to the generalized Yule model. Columns 2 and 5 show that this addition improves the fit of the models significantly.[8] So the null hypothesis that density dependence is monotonic turns out to be very implausible given these data. In other words, the data strongly prefer the non-monotonic model over the monotonic one.

Do the estimated effects of density agree with the predictions of the model in (9.4b)? Columns 2 and 4 show that the answer is yes. The effects of density have the predicted signs: the first-order effect, α, is positive and the second-order effect, γ, is negative.

The second question concerns the effect of recent foundings. Columns 3 and 6 report estimates of the parameters of model (9.6a), which adds a log-quadratic specification of the number of foundings in the prior year. In each case, the null hypothesis of no effect of recent foundings can be rejected at the .01 level.[9] So the hypothesis advanced by Delacroix and Carroll (1983) in analyzing founding rates of Argentinean and Irish newspapers finds support here.

Next we consider the effects of the periods. As we noted earlier, the antilogs of the period effects are the ratio of the rate in the period in question to that in the preceding period. Estimates of the period effects in Table 9.1 reveal that the founding rate rose in the second period, following the founding of the AFL. According to the sixth column of Table 9.1, the rate was exp(.615) = 1.85 higher in the second period than in the first. It also rose significantly in the third period, which marks the New Deal. The multiplier for the third period is exp(.379) = 1.46, which means that the founding rate during the New Deal was 46 percent higher than in the second period. The estimated effect of the fourth period, beginning with the Taft–Hartley Act, does not differ significantly from zero. But the rate did drop sharply and significantly after the merger of the AFL and the CIO, the start of period 5. The estimates imply that the rate in the fifth period was about a third as large as that in the fourth period.

---

8. A likelihood ratio test of the model in column 2 against that in column 1 equals 44.6 with one degree of freedom, which is significant at the .01 level. Similarly, a test of the model in column 5 against that in column 4 equals 63.8 with one degree of freedom.

9. A likelihood ratio test of the null hypothesis that prior foundings have no effect equals 10.1 with two degrees of freedom when the second and third columns are compared. It equals 20.9 with two degrees of freedom when the fifth and sixth columns are compared.

Apparently the five periods do a reasonably good job of representing the broad secular changes in the founding rate. When these four period effects are included in the models, none of the environmental covariates listed earlier has an effect that differs significantly from zero at the .10 level. If we were interested primarily in describing the effects of particular environmental variations, we might prefer to begin with models that contain effects of these covariates before adding period effects. However, our experience with many different specifications is that the findings about the theoretically relevant processes of density dependence and rate dependence are not sensitive to choice of which covariates to use as long as the period effects are included.

From the perspective of ecological theory, the most important result is that using many different representations of environmental variations does not eliminate or even diminish the effects of density and recent foundings. Estimates very similar to those in Table 9.1 are obtained when the environmental covariates listed earlier (and the period effects for wars and "employer offensives") are included in the models. Our provisional conclusion is that estimates of effects of density and recent foundings are quite robust with respect to specification of the effects of environmental conditions on the founding rate.[10]

Next we consider the dependence of founding rates on the length of time since the most recent founding and on unobserved heterogeneity in order to check the sensitivity of the basic findings. We have presumably taken care of possible duration dependence in the rate by using partial likelihood estimators.[11] However, the models whose results we just discussed assume that the founding rate (conditional on the covariates and the period effects) is not affected by unobserved heterogeneity. In order to evaluate the sensitivity of our findings with respect to this assumption, we estimated the generalized gamma model (of Weibull time dependence) and (gamma distributed) unobserved heterogeneity discussed in Chapter 8.[12] It turns out that the special case of the Weibull model fits essentially as well as the

---

10. However, some of the key results regarding competition between populations of craft and industrial unions are sensitive to specifications of periods.

11. Since we have ordered the intervals between foundings by duration in forming PL estimators, we obtain estimates of effects of covariates and periods that are nonparametric with respect to effects of duration on the rate, as we explained in Chapter 8.

12. The fact that we assigned founding times within years from a uniform distribution for roughly half of the cases should worsen the fit of all models in the exponential family.

generalized gamma model. This result suggests that there was duration dependence in the founding rate but that there is little effect of unobserved heterogeneity in these models. So we present the results of the Weibull models rather than those of the generalized gamma model.[13]

The results of estimating Weibull models with the same causal structure as the models in columns 3 and 6 in Table 9.1 appear in Table 9.2. Several features of these estimates are noteworthy. First, the Weibull model improves significantly over an exponential (time-independent) model with the same specification of the effects of the covariates. There does appear to be duration dependence in the founding process. The estimated scale parameter, $\hat{\sigma}$, exceeds unity. Since $\sigma = \rho^{-1}$ (see equation 8.12), $\hat{\rho} = 1/1.2 = .83$. This estimate of the Weibull parameter implies that the founding rate declines slowly with the passage of time since the previous founding. The less time that has elapsed since the last founding, the lower is the probability of a founding in the near future. Second, the estimates of density dependence and rate dependence are quite similar to those in Table 9.1. Adding explicit duration dependence does not alter substantive conclusions about these ecological processes.

Qualitative Implications

Substantive implications of these findings for the ecology of unions can be seen in plots of the estimated relationships. Because the various estimators agree substantially about the effect of density, it does not matter for qualitative conclusions which of the estimates we use. Figure 9.3 plots the estimated relationship using the estimates in column 3 in Table 9.1. The vertical axis tells the *multiplier*[14] of the rate, that is, the coefficient that is multiplied by the effects of other covariates in the model. The multiplier of density exceeds unity over the observed range of density, [0, 211], which is indicated by the vertical dashed line. At its maximum, when $N \approx 70$, the rate is 3.6 times larger than the rate at $N = 0$.

Because the estimated rate rises very sharply with increasing density in the range near $N = 0$, it is more informative to use the multiplier at some non-zero level of N as the point of comparison. For instance, take the level

13. Choice between the two makes almost no difference in deriving inferences about density dependence and rate dependence.

14. The multiplier of density is $N_t^\alpha \exp(-\gamma N_t^2)$, where α is the coefficient corresponding to the log $N(t)$ and $-\gamma$ multiplied by .0001 is the coefficient corresponding to $N^2/1000$.

Table 9.2.   ML estimates of Weibull model of the founding rate of national labor unions, 1836–1985

Independent variable	(1)	(2)	(3)
Intercept	.222	−.246	−.327
	(.214)	(.274)	(.269)
log $N(t)$	.233[c]	.427[c]	.367[c]
	(.072)	(.091)	(.091)
$N^2(t)/1000$	—	−.053[c]	−.041[c]
		(.007)	(.006)
$B(t)$	—	—	.114[b]
			(.044)
$B^2(t)$	—	—	−.004[a]
			(.002)
Period 2	.516[c]	1.11[c]	.726[c]
(1896–1985)	(.254)	(.245)	(.266)
Period 3	−.211	.611[c]	.436[b]
(1932–1985)	(.167)	(.203)	(.209)
Period 4	−.337	−.078	.018
(1947–1985)	(.300)	(.285)	(.283)
Period 5	−.975[c]	−1.47[c]	−1.17[c]
(1955–1985)	(.334)	(.322)	(.333)
Scale parameter	1.29[c]	1.21[c]	1.20[c]
	(.045)	(.043)	(.042)
Number of cases	497	497	497
Log-likelihood	−865.12	−841.79	−836.13
Degrees of freedom	7	8	10

Note: Figures in parentheses are asymptotic standard errors.
a. $p < .10$.
b. $p < .05$.
c. $p < .01$.

$N = 5$ as the baseline; then the multiplier is 1.73 higher than the rate at $N = 0$. So a value of 1.73 becomes the baseline for comparison here. When density increases to the historical maximum $N = 211$, the multiplier equals 1.30. In other words, our estimates imply that the founding rate in populations with 5 national unions was higher than that in a population of 211

MULTIPLIER OF THE RATE

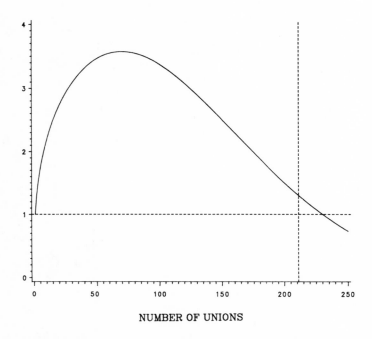

NUMBER OF UNIONS

Figure 9.3   Effect of density on union founding rate (estimates from model
3 in Table 9.1)

unions, since 1.73 is larger than 1.30. Put differently, the founding rate
when there were only 5 unions was 33 percent larger than it was at the
historical high of density. These comparisons, which hold exactly for the
first period and no foundings in the prior year, show that density drives the
founding rate in a large population down to the level that holds in a very
small population of unions. The rate rises sharply with increasing density
in the lower range and drops sharply with increasing density in the higher
range, indicating that the founding rate is very sensitive to density.

Figure 9.4 plots the effect of prior foundings, again using the estimates
from column 3 in Table 9.1. As in Figure 9.3, the implied effect is positive
over the observed range. This effect is weaker than the effect of density,
but it is still considerable. The multiplier due to prior foundings is largest
when $B \approx 15$, at which point the multiplier is 1.9 times that when $B = 0$,

MULTIPLIER OF THE RATE

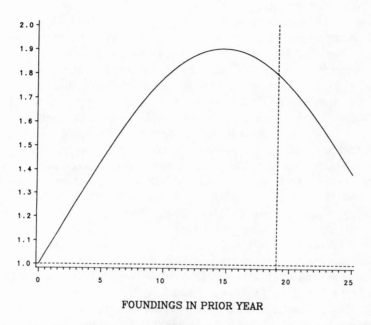

FOUNDINGS IN PRIOR YEAR

Figure 9.4   Effect of prior foundings on union founding rate (estimates from model 3 in Table 9.1)

which is a useful baseline since many years had zero foundings. From that level, the multiplier drops with additional prior foundings, but it is roughly 1.8 when the number of foundings reached its maximum level of 19. The strong effect of prior foundings on the founding rate may have contributed to the wavelike pattern of observed foundings. When the population is below the carrying capacity, a perturbation that produced a high level of founding activity in one year seems to have raised the rate for the next year substantially.

Interactions between Craft and Industrial Populations

The final part of this analysis considers founding rates of craft and industrial unions. It has two objectives: (1) to learn whether the processes differ by form; and (2) to examine competition between forms. We start by estimating models for each population using the non-monotonic model discussed to this point. Then we estimate model (9.7), which incorporates interpopulation effects. Tables 9.3 and 9.4 report the results for craft unions and industrial unions respectively. Again we use both PL analysis of durations between foundings and ML analysis of Poisson regressions of yearly counts of foundings. However, we now calculate durations and yearly counts separately for each subpopulation. This is the sense in which we treat the two forms as possibly having different dynamics.

The results for the craft founding rate can be seen in Table 9.3. The models in columns 1 and 4 in this table mimic the models in columns 4 and 6 in Table 9.1, but with one important difference: counts of all unions (N) and of all prior foundings (B) are replaced by counts of craft unions (N_C) and craft foundings (B_C). This specification allows us to consider how the founding rate of craft unions depended on the density and recent foundings in this subpopulation. We find that craft density and number of recent craft foundings have the predicted non-monotonic effects. Indeed estimates of these effects are fairly similar to those for the entire population of unions in Table 9.1, which is not surprising since craft unions constituted such a large share of the total population of unions.

What happens when the cross-effect of density of industrial unions (N_I) is added to the model? Columns 2 and 5 in Table 9.3 give the answer. In this case, choice of estimator makes a difference, but it turns out that the difference is not substantively important. The PL estimates tell that N_I had a negligible effect on the craft founding rate. This estimated cross-effect is much smaller than its standard error. The ML estimates of Poisson regressions, however, indicate that the cross-effect is *negative* and significant. Thus the competitive effect between subpopulations was a strong one according to the Poisson regressions. The estimate in the fourth column implies that the founding rate of craft unions was negligible when there were 50 industrial unions (since $\exp(-.304*50) \approx 0$). Put differently, growth in the density of industrial unions from zero to its historical maximum eradicated the founding rate of craft unions, according to the Poisson regression estimate.

In the final step, we allowed the craft founding rate to depend loglinearly on both N_I and N_I^2. That is, we added N_I^2 to the models in columns 2 and 5. The results, which are reported in columns 3 and 6, indicate that this alteration improves the fit significantly at the .01 level in the case of the PL estimator.[15] The estimated effect of N_I is positive; the effect of N_I^2 is

---

15. The likelihood ratio test statistic evaluating improvement over the model without N_I^2 equals 16.1 with one degree of freedom.

Table 9.3.   Density dependence in the founding rate of craft unions, 1836–1985

Independent variable	PL estimates			Poisson regression estimates		
	(1)	(2)	(3)	(4)	(5)	(6)
Intercept	—	—	—	$-.646^c$ (.250)	$-.662^c$ (.256)	$-.641^c$ (.253)
$\log N_C(t)$	$.397^c$ (.094)	$.389^c$ (.095)	$.256^c$ (.090)	$.371^c$ (.085)	$.400^c$ (.088)	$.379^c$ (.094)
$N_C^2(t)/1000$	$-.067^c$ (.019)	$-.076^c$ (.028)	$-.159^c$ (.034)	$-.049^b$ (.020)	$-.017$ (.026)	$-.026$ (.030)
$B_C(t)$	$.188^c$ (.051)	$.191^c$ (.051)	$.186^c$ (.051)	$.204^c$ (.047)	$.194^c$ (.048)	$.195^c$ (.048)
$B_C^2(t)$	$-.010^c$ (.003)	$-.010^c$ (.003)	$-.010^c$ (.003)	$-.008^c$ (.003)	$-.008^c$ (.003)	$-.008^c$ (.003)
$N_I(t)$	—	$.010$ (.020)	$.171^c$ (.044)	—	$-.034^a$ (.019)	$-.013$ (.040)
$N_I^2(t)/1000$	—	—	-2.42^c (.602)	—	—	$-.326$ (.559)
Period 2 (1896–1985)	$.507^a$ (.299)	$.527^a$ (.302)	$.508^a$ (.298)	$.529^a$ (.303)	$.477$ (.303)	$.461$ (.303)
Period 3 (1932–1985)	$-.062$ (.191)	$-.291$ (.521)	$-.271$ (.447)	$-.101$ (.181)	$.678$ (.464)	$.709$ (.456)
Period 4 (1947–1985)	$-.123$ (.294)	$-.140$ (.296)	$.241$ (.323)	$-.220$ (.294)	$-.170$ (.296)	$-.123$ (.308)
Period 5 (1955–1985)	$-.721^b$ (.346)	$-.751^b$ (.352)	-1.69^c (.428)	$-.848^b$ (.353)	$-.753^b$ (.357)	$-.871^c$ (.411)
Number of cases	355	355	355	150	150	150
Log-likelihood	$-1,683.09$	$-1,682.98$	$-1,674.96$	—	—	—
G^2	—	—	—	240.5	237.2	236.85
Degrees of freedom	8	9	10	9	10	11

Note: Figures in parentheses are asymptotic standard errors.
a. $p < .10$.
b. $p < .05$.
c. $p < .01$.

negative. These estimates imply that increasing density of industrial unions raised the craft founding rate until $N_I = 35$. From that point on, increasing numbers of industrial unions depressed the craft founding rate strongly. In fact, the implied multiplier for industrial density is essentially zero when $N_I = 50$.

In contrast to the case for the PL estimates, adding N_I^2 does not significantly improve the fit of the Poisson regression model in column 6 (at the .10 level). So within the hierarchy of models we have chosen, the two estimators favor different specifications: the model whose estimates appear in the third column for PL and the one in the sixth column for the Poisson regression.[16] But this difference does not mean much substantively. Estimates of the two models tell the same qualitative story: over most of the range of variation, increasing density of industrial unions strongly depressed the founding rate of craft unions. Thus the rise of the industrial form of union organization and the spread of industrial unions appear to have played a major role in depressing the founding rate of craft unions.

We turn finally to the results for industrial unions in Table 9.4. The PL estimates in column 1 give the predicted non-monotonic pattern of dependence on own density. The first-order effect of industrial density is positive, the second-order effect is negative. The Poisson ML estimates have the same signs, but are just significant at the .10 level or not significant.

Next we add the cross-effect of craft density (N_C). According to the PL estimate in the second column, the cross-effect of N_C is negative and significant. According to the Poisson regression in column 5, this cross-effect is negative but insignificant.[17] However, the point estimates are quite similar for the two estimators. Adding a second-order effect of N_C (in the third and sixth columns) does not improve the fit much with either estimator. So the density of craft unions appears to have had a negative effect on the industrial founding rate. According to column 2, this effect was a strong one even though it was just barely significant. When craft density reached its peak of 156, the multiplier of the cross-effect equals $\exp(-.026 * 156) = .017$. As was the case for the craft union form, the founding rate of the industrial unions form was close to zero when its

16. Results of Weibull and gamma specifications again agree closely with the PL estimates. In particular, they indicate a significant quadratic effect of N_I on the rate.

17. Estimates of Weibull and gamma specifications indicate a significant negative effect of craft density on the industrial founding rate. Again they agree closely with the PL estimates.

Table 9.4. Density dependence in the founding rate of industrial unions, 1836–1985

Independent variable	PL estimates			Poisson regression estimates		
	(1)	(2)	(3)	(4)	(5)	(6)
Intercept	—	—	—	-2.14^c (.421)	-1.79^c (.491)	-1.87^c (.689)
$\log N_I(t)$	$.390^b$ (.172)	$.876^c$ (.331)	.630 (.461)	$.711^a$ (.233)	1.28^c (.483)	1.22^a (.645)
$N_I^2(t)/1000$	-1.83^c (.421)	-1.81^c (.413)	-1.67^c (.452)	$-.224$ (.316)	$-.320$ (.323)	$-.288$ (.385)
$B_I(t)$	$.392^b$ (.184)	$.380^b$ (.183)	$.370^b$ (.182)	$.631^c$ (.185)	$.624^c$ (.184)	$.624^c$ (.184)
$B_I^2(t)$	$-.037$ (.026)	$-.039$ (.026)	$-.038$ (.026)	$-.082^c$ (.032)	$-.084^c$ (.032)	$-.084^c$ (.032)
$N_C(t)$	—	$-.026^a$ (.014)	$-.001$ (.036)	—	$-.021$ (.013)	$-.016$ (.033)
$N_C^2(t)/1000$	—	—	$-.111$ (.149)	—	—	$-.021$ (.135)
Period 2 (1896–1985)	.516 (.441)	1.86^b (.855)	1.89^b (.827)	$-.475$ (.457)	.421 (.726)	.452 (.749)
Period 3 (1932–1985)	2.89^c (.625)	2.73^c (.622)	2.77^c (.627)	.555 (.534)	.455 (.518)	.461 (.521)
Period 4 (1947–1985)	.166 (.536)	.196 (.529)	.194 (.525)	$-.811^a$ (.411)	$-.750$ (.442)	$-.745^a$ (.433)
Period 5 (1955–1985)	-2.43^c (.890)	-2.93^c (.959)	-3.05^c (.976)	-1.50^b (.651)	-2.11^c (.773)	-2.13^c (.786)
Number of cases	96	96	96	150	150	150
Log-likelihood	-316.76	-315.01	-314.75	—	—	—
G^2	—	—	—	114.58	112.01	111.99
Degrees of freedom	8	9	10	9	10	11

Note: Figures in parentheses are asymptotic standard errors.

a. $p < .10$.

b. $p < .05$.

c. $p < .01$.

competitor's density reached its historical maximum. However, this conclusion must be tempered by the fact that the effect is significantly different from zero for only one of the estimators.

The pattern of period effects parallels that for craft unions with one important exception. The similarities are that the rate rose significantly in the second period and dropped significantly in the fifth period. The exception concerns the effect of the New Deal, in period 3. Although this period had a lower rate for craft unions, the founding rate of industrial unions jumped enormously during the New Deal: the estimates imply that the industrial founding rate during the New Deal was 15 times higher than in the previous period. As numerous commentators have noted, the protections for union organizing incorporated into New Deal legislation were especially important in stimulating the foundings of industrial unions. However, the large negative effect of the fifth period cancels all of the gains of the second and third periods. The estimated rate of industrial founding in the fifth period is slightly less than that in the baseline first period.

As a final step in analysis, we tried pooling the data used separately in the analyses just discussed. Estimates of the pooled models can be used to test whether the pattern of effects differs overall for the two populations— whether the ecologies of the two populations differ with respect to foundings. The pooled models use the specifications discussed thus far but add a covariate that distinguishes craft from industrial unions. That is, the pooled models specify an additive effect (in the log-linear model) of the industrial form. We find for all models that the pooled models fit significantly more poorly than the less constrained separate models that allow different effects for the two populations. We conclude, therefore, that there really has been a difference in the founding processes of these two subpopulations. This result suggests that we have in fact identified meaningful subpopulations.

Entry Rates of Semiconductor Manufacturing Firms

We next consider the same set of issues for a very different kind of organizational population: semiconductor manufacturing firms. Since there are many obvious technical, environmental, and operating differences between national labor unions and semiconductor companies, comparing the dynamics of the founding and entry rates in the two populations provides a strong test of the generality of our model. In particular, this comparison (along with the one in the next section on newspaper publishing firms) allows us to assess possible differences in the entry and founding processes for market and non-market organizations.[18]

The comparison is complicated because there are important differences in the data available on the two populations. These differences led to modifications in the operations used to define both events and variables for study. As we discussed in Chapter 7, we do not necessarily observe the foundings or start-ups of firms in the semiconductor industry. Rather, we observe the entry of firms into the merchant semiconductor market. Some of these firms may be new organizations, so that entry and founding are equivalent events. However, some new entrants have a prior organizational existence. The dynamics of entry must differ from the dynamics of founding if only because foundings involve most of the same requirements as entries, but in addition involve organization-building activities that entries do not necessarily involve.

Another difference between the two populations is the length of the historical record. The semiconductor industry has existed for only about 40 years, as compared to the 150 years of national union history. Consequently, the maximum number of yearly observations is much smaller. On the other hand, the population of semiconductor firms has been much more volatile. For example, while the peak years for labor unions saw 19 foundings, there were 78 entries for semiconductors in the peak year, 1969.

We do not have precise data on the timing of entry. Our method of data collection allows recording only the year of entry. Therefore, we use only one of the methods we employed in analyzing founding rates of labor unions: maximum likelihood estimation of Poisson regressions based on yearly counts of foundings. We have compared annual listings of firms in 40 adjacent years to determine entries; thus we have 39 years for which entries and exits were observed. Since our models predict entries using variables measured in the prior year, the number of observations is actually 38. This small number of observations severely constrains the complexity of the models that can be estimated and makes insignificant effects likely.

Referring to equations (9.6) and (9.7), we define density (N_t) as the number of firms in the list of semiconductor manufacturers in the *Electronics Buyer's Guide* in a given year. The number of entries is the number of firms appearing in the *Guide* in a given year that had not appeared for at

18. Nelson and Winter (1982) claim that only organizations that operate in explicit markets can usefully be analyzed with a selection logic.

least the two previous years. All variables defined in terms of life events, such as density, number of entries, and number of exits, are measured at the beginning of the year for which a count of entries applies.

We also include two other variables in some specifications to reflect variations in economic conditions. These are indicators of two crucial resources used to found (and maintain) semiconductor firms: the total sales of semiconductor devices in North America and the cost of capital, measured at year-end by Moody's AA corporate bond interest rate. Both of these variables were measured in the year prior to the year in which foundings were counted.

We recorded 1,197 entries into the semiconductor industry between 1946 and 1984. Figure 9.5 shows the variation over time in number of entries. The entries seem to come in waves; note that the four-year period between 1969 and 1973 contains almost 28 percent of all entries. Figure 9.6 shows yearly variations in population density. The number of firms in the industry rose more or less linearly from 1945 to a peak of 335 in 1970, then stabilized and declined slightly over the subsequent 15 years. The general

ENTRIES

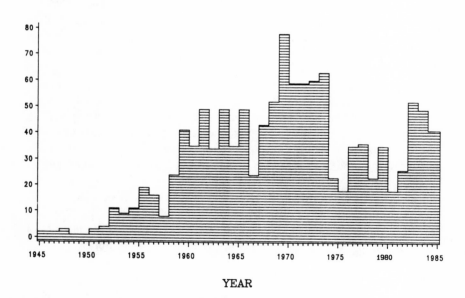

YEAR

Figure 9.5　Semiconductor firm entries by year

pattern is surprisingly similar to that for national labor unions in Figure 9.2. Despite the many differences between the organizations in the populations, at least some observable features of the population dynamics have been quite similar.

A comparison of Figures 9.5 and 9.6 shows that the period of highest density corresponds to the peak period of entry. This contrasts sharply with the union pattern, in which the peak period of foundings occurred during a time of only moderate density. Figures 9.5 and 9.6 suggest that density dependence in the entry may have been *monotonic* in the semiconductor industry. We check in subsequent analyses to see whether this is the case once period effects and economic conditions have been taken into account.

Figure 9.7 shows that sales of semiconductor products have grown almost exponentially over the history of the industry, which comes as no surprise. Clearly the drop in entries toward the end of the series in Figure 9.6 cannot be explained in terms of a drop in demand for the products of the industry.

As in our analysis of union foundings, we control for some environmental changes by using period effects. The substantive status of the periods differs somewhat between the two analyses. The definition of periods for

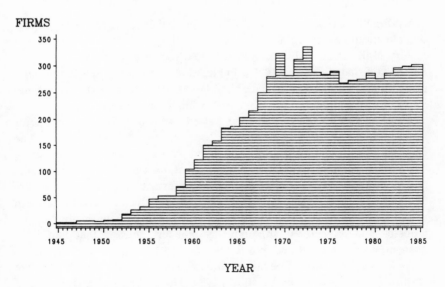

Figure 9.6   Density of semiconductor firms by year

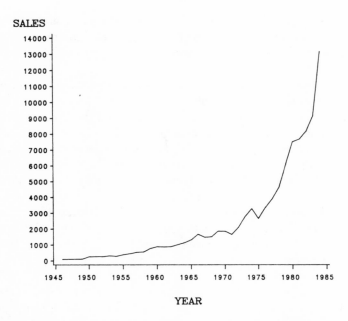

Figure 9.7   Semiconductor firm sales by year (in millions of dollars)

analyzing labor unions follows policies and legislation designed to hinder or help the union movement, while the events that we use to mark the history of the semiconductor industry are discoveries and inventions. It is not certain that these events had implications for entries into the population of merchant market producers, although we think that they did. Such implications are much more obvious for foundings of labor unions.

Another difference between the periods specified for semiconductor firms and for national labor unions concerns the clarity of dates. The enactment of legislation can be associated with a precise date much more easily than can the introduction of an innovation. Diffusion of innovations is a continuous process that does not conform completely to the step deviations; thus it is somewhat arbitrary to pick a given year as the point in which innovations occur. Nonetheless, our reading of the history of the industry and interviews with industry pioneers suggest that important changes were concentrated in a few years.

As with unions, we define these periods so that they proceed from some starting date to the end of the study, 1984. The first period (suppressed in the analysis) starts at the beginning of the industry in 1945. The second period begins in 1960. Its beginning is marked by the introduction of the integrated circuit and the development of some important innovations in production processes that reduced the cost and risk of manufacturing these devices. The third period begins in 1970. Between 1970 and 1972 the first thousand-bit MOS dynamic random access memory (RAM) chip, the bipolar RAM, and the microprocessor were all introduced (Wilson, Ashton, and Egan 1980, p. 41). With these innovations, computers became much less costly and more powerful. The exploding market for computers spilled over into the market for the vital semiconductor components.

Inspection of Figure 9.6 shows that the middle period was marked by frequent entry into the industry. During the third period the rate of entry dropped in spite of the expansion in the market, as we noted earlier. Because these periods are defined as partially overlapping time intervals, the antilog of each period effect tells the ratio of the rate in that period relative to the rate in the previous period.

Results

For continuity, we organize the exposition of our analysis around the same questions we asked concerning the union data. The first empirical question is whether the rate of entry has had a pattern of *density dependence* such as that found for national labor unions. The first column in Table 9.5 reports estimates of the generalized Yule model; it reveals that density has a strong and significant effect on the entry rate. According to this estimate, the rate rises sharply with density but at a slowly decreasing rate. The model whose estimates are found in column 2 adds the second-order effect of density to the model in the first column. This addition does not improve the fit significantly, since the drop in G^2 is only 1.47. Moreover, the second-order effect of density, which is positive in opposition to our hypothesis, is no larger than its standard error. So with this simple specification of the model, we find no evidence that the entry rate has been subject to non-monotonic density dependence. Columns 3 and 4 add additional covariates to the basic model. Adding effects of total sales, interest rates, and recent entries makes both the first- and second-order effects of density positive and significantly different from zero.[19]

---

19. For a model like that in column 4 but excluding log N and $N^2(t)/1000$, G^2 equals 176.6. The addition of log N and N^2 thus lowers G^2 by 44.2, which is significant at better than the .01 level.

Table 9.5. Poisson regression estimates of density dependence in the entry rates of U.S. semiconductor companies, 1947–1984

Independent variable	Model			
	(1)	(2)	(3)	(4)
Intercept	.078	.249	.359	.567[a]
	(.281)	(.304)	(.312)	(.313)
log $N(t)$	.756[c]	.708[c]	.741[c]	.535[c]
	(.073)	(.081)	(.083)	(.112)
$N^2(t)/1000$	—	.002	.004[b]	.006[b]
		(.002)	(.002)	(.003)
Entries (t)	—	—	—	.029[c]
				(.011)
Entries $(t)^2/1000$	—	—	—	−.310[b]
				(.132)
Aggregate sales (billions of dollars)	—	—	.031	−.002
			(.025)	(.028)
Interest rate	—	—	−.070[b]	−.022
			(.033)	(.038)
Period 2 (1960–1984)	−.249[a]	−.271[a]	−.306[b]	−.349[b]
	(.148)	(.149)	(.151)	(.151)
Period 3 (1970–1984)	−.465[c]	−.518[c]	−.420[c]	−.466[c]
	(.067)	(.079)	(.096)	(.112)
Number of cases	38	38	38	38
G^2	147.0	145.53	139.7	132.4
Degrees of freedom	4	5	7	9

Note: Figures in parentheses are asymptotic standard errors.
a. $p < .10$.
b. $p < .05$.
c. $p < .01$.

Figure 9.8 displays the effect of density using the estimates in column 4. We see that the entry rate increased as an approximately linear function of density over the observed range. Although N^2 has a positive effect, the coefficient's magnitude is small relative to that of log N. Over the range of variation in our data, the curve does not show a pronounced tendency to bend upward. These data show no evidence of non-monotonic density

MULTIPLIER OF THE RATE

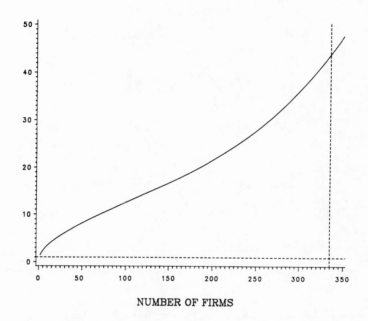

NUMBER OF FIRMS

Figure 9.8 Effect of density on entry rate of semiconductor firms (estimates from model 4 in Table 9.5)

dependence. So our suspicion, based on visual inspection of the raw counts of entries, that density dependence is monotonic is confirmed for semiconductor firms. Nonetheless, the monotonic effect of density is extraordinarily powerful. At high density, the entry rate is over forty times higher than the rate at zero density. These results suggest that growth in the number of firms in the industry accelerated the rate of entry by increasing the number of potential organization builders with appropriate technical background and perhaps by legitimating the industry and its organizational form.

Adding measures of environmental variables to the model (in column 3 of Table 9.5) improves the fit, but only at the .10 level. According to these estimates, growth in aggregate sales increased the rate of entry and high interest rates depressed it, as expected.

MULTIPLIER OF THE RATE

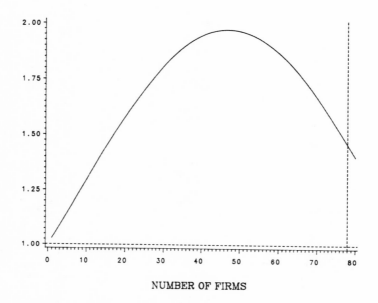

NUMBER OF FIRMS

Figure 9.9   Effect of prior entries on entry rate of semiconductor firms
(estimates from model 4 in Table 9.5)

The second question involves *rate dependence*, the effect of the flow of recent entries on the entry rate. The fourth column of Table 9.5 reports estimates of a model that includes effects of the previous year's number of entries and its square. The addition of these regressors improves the fit significantly.[20] And the first-order effect of recent entries is positive and the second-order effect is negative, as predicted.

In Figure 9.9 we can see that as the number of recent entries increases, the rate of entry rises and then falls. This wavelike pattern of entry may reflect the effects of variables not included in our models. For example, the availability of venture capital rises and falls with government tax policy, and its variations are not adequately captured by the bond interest rate. Our expectation of wavelike patterns in entry rates is based on our view that recent entries can provide a signaling function, encouraging other

20. This addition of B and B^2 to the model in column 4 lowers G^2 by 7.3, which is significant at the .05 level with two degrees of freedom.

entries; this continues until the resources needed to build organizations begin to run out.

The period effects in Table 9.5 are consistently negative. They show a decline in the 1970s and the first part of the 1980s. According to the estimated effect of the second period in column 4, the rate was only $\exp(-.349) = .705$ as large as the rate in the first period. So the rate of entry dropped by almost 30 percent after 1960. After 1970, it dropped by another 37 percent. Looking back at Figure 9.5, we can see that the crude number of entries actually rose during the 1960s. The analysis in Table 9.5 shows that this is misleading, however. Even without controls for sales, interest rates, and previous entries, the rate of entry drops. We suspect that the increased technological complexity represents increases in cost of entry as well as in opportunity. Of course, other events such as the rise of foreign competition could explain this decline.

Qualitative Implications

There is a clear difference in the qualitative patterns of density dependence in founding rates for national labor unions and in entry rates for semiconductor manufacturing firms. Recall that the founding rate of unions rose with density over roughly half of its observed range, and that the multiplier of density at the maximum was about four times the multiplier at zero density. Here we see that for the population of semiconductor firms, the positive effect of density operated over the full range of density. If the population as a whole is well below its carrying capacity at all times, a growing population creates opportunities. Growing firms provide more people to serve as trained entrepreneurs and more opportunities based in technologies that have not yet been commercialized.[21]

Another interpretation is that this difference between unions and semiconductor firms reflects mainly the difference in the kind of event under study. Semiconductor firms are observed upon entry to the industry, not necessarily when the corporations are first set up. Entry into an industry may well be an easier process than founding a firm.

Interactions between Subsidiary and Independent Firms

Next we turn to interactions between two substantively interesting subpopulations: subsidiary and independent firms. Some semiconductor firms

---

21. See Brittain and Freeman (1980) for a discussion of such opportunities.

are organized as free-standing corporations; others are corporate divisions, embedded in larger organizations. The potential advantages to organization as a free-standing corporation are the capacity for quick adjustment to changing conditions and a more single-minded attention to the interests of the organization. Corporate divisions enjoy the advantage of buffering by the parent firm, which allows them to tolerate short-run downturns in business. In addition, they can use the parent firm's superior ability to make claims on the resource environment. For example, such divisions have access to capital markets through the parent firm to support expansion in capital investment or research and development. Indeed, such access is one of the common reasons why free-standing firms accept offers to be acquired and made part of a multidivisional firm.

Since the two kinds of firms rely on different kinds of resources and have different organizational structures, it seems likely that the entry process differs for the two subpopulations. So in the next step we investigate whether the processes do differ and whether there is any competition between subpopulations. As in the case of labor unions, we analyze yearly counts of entries in each subpopulation as functions of the density of the subpopulation, the number of recent entries into the subpopulation, and the density of the other subpopulation.

Table 9.6 reports estimates of parameters of models of entry into the population of subsidiary firms. Unlike the full-population estimates reported in the previous table, subsidiary firm entries show strong non-monotonic density dependence. As was the case for unions, the first-order effect of own density is positive and the second-order effect is negative. The rate rises with low-level increases in density, but then declines with further increases at high density. So there has been *intraform* competition within the population of subsidiary firms, and the expected non-monotonic pattern is evident in this subpopulation.

On the other hand, competition between the forms does not appear to have characterized the dynamics of entries into the population of subsidiary firms. In fact, there is evidence of mutualism. The number of independent firms has a positive and significant effect on the entry rate of subsidiary firms.[22] If independent firms provide support for the subsidiary firms, for example by serving as second sources or as scouts who identify new applications and markets, growth in the size of this population should

---

22. When N_i^2 is added to the model in column 2, both it and the first-order effect of N_I are insignificant.

Table 9.6. Poisson regression estimates of density dependence in the founding rates of subsidiary firms, 1947–1984

Independent variable	Model	
	(1)	(2)
Intercept	−.485	−.443
	(.518)	(.511)
log $N_S(t)$	.596[c]	.404[b]
	(.178)	(.180)
$N_S^2(t)/1000$	−.096	−.423[c]
	(.092)	(.122)
$N_I(t)$	—	.014[c]
		(.003)
Aggregate sales	−.111	−.238[b]
(billions of dollars)	(.090)	(.096)
Interest rate	.095	.150
	(.098)	(.103)
Period 2	.172	−.081
(1960–1984)	(.362)	(.376)
Period 3	−.263	−.013
(1970–1984)	(.283)	(.277)
Number of cases	38	38
G^2	68.6	52.4
Degrees of freedom	7	8

Note: Figures in parentheses are asymptotic standard errors.
a. $p < .10$.
b. $p < .05$.
c. $p < .01$.

increase the rate of entry into the population of subsidiary firms, and this is what we find here. Another interpretation is that the independent firms absorb uncertainty for the subsidiary firms by expanding and contracting the population as business competition rises and falls. If this is true, we would expect to see more competition in the entry rate dynamics of independent firms. This has indeed been the case.

Table 9.7 reports parallel results for the rate of entry into the other subpopulation, independent firms. Note first that the effect of own density

Table 9.7.   Poisson regression estimates of density dependence in the founding rates of independent firms, 1947–1984

Independent variable	Model	
	(1)	(2)
Intercept	.588[b]	.486
	(.296)	(.337)
log $N_I(t)$	.692[c]	.516[c]
	(.088)	(.167)
$N_I(t)^2/1000$	.007[b]	.018[c]
	(.003)	(.005)
$N_S(t)$	—	.029
		(.020)
$N_S^2(t)/1000$	—	−.387[b]
		(.157)
Aggregate sales (billions of dollars)	.023	−.084[b]
	(.025)	(.039)
Interest rate	−.063[a]	.033
	(.034)	(.043)
Period 2 (1960–1984)	−.228	−.192
	(.166)	(.239)
Period 3 (1970–1984)	−.384[c]	−.149
	(.102)	(.123)
Number of cases	38	38
G^2	122.9	109.5
Degrees of freedom	7	9

Note: Figures in parentheses are asymptotic standard errors.
a. $p < .10$.
b. $p < .05$.
c. $p < .01$.

is monotonic, as was the case for the population as a whole. Both first-order and second-order effects of density are positive and significantly different from zero.

Next we consider the cross-effect, the effect of the density of the other subpopulation. Analysis reveals that this cross-effect is non-monotonic. The first-order cross-effect is positive, and the second-order effect is negative. It seems that increasing numbers in the subpopulation of subsidiary firms initially increased the rate of entry of independent firms; but, as the density of subsidiary firms increased at higher levels, the entry rate of independent firms dropped off rapidly.

In fact, Figure 9.10 shows that the estimated cross-effect at high observed levels of density of subsidiary firms falls below the effect at low density. At its minimum, the cross-effect has cut the entry rate of independent firms by roughly 30 percent. So we find that competitive effects on the entry rate of subsidiary firms concern processes *within* the subpopulation. But the competitive effect for independent firms comes primarily from the subpopulation of subsidiary firms.

In Tables 9.6 and 9.7 rate dependence is not estimated because it is not significant for either subpopulation. We can only speculate that the apparent rate dependence in the analysis of the full population (in Table 9.5)

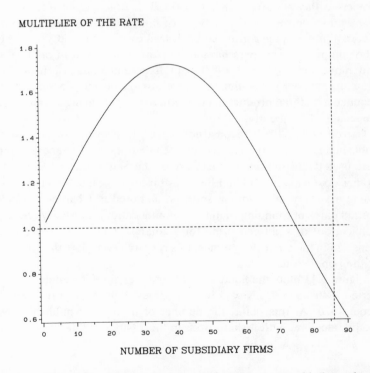

Figure 9.10   Effect of subsidiary firm density on entry rate of independent firms (estimates from model 2 in Table 9.7)

actually reflects the aggregation of competitive relationships between the two populations. The effect of "other" population density on "own" entry rate net of own density must be highly correlated with own lagged entry rate.

The period effects for both populations are not significant. The addition of total sales of semiconductor devices in North America to the models in Tables 9.6 and 9.7 improves the fit significantly. When the entire population is studied, total sales have insignificant effects. In Tables 9.6 and 9.7, its effects are negative. However, the industrial bond interest rate does not seem to have affected the rate at all.

Founding Rates of Newspaper Firms

Finally we consider the result of fitting the same basic models to data on founding rates of organizations that published local newspapers in the San Francisco Bay area from 1840 to 1975. This organizational form provides interesting contrasts with the two just considered. As with labor unions, records on newspaper firms go back well over a hundred years. And like labor unions, newspapers have been heavily involved in political events and movements (Carroll 1987). But like semiconductor manufacturing firms, newspaper publishing organizations are business organizations that produce a material product in competitive markets using a technology that has changed frequently.

Carroll (1985, 1987) reconstructed the life histories of all newspapers published in seven urban areas in the United States. The analysis reported here uses data from one of these areas, the San Francisco Bay area (San Francisco, Oakland, and San Jose), by far the largest of the areas studied.[23] Using a variety of historical sources, as noted in Chapter 7, Carroll recorded dates of founding (initiation of publication), mortality (cessation of publication) or right-censoring for a total of 2,170 newspaper organizations. As in the other two studies, this research considers the entire history of the population.

Figure 9.11 plots the fluctuations in numbers in this population over the period 1840–1975. Density grew more or less linearly over the period up to about 1920. At this point, the number of newspaper publishers began a gradual decline, with a sharp drop in the 1940s and a temporary rebound

---

23. The research reported in this section was done jointly with Glenn Carroll. For more details, see Carroll and Hannan (1988).

FIRMS

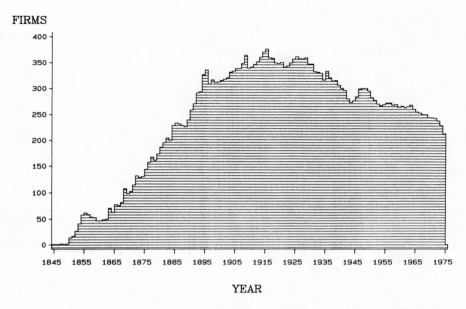

YEAR

Figure 9.11   Density of newspaper publishing firms by year (San Francisco
Bay area)

during the 1950s. It is worth noting that growth in density of newspaper
organizations does not track the growth of population and commercial
activity in the region. Density peaked while these resource dimensions
were just beginning explosive growth; density leveled off and then declined during a time when newspaper circulation and advertising revenues
showed continued strong growth. Thus, this pattern of growth and decline
in density does not appear to reflect fluctuations in availability of resources
or obsolescence of social and material technologies.

Figure 9.12 shows yearly fluctuations in the number of foundings in this
population. Notice that the peak period of foundings was the 1890s, and
that the number of foundings dropped sharply during the period of high
density. This comparison suggests that the relationship between density
and the founding rate may have been non-monotonic in this population.

Estimates of models for founding rates are obtained by treating the
process as a point process and using the intervals between events to estimate the rate with partial likelihood estimators, which is one of the methods used earlier in analyzing founding rates of unions. Here the observa-

FOUNDINGS

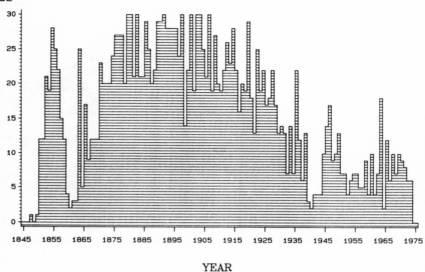

YEAR

Figure 9.12   Foundings of newspaper publishing firms by year (San Francisco Bay area)

tions are the durations between the 2,170 foundings. All but the last of these spells ends with an event; the last is censored on the right at the end of 1975.

Carroll and Huo (1986) previously analyzed yearly counts of foundings in this population without considering effects of density. They used models in which the count in any year was regressed on the count for the previous year and the square of the previous year's count of foundings. They found that lagged foundings tended to have the non-monotonic pattern of effects found earlier in studies of the ecology of Argentinean and Irish newspaper populations (Delacroix and Carroll 1983). They also found that the number of foundings was affected significantly by several environmental covariates and that counts of foundings rose significantly during years of political turmoil (mainly anti-Chinese riots, general strikes, and strike-related violence). So we include in our analyses a variable that distinguishes years of such political turmoil.

Table 9.8 reports PL estimates of models of density dependence in founding rates in the San Francisco Bay area newspaper publisher population. The first column contains estimates of our basic model of density

Table 9.8. PL estimates of density dependence in the founding rate of newspaper publishers in the San Francisco Bay area, 1840–1980

Independent variable	Model		
	(1)	(2)	(3)
log $N(t)$	.226[c]	.095[a]	—
	(.049)	(.056)	
$N(t)$	—	—	.003[c]
			(.001)
$N^2(t)/100$	−.0003[c]	−.0002[c]	−.0008[c]
	(.0001)	(.0001)	(.0003)
$B(t)$	—	.106[c]	.113[c]
		(.009)	(.009)
$B^2(t)$	—	−.0010[c]	−.001[c]
		(.0002)	(.0002)
Year of political turbulence	.342[c]	.032	.012
	(.053)	(.054)	(.055)
Degrees of freedom	3	5	5
Log likelihood	−14,839.21	−14,577.12	−14,509.59
Number of events	2169	2169	2169

Note: Figures in parentheses are asymptotic standard errors.
a. $p < .10$.
b. $p < .05$.
c. $p < .01$.

dependence (9.4a). The model also contains the effect of political turbulence. Again we find that the effect of density was non-monotonic. The estimated first-order effect of density is positive, and the second-order effect is negative. Both point estimates differ significantly from zero at the .01 level. In addition, political turbulence raised the rate significantly, as Carroll and Huo (1986) found with a different model and estimator. According to the estimate in column 1, the founding rate of newspaper publishing firms was 40 percent higher in years of marked political turbulence.

The second column contains estimates of a model that adds the effect of foundings in the prior year, as in equation (9.6a). The effects of density still have the predicted signs, and both point estimates still differ significantly from zero. Prior foundings also have the predicted effect on the founding rate: the first-order effect is positive and the second-order effect is negative. Both of these point estimates also differ significantly from zero.

In exploring alternative specifications, we found that a better fit can be obtained by using a log-quadratic effect of density.[24] In the log-quadratic model the log of the founding rate is a linear function of density and its square. This model has essentially the same qualitative interpretation as the one discussed to this point. Column 3 in Table 9.8 reports estimates of this model. Again the relationship between the founding rate and density is non-monotonic: the first-order effect is positive and the second-order effect is negative. Both point estimates are significant at the .01 level. The effects of prior foundings are essentially unchanged from those in column 2.

In both columns 2 and 3 the estimated effect of political turmoil is much lower than in column 1, and the point estimates are smaller than their standard errors. We are not sure why adding the flow of recent foundings depresses the effect of political turmoil, given the fact that Carroll and Huo (1986) find a significant effect of this variable in models that include the effects of prior foundings. Perhaps the difference is due to the fact that our models also contain the effect of density, or it may reflect differences in the estimators used or in other details of the specifications.

The estimated effects of density in Table 9.8 imply that the effect of density is non-monotonic within the observed range of density.[25] In the case of the best-fitting model, the estimated effects of density in the third column show that the founding rate rose with increasing density until $N = 206$ and then declined. The founding rate at this maximum was 41 percent larger than at $N = 0$. At the historical maximum of density ($N = 377$) the rate was only 17 percent higher than the rate at zero density. Put differently, the founding rate in a population with 377 newspaper publishers was about the same as that in one with 70 newspaper publishers.

However, the estimates in Table 9.8 imply that growth in the founding rate has been monotonic over the historical range of variation in number of recent foundings. That is, the estimates tell that the founding rate was at a maximum when $B = 51$, while the historical high was $B = 47$. So these results suggest that the founding rate increased at a decreasing rate with the number of foundings in the previous year.

24. We did not find this to be the case in analyzing either the union or the semiconductor manufacturer founding rate.
25. Carroll and Hannan (1988) report similar results for the populations of newspaper publishing firms in Argentina and Ireland.

Comparisons and Contrasts

Have entries into populations of labor unions, semiconductor firms, and newspaper publishers been subject to similar processes of density dependence? In a general sense the answer appears to be yes. For all three kinds of organizations, rates of founding depend on density. For unions and newspaper publishers the founding rates rise with increasing density to a point and then decline with further increases in density. For semiconductor firms this non-monotonic pattern characterizes only the subsidiary firms. The entry rates of independent firms do not behave as if they have encountered a carrying capacity.

We should note that because of imprecise founding dates, we were forced to rely on aggregate analyses of entry processes in the semiconductor analysis. The small number of time points available makes this a risky procedure. We should also note that we are studying entries into the semiconductor business, not foundings. In this sense, the semiconductor study may very well produce different results because the phenomenon under investigation is conceptually different.

Both labor unions and semiconductor firms display competition between forms, and in both studies the competition is asymmetric. The number of industrial unions has strong negative effects on the founding rate of craft unions, but the number of craft unions has no effect on the founding rate of industrial unions. Among semiconductor firms, the density of subsidiary firms has strong competitive effects on the entry rate of independent firms, but not the reverse.

In Chapter 11 we consider the same issues in the context of rates of failure. But before doing so, we turn to consideration of the prior issue of age variation in failure rates.

10 | Age Dependence in Failure Rates

This is the first of three chapters on the other side of the selection process: organizational mortality. Analyzing mortality is more complicated than analyzing founding and entry. Processes of founding and entry, at least as we have viewed them, are attributes of a population alone.[1] But interesting mortality processes occur at both the organizational and the population levels. In analyzing mortality even at the population level, we are dealing with organizations that have histories and concrete structures. These characteristics may often be distributed in ways that confound processes at the individual and population levels. If so, useful analysis needs to consider processes at both levels.

In Chapter 1 we referred to studies of the effects of organizational characteristics on mortality rates as *demographic* analysis. Recent research has shown that the most important demographic issue from the perspective of ecological analysis is age variation in mortality rates. There are good reasons for thinking that this demographic issue is linked tightly with the ecological issues of interest. One of the most important links involves the likelihood that susceptibility to environmental shocks varies with age. The same shock, say a coup d'état, a financial panic, or a major strike, apparently has much more devastating effects on new organizations than on old ones. If so, the effect of a particular shock on an organizational population depends on the age distribution of the population and the relationship between age and mortality rates.

---

1. In particular, one does not know how to attach the outcome of no foundings or entries in a period to any particular organization(s).

Indeed, we have found that the effects of age on failure rates are so powerful that it is extremely difficult—if not impossible—to obtain useful estimates of ecological processes if aging is not taken into account. Therefore, before addressing questions about competition and environmental pressures, we consider baseline models of age dependence in failure rates.

We give considerable attention to the mortality of labor unions since we have detailed data on both the timing of events and distinctions among the types of starting and ending events.[2] The analysis of unions is followed by a brief analysis of semiconductor manufacturing firms. We do not present results on age dependence in populations of newspapers because Carroll (1987) has thoroughly documented the existence of such effects.

The Liability of Newness

Stinchcombe (1965, pp. 148–150) claimed that organizations face a liability of newness: new organizations fail at higher rates than old ones. His arguments supporting this claim pertain to both internal organizational matters and environmental relations. New organizations are vulnerable because their participants are strangers. Efficient organization requires trust among members; and trust takes time to build. New organizations are also vulnerable because they have to create organizational roles and routines. Inventing and refining roles and routines take time and effort precisely when organizational resources are stretched to the limit.

These considerations direct attention to the effects of environments because new organizations, particularly those with a new form, must socialize members into new roles and routines. They cannot rely on generalized skills and experience available in the labor market. New organizations also have to develop relationships with existing organizations on which they rely for resources. So trust, which as we noted takes time to build, is important in organization–environment relationships too.

In Chapter 4 we derived the liability of newness from fundamental propositions about the nature of selection processes in the modern world of organizations. We argued that social selection processes favor organizations and organizational forms that have high levels of reliability of performance and accountability, and that reliability and accountability in turn depend on a capacity to reproduce structure with high fidelity. By all accounts, new organizations have lower fidelity in reproducing structure

2. Chapter 12 shows that restaurants also face a liability of newness.

from day to day. That is, fidelity of reproduction increases with age. So reliability and accountability increase with age; and mortality rates decrease with age. Empirical indications of a liability of newness provide indirect support for this line of argument.

In recent years evidence has accumulated in support of Stinchcombe's hypothesis. In the broadest study, Carroll (1983) examined the liability of newness in 52 populations of firms in such diverse industries as retail sales, printing, chemical manufacturing, metal industries, and saloons. He used Gompertz and Makeham models to estimate the rate of decline in mortality rates with age and found that the rates do tend to drop sharply with aging. Freeman, Carroll, and Hannan (1983) explored these issues using richer data on newspaper firms, labor unions, and semiconductor manufacturing firms. They also used Gompertz and Makeham models and found that mortality rates drop sharply with age even when the initial size of organizations is taken into account.

The study by Freeman, Carroll, and Hannan (1983), hereafter cited as the FCH study, used preliminary and partial data on unions and semiconductor firms. They analyzed the histories of 476 national unions, the set of members of the AFL, the CIO, and the AFL/CIO along with some "major independent unions." Here we update and replicate these analyses using somewhat more complete data, not restricted to the longer-lived, more successful members of the population. We also use different parametric models. We devote considerable attention to contrasting alternative representations of age dependence in failure rates because, as we noted earlier, the effects of aging are so strong that it is difficult to obtain meaningful estimates of other processes affecting mortality unless age dependence has been well represented.

One important issue has not been addressed in previous research on the liability of newness. This is the plausible possibility that age variation in mortality rates is "spurious" in the sense that it reflects only the operation of unobserved but age-independent heterogeneity in cohorts of organizations. Suppose that each cohort of organizations differs in terms of difficult-to-observe characteristics such as managerial competence, political harmony among departments, and so forth. Assume further, contrary to Stinchcombe's thesis, that these characteristics do not change with aging. Then those organizations with the characteristics that make them ill-suited to surviving in the socioeconomic environment will tend to experience mortality at early ages. As these events of mortality occur, the average mortality rate in the population will fall as a result of the loss of organizations with very high mortality rates. Since this process occurs on a time scale measured in age, the result of the unobserved heterogeneity is to give the empirical indications of age dependence in the rate. This is an instance of the general rule that unobserved heterogeneity and time dependence have similar empirical indications. The best way to combat this problem is to measure the relevant factors and include them as observed covariates, and we have indeed tried to do so. But it is also useful to examine the consequence of estimating models that allow the rate to depend on unobserved heterogeneity as well in order to see whether apparent age dependence is eliminated. We do so in this chapter using a parametric representation of the unobserved heterogeneity.

National Labor Unions

We analyze the questions about the liability of newness in terms of effects on the mortality rate. To begin with the simplest possible model as a baseline of comparison, assume that there is a single overall mortality process driven by a *constant* rate. In other words, assume that there is a single process by which unions disappear and that it is a Poisson process. The maximum likelihood estimator of the Poisson rate is 0.027. This estimate implies that the expected lifetime of a labor union was 37 years and that the half-life (the age by which half the unions would have experienced mortality) was roughly 26 years.

The claim that organizations face a liability of newness implies that the mortality rate is *not* constant over age. A nonparametric procedure for exploring whether the mortality rate varies with age is with estimates of the integrated mortality rate (see equation 8.1). Figure 10.1 plots an estimate of this function for the population of labor unions and a 95 percent confidence interval, using Aalen's (1978) estimator. Recall from Chapter 8 that the integrated rate is approximately a *linear* function of age if the mortality rate is constant. Clearly the estimated integrated rate is not linear over the age range in Figure 10.1; the integrated rate rises steeply over the first few years of life and then begins to level off. The (pointwise) 95 percent confidence interval is narrow enough that no linear relationships fall within the interval over any considerable age range. So the overall pattern agrees with the argument that organizations have a liability of newness.

In order to describe the process, the integrated mortality rate provides all that we need to know about age variation in the rate for the population taken as a whole. But we want more than description: we want to control for observed characteristics of unions and for unobserved heterogeneity in

INTEGRATED HAZARD

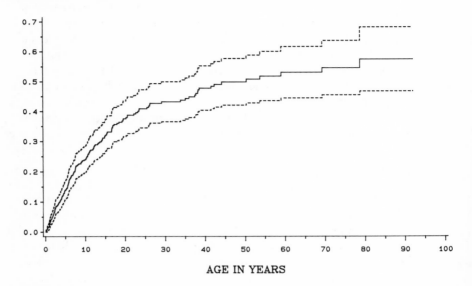

AGE IN YEARS

Figure 10.1   Integrated hazard of mortality of unions (dashed lines indicate
95% confidence interval)

order to learn whether the age variation apparent in the plot of the integrated rate reflects real aging processes. If there does seem to be a real
aging process, we want to explore whether we can summarize the aging
process with a simple parametric model. If we can, the task of taking aging
into account in studying ecological processes will be greatly simplified.

Before turning to the effects of observed and unobserved heterogeneity,
we need to discuss the choice of families of parametric models in which to
embed the effects of covariates. The recent empirical literature on organizational mortality has used the Gompertz model of age dependence and its
extension, the Makeham model. As we show next, our research reveals
that the Gompertz model does not fit our data as well as the equally simple
Weibull model.

In Chapter 8 we pointed out that the Gompertz process implies that the
logarithm of the hazard is a linear function of age. So one way to explore
the fit of this model is with plots of the logarithm of the estimated values of
the hazard against age. This procedure requires that the hazard be evaluated over particular intervals of the time axis. We do so using the classical

LOG OF HAZARD

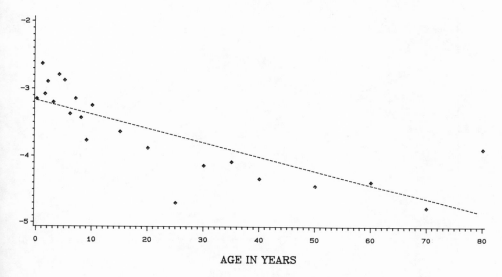

Figure 10.2 Log-hazard of mortality by age for unions

actuarial estimator of the hazard (Cox and Oakes 1984, pp. 53–56). Figure 10.2 plots the log of the actuarial estimator of the hazard of mortality for national labor unions. If the data were generated by a Gompertz process, this plot would be approximately linear. Rather, the estimated relationship between the log-hazard and age appears to be nonlinear. At young ages, the log-hazards fall above the least squares regression (dashed) line. At middle ages, they fall below the regression line. This poor fit is typical of the results of our explorations with the data described in the previous chapter (Hannan 1988b provides details).

The Weibull model implies a linear relationship between the log-hazard and log-age. Figure 10.3 plots this relationship, again using the actuarial estimator of the hazard. The implied linear relationship seems to hold in Figure 10.3, though it is far from exact. Nonetheless, the fit is better than was the case for the Gompertz model in Figure 10.2. Not only are the observations spread more evenly around the least squares regression line, but the correlation is stronger (−.88 versus −.78). Since the Weibull and Gompertz models have similar qualitative behavior and the Weibull fits these data better, we rely on the Weibull model as the leading alternative to

LOG OF HAZARD

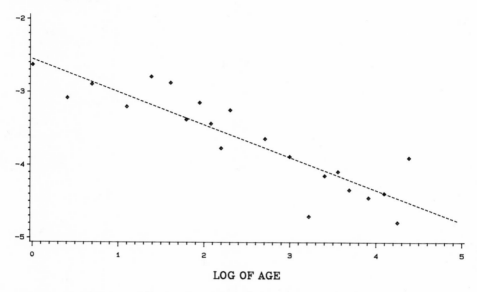

Figure 10.3 Log-hazard of mortality by log-age for unions

the exponential model as a representation of age dependence in rates of the mortality of labor unions. In so doing, we depart from what has recently become standard practice in organizational demography and ecology.

The mortality of labor unions includes three separate processes: merger, absorption, and dissolution. There is no reason to suspect that each subprocess bears the same relationship to age. In fact, the results at every stage in our analysis suggest that the three subprocesses differ substantially. Therefore, we consider them separately in the remainder of this section.

The Rate of Disbanding

By disbanding we mean that a labor union dissolved its structure without becoming part of another union. This was clearly the most catastrophic event that could befall a union. The ML estimate of the (constant) rate of disbanding is .011 per year. This rate implies that the expected age of disbanding is 90 and the half-life of unions up to the time of disbanding is about 63 years. But the constant rate understates the importance of this event in the population if there is a liability of newness, since it averages long periods with low rates with the brief periods of very high rates.

Figure 10.4 plots the integrated rate of disbanding against age. Again there is evidence of a strong age dependence: the integrated hazard rises steeply at young ages and then flattens out. This means that the disbanding rate is high at young ages and declines with aging.

Given the results of contrasting the Gompertz and Weibull models discussed above, we begin with the Weibull model of age dependence as an alternative to the exponential (age-independent) model in exploring the effects of covariates. Then we contrast the fit of a model that adds unobservable heterogeneity in the rate, the gamma model. We also report estimates of a generalized gamma model that combines the gamma and Weibull processes. Finally, we examine the results of fitting a model in which the rate can have a non-monotonic relationship with age, the loglogistic model.

As we discussed in Chapter 8, the general model used (from equation 8.12) is

(10.1) $\log T = -\boldsymbol{\beta}^* \mathbf{x} + \sigma W,$

INTEGRATED RATE OF DISBANDING

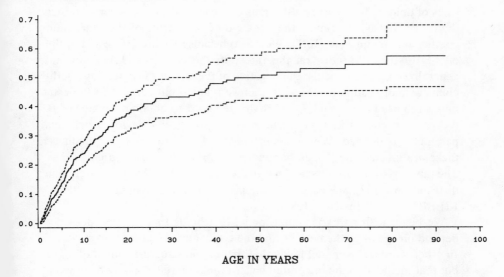

AGE IN YEARS

Figure 10.4   Integrated rate of union disbanding (dashed lines indicate 95% confidence interval)

where T denotes age at mortality or censoring in this section. The various models we use are special cases of this model. In the case of the exponential (age-independent) model, $\beta^* = \beta$, where β is the vector of effects of interest, $\sigma = 1$, and W has the extreme value distribution (8.5). In the case of the Weibull model, $\sigma = \rho^{-1}$, $\beta^* = \beta\sigma$, and W again has the extreme value distribution. In the case of the pure gamma model, $\beta^* = \beta$, $\sigma = 1$, and W has the gamma distribution given in (8.14) with shape parameter k. The generalized gamma model has the same form but without the restriction that $\sigma = 1$. Finally, the log-logistic model has $\beta^* = \beta$, and W has the logistic density (8.17).

In each stage of the analysis we include six covariates in the models. Two are dummy variables that describe the nature of the starting event. The first (FOUNDING) indicates that the union began with a founding event, as discussed in the previous chapter. The second (SECESSION) tells that the union began when some members left an existing national union and formed a new one. The omitted category includes unions that began with mergers between existing unions and four cases in which professional associations became labor unions. The remaining covariates are four dummy variables that distinguish periods. We use the same set of five periods as in the previous chapter.

Table 10.1 reports ML estimates of the relevant models for disbanding rates of unions. In reporting estimates of these models, we report $\hat{\beta}$ rather than $-\hat{\beta}$; that is, we report the negative of the vector of the regression coefficients in equation (10.1). We do so because we are interested in the effects of the covariates on the rates. In the case of the Weibull and generalized gamma models, the negative of the vector of regression coefficients actually estimates $\beta^* = \beta\sigma$, as we pointed out earlier. So the estimates reported in the tables can be divided by $\hat{\sigma}$ to obtain estimates of β.

As we discussed in Chapter 8, $\sigma = \rho^{-1}$ in all models for which this parameter is defined. We report estimates of σ in the tables of findings; these are labeled the "scale parameters." ML estimates of ρ equal $\hat{\sigma}^{-1}$. The tables also report a "shape parameter" for models that use the gamma distribution. The shape parameter equals $1/k^2$ in the conventions of PROC LIFEREG (SAS Institute 1985).

We begin with an exponential model that holds that the rate does not depend on age once the periods and the covariates are taken into account. In other words, this model holds that there is no structural effect of aging but that the bend in the integrated hazard function reflects only the uncontrolled effects of periods and observed covariates. Estimates of this model can be found in the first column of Table 10.1. The second column reports estimates of a comparable Weibull model, which allows the rate to vary by

Table 10.1. ML estimates of models of age dependence in rates of disbanding of labor unions, 1836–1985

Independent variable	Exponential	Weibull	Gamma	Generalized gamma	Log-logistic
Intercept	−6.85[c]	−8.57[c]	−8.71[c]	−6.22[c]	−7.60[c]
	(.583)	(1.02)	(1.20)	(.722)	(.876)
Founding	2.33[c]	3.73[c]	3.71[c]	2.92[c]	3.58[c]
	(.583)	(.998)	(1.16)	(.575)	(.852)
Secession	1.82[c]	2.58[b]	2.75[c]	2.15[c]	2.40[c]
	(.632)	(1.07)	(1.21)	(.633)	(.924)
Period 2	.633[c]	.744[c]	.101	.593[b]	.629[b]
(1886–1985)	(.158)	(.266)	(.266)	(.285)	(.283)
Period 3	−1.32[c]	−2.21[c]	−1.68[c]	−2.09[c]	−2.24[c]
(1932–1985)	(.296)	(.512)	(.542)	(.391)	(.466)
Period 4	.868[a]	1.17	1.25	.525	1.08
(1947–1985)	(.469)	(.786)	(.827)	(.658)	(.721)
Period 5	.011	−.304	−.372	.191	−.215
(1955–1985)	(.518)	(.858)	(.920)	(.706)	(.791)
Scale parameter	—	1.67	—	2.70	1.37
		(.103)		(.155)	(.083)
Shape parameter	—	—	2.00	−.961	—
			(.152)	(.315)	
Log-likelihood	−671.10	−626.81	−644.09	−604.93	−616.61
Number of cases	621	621	621	621	621
Number of events	191	191	191	191	191

Note: Figures in parentheses are asymptotic standard errors.
a. $p < .10$.
b. $p < .05$.
c. $p < .01$.

age. Note that the Weibull model fits significantly better than the exponential model.[3] So with this particular model the null hypothesis of age independence, conditional on the covariates, is rejected decisively.

Next we consider what happens when we add unobserved heterogene-

3. The likelihood ratio test of the Weibull model of age dependence against the exponential model of age independence equals 88.6 with one degree of freedom, which is significant at the .01 level.

ity. We begin with a pure gamma model (8.14) which implies that the apparent age dependence reflects the observed covariates and period effects as well as a set of unobserved differences among organizations that have a gamma distribution. The third column in Table 10.1 contains estimates of this model. Although this model represents a significant improvement over the exponential model, it does not fit nearly as well as the Weibull model.

Since both the Weibull and the gamma models improve over the exponential model, we are especially interested to learn what happens when we estimate a model that includes both real aging and unobserved heterogeneity. Will the apparent age dependence disappear in such a model? The answer can be found in column 4, which reports estimates of the generalized gamma model. This model does indeed improve the fit significantly compared to the Weibull model.[4] So introducing unobserved heterogeneity with a gamma distribution into a Weibull model with these covariates gives a better representation of the process at the cost of a single degree of freedom. However, introducing the unobserved heterogeneity does not eliminate age dependence. A 95 percent confidence interval around the ML estimate of the Weibull scale parameter does not include unity, the value under the null model of an age-independent gamma model. So adding unobserved heterogeneity does not eliminate age dependence—it actually makes it stronger.

The ML estimate of the scale parameter in column 4 of Table 10.1 is $1/2.70 = .37$. Figure 10.5 illustrates the average age dependence in the disbanding process implied by this estimate.[5] Age dependence in the disbanding rate has been considerable in substantive terms as well as in terms of statistical significance. For example, the figure shows that the implied rate of disbanding at 2.5 years of age is only half the rate at one year. That is, surviving from age one to age three reduces a union's disbanding rate by half. Even when observable and unobservable causes of disbandings are taken into account, there is still a substantial liability of newness.

Next we consider the possibility that the rate has a non-monotonic relationship with age. Two previous studies of mortality of labor unions report that mortality rates for unions in the service sector (Langton 1984) and for

---

4. The likelihood ratio test of the model in column 4 against its special case in column 2, that is the null hypothesis that $k = 1$ (no unobservable heterogeneity), equals 43.7 with one degree of freedom, which is significant at the .01 level.

5. More precisely, it plots the age dependence at the mean of the distribution of the unobservables.

RATE OF DISBANDING

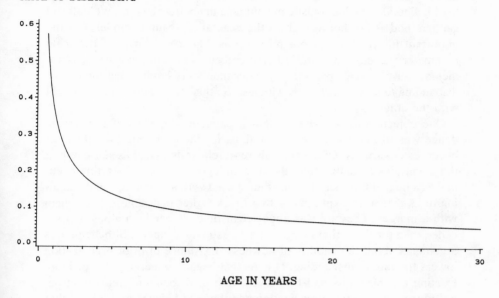

Figure 10.5 Estimated Weibull disbanding rate

unions affiliated with the Knights of Labor (Carroll and Huo 1988) declined with age but were *lower* during the first year than in subsequent years. The possibility that mortality rates are low during the first year makes sense in the case of voluntary associations like labor unions. National unions usually hold annual conventions at which results for the year and prospects for the next year are evaluated. If a union has fared poorly during its initial year, the lack of success becomes particularly apparent at the time of the first convention (the end of the first year). When representatives return to report to the locals, their bad news probably spreads discouragement and speeds the demise of the union.

We noted in Chapter 8 that the log-logistic model is a useful one for exploring these questions because it can imply either monotonic or non-monotonic age dependence depending on the value of the shape parameter. In particular, it implies a non-monotonic pattern of age dependence if the scale parameter is less than unity (or equivalently if $\rho > 1$; see equation 8.16). Since none of the models other than the exponential is a special case of the log-logistic model, we cannot construct a likelihood ratio test of this model against the Weibull or generalized gamma model. Judging from the log-likelihoods, the log-logistic in column 5 fits better than the Weibull and gamma models but not as well as the generalized gamma model. But the important information for our purposes is that the estimate of the scale parameter exceeds unity. Indeed, a 95 percent confidence interval does not include unity. A scale parameter greater than unity implies that the rate of disbanding *falls monotonically* with age. So this model agrees qualitatively with the others.

One objective of this search among parametric models of age dependence was to find useful representations for incorporating the effects of observed covariates. Of course, this research strategy makes sense only if the covariates actually affect the disbanding rate. Type of starting event makes a huge difference. Unions that started with a founding had disbanding rates that were exp(2.92) = 18.5 times higher than unions that began with a merger. The rate was about eight times larger for unions that seceded than for those that merged. These estimates support Stinchcombe's arguments about the liability of newness. Existence of prior organization lowers the rate of disbanding. Unions that began by merging two or more existing organizations had the lowest rate of disbanding; those that seceded from an existing organization had the next lowest. And unions that started from scratch as national organizations had the highest disbanding rates.

Although only two of the periods differ significantly from the baseline period running from 1836 to 1886, these differences are also large. Unions that began during the second period, from the start of the American Federation of Labor in 1886 to the start of the New Deal, had disbanding rates about twice as high as those formed during the preceding 50 years. Unions that started during the third period, the New Deal, had disbanding rates that were only a tenth as large as for those formed during the baseline period.

The effect of another covariate, initial size of the union, has special interest. As we mentioned earlier, previous research suggests that the apparent liability of newness may really be a liability of smallness, because new organizations tend to be small and small organizations typically have high mortality rates. If initial size is not considered explicitly, small organizations may exit from the population rapidly, driving the average rate in the population down. This is another instance of the general problem that unobserved heterogeneity may give the appearance of negative age dependence in transition rates.

Does age dependence persist when we adjust for the size of each union at the time of founding? In order to answer this question, we use data on size of membership in (or near) each union's initial year, as in the FCH study. Complete information on variations in size after founding is unavailable for many unions. However, given the importance of variations at early ages, use of initial size probably does not seriously limit the scope of our analysis. Even with the use of this more limited measure, cases are lost because initial size is known for only 507 of the 621 unions (this number excludes the 12 unions in the Trade Union Unity League, as noted in Chapter 7).

FCH argued that increasing size affects rates of disbanding at a decreasing rate—that there are diminishing returns to initial scale. They estimated models in which the relationship between size and the rate of disbanding (and merger) was a power function:

$$r(t \mid S_0) = S_0^\beta r^*(t),$$

where S_0 is initial size and $r^*(t)$ is the rate implied by age dependence and the effects of the covariates. FCH found that initial size had a negative and significant effect on the rate of disbanding and a negative but insignificant effect on the rate of merger.

We use the same specification of the effect of initial size here. We add the logarithm of initial size to the vector of covariates for the generalized gamma model, which has the best fit of the models considered. Since the covariates are constrained to affect the rate log-linearly, this is equivalent to specifying a "power law" relationship between size and the rate of disbanding.

Table 10.2 reports results on the effect of initial size. The first question is whether the subset of cases for which size is known differs systematically from the others. The first column shows that estimating the model in the fourth column of Table 10.1, using only the cases for which initial size is known, produces estimates that are quite similar to those in column 4 of Table 10.1. Although the presence of information on initial size is unlikely to be random, it does not appear that the process of interest differs substantially for the set of unions for which size is known.

The second column in Table 10.2 shows that adding size improves the fit significantly.[6] The point estimate of the effect of size, which differs signifi-

---

6. The likelihood ratio test against the comparable model without size effects in column 1 equals 4.5 with one degree of freedom, which is significant at the .05 level.

Table 10.2.   ML estimates of generalized gamma models of disbanding rates of labor unions with effects of initial size of membership

Independent variable	Model		
	(1)	(2)	(3)
Intercept	−6.13[c]	−7.38[c]	−8.82[c]
	(.790)	(.991)	(1.48)
Founding	2.79[c]	3.04[c]	4.98[c]
	(.591)	(.595)	(1.55)
Secession	1.55[b]	1.61[b]	1.73[c]
	(.676)	(.666)	(.668)
Period 2	.930[c]	.776[b]	.797[b]
(1896–1985)	(.326)	(.330)	(.327)
Period 3	−2.36[c]	−2.44[c]	−2.48[c]
(1932–1985)	(.450)	(.444)	(.440)
Period 4	−.663	−.555	−.578
(1947–1985)	(.739)	(.726)	(.712)
Period 5	−.161	−.196	−.306
(1955–1985)	(.793)	(.774)	(.761)
Log-size	—	.179[b]	—
		(.085)	
Log-size × founding	—	—	.119
			(.094)
Log-size × (1 − founding)	—	—	.359[b]
			(.156)
Scale parameter	2.84	2.80	2.78
	(.178)	(.175)	(.174)
Shape parameter	−1.30	−1.36	−1.43
	(.372)	(.361)	(.363)
Log-likelihood	−474.56	−472.31	−471.40
Number of cases	507	507	507
Number of events	146	146	146

Note: Figures in parentheses are asymptotic standard errors.
a. $p < .10$.
b. $p < .05$.
c. $p < .01$.

cantly from zero at the .05 level, is *positive*—it indicates that initially large unions had higher disbanding rates than smaller ones. This result is the opposite of what FCH found using the subpopulation of large and successful unions.

Because unions that began by merger and secession were much bigger initially on average than those that began with a founding, we explored the possibility that the effects of size differ by type of starting event. The third column in Table 10.2 reports estimates of a model with two effects of size, one for unions that began with a founding and one for unions that began with either a merger or a secession. Using two parameters to represent the effect of size on the disbanding rate does not improve the fit significantly at even the .10 level. Still, the point estimates provide interesting information. The effect of size is positive, strong, and significantly greater than zero for unions that began by merger or secession. The effect is smaller and insignificant, though still positive, for unions that began by founding. These results suggest that initial size did not have much impact on the disbanding rates of newly founded unions but that very big unions created by mergers and secessions faced a strong liability. Perhaps the combination of large membership size and ill-formed organizational routines and structures was especially destabilizing.

From the perspective of this chapter, the most important results in Table 10.2 concern age dependence. Here the pattern is clear: introducing size dependence does not diminish the strength of age dependence. The estimated scale parameters in columns 2 and 3 in Table 10.2 imply that the Weibull parameter is approximately 0.36, which is very close to the level estimated for the entire population without controls for initial size. We conclude that the liability of newness is not an artifact due to omission of initial size (or attributes strongly correlated with initial size) from models for mortality rates.

Rates of Absorption

Absorption by another union, with the implied loss of organization, was the second most common ending event for national labor unions. The ML estimate of the constant rate of absorption is 0.08, which implies a half-life to absorption of 86 years. Figure 10.6 plots the integrated rate of absorption by age. Age dependence is again apparent in the nonlinearity of this plot, although the nonlinearity is less pronounced than in the case of disbanding.

INTEGRATED RATE OF ABSORPTION

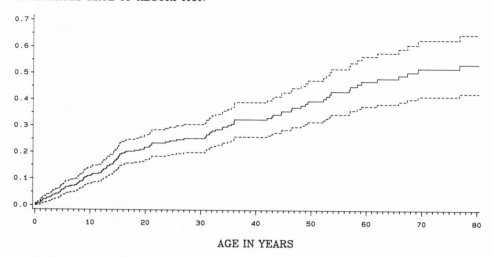

Figure 10.6 Integrated rate of absorption of unions by age (dashed lines indicate 95% confidence interval)

Table 10.3 reports estimates of the models for the rate of absorption that parallel those used for rates of disbanding. Again the Weibull model, which allows the absorption rate to vary with age, improves significantly over the exponential model of age independence. The estimated scale parameter for the Weibull model in column 2 implies that the rate decreases slowly with age—the ML estimate of ρ is $1/1.15 = .87$. According to this estimate, the implied age dependence is much less severe than for disbanding.

Unlike the case of disbanding, the pure gamma model of unobserved heterogeneity in the rate of absorption does not improve significantly over the exponential model. Yet the generalized gamma model, which adds unobserved heterogeneity to the Weibull model of age dependence, does fit significantly better than the pure Weibull model. According to the estimates in the fourth column of Table 10.3, the Weibull parameter (ρ) in this complicated model is $1/1.84 = .54$. This means that the rate drops with age even when the effects of unobservables are taken into account. The ML estimate of the gamma shape parameter (.01) implies that there is a large variance in ending times around the distribution implied by the Weibull model.

Table 10.3. ML estimates of models of age dependence in rates of absorption of labor unions, 1836–1985

Independent variable	Exponential	Weibull	Gamma	Generalized gamma	Log-logistic
Intercept	−5.19[c]	−5.33[c]	−5.29[c]	−5.25[c]	−5.06[c]
	(.376)	(.438)	(.412)	(.502)	(.462)
Founding	−.030	−.054	−.058	.029	−.013
	(.275)	(.315)	(.297)	(.363)	(.334)
Secession	.537[a]	.581	.512	.915[b]	.818[b]
	(.315)	(.362)	(.339)	(.445)	(.395)
Period 2	.266	.267	.259	.273	.304
(1896–1985)	(.288)	(.331)	(.311)	(.366)	(.350)
Period 3	.330	.334	.343	.322	.309
(1932–1985)	(.215)	(.246)	(.232)	(.283)	(.265)
Period 4	.321	.319	.285	.601	.493
(1947–1985)	(.366)	(.420)	(.400)	(.482)	(.462)
Period 5	−.894	−1.11[a]	−1.01	−1.48[b]	−1.29[b]
(1955–1985)	(.550)	(.642)	(.621)	(.637)	(.636)
Scale parameter	—	1.15	—	1.84	1.02
		(.079)		(.327)	(.070)
Shape parameter	—	—	1.17	.010	—
			(.114)	(.408)	
Log-likelihood	−447.55	−445.41	−446.38	−442.09	−443.26
Number of cases	621	621	621	621	621
Number of events	140	140	140	140	140

Note: Figures in parentheses are asymptotic standard errors.
a. $p < .10$.
b. $p < .05$.
c. $p < .01$.

The substantive case for a non-monotonic pattern of age dependence is stronger in the case of absorption (and the case of equal-status merger, discussed in the following section) than for disbandings. It presumably takes time for these organizational agreements to be worked out and to take effect. Leaders must negotiate agreements, and the membership typically must ratify the agreements before the actual absorption (or merger) takes place. So it would not be surprising if the rate were low initially and then rose with age for a period before beginning its decline with further aging.

Again, we explore the possibility that the absorption rate is low initially, rises with age, and then declines by using the log-logistic model. The fifth column in Table 10.3 reports ML estimates of this model. Note that the log-logistic model fits better than the Weibull model and almost as well as the generalized gamma model (which has one additional parameter). But the estimated scale parameter is very close to unity and its standard error is large, which means that we cannot reject the null hypothesis that the scale parameter equals unity. At the value of unity, the log-logistic model implies *monotonic* decline from the level implied by the exponential function of the covariates. So there is no suggestion here that the scenario painted above actually characterized the absorption process for unions. We conclude that there was substantial age dependence in the rate of absorption and that this dependence was monotonic-negative. The liability of newness apparently characterized the absorption process as well as the disbanding process.

Effects of several covariates deserve mention. Unions that began with foundings did not differ much, if at all, in absorption rates from those that began with mergers. However, unions that started as secessions were significantly more likely to be absorbed. This makes sense in the context of labor history. Numerous secessions took place over struggles for leadership and over political programs. Seceding groups could sometimes be reincorporated easily into the original union once the disputes had cooled, especially if the protagonists in the original dispute had lost power.

Only one of the periods differs systematically from the baseline: the rate of absorption seems to have dropped sharply during the most recent period. The rate from 1955 to 1985 was only about a fifth as large as during the preceding period.

What happens when we add initial size? Table 10.4 reports our findings. Again the first column reports estimates of the baseline generalized gamma model for the restricted set of cases for which initial size is known. The second column shows the effect of adding size to the model. As was the case for the rate of disbanding, initial size has a strong effect on the rate of absorption. But this time the effect is *negative*: the rate of absorption for initially large unions was significantly lower than the rate for small ones. Column 3 replaces the single measure of size with separate ones for unions that began with foundings and those that began with some other kind of event. As was the case in our analysis of disbandings, this model does not

Table 10.4.   ML estimates of generalized gamma model of absorption of labor unions with effects of initial membership

Independent variable	Model		
	(1)	(2)	(3)
Intercept	−5.27[c]	−4.40[c]	−3.59[c]
	(.370)	(.518)	(.731)
Founding	−.032	−.187	−1.43[a]
	(.307)	(.303)	(.859)
Secession	.412	.326	.278
	(.384)	(.370)	(.371)
Period 2	.570[b]	.660[b]	.614[b]
(1896–1985)	(.266)	(.295)	(.262)
Period 3	.131	.289	.280
(1932–1985)	(.283)	(.277)	(.278)
Period 4	.321	.327	.374
(1947–1985)	(.468)	(.453)	(.454)
Period 5	−.710	−.670	−.608
(1955–1985)	(.583)	(.589)	(.586)
Log-size	—	−1.28[b]	—
		(.059)	
Log-size × founding	—	—	−.058
			(.073)
Log-size × (1 − founding)	—	—	−.229[c]
			(.087)
Scale parameter	1.43	1.26	1.25
	(.322)	(.356)	(.361)
Shape parameter	.208	.452	.457
	(.457)	(.483)	(.510)
Log-likelihood	−302.46	−300.11	−298.90
Number of cases	507	507	507
Number of events	100	100	100

Note: Figures in parentheses are asymptotic standard errors.
a. $p < .10$.
b. $p < .05$.
c. $p < .01$.

improve significantly over the model with a single effect of initial size. Nevertheless, the point estimates are again interesting from a substantive perspective. Initial size does not have a significant effect on the absorption rate for unions that began with foundings. However, initial size does have a strong, significant effect for unions that began with mergers or secessions. Most important, adding initial size to the model does not eliminate the apparent age dependence in the rate of absorption. Taking into account the fact that initially larger unions were much less likely to be absorbed, the absorption rate still falls with age.

Rate of Equal-Status Merger

The third kind of *organizational* mortality for labor unions is the merger between two (or more) national unions of roughly equal status that creates a new national union combining the structures into one. The ML estimate of the (constant) rate of merger is 0.08, essentially the same as the rate of absorption. Figure 10.7 reports the estimated integrated rate of equal-status merger by age. Again a pattern of age dependence is apparent in the nonlinearity of this plot. The rate during the early years seems higher than in later years. The pattern resembles that for absorption and is again weaker than for disbanding.

Table 10.5 reports ML estimates of models of the rate of equal-status merger. Since the pattern of effects is fairly similar to those just discussed for absorption, we do not discuss them in detail.[7] According to the Weibull model, the rate of equal-status merger declines with age.

While the pure gamma model fits about as well as the Weibull model, we never succeeded in obtaining estimates of the generalized gamma model for this outcome. So we do not have any formal way to examine whether the merger process reflects both a liability of newness of the Weibull form and unobservable heterogeneity.

As was the case for the other two rates, the estimated log-logistic model implies that the rate of equal-status merger declines monotonically with age, because the estimated scale parameter exceeds unity. Therefore, as in the case of the other two rates, we conclude that labor unions have faced a liability of newness with respect to the merger process and that this liability falls monotonically with age.

---

7. A more detailed account can be found in Hannan (1988b).

INTEGRATED RATE OF MERGER

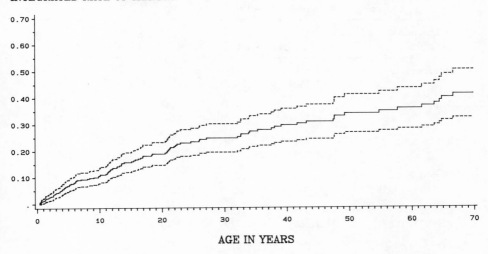

AGE IN YEARS

Figure 10.7   Integrated rate of equal-status merger by age (dashed lines indicate 95% confidence interval)

Comparisons with Previous Findings

This replication of the FCH analysis of age dependence in the mortality of national labor unions finds one major consistency with the earlier work and one major difference. The consistency concerns the main question. The research reported here agrees with FCH that Stinchcombe (1965) was right—the demography of national labor unions has been characterized by a strong liability of newness. This liability of newness applies to the overall process of mortality and to each of the three component processes: disbanding, absorption, and merger.

The divergence from FCH concerns the effects of size on mortality. Although both studies found that the liability of newness was not primarily a liability of smallness, the findings about the effects of size differ considerably. FCH found that larger unions had smaller rates of disbanding; the present research finds the opposite pattern. FCH found no significant effect of size on the merger rate; the present study, which uses more complete data, finds that size has strong and significant effects on one component of the overall merger rate, the rate of absorption into other unions. Larger unions had significantly lower rates of absorption than smaller

Table 10.5. ML estimates of age dependence in the rate of equal-status merger of unions, 1836–1985

Independent variable	Exponential	Weibull	Gamma	Log-logistic	Weibull
Intercept	−4.62[c]	−4.69[c]	−4.82[c]	−4.25[c]	−4.07[c]
	(.250)	(.308)	(.405)	(.366)	(.555)
Founding	−.481[b]	−.631[b]	−.584[b]	−.690[b]	−.716[b]
	(.242)	(.304)	(.286)	(.347)	(.312)
Secession	.181	.150	.170	.083	.207
	(.293)	(.360)	(.332)	(.413)	(.354)
Period 2	.096	.007	.079	−.060	.015
(1896–1985)	(.205)	(.254)	(.328)	(.283)	(.261)
Period 3	.093	−.133	−.116	−.126	.017
(1932–1985)	(.268)	(.329)	(.300)	(.348)	(.353)
Period 4	.037	−.028	−.012	−.053	.211
(1947–1985)	(.500)	(.614)	(.603)	(.628)	(.609)
Period 5	.202	.113	.164	.029	.077
(1955–1985)	(.572)	(.703)	(.694)	(.707)	(.683)
Log-size	—	—	—	—	−.079
					(.066)
Scale parameter	—	1.23	—	1.12	1.19
		(.089)		(.08)	(.092)
Shape parameter	—	—	1.31	—	—
			(.118)		
Log-likelihood	−439.29	−434.99	−435.24	−435.53	−385.44
Number of cases	621	621	621	621	507
Number of events	130	130	130	130	120

Note: Figures in parentheses are asymptotic standard errors.
a. $p < .10$.
b. $p < .05$.
c. $p < .01$.

ones. However, this research finds no strong evidence that size affected the rate of equal-status merger.

Interestingly, initial size did not affect any of the rates for unions that began with a founding, according to our estimates. The significant positive effect of size on the disbanding rate and the significant negative effect of size on the absorption rate seem to have held mainly for unions that began with a merger or a secession. Perhaps large unions starting through such processes tend to be weak. Since large unions can only be absorbed by other large unions, a big union in trouble is more likely to disappear through disbanding than through merger.

The set of parametric models used here also differs from those used by FCH. While FCH used Gompertz and Makeham models, this research finds that Gompertz models fit data on union lifetimes less well than comparable Weibull models. This research also estimated models that combined unobserved heterogeneity, a generic cause of "spurious age dependence" with aging. Even though adding unobserved heterogeneity (assumed to follow a gamma distribution) typically improves the fit of a Weibull model significantly, it does not eliminate the significant age dependence in these mortality processes. So we have some evidence that the liability of newness concerns real effects of aging rather than simply the early loss of unions with (unobserved) low levels of fitness.

Finally, we explored the reasonable supposition that organizational mortality rates increase with age initially before beginning to decline with aging. We did so using the log-logistic model. Although this model often fit the data as well as the others, estimates of its parameters suggest that the age dependence in these rates was monotonic.

Exits of Semiconductor Manufacturing Firms

Next we consider the lengths of "careers" in the semiconductor industry, the length of time between entry and exit of firms. Limitations on the data preclude an analysis with as much detail as just reported for labor unions. Entries and exits are recorded only at yearly intervals in the data we used; so observed durations in the industry are also aggregated in time. Since more than half the firms in the population had observed durations of three or fewer years in the semiconductor industry, the temporal aggregation is large relative to the time scale of events.[8]

Given the temporal aggregation of these data, we display the qualitative pattern of variation in exit rates with length of time in the industry using the actuarial estimator of the hazard. Figure 10.8 plots the estimated haz-

8. The difference between failures and exits parallels the difference between foundings and exits discussed in Chapter 7. Exits include two kinds of events: failures and semiconductor industry exits. This analysis assumes that the organizational routines necessary for semiconductor production are sufficiently unique that exiting the industry can be viewed as a kind of failure.

INTEGRATED HAZARD

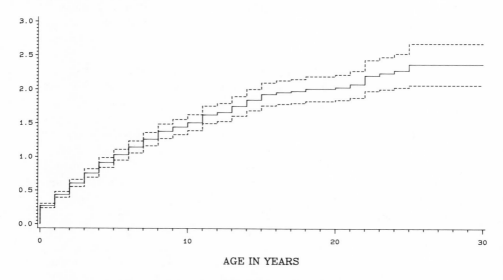

Figure 10.8   Integrated hazard: semiconductor firm mortality (dashed lines
indicate 95% confidence interval)

ard by years in the industry over the observed range. This plot suggests
a pronounced liability of newness. The hazard during the first year in
the industry is considerably larger than for any other year. From this
initial high level, the hazard of exit drops fairly consistently with number
of years in the industry, falling to zero toward the upper end of the observed range. In other words, the rate of exit drops roughly monotonically with time in the industry. There does seem to have been a liability
of newness.

In the spirit of the previous section, we next explore whether the pattern
of decline in the rate agrees with a Gompertz or a Weibull model. Recall
that the Gompertz model implies that the log-hazard is a linear function of
elapsed time and the Weibull implies that it is a linear function of the
logarithm of elapsed time. Figures 10.9 and 10.10 display these two plots.
Both plots seem to fit reasonably well. The correlation is slightly higher for
the relation of the log-hazard to log-time (−.84 versus −.82), but this
difference is too small to form the basis of a choice of specifications.
However, the linear relationship between the log-hazard and elapsed time,
which follows from the Gompertz model, does not fit well in the lower

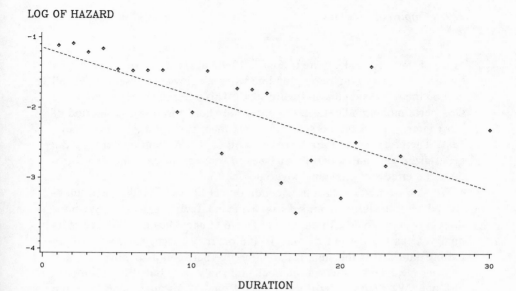

Figure 10.9 Log-hazard of semiconductor firm exiting by duration

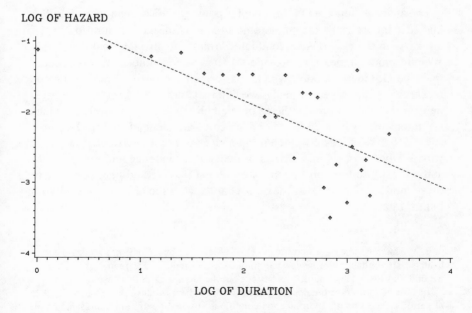

Figure 10.10 Log-hazard of semiconductor firm exiting by log-duration

range of the time scale. Note in Figure 10.9 that the first five observations (in time) fall above the regression line whereas the same observations fall around the regression line in Figure 10.10. This difference suggests that the Gompertz model understates the hazard at short durations, the period of most interest from the perspective of arguments about a liability of newness. Therefore we use an approximation of the Weibull model (and the generalized gamma model) in analyses in subsequent chapters that introduce the effects of changing covariates.[9]

We also wanted to learn how conditions at time of founding and unobserved heterogeneity combined with aging in affecting exit rates. We have done this in two ways. In one, we assigned to each firm the midyear of its final year as the date of exiting. In the other, we assigned each firm an exiting date that is the sum of the difference between its exiting year and entering year and a random number uniformly distributed between zero and one. We then applied the variety of models discussed earlier in the chapter to these two sets of observations. The two analyses agree that the generalized gamma model fits significantly better than any of its special cases. In particular, the results tell that there was substantial unobserved variation in exit rates and a strong liability of newness.[10]

The analyses reported in this chapter point in a fairly clear direction. We find that failure rates are monotonic functions of age (or duration in the industry, in the case of semiconductor firms). We also find that the simple Weibull model appears to provide a better representation of this process than the Gompertz model, which has formed the basis of most previous research on this subject. Finally, we find that adding unobserved heterogeneity sometimes improves the fit of Weibull models significantly but does not alter conclusions about the presence of age dependence in the rates. We build on these results in the remaining chapters. In particular, we begin with Weibull models in analyses of density dependence and niche width, and we explore the consequences of adding unobserved heterogeneity to these models. We begin in the next chapter with the effects of density on failure rates.

9. We mentioned earlier that Carroll (1987) has relied on a Gompertz model in establishing a strong liability of newness in the newspaper industry. In reanalyzing his data, we find that the Weibull model fits better than the Gompertz in this case as well.

10. We do not report the details of these analyses here because the estimated effects of period effects and of environmental conditions at time of entry are quite sensitive to the assumptions made about the exact timing of exits, which is of course unknown.

11 | The Population Ecology of Organizational Mortality

This chapter explores empirically the effect of population ecology processes on failure rates. It considers different kinds of failure rates in populations of three kinds of organizations: disbandings of national labor unions, exits from the industry by semiconductor firms, and cessation of publication for newspaper publishing firms. The structure of the argument and much of the analysis parallels that of Chapter 9, which considered rates of founding and entry for the same populations. However, because of the added complexity of failure processes, we consider more kinds of effects here. In particular, we study the effects of (1) aging, (2) density, (3) recent failures, (4) organizational characteristics, (5) periods, and (6) environmental conditions. Given the theoretical importance of density dependence, we organize much of the discussion and analysis of these factors within the context of models for the effects of density on failure rates.

As we discussed at length in Part I, we have conceptualized and measured the density of organizational populations in terms of the *number of organizations in the population*. The arguments in Chapter 6 imply that the effect of density on failure rates is non-monotonic. We suggest that legitimation processes cause the rate to fall with increasing density in the lower range but that competition processes eventually cause the rate to rise with increasing density, when levels of relevant resources have been taken into account. In other words, we predict that the failure rate falls with increasing density up to a point (the neighborhood of the carrying capacity) and then rises with increasing density. We specified this process using models of the general form:

$$(11.1) \quad \mu_p(u) = u^{\rho-1} \cdot \exp(\beta_1 N_u + \beta_2 N_u^2) \cdot \exp(\boldsymbol{\pi}' \mathbf{x}_u + \phi_p),$$

where $\mu_p(u)$ is the failure rate of an organization of age u during period p. N_u is the number of organizations in the population at the beginning of the year in which the organization reaches age u, $\mathbf{x}_u$ is a set of relevant organizational characteristics and environmental conditions measured at that time, and ϕ_p are a set of period effects. Note that we use a Weibull representation of aging, based on the results of the previous chapter.

Our model of opposing processes of legitimation and competition implies that

(11.2) $\beta_1 < 0$ and $\beta_2 > 0$,

and that the values of these parameters are such that the function relating mortality rates to density actually changes from negative to positive within the range of variation in density observed. That is, our prediction is that the function has a U-shape over the history of the population. So the first set of questions explored here concerns the implications of this model. Does density have a non-monotonic effect on failure rates in populations of labor unions, semiconductor manufacturing firms, and newspaper firms? And do such effects hold when effects of aging, organizational characteristics, environmental conditions, and periods are controlled?

We also examine the effects of recent mortality experience on the mortality rate. We have learned that founding (and entry) rates varied with the number of recent foundings (or entries) for all three populations. It appears that potential organization-builders regard a surge in foundings as a sign that the times are propitious for new ventures. Is there a parallel effect on the failure rate? Perhaps a wave of failures signals that times are bad for the organizational form, thereby making it more difficult to obtain resources from other organizations. That is, a high level of mortality may accelerate processes of decline, thereby increasing the failure rate. Does this kind of process characterize failure rates in the three populations?

We explore this question by adding a count of the number of failures in the previous calendar year to models with the form of (11.1). We predict that the effect of the number of recent failures on the rate is positive.[1] In

---

1. As we noted in Chapter 9, support for such a hypothesis does not unambiguously confirm the notion that waves of failures accelerate processes of decline by diminishing chances of obtaining resources. Perhaps some unobserved factors operate similarly over adjacent years—the factors that caused last year's rate to be high also cause this year's rate to be high. In either case, adjusting for the effect of recent failures will improve the quality of estimates of density dependence.

addition, we have also tried adding the square of the number of recent failures in order to allow rate dependence to be non-monotonic.

In addition to studying the effects of these processes at the population level, we also consider the effects of organizational characteristics, environmental factors, and period effects on failure rates. Of course, different organizational characteristics, environmental factors, and periods are relevant for unions, semiconductor firms, and newspapers. We discuss these factors separately in considering each kind of organizational population.

Finally, we study competition between forms by examining the effects of the density of subpopulations on the mortality rates of other subpopulations. We compare these effects of competition within and between subpopulations using models of the form:

$$(11.3) \qquad \mu_{pi}(u) = u^{\rho_i - 1} \cdot \exp(\beta_{1i} N_{iu} + \beta_{2i} N_{iu}^2 + \theta_i N_{ju} + \pi_i' x_u + \phi_p),$$

where $\mu_{pi}(u)$ is the disbanding rate of an organization of age u in the ith population during period p and N_{iu} and N_{ju} are the sizes of the ith and jth populations at the beginning of the year in which the organization in question reached age u.[2]

Disbanding Rates of Labor Unions

We begin with national labor unions. As we have noted in earlier chapters, ecological analysis of unions has special sociological interest because unions have combined elements of social movement and bureaucracy. The fact that unions have often had the character of social movements allows a range of sociological theory to be used in analyzing their life histories in addition to the theories we have emphasized.

We set the stage for our treatment of the life chances of unions by restating the implications of Michels' famous analysis of oligarchical tendencies in labor unions. We suggest that his views can be recast with profit into the framework of organizational ecology. In particular, we suggest that Michels' theory has implications for density dependence in the disbanding rates of labor unions and other kinds of social-movement organizations.

---

2. We have investigated whether adding second-order cross-effects improves the fit of models. For semiconductor firms, the addition of second-order cross-effects improved the model's fit; for the others, it did not.

Many sociological analyses of the labor movement emphasize *organizational* aspects of the history of the labor movement. Much of this literature concentrates on the observation that social movements increase their chances of wide-scale coordinated action by developing formal organizations with differentiated administrative structures and procedures for maintaining flows of resources and taking collective action (Tilly 1978). Although building a permanent organization facilitates collective action, it also imposes constraints on action. The classic statement on the consequences of organization-building for social movements is Michels' thesis of the iron law of oligarchy (1915/1949, p. 70): "Organization implies the tendency to oligarchy. In every organization, whether it be a political party, a professional union, or any other association of the kind, the aristocratic tendency manifests itself very clearly. The mechanism of the organization, while conferring a solidity of structure, induces serious change in the organized mass, completely inverting the position of the leaders and the led."

Subsequent research has shown that Michels' claim of the inevitability of oligarchy in trade unions is not quite an iron law. For example, Lipset, Trow, and Coleman (1956) showed that the International Typographic Union has maintained a competitive two-party system. Yet the ITU stands alone among American unions in having a competitive political structure. Other American unions have exhibited contested politics at various times as insurgent groups challenged leadership. The political turbulence occasioned by such insurgencies gives testimony to the strength of oligopolistic tendencies in the American labor union movement over most of its history.

We concentrate on a less well remembered aspect of Michels' theory (1915/1949, pp. 338–340) as it pertains to unions: "From a means, organization becomes an end . . . The sole preoccupation is to avoid anything that may clog the machinery. Thus the hatred of the party is directed, not in the first place against the opponents of its own view of the world order, but against the dreaded rivals in the political field, against those who are competing for the same end—power . . . Evidently among the trade unions of diverse political coloring, whose primary aim is to gain the greatest possible number of new members, the note of competition will be emphasized more."

This section follows the Michelsian tradition by analyzing the consequences of competition among unions for their life chances. In doing so, it examines unions both as social movements and as organizations. It takes seriously the idea from labor history and social movement research that the life chances of unions have been affected by environmental events that altered the resources available to the union movement and by competition between unions and management. It also uses Michels' notion that competition among unions for members and political power also affected the life chances of unions profoundly. In particular, this section asks whether competition among unions has played a role in stalling the growth of the union movement. It does so by examining the effects of competition among unions on the rates at which unions disbanded.

We recast Michels' views about competition among rival social-movement organizations in ecological terms. However, we think that Michels considered only one side of the process. In our view, rivalry does affect the fates of social-movement organizations when density is high and the field is crowded. Yet this is not the only way in which density affects the life chances of these and other kinds of organizations. We suggest that there are two opposing processes by which density affects life chances: first, growth in numbers in organizational populations provides legitimacy and political power; second, increasing density exhausts limited supplies of resources for building and maintaining organizations and thereby increases both direct and diffuse competition. Our theory holds that the first process dominates at low densities and the second (Michelsian) process dominates at high densities.

The Etiology of Disbandings: Views from Labor History

We begin by reviewing common arguments in labor history about the causes of disbandings. This review provides some institutional context for our ecological analysis, giving numerous concrete examples of the phenomena of interest. It also has implications for the design of our research. We are not interested primarily in evaluating whether these historical claims stand up in the face of systematic comparative analysis. However, we do want to control for the effects of relevant causal factors other than those identified by ecological theory. So this discussion identifies a set of covariates to be used as "control variables" in our analysis and also suggests some potential alternative explanations.

Labor historians sometimes explain union disbandings by alluding to particular catastrophes. These include misjudged or mistimed actions by the union, actions of those in other organizations such as the state or federations of employers, and sharp, unexpected swings in the economy. The most vivid examples of catastrophes involving the actions of unions and their opponents are large, often violent, strikes in which a union is crushed. When the famous Pullman strike occurred in 1894, the radical

American Railway Union had grown to roughly 140,000 members since its founding the year before. The union was destroyed by federal troops enforcing court injunctions. Union leaders were jailed and eventually convicted, and the American Railway Union disbanded. In a recent case, the Professional Air Traffic Controllers Organization, founded in 1970, disbanded in 1982 after striking controllers were fired and replaced at the order of President Reagan.

Some catastrophes involved concerted action by employers and by associations of employers during periods in which unions were weak or public opinion seemed to have turned against them. Taft (1964, pp. 212–229, 361–371) describes widespread employer offensives between 1903 and 1908 (led by the Citizens Industrial Association, the American Anti-Boycott Association, and the National Council of Industrial Defense) and in the period 1919–1929 (with the American Plan of Employment, an open shop campaign mounted by a national conference of state manufacturing associations). Unions such as the Oil and Gas Well Workers (1889–1905) and the Timber Workers (1917–23) have been depicted as victims of the success of these employer offensives (Fink 1977).

Actions by agencies of government also have proved catastrophic to unions at times. An interesting case concerns the Foremen's Association of America, founded in 1941. By 1947 this union had organized 28,000 supervisory employees, mainly in the auto industry. After passage of the Taft–Hartley bill that year, which held that existing labor laws no longer applied to supervisory employees, numerous firms declared their contracts with the Foremen's Association to be void. The union disbanded shortly thereafter. On the other hand, some governmental actions apparently lowered the risk of disbandings. It is widely agreed that the Wagner Act, which institutionalized collective bargaining and legitimized business unions, had such a stabilizing effect.

Many disbandings have been attributed to economic upheavals. During financial panics, such as the panics of 1837, 1853, and 1873, many businesses failed and unemployment surged. Apparently, union members deserted unions in the interest of finding or keeping scarce jobs during these crises.

Labor leaders and scholars have emphasized the role of immigration in disrupting the union movement. Although the pool of immigrant labor provided many labor leaders and large numbers of class-conscious workers, immigration reduced the power of unions by providing a source of cheap (and nonunionized) labor and by supplying a ready pool of strikebreakers (Bonacich 1976). Foner (1975, p. 17) asserts that "all too frequently newly-arrived immigrants of every nationality made their first entrance into American industry as strikebreakers . . . To list the unions weakened or destroyed or the strikes broken in the 'eighties by industry's policy of introducing immigrant labor or strikebreakers would require many pages."

Historians have often argued that such catastrophes destroyed unions that were already vulnerable for other reasons, such as youth, declining membership, and inability to adjust to technical change. The following are the most widely cited causes of long-term decline of the kind that would make unions susceptible to disbanding in the face of environmental catastrophe.

Some unions never developed effective routines for organizing members, collecting dues, and engaging in collective bargaining. Such failure to develop procedures for sustaining an organization made some unions highly vulnerable to internal and external shocks. At least three unions disbanded in rancorous internal conflict after officers embezzled their treasuries: the American Longshoremen's Union (1897–8), the Journeymen Tailors' National Trades Union (1865–76), and the Switchmen's Mutual Aid Association (1886–94).

Inability to adapt to technical change or to control it is often cited as a cause for the downfall of unions that organized a set of named crafts or jobs. As employers adopted new technologies, the distinctions among jobs changed quickly and crafts became obsolete. The titles of some disbanded labor unions from the nineteenth and early twentieth century illustrate the problem: the Horse Collar Makers' National Union (1888–93), the Window Glass Snappers' Union (1902–8), the Associated Brotherhood of Iron and Steel Heaters, Rollers, and Roughers (1872–6), the Brotherhood of Tanners and Furriers (1892–5), the Gold Beaters' Protective Union (1897–1907), and the Union of Shipwrights, Joiners and Caulkers (1902–11).

Even old, successful unions of skilled workers, such as the International Typographic Union (1850–1985), managed only to slow the tide of technical changes that eventually made their crafts obsolete (Wallace and Kalleberg 1982). More typical is the case of the Knights of Saint Crispin (1867–78), the first really large union in the United States. The Knights organized skilled workers in the shoe industry in order to forestall competition from semi-skilled workers ("green hands") on machines. The tactic used to forestall technical change was to prohibit members from offering instruction to green hands in any of the techniques of shoe making. Since machine workers did not need to learn craft skills, the tactic failed. Although the Knights grew very rapidly (its peak membership was estimated to be

50,000 to 80,000), it also declined very quickly when it became apparent that the strategy could not slow the mechanization of shoe making (Lescohier 1910). The combination of organizational inertia and rapid technical change apparently caused the downfall of many craft unions.

Labor historians have also stressed the role of *direct competition*, sometimes called interunion rivalry, as a cause of decline and eventual disbanding or merger (Galenson 1940, 1960). It was common for two or more unions to attempt to organize the same set of workers. Such rivalry was sometimes due to expansion of unions that had begun in different sections of the country; for example, the Western Federation of Miners (1893–1982) competed with the (mainly Eastern) United Mine Workers (1890–1985) before merging with the United Steelworkers. Sometimes the rivalry reflected disagreements over politics or tactics, as in the case of the conservative Journeymen Tailors' Union (1883–1914) and the mainly socialist Tailors' National Progressive Union (1885–9). At other times a national federation created an affiliated union to compete with an independent union. For example, the American Federation of Labor created the American Federation of Musicians (1896–1985) to compete with the National League of Musicians (1886–1904) after the NLM repeatedly refused to affiliate with the AFL.

Another kind of head-to-head competition pitted craft unions against industrial unions and against unions that organized multiple crafts, the so-called compound craft unions (Ulman 1955). For example, as mentioned in Chapter 7, the United Brotherhood of Carpenters and Joiners (1881–1985) claimed jurisdiction over all wood workers. The UBC fought jurisdictional battles with and raided the membership of unions such as the International Union of Timber Workers (1917–23), the Furniture Makers' Union (1873–95), the Laborers International Union (1903–85), the Association of Sheet Metal Workers (1888–1985), the Alliance of Theatrical Stage Employees and Moving Machine Operators (1893–1985), the Woodcarvers' Association (1883–1945), and the International Woodworkers of America (1936–85). Interestingly, even though the UBC was a major element in the AFL, it took most of these actions over the strong objections of the federation (see Christie 1956).

Much rival unionism involved competition between national federations promoting different forms of unionization. The most important example was the competition of the Congress of Industrial Organizations, a federation of industrial unions, with the American Federation of Labor, a federation of craft unions. After the founding of the CIO within the AFL in 1936 and its expulsion in 1938, the CIO was instrumental in founding industrial unions to compete with AFL unions (Galenson 1940, 1960). For example, the CIO created the United Paperworkers' International Union (1944–57) to compete with the AFL-affiliated Brotherhood of Paper Makers (1902–57) and the Retail, Wholesale, and Department Store Union (1937–79) to compete with the Retail Clerks' International Association (1890–1979). Sometimes jurisdictional struggles and raids on memberships of rival unions were resolved by a merger of the competing parties. However, in many cases one of the competitors was destroyed and its members absorbed individually.

Population Ecology Analysis

Historical accounts of disbandings are useful for identifying factors that appear to affect union mortality. But they are not appropriate for assessing competing arguments about the causal structure. Meaningful causal analysis requires study of unions that faced comparable catastrophes and did not disband. That is, restricting analysis to unions that disbanded distorts causal inferences about the causes of disbanding. This is a clear instance of sample selection bias (Heckman 1979; Berk 1983). We depart from the labor history tradition by analyzing the entire population of national unions over the full 150-year historical period. This strategy avoids problems of selectivity bias and permits consideration of the joint operation of the various hypothesized causes of disbanding.

Our first objective is to learn whether density affected disbanding rates in the predicted non-monotonic manner. Figure 11.1 shows variation in the yearly count of disbandings over the period. As in the case of union foundings (Figure 9.1), the peak occurs in the middle of the series. Given the strong liability of newness, this is not surprising. Periods of peak foundings will tend to be followed by periods of high rates of disbandings as a result of the presence of many youthful organizations. As we insisted in the previous chapter, the effect of aging must be taken into account in assessing the effects of density and other factors.

Effects of aging are included in all models estimated in this section. Given the findings of the previous chapter, we use a Weibull model of age dependence. More precisely, we use a step-function approximation to the Weibull model. This approximation uses the logarithm of age at the beginning of each year as a covariate in the log-linear model. We break each union's entire history into P_i periods, where P_i is the completed age of the union in years, and we update the union's age (and all time-varying covariates) at the beginning of each year. In other words, the history of a union

DISBANDINGS

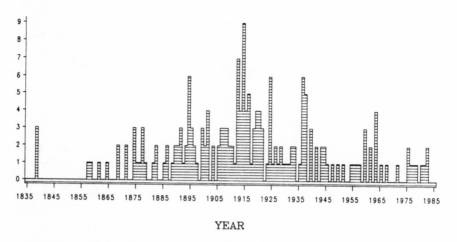

YEAR

Figure 11.1   Labor union disbandings by year

that existed for 15 years is represented by 15 spells.[3] Let p denote the union's age at the beginning of each of these spells. Then we approximate the Weibull model of age dependence with

$$\mu(p) = \lambda p^\alpha, \qquad p = 1, \ldots, P_i.$$

To a reasonable approximation, $\alpha = \rho - 1$, where ρ is the parameter of the Weibull model defined in Chapter 8.

Properties of individual unions considered include the type of starting event. We distinguish unions that began with foundings and those that began with secessions from those that began with mergers (the excluded category). In addition, we construct simple measures of each union's form. These are dummy variables that distinguish: (1) craft unions (those that organized on the basis of occupation or craft) from industrial unions, (2)

---

3. This procedure does not change the number of events since each spell but the last is censored on the right. The ML estimators we use handle such multiple spells per case in a natural way (see Tuma and Hannan 1984).

unions whose target membership consisted solely of unskilled and semi-skilled workers from those that organized at least some skilled workers, and (3) independent unions from those that belonged to any of the national federations such as the AFL and CIO. Because these characteristics can and do change over the lifetime of a union, we treat them as *time-varying* covariates. Their values were updated at the beginning of each year for each union. In addition to these characteristics, we also explore the effects of each union's initial membership size.

We also include the effects of conditions in the economic and political environments. Our records on foundings, mergers, and disbandings of unions begin in 1836, more than 20 years before the first census of business and manufacturing. Even when such censuses began in 1859, coverage of firms and establishments was spotty and accuracy of information was doubtful. Still, as we argued earlier, it is crucial to include information on disbanding rates for the full period. Our insistence on using the full 1836–1985 period places strong constraints on choice of measures of environmental conditions. The set of measures used is listed below. Unless noted otherwise, the source is the U.S. Bureau of the Census, especially *The Historical Statistics on the United States: Colonial Times to 1970*.

Economic catastrophes are measured with an index that identifies depression years, taken mainly from Thorp and Mitchell (1926). This measure records eight depressions during the 1836–1899 period and four between 1900 and 1985. Other measures of swings in general economic conditions include the number of business failures (1857–1984), the unemployment rate (1890–1984), gross national product per capita (1889–1984), and the real wage rate of common laborers (1836–1974), taken from David and Solar (1977).

Some analyses of labor union history have stressed the importance of the rise of a *national* market for the success of national unions. It is difficult to find indicators of the nationalization of economic activity over this long period. We have tried to address these issues by considering the effects of the extension of transportation services essential to the rise of national markets. The relevant transportation indicators change from period to period—first canals, then railroads, then interstate trucking and airlines. Because the crucial period of the expansion of the union movement occurred during the railroad era, we focused on the expansion of this form of transportation, using a measure of miles of railroad track constructed per year. Unfortunately the available series, which begins before 1836, has a gap between 1880 and 1893 and ends in 1925. So use of this indicator leads to a major loss of observations. This does not appear to be a serious problem, however, because other indicators such as GNP and the period effects are likely to pick up the effects of major changes in the speed and cost of transportation and communication.

Technical change and intensification of production are measured on the basis of capital investment in plant and machinery (1863–1971) and patents issued for inventions (1836–1984). We also use a measure of the total yearly flow of immigrants (1836–1984) as well as year-to-year changes in levels of immigration in some analyses. Our data do not contain information about the timing of strikes for a particular union. Instead, we used a measure of aggregate strike activity: number of strikes in a year (1881–1980).

We also explore the effects of historical periods. Claims that the political and economic structures facing unions changed qualitatively at certain points in history are addressed by using "period effects." That is, we specified models that allow the rate to shift at certain specified dates. We have tried several sets of periods. Most do not improve the fit of the models significantly (at the .10 level) over models that contain the other covariates of interest (including density, age, and type of founding). Nonetheless, we include a set of period effects in all models we estimated in order to ensure that the estimated effects of density do not reflect unobserved effects of secular changes in the society or of changes in the legal and political standing of unions. The analysis reported below breaks the 150-year history into the same five periods used in previous chapters.

We also used period effects to deal with the claim that coordinated nationwide offensives by employers raised disbanding rates. Although it is difficult to find agreement on the precise dates of these offensives, it seems clear that the peak periods were 1903–1908, the period of a national "open shop" drive, and 1919–1929, the period of the so-called "American Plan of Employment" campaign led by the National Association of Manufacturers (see especially Taft 1964, pp. 212–229, 361–371). We constructed a dummy variable that distinguished years of these employer offensives from other years. Finally, we also used period effects to deal with the possibility that wartime conditions affected the life chances of unions. We used periods that distinguished years during the Civil War, the two world wars, the Korean War, and the Vietnam War as well as periods that distinguished only the two world wars (during which unions were given a relatively protected status under wartime production controls).

As in analysis of foundings, density is measured as the number of unions in existence at the beginning of each calender year. The count of recent disbandings is the number of disbandings recorded in the previous calender year.

Estimation

In order to allow values of the covariates to vary over the lifetimes of unions, we broke each union's history into a sequence of yearly spells. The histories of the 621 unions (which number excludes the 12 Trade Union Unity League unions) provide 17,896 spells. Only 191 of them end with a disbanding; the rest are censored on the right. Age and the values of all covariates are updated at the beginning of each year for each union. However, all covariates are constant within years.

In some analyses, we also added a gamma-distributed disturbance term to the Weibull model in order to represent the effects of unobservable heterogeneity. That is, we estimated generalized gamma models. Surprisingly, we found that this more complicated model did not improve the fit significantly at even the .10 level over the Weibull model. Apparently the set of covariates in our models does an adequate job of picking up the main heterogeneity in the population. Therefore, we rely on the Weibull model.[4]

Results

We begin analysis with a baseline model that includes the effects of aging, type of starting event, waves of disbandings, and several environmental factors. Then we add density dependence to the baseline. Next we add other characteristics of the individual union as covariates. Finally, we explore the consequences of altering the representation of environmental processes.

The estimates of the baseline model appear in the first column of Table 11.1. The effect of aging is strong, as would be expected given the findings of the previous chapter. The estimated scale parameter indicates that the rate of disbanding drops sharply with aging. Even when these various time-varying covariates are included in the model, we continue to find a strong liability of newness.

The first column of Table 11.1 also reports the effects of a core set of covariates. This set includes only those covariates that are available for the whole period (1836–1985), meaning that the estimates of these models use the entire set of observations. In addition, only estimates of those covariates appearing to have systematic effects on the rate are included in the baseline model. These are type of starting event, indicated by the pair of

---

4. The effects of density are insensitive to the specification of age dependence. For example, the estimated effects of density with a Gompertz model are almost identical to those reported here (Hannan and Freeman 1988).

Table 11.1. ML estimates of effects of density on disbanding rates of labor unions, 1836–1985

Independent variable	Model			
	(1)	(2)	(3)	(4)
Intercept	−5.35[c]	−4.56[c]	−4.85[c]	−5.48[c]
	(.609)	(.655)	(.789)	(.816)
$N(t)$	—	−.022[c]	−.023[c]	−.020[b]
		(.007)	(.007)	(.009)
$N^2(t)/1000$	—	.094[c]	.097[c]	.080[b]
		(.036)	(.038)	(.041)
Log-age	−.310[c]	−.311[c]	−.294[c]	−.338[c]
	(.044)	(.044)	(.050)	(.051)
Founding	2.05[c]	2.02[c]	2.27[c]	2.04[c]
	(.583)	(.584)	(.715)	(.589)
Secession	1.45[b]	1.44[b]	1.81[b]	1.22[a]
	(.633)	(.633)	(.755)	(.659)
Depression (t)	.314[a]	.371[b]	.347[a]	.299
	(.174)	(.173)	(.185)	(.201)
Period 2	−.162	.012	−.061	.028
(1896–1985)	(.199)	(.501)	(.540)	(.559)
Period 3	−.658[c]	−.994[c]	−.854[c]	−1.33[c]
(1932–1985)	(.235)	(.301)	(.323)	(.360)
Period 4	−.709	−.827	−.723	−.351
(1947–1985)	(.553)	(.562)	(.570)	(.594)
Period 5	.577	.937	.768	.581
(1955–1985)	(.542)	(.581)	(.595)	(.605)
Disbandings $(t-1)$	.032	.044	.053[a]	.054
	(.029)	(.029)	(.030)	(.034)
Independent (t)	—	—	.121	—
			(.185)	
Craft (t)	—	—	.096	—
			(.221)	
Low skill (t)	—	—	−.150	—
			(.193)	
Log-size (t_0)	—	—	—	.102[a]
				(.053)
Log likelihood	−1,168.73	−1,164.17	−1,026.91	−893.52
Number of spells	17,896	17,896	16,958	16,157
Number of events	191	191	166	146

Note: Figures in parentheses are asymptotic standard errors.
a. $p < .10$.
b. $p < .05$.
c. $p < .01$.

dummy variables that distinguish foundings and secessions from mergers, a dummy variable that equals unity for depression years, and the four period effects.

As we saw with somewhat different models in the previous chapter, type of starting event has a powerful effect on disbanding rates. Unions whose starting event was a founding had disbanding rates roughly eight times larger than those beginning with a merger, while unions whose starting event was a secession had rates about four times higher than the merged unions. Disbanding rates rose during economic depressions, as labor historians have noted. Adjusting for age and other covariates, disbanding rates were 37 percent higher during depression years.

It is worth considering the estimated effects of periods in some detail because they have a different meaning from that in the previous chapter. In Chapter 10, the periods were defined as the period in which a union started; so the effect of a period was the effect of having begun in that period. Here period effects are defined for each year of a union's existence. That is, each union's disbanding rate is allowed to change across the periods that its existence spans. So in this chapter period effects tell the effect of a period on all unions in existence in a period, regardless of their period of beginning.

Estimates of the period effects tell that the rate did not change appreciably from the first to the second period, beginning in 1887. Net of other included factors, the disbanding rate seems to have been constant over the first century of the national union movement. But the onset of the New Deal, Period 3, had a powerful effect, reducing the rate to about half of its previous level. Extensive legal protection for union organizing seems not only to have stimulated membership growth of unions, as many have noted, but also to have depressed the disbanding rate of unions.

Somewhat surprisingly in view of the negative implications of the Taft–Hartley Act for unions, the period beginning in 1947 had an even lower disbanding rate than the New Deal period. However, the estimated negative effect of the fourth period does not differ significantly from zero. So a cautious conclusion is that the rate during the brief fourth period did not differ from the New Deal rate. Finally, the rate seems to have jumped during the final period, whose start marks the merger of the two major federations of unions and the beginning of long-term decline in the share of the work force represented by unions. However, the rate in the fifth period does not differ significantly from that of earlier periods.

The number of disbandings in the previous year also has a positive effect, as predicted. However, it does not differ significantly from zero in this and most other models we estimated. There is no strong evidence here that waves of disbandings affected the subsequent rate, when other relevant variables are controlled.[5]

Next we turn to density dependence. The results of many different analyses reveal that the effect of density on the disbanding rate is indeed non-monotonic, as predicted. For instance, a comparison of columns 1 and 2 in Table 11.1. shows that adding the log-quadratic effect of density improves the fit significantly.[6] More important, the estimated effect of density in the second column has the signs predicted in (11.2): the first-order effect, β_1, is negative and the second-order effect, β_2, is positive.

It is worth emphasizing that estimates of the effects of density are stable and significant even in the presence of strong effects of aging, periods, environmental conditions, and founding conditions. Moreover, as we show later in this section, the estimated effects of density are quite robust with respect to specification of the environmental determinants of disbanding rates.

The third column of Table 11.1 adds three covariates describing a union's organizational form: (1) craft versus industrial form; (2) organizing only less skilled workers versus organizing some skilled workers; and (3) independence versus membership in a national federation. Since measures of the first two distinctions are unavailable for some unions, the number of spells used to estimate the model is smaller than in the first two columns. According to the table, none of the three measures of form affects the disbanding rate strongly or significantly.

Finally, the fourth column adds the log-size of initial membership to the model in the second column. Because information on size is unavailable for some unions, this addition too causes some loss of observations. As in the analysis in the previous chapter, which did not incorporate time-varying covariates, initial size has a significant *positive* effect on the disbanding rate.

The estimated parameters in columns 2–4 in Table 11.1 imply that the effect of density changes sign within the historical range of density [0,211]. The point of inflection implied by these estimates and the relationship in (4.3) is $N \approx 122$. Figure 11.2 plots the estimated effect of density on the disbanding rate, using the estimates from the second column of Table 11.1. The effect of density, the multiplier of the rate, reaches a minimum of 0.26 at $N = 122$. This means that the implied rate when there were 122 unions in

---

5. This is also true when a quadratic effect of prior disbandings is used.

6. The likelihood ratio test statistic equals 9.12 with two degrees of freedom, which is significant at the .01 level.

MULTIPLIER OF THE RATE

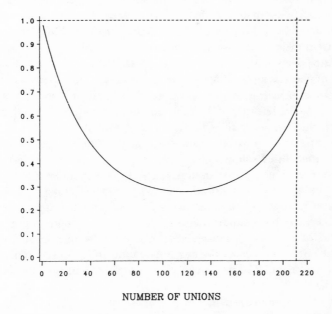

NUMBER OF UNIONS

Figure 11.2 Effect of density on disbanding rate of unions (estimates from model 2 in Table 11.1)

the population was only a quarter as large as at a density of zero (for any combination of age and covariates). When density equals its historical maximum ($N = 211$), the multiplier equals 0.59. In other words, as the number of unions rose from 122 to 211, the disbanding rate more than doubled in the sense that the multiplier rises from 0.26 to 0.59. In fact, the estimated multiplier at the observed maximum of density is the same as when $N \approx 20$. The process has come almost full circle. This pattern provides strong support for the theory developed in Chapter 6.

We also explored the consequences of adding each of the environmental covariates discussed earlier. We added each covariate in turn to the model whose estimates appear in the fourth column of Table 11.1.[7] That is, we

---

7. We have also added the variables in various combinations. The main results discussed in the text hold up for many different specifications.

added each covariate in turn to a model that contains the effects of age, type of starting event, independence, depression year, and the period effects. The results of a portion of this exercise appear in Table 11.2. This table reports estimates of the effects of the two density terms and each covariate, but not the effects of all the other variables in each model because they are quite stable from model to model and differ little from the estimates discussed above. Table 11.2 lists the environmental variables in order of decreasing coverage of the historical period (in terms of number of events excluded when the covariate is entered into the model). So the columns to the left side of the table contain estimates that used more of the historical information than those to the right.

The effects of most covariates are slight. Only three have estimated effects that differ significantly from zero at the .10 level: periods of employer offensives against unions, capital investment in plant and equipment, and gross national product per capita. The finding regarding capital investment suggests that the spread of mechanized factory production enhanced the life chances of labor unions. This finding agrees with the general thrust of Marx's model of mobilization—concentration of workers in large enterprises eases the communication and interaction necessary for collective action. The negative effect of GNP can be given a similar interpretation.

The other significant effect is puzzling: it indicates that disbanding rates *fell* during periods of nationwide employer offensives. It is hard to believe that these offensives actually reduced the rate, unless the offensives somehow caused unions to take defensive actions that gave them a resistance to disbanding that they would otherwise not have possessed. More plausibly, other changes occurring during the first and third decades of this century may have lowered the disbanding rate. Nonetheless, this finding raises questions about the claim that employer offensives had powerful negative effects on the union movement (Griffin, Wallace, and Rubin 1986).

We find no evidence that disbanding rates were affected by wars, immigration flows, strike waves, or size of the labor force. Likewise, the variety of indicators of economic activity (the real wage rate of common laborers and the unemployment rate) fail to affect the rate significantly when union characteristics, density, the occurrence of economic depressions, and the differences among periods are taken into account. The same is true when levels of economic conditions are replaced by variables measuring year-to-year changes in these conditions.

Given the objectives of this chapter, the behavior of the estimated effect of density when the covariates are entered into the model is particularly

...r and add additional covariates to model (2) in Table 11.1

Independent variables	(1)	(2)	(3)	(4)	(5)	(6)	(7)	(8)	(9)	(10)	(11)	(12)
$N(t)$	-.023c (.007)	-.021c (.007)	-.022c (.007)	-.020c (.007)	-.019b (.008)	-.015a (.008)	-.019b (.007)	-.011 (.009)	-.014 (.015)	-.100b (.046)	-.070a (.039)	-.022c (.008)
$N^2(t)/1000$	.098c (.036)	.091b (.037)	.096c (.035)	.090b (.035)	.087b (.037)	.068b (.038)	.093b (.037)	.063 (.041)	.075 (.056)	.348b (.150)	.261b (.130)	.100b (.046)
War (t)	-.224 (.267)											
Employer offensive (t)		-.399a (.029)										
Labor force (t)			.008 (.010)									
Immigration (t)				-.010 (.029)								
Patents (t)					.013 (.011)							
Business failures (t)						.572 (1.66)						
Real wage (t)							-.454a (.245)					
Capital investment (t)								-.094a (.049)				
Strikes $(t)/1000$									-.078 (.086)			
Unemployment rate (t)										.032 (.026)		
GNP per capita $(t)/1000$											-.558a (.360)	
Railroad track construction (t)												-.070 (.056)
Log-likelihood	-1,163.80	-1,162.48	-1,163.91	-1,163.31	-1,142.22	-1,144.75	-1,114.21	-1,079.51	-1,031.62	-969.87	-999.19	-642.26
Spells	17,896	17,896	17,896	17,596	16,876	17,556	16,230	15,743	16,605	16,289	15,223	5581
Events	191	191	191	191	188	186	184	176	166	157	154	114

Note: All models contain all the variables in Model (2) in Table 11.1. Figures in parentheses are asymptotic standard errors.

a. $p < .10$.
b. $p < .05$.
c. $p < .01$.

important. The non-monotonic pattern of density dependence is quite robust. In all 12 models in Table 11.2, the first-order effect of density is negative and the second-order effect is positive, as predicted.

Although the qualitative pattern is stable, the point estimates differ among specifications. We think that there are two sources of such variation. The first source is sampling error due to the fact that the cases used in each analysis differ because of missing values on covariates. The second source is that the relevant range of variation in density differs from column to column as the years of coverage change (also because of missing values on covariates). Consider, for example, the results in the model that contains the effect of gross national product per capita. If the estimated effect of density is evaluated over the entire range of density, it implies that the disbanding rate declines sharply beginning at $N = 0$ and rises only slightly at high density. But the relevant range of variation in density in this analysis does not include the region of low density. Since data on GNP are available beginning only in 1889 when the level of density was $N = 79$, the estimated effects of density should be evaluated only over the restricted range [79,211]. And over this range, the effect of density is indeed non-monotonic.

In all but two cases, both the first-order and second-order effects of density differ significantly from zero. The exceptional cases are the models in columns 8 and 9, which include the effects of capital investment and counts of strikes. These indicators are missing in years in which the density of unions is far below the apparent carrying capacity. The estimated first-order effects and, to a lesser extent, the second-order effects are somewhat diminished relative to other models. However, it is clear that the necessity of dropping a large part of the historical record increases the standard errors of estimate. For this reason we do not think that these exceptions cast serious doubt on the pattern that holds with the alternative specifications. In our view, analysis of this set of possible covariates does not alter the conclusion reached above. Density, measured in terms of number of unions, affects the disbanding rate in the predicted way. These effects are large in substantive terms, and they differ significantly from zero in all but two models.

Competition between Populations

Finally, we explore the effects of competition between populations. We continue to distinguish craft unions, which organized a named set of occupations or jobs, and industrial unions. In preliminary analysis we found that the effects of age and the covariates were fairly similar for the two populations. Therefore, we have pooled them together and estimated models in which the effects of age, periods, and covariates are constrained to be the same for both craft and industrial unions. However, we have allowed the effects of density to differ for the two subpopulations. That is, we specify that the disbanding rate in each population depends on its own density (in log-quadratic form) and on the density of the other population as in equation (11.3), and that the parameters indexing these dependencies may differ between subpopulations. We also allow for a main effect of the difference between craft and industrial unions, using a dummy variable that equals one for industrial unions. Table 11.3 reports ML estimates of this model.

Consider first the effects of own density. For both craft and industrial subpopulations, own density has a negative first-order effect and a positive second-order effect, as predicted. However, the effects differ considerably between the subpopulations. The estimated effect of own density (N_C) for craft unions implies that the disbanding rate falls with increasing own density until $N_C = 77$. This point of inflection falls roughly halfway between zero and the observed maximum of 156. At this level of craft density, the multiplier reaches its minimum level of 0.46. This means that legitimation processes associated with increasing density have cut the disbanding rate by slightly more than one-half when density equals 77. From that point on, growth in N_C *increases* the disbanding rate. When N_C reaches its observed maximum, the multiplier is close to unity (1.03), which means that the disbanding rate is essentially the same in a population of 156 craft unions as in a population with zero density. Thus, competition within the population of craft unions had eroded all of the disbanding-reducing effects of legitimation when craft density reached its peak level.

Legitimation apparently has had a much stronger effect in the population of industrial unions. The estimates in Table 11.3 imply that the disbanding rate of industrial unions reaches its minimum at $N_I = 50$, just below its peak level of 52. So the disbanding rate of industrial unions falls with increasing density over almost the entire range. In fact, the rate has been driven close to zero at this point. Legitimation processes have clearly dominated processes of intra-population competition for industrial unions.

Next consider the effects of competition between subpopulations, as indicated by the cross-effects of density. Density of craft unions (N_C) has a significant *positive* effect on the disbanding rate of industrial unions. But N_I has a *negative* and insignificant effect on the disbanding rate of craft

Table 11.3. ML estimates of density on disbanding rates of populations of craft and industrial unions

Independent variable	Population	
	Craft	Industrial
Intercept	-4.88^c	*
	(.778)	
$N_C(t)$	$-.020^b$	$.025^a$
	(.010)	(.015)
$N_C^2(t)/1000$	$.130^b$	
	(.006)	
$N_I(t)$	$-.042$	$-.223^a$
	(.026)	(.125)
$N_I^2(t)/1000$		2.23
		(1.83)
Log-age	$-.294^c$	*
	(.049)	
Industrial (t)		$-.557$
		(.747)
Founding	2.32^c	*
	(.714)	
Secession	1.85^b	*
	(.758)	
Period 2	.008	*
(1896–1985)	(.506)	
Period 3	.477	*
(1932–1985)	(.646)	
Period 4	$-.643$	*
(1947–1985)	(.568)	
Period 5	.713	*
(1955–1985)	(.592)	
Log-likelihood	$-1,052.01$	
Number of cases	17,185	
Number of events	171	

Note: Figures in parentheses are asymptotic standard errors.
* Coefficients are constrained to be the same for the craft and industrial populations.
a. $p < .10$.
b. $p < .05$.
c. $p < .01$.

unions. So again we find that competition processes in the world of national unions have been asymmetric. Craft unionism suppressed industrial unionism, but the reverse was not true.

The estimated effect of craft density on industrial disbandings is strong. When the number of industrial unions reached its peak in 1939, the number of craft unions was also large by historical standards. We have already noted that the negative effect of own density drives the industrial union disbanding rate close to zero under these conditions. But this effect is partly offset by a strong positive effect of craft union density. Still the effect of N_I dominates, and the implied disbanding rate was only 20 percent as large as under zero density in each population. Yet these estimates also suggest that the density of craft unions strongly affected the life chances of industrial unions when industrial unions were not large in numbers. That is, in periods when industrial density was low, the high density of craft unions increased disbanding rates of industrial unions strongly. Still, the competitive effect was dwarfed by the strong legitimating effect of increasing density within the population of industrial unions.

We have emphasized the role of density in affecting disbanding rates as a way to explore the effects of diffuse competition and legitimation. As we had hypothesized, density of unions does affect disbanding rates strongly. It is clear that whatever else affected union disbanding rates—and economic and political conditions surely did—these rates were strongly affected by competition *among* unions. As Michels pointed out, the struggle was not simply one of conflict with employers or the state, as many discussions suggest. Rather, there has been intense competition *within* the population of unions over the 150-year period we studied. There has also been competition between craft and industrial unions. Yet density dependence also seems to reflect processes of legitimation. And we find strong evidence that increases in density lowered disbanding rates before density reached a high level.

Exit Rates of Semiconductor Firms

Now we turn to a quite different application of our approach and models: the rate at which firms leave the semiconductor industry. Opportunities in this industry, emanating from changing technology and markets, are seized by venture capitalists and entrepreneurs in ways that have attracted much publicity and created a few large personal fortunes. The popular press often depicts the scientist-entrepreneur as a romantic figure, a modern explorer taking great risks for high stakes. There does appear to have been great risk. But in the semiconductor business a failed venture appears to be less a black mark than a sign of experience. Venture capitalists seem willing to provide funding for a new venture on the heels of a recent failure. T. J. Rogers, for example, persuaded his employer, American Microsystems, Inc., to spend (and lose) $25 million on a technology called VMOS. After changing jobs, Rogers succeeded in acquiring venture capital to start Cypress Semiconductor only a few years later, in 1983. Three years after founding, the company's stock was valued at $300 million (*Fortune* 1987). The same instabilities in the market and the technology that generate opportunity impose these risks on entrepreneurs. Moreover, as we indicated in the previous chapter, there is a substantial liability of newness in the semiconductor business.

From an ecological point of view, the issue is how the probabilities of failure are influenced by the dynamics of the population of firms and the conditions under which they operate. In particular, competition within and between populations has obviously affected the life chances of firms in this industry. One of the major goals of this chapter is to show that such competitive processes can be understood and analyzed empirically with the same approach that we used to study such nonmarket organizations as labor unions. So the question is: Does market competition, for which the semiconductor industry is justly renowned, yield similar processes of organizational competition to those we just reported for unions, which do not operate in such a clear market context?

We recorded histories of participation of 1,197 firms in the U.S. semiconductor industry between 1946 and 1984. Of these, 302 firms were still operating in 1984, which means that we treat them as censored on the right. The remaining 895 firms exited (either went bankrupt, were absorbed by other firms, or left the industry). Yearly counts of exits rise and fall over time, as Figure 11.3 shows. If anything, the variability in exit rates over time is stronger than for entries. In the peak year, 1972, there were 110 exits, fully one-eighth of the total. Comparing fluctuations in exits in Figure 11.3 with variations in density in Figure 9.6 suggests that the effect of density on the exit rate was non-monotonic. The exit rate peaks at the same time that density peaks. We examine later in this section whether this pattern holds under controls for environmental conditions.

Estimation

We analyze the rate of exiting using models of the form in equation (11.1). Since the exact dates of semiconductor firm exits are not available, we do

EXITS

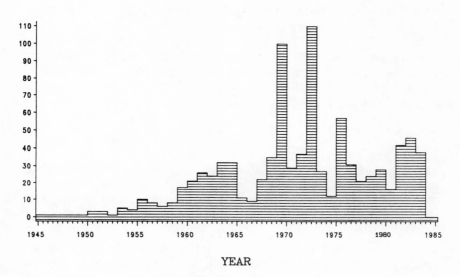

YEAR

Figure 11.3   Semiconductor firm exits by year

not try to use parametric models of time dependence. As in the previous chapter, we use partial likelihood estimators which treat the effects of time in the industry nonparametrically. As in the analysis of unions, we broke each spell between the firm's first and last appearance into yearly spells.[8] Spells not ending in an exiting event are censored on the right. This procedure generated 6,856 spells for analysis. Values of several time-varying covariates were associated with each spell, updated at the beginning of each year. These include time since entry, counts of firms (density), or counts of life events such as number of exits. Variables describing economic conditions were measured in the year covered by the spell.

For example, a firm might first have appeared in the *Electronics Buyer's Guide* in 1958. Suppose its last year of appearance was 1961. Its starting

---

8. To break ties in durations, a uniform random number between zero and one was added to the starting time of the first spell. For the last subspell, a uniform random number between zero and one was subtracted from the ending time. When the firm appeared in only one year, a similar random number was generated. Half of that number was added to the starting time; the other half was subtracted from the ending time.

and ending times would be something like 1957.53 and 1960.48. The first spell would be 1957.53 to 1958; the second, 1958 to 1959; the third, 1959 to 1960. Each of these spells would be right-censored. The last spell would be 1960 to 1960.48 and would not be censored. A series of independent variables would be attached to each spell, as described in the previous paragraph. For the first spell, the number of firms observed in the year 1957 would be entered (53), and the total sales for 1958 would be added ($571 million). Time since entry for this spell is zero, because at the start of the year, the firm had not yet entered the population.

Results

Table 11.4 presents the results of our analysis, proceeding from simple to complex as before, with models to the right adding regressors so that likelihood ratio tests can be performed. We begin by asking whether density has the predicted non-monotonic effect on the exit rate of semiconductor firms. As before, we expect that the coefficients representing the effects of density and its square in equation (11.1) will satisfy the inequalities $\beta_1 < 0$ and $\beta_2 < 0$. In each column of Table 11.4, the first-order and second-order effects of density are statistically significant, and their signs are in the predicted direction.[9]

The next step is to see whether the estimated effect of density has the predicted non-monotonic form over the range of variation in our data. Figure 11.4 plots the effects of density on the rate of exiting. As expected, the multiplier drops as density increases at the low end of its range, but then rises. At its minimum (when $N = 191$), the exit rate is only 3 percent as large as a zero density. As density increases above 191 to its maximum value of 335, the multiplier rises to 0.22. Although the exit rate at $N = 335$ is only about a quarter as large as at zero density, the multiplier has still risen seven-fold from the minimum at $N = 191$.

We conclude that there is strong evidence of density dependence in exit rates in the semiconductor industry. The predicted non-monotonic pattern of this dependence is stronger in the best-fitting model than it is in the simpler specifications. This pattern differs from the pattern for labor unions in Figure 11.2 in that the semiconductor exit rates drop much more

---

9. If the model in column 1 is compared with a simpler model excluding the two density variables, the improvement of fit provided by the inclusion of N and N^2 is not significant. When the same comparison is made with the best-fitting model (column 4), the difference is 27.1, which is significant at the .01 level.

Table 11.4.   PL estimates of effects of density on exit rates of semiconductor firms, 1946–1984

Independent variable	Model			
	(1)	(2)	(3)	(4)
$N(t)$	$-.011^c$	$-.030^c$	$-.036^c$	$-.037^c$
	(.004)	(.005)	(.005)	(.005)
$N(t)^2/1000$	$.029^c$	$.078^c$	$.094^c$	$.097^c$
	(.009)	(.011)	(.012)	(.012)
Log of time since entry	$-.115^c$	$-.115^c$	$-.116^c$	$-.110^c$
	(.006)	(.006)	(.006)	(.006)
Exits (t)	—	$.030^c$	$.030^c$	$.031^c$
		(.007)	(.007)	(.007)
Exits $(t)^2/1000$	—	$-.359^c$	$-.333^c$	$-.337^c$
		(.054)	(.054)	(.054)
Entries (t)	—	—	$.047^c$	$.046^c$
			(.015)	(.015)
Entries $(t)^2/1000$	—	—	$-.653^c$	$-.647^c$
			(.182)	(.183)
Subsidiary	—	—	—	$-.605^c$
				(.092)
Period 2 (1960–1984)	.480	1.111^c	1.080^c	1.101^c
	(.311)	(.349)	(.348)	(.349)
Period 3 (1970–1984)	$-.670^c$	$-.749^c$	$-.666^c$	$-.683^c$
	(.135)	(.125)	(.128)	(.128)
Aggregate sales (billions of dollars)	$-.259^c$	$-.287^c$	$-.357^c$	$-.360^c$
	(.038)	(.040)	(.047)	(.047)
Interest rate	$.267^c$	$.260^c$	$.303^c$	$.303^c$
	(.040)	(.043)	(.050)	(.050)
Log-likelihood	$-7,549.3$	$-7,507.5$	$-7,498.7$	$-7,474.2$
Number of spells	6,856	6,856	6,856	6,856
Number of events	895	895	895	895
Degrees of freedom	7	9	11	12

Note: Figures in parentheses are asymptotic standard errors.
a. $p < .10$.
b. $p < .05$.
c. $p < .01$.

MULTIPLIER OF THE RATE

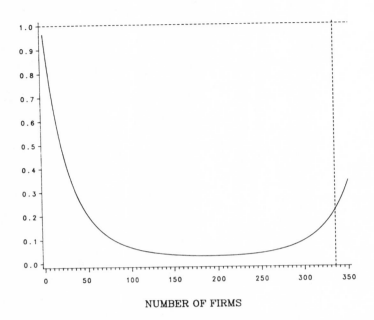

Figure 11.4 Effect of density on exit rate of semiconductor firms (estimates from model 4 in Table 11.4)

sharply at low levels of density. This is surprising because one would expect that legitimacy problems would be much more salient for labor unions than they are for semiconductor companies. On the other hand, when semiconductor firms were rare, the technology was new. For this population, low levels of density occur early in historical time. Our controls for periods may not be fine enough to remove the historical time dependency from the analysis. If this is true, the steep decline in the rate of exiting reflects the vulnerability of organizations without well-established routines for dealing with a radically new technology. Such a perspective fits the arguments of Tushman and Anderson (1987) that fundamental technical innovations often destroy organizational competence.

The second research question is whether experience in the industry also affected the failure rates of these firms. We do not have data on the ages of these organizations. Rather, we observe the time since entry into the semiconductor industry. Following the arguments and results of Chapter 10, we expect that the time since entry of the firm, "experience," will have a negative effect on the rate of exiting. We estimated effects for the logarithm of time since entry and found strong evidence supporting our expectation of experience dependence in rates of exiting from the semiconductor industry. Each model in Table 11.4 includes the log of time since entry. All estimates of this effect are negative, as we would expect if a liability of newness is operating. These coefficients are always many times their standard errors. Apparently the risks of failure that such new high-technology ventures suffer drop off quite quickly as the firms develop experience.

The third question concerns the effects of environmental conditions. We expect industry sales to have a negative effect on the rate of exiting but the interest rate of corporate bonds to have a positive effect on the rate, indicating that when the cost of capital is high, the highly capitalized semiconductor firms suffer. Both of these predictions are supported by the analyses reported in Table 11.4.

Finally, we expected that growth in applications for semiconductor technology would lower the exiting rate. Technical innovations generate opportunities for firms manifesting various subforms, and these should make survival easier than when the technology only provides a few viable niches. We try to control for these changes by including period effects in the model. A glance at Figure 11.3 would suggest that the 1960–1969 period would show higher exit rates than the 1946–1969 period, and that the 1970–1983 period would be higher still. In fact, the antilog of the coefficient for the second period in column 4 of Table 11.4 is 2.78, which means that the exit rate in the second period is 178 percent higher than that in the prior period. In the third period, the rate rises by a further 55 percent. So proliferation of applications does not appear to have improved life chances in this industry. As the industry has developed, the exit rate has risen sharply.

Column 2 in Table 11.4 adds effects of rate dependence. We want to see if the pattern of change in exit rates has the wavelike pattern previously observed for the founding and entry rates of unions and semiconductor firms but not for the disbanding rates of labor unions. We expect that number of exits in the previous year would show a non-monotonic pattern like that found for density dependence. The function should turn down at high prior rates of exiting as the negative signaling begins to wear off. Another way of looking at this is to note that if the prior rate has a positive monotone effect on current rate of exit, the rate would continue to acceler-

MULTIPLIER OF THE RATE

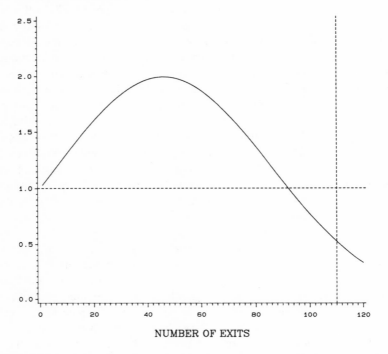

Figure 11.5   Effect of prior exits on exit rate of semiconductor firms (estimates from model 4 in Table 11.4)

ate. Unless the entry rate accelerated at the same time or the effect were
offset by environmental changes, the population would vanish.

The coefficients in column 2 of Table 11.4 have the signs that we expected. The estimated effects differ significantly from zero, and the model
improves significantly over the model that excludes the effect of prior
exits.[10]

Figure 11.5 shows how the multiplier of the rate varies with the number
of exits in the previous year. It shows that the effect of recent exits has
been a strong one. At its peak, when roughly 50 firms had exited in the
previous year, the multiplier is about 2, which means that a firm's rate of
exit in such a year is double the rate that would hold if no firms had exited

10. The likelihood ratio test comparing the fit of the models in columns 1 and 2 is
significant at the .01 level.

in the previous year. The multiplier diminishes as the number of prior exits ranges higher and eventually falls below unity.

An additional issue we explored with these data is the relationship between waves of prior entries and the exit rate. One way to view this is that when entry rates are high, a larger number of firms enter the industry with fatal flaws in their design, in business strategy, or in managerial expertise. If such a defect results in a higher exit rate, it should produce two results in our model: it should increase apparent experience dependence, and it should also produce an effect of prior entries with the quadratic function we observe. However, the two are difficult to untangle with our data because we have imprecise information on timing of entry and exit. A more elaborate specification of experience dependence might, in fact, wipe out the effect of entries. Consequently, these effects should be interpreted with caution.

Column 3 of Table 11.4 shows estimates of the model with the addition of number of entries and its square. The increase in the log-likelihood of 8.8 is significant at the .05 level. Waves of exits do seem to follow waves of foundings.

A fourth question is whether exit rates differ by form. The last column in Table 11.4 adds a binary variable that indicates whether the firm is a subsidiary of a larger corporation or whether it is an independent firm. We expected to find that the exit rate of subsidiary firms would be lower because these firms are buffered from many of the contingencies that vary so dramatically over the short run in the semiconductor industry. Furthermore, the superior access to resources afforded by the parent firm makes exiting due to scarce resources less likely. On the other hand, subsidiary firms tend to be much smaller organizations, as we indicated in Chapter 7. Adding the distinction between subsidiaries and independents to the model improves the fit significantly. The coefficient for SUBSIDIARY is negative and significant, as expected. The point estimate implies that the exit rate of subsidiary firms was only about half as large as that of independent firms.

The last set of issues concerns interactions between subpopulations of subsidiary and independent firms. We have already shown that the exit rates of subsidiary firms are lower than those of independent firms. But is this protected status achieved at the expense of the independent firms? When we explored this question in the context of entry rates, we found that the dynamics of the two populations were quite different. In fact, most of the variables that had significant effects on entry rates of the independent firms did not have significant effects for the subsidiary firms. This same situation obtains for exits, albeit less strongly.

Table 11.5 reports the results on competition between subpopulations. It gives two sets of results, one for each subpopulation. The models are based on the one reported in column 3 of Table 11.4. Table 11.5 excludes the effect of SUBSIDIARY, of course; and it adds a cross-effect of the other subpopulation's density.

This model predicts the exit rate of independent firms much better than that of subsidiary firms. All coefficients in the independent-firm column are significant, except for the effect of the second period. In the subsidiary-firm model, most coefficients are not significant. There is no apparent density dependence in this subpopulation, nor is there any rate dependence. We do see evidence that effects of time in the industry and of the measures of business conditions are similar in the two subpopulations. We tried various simplified versions of the model on this subpopulation, with no better success.

We are most interested in examining the competitive relationship between these two subpopulations. When we analyzed unions we found an asymmetric pattern: the number of craft unions had a positive effect on the disbanding rate of industrial unions, but not the reverse. Table 11.5 shows a very similar pattern. There is a powerful effect of the number of subsidiary firms on the exit rate of independent firms, but not the reverse. However, unlike the results for labor unions, the cross-effect is log-quadratic. Both the first-order and second-order cross-effects differ significantly from zero.

Figure 11.6 plots the implied cross-effect of the density of subsidiary firms on the exit rate of independent firms. Over most of the range of density of subsidiary firms, the cross-effect is positive. That is, a high density of subsidiary firms *increased* the exit rate of independent firms. At its peak, when $N_S = 66$, the multiplier is 38. This means that the implied exit rate of independent firms is almost forty times higher the rate that would hold if there were no subsidiary firms in the industry. Eventually, when the subsidiary firm population approaches its maximum, the function turns down. But even at the maximum observed level of N_S, the multiplier is still about 20.

Given that the density of subsidiary firms has such a powerful deleterious effect on the life chances of independent firms, why does the effect diminish at high density? Perhaps competitive pressures have their greatest effect when there are many marginal firms in the population, but the vulnerable firms exit as density of the competing form rises. Perhaps rising competition from subsidiary firms leads the independent firms to develop competitive responses. Such companies often develop alliances (joint ven-

Table 11.5. PL estimates of density on exit rates of subsidiary and independent semiconductor firms, 1946–1984

Independent firms		Subsidiary firms	
$N_I(t)$	−.086[c] (.014)	$N_S(t)$	.053 (.100)
$N_I(t)^2/1000$	.291[c] (.039)	$N_S(t)^2/1000$	−.209 (.664)
Log time since entry	−.109[c] (.007)	Log time since entry	−.108[c] (.016)
$\text{Exits}_I(t)$	.033[c] (.008)	$\text{Exits}_S(t)$	−.156 (.117)
$\text{Exits}_I(t)^2/1000$	−.505[c] (.077)	$\text{Exits}_S(t)^2/1000$	6.470 (6.921)
$\text{Entries}_I(t)$	.061[c] (.022)	$\text{Entries}_S(t)$	.144 (.160)
$\text{Entries}_I(t)^2/1000$	−1.209[c] (.318)	$\text{Entries}_S(t)^2/1000$	−13.229 (10.986)
$N_S(t)$	.110[c] (.035)	$N_I(t)$	−.045 (.035)
$N_S(t)^2/1000$	−.833[c] (.241)	$N_I(t)^2/1000$	.137 (.095)
Period 2 (1960–1984)	.759[b] (.348)	Period 2 (1960–1984)	2.084[b] (1.048)
Period 3 (1970–1984)	−.297 (.222)	Period 3 (1970–1984)	−.734 (.534)
Aggregate sales (billions of dollars)	−.472[c] (.065)	Aggregate sales (billions of dollars)	−.306[b] (.129)
Interest rate	.352[c] (.061)	Interest rate	.335[c] (.121)
Log-likelihood	−6,015.3		−1,038.2
Number of spells	5,000		1,856
Number of events	750		145
Degrees of freedom	13		13

Note: Figures in parentheses are asymptotic standard errors.

a. $p < .10$.

b. $p < .05$.

c. $p < .01$.

MULTIPLIER OF THE RATE

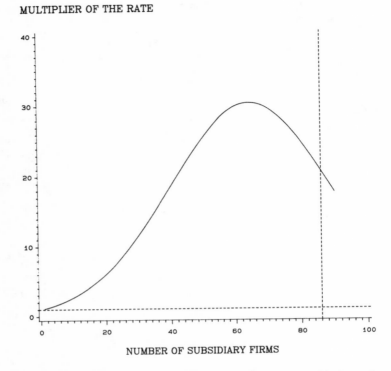

Figure 11.6 Effect of subsidiary firm density on exit rate of independent
firms (estimates from Table 11.5)

tures, second sourcing arrangements, and exchanges of technical information) with members of the competing population to gain some of the advantages of the subsidiary form without actually adopting it. Finally, they may develop alliances with firms in the captive side of the business, or with important customers, which provide the buffering and factor market presence whose absence threatens their viability. "Strategic alliances are a partial substitute for deep pockets and vertical integration. They entail exchanges of precious masks—the photographic negatives of a chip's layout—and even more precious secrets of design and production technology. For example, in 1984 Advanced Micro Devices agreed to give LSI Logic Corp. some of its own chip designs in exchange for access to LSI Logic's software for designing chips" (*Fortune* 1986).

A notable example of such strategic moves among independent firms is the alliance between IBM and Intel. Intel is a major supplier of microcomputer microprocessor chips to IBM. When Intel was suffering from cash shortages during the 1983 recession in semiconductors, IBM invested $250 million in Intel with an explicit agreement not to acquire a controlling interest, and Intel weathered the storm without becoming one of IBM's divisions. The change in form that absorption would imply was widely described as a likely death knell for Intel, and perhaps for the independent form itself (*San Jose Mercury* 1984).

Whatever the source of this drop in the multiplier due to cross-effects of the density of subsidiary firms, we should not make too much of it. In fact, the decline in the cross-effect at high density of subsidiary firms is small in substantive terms since the exit rate remains roughly twenty times higher than the rate at low densities. It is interesting to contrast this very powerful interpopulation competitive effect with the modest difference in the life chances of individual members of the two subpopulations noted earlier. Recall that the exit rate of subsidiary firms is about half as large as that for independent firms. But here we see that the exit rate of independent firms rises almost forty-fold when the density of subsidiary firms grows large.

Failure Rates of Newspaper Firms

The third empirical test of the model of density dependence in rates of organizational mortality concerns the population of firms publishing newspapers in the San Francisco Bay area (in collaboration with Glenn Carroll). Partial likelihood (PL) is used in much the same manner as just described for the semiconductor firms. Lifetimes are broken into yearly segments, producing 30,781 observations. The values of all covariates are updated at the beginning of each calendar year: age, density, number of foundings in the prior year, and the index of political turmoil. All but the last observation for each publisher is censored on the right. For the 1,837 publishers that ceased publishing during the period of study, the last observation ends with an event; the spell is not censored. For the 333 publishers still in existence at the end of 1975, the last observation is censored on the right as well. The specification of dependence on time since entry in the mortality rate is an approximation to the Weibull model obtained by including the log-age at the beginning of each yearly spell as a covariate in the log-linear model, as described earlier.

Figure 11.7 shows the fluctuations in the mortality of newspaper publishers over the period. The peak period for mortality is slightly later than

DEATHS

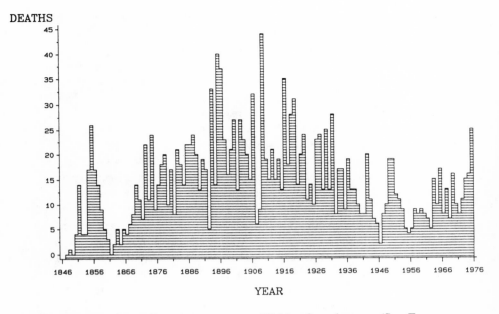

YEAR

Figure 11.7 Mortality of newspaper publishing firms by year (San Francisco Bay area)

that for foundings. Indeed, it is partly a reflection of the fluctuations in foundings because young newspaper publishers have a much higher rate of mortality than older ones, as we noted in the previous chapter.

Now we explore the consequences of adding measures of density to models for the rate of mortality of newspaper publishers.[11] Table 11.6 contains estimates of the basic model in equation (11.1). These estimates tell that both aging and density had strong effects on the mortality of publishers. Since the effects of aging in this population have been considered at length elsewhere, we concentrate on the effects of density. As predicted, the effect of density on the mortality rate is non-monotonic. The first-order effect is negative, and the second-order effect is positive. Both effects differ significantly from zero at the .01 level.

According to these estimates, the mortality rate fell and then rose with increasing density over the historical range. The minimum rate, at $N =$

11. Carroll and Hannan (1988) provide more detail about this analysis as well as applications of the model to other populations of newspaper publishing firms.

Table 11.6.   PL estimates of the effect of density on the mortality rate of newspaper publishers in the San Francisco Bay area, 1840–1980

Independent variable	
Log-age	-1.02^c
	(.036)
$N(t)$	$-.0079^c$
	(.0013)
$N^2(t)/100$	$.0014^c$
	(.0003)
Year of political turbulence	$.104^a$
	(.055)
Log-likelihood	$-18,463.11$
Number of spells	30,781
Number of events	1,837
Degrees of freedom	4

a. $p < .10$.
b. $p < .05$.
c. $p < .01$.

282, was only a third as large as the rate at zero density. From this point on, the mortality rate rose gradually with increasing density. By the time the historical maximum ($N = 377$) was reached, the rate was 13 percent higher than the minimum rate. Figure 11.8 illustrates the estimated relationship between density and the mortality rate.

As was the case with labor unions but not with semiconductor firms, we found no evidence that the number of recent failures in the population affected the failure rate of newspapers (estimates are not reported here). This result stands in sharp contrast to the findings for the founding rate in this population, which showed a strong dependence on the number of recent foundings.

Finally, as Carroll and Huo (1986) found, political turmoil increased the mortality of newspaper publishing firms significantly. The estimated effect implies that the mortality rate rose almost three-fold during years characterized by riots, ethnic violence, and violent labor unrest.

MULTIPLIER OF THE RATE

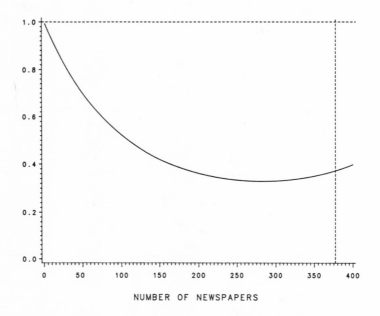

NUMBER OF NEWSPAPERS

Figure 11.8   Effect of density on mortality rate of newspapers (estimates from Table 11.6)

Comparisons and Contrasts

Have populations of labor unions, semiconductor firms, and newspapers been subject to similar processes of density-dependent growth? In a general sense the answer appears to be yes. For each population, rates of mortality depended on density in essentially the same way. In all three studies the mortality rate fell with growing density to a point and then rose with further increases in density. Populations of dissimilar kinds of organizations have been subjected to similar processes of legitimation and competition, as can be seen by comparing Figures 11.2, 11.4, and 11.8.

Despite the importance of the consistency among the findings about density dependence in the three populations, differences in the strength of the effects deserve note. The effect of legitimation conveyed by growing numbers was quite similar for the populations of newspaper publishers, semiconductor firms, and labor unions: the mortality rate dropped sharply with increasing density for all three populations. At the minimum, the implied mortality rate was 0.33 times as large as the zero density rate for newspaper publishers, 0.41 times as large as the zero density rate for unions, and 0.03 times as large as the zero density rate for semiconductor firms. Given the numerous differences among populations and the definitions of ending events, this strikes us as an important consistency.

On the other hand, the effect of competition on the mortality rate differed considerably among the three populations. Competitive pressures were apparently strongest for unions. When density grew from the point of minimum mortality, the implied mortality rate more than doubled in the population of unions. At this point it was about 60 percent as large as the zero density rate. For semiconductor firms the rate grew about seven-fold from its minimum when density reached its observed maximum. At this point it was only 22 percent of its zero-density level. But for the population of newspaper publishers, the rate grew only 13 percent as density grew from the point of minimum mortality to the historical maximum. Thus the competitive process seems to have been much stronger for labor unions and semiconductor manufacturing firms than for newspaper publishing firms. It is interesting to note that these findings do not agree with the view that nonmarket organizations do not face competitive pressures.

In analyzing the mortality of labor unions and exits of semiconductor firms, we also explored competition between subpopulations. We found strongly asymmetric competition in each case. For national labor unions, the density of craft unions had a strong positive effect on the disbanding rate of industrial unions, but the reverse was not the case. For semiconductor merchant producers, the density of subsidiary firms had a strong positive effect on the exit rate of independent firms, but the reverse was also not true. These analyses show some of the promise of our approach for analyzing competitive links between populations empirically.

12 | Dynamics of Niche Width and Mortality

In earlier chapters we discussed applications of modern theories of niche width, such as Levins' (1968) fitness set theory, to explain the distribution of specialist and generalist organizations across social environments. This chapter pursues such applications empirically.

We have argued that many of the classic problems concerning environmental uncertainty and organizational structure can be recast profitably as problems of organizational niche width (Hannan and Freeman 1977; Freeman and Hannan 1983). Organizations clearly vary on this dimension. For example, our study of the semiconductor industry finds firms that produce a single product and others that produce a great range of products. The connection between niche width and diversity is straightforward. To the extent that larger social trends favor generalist organizations, organizational diversity will decline. But if specialist organizations have adaptive advantages, the society will contain many diverse specialists. In other words, the dynamics of organizational niche width constrain organizational diversity.

In Chapter 5 we adapted Levins' (1968) approach to analyzing niche width to develop models of the effects of various forms of environmental variation on the life chances of populations of organizations that varied in degree of specialization of structure (Hannan and Freeman 1982; Freeman and Hannan 1983). The equilibrium implications of Levins' theory, summarized in Figure 12.1, agree in part with the existing literature on organizations but differ in one important respect. The conventional wisdom holds that uncertain environments always favor generalist organizations (see, for example, Katz and Kahn 1966, p. 131; Lawrence and Lorsch 1967, p. 8; Thompson 1967, pp. 34–37; and Pfeffer and Salancik 1978).

CONCAVE FITNESS SET   CONVEX FITNESS SET

	HIGH VARIABILITY	LOW VARIABILITY	HIGH VARIABILITY	LOW VARIABILITY
COARSE GRAIN	GENERALIST (POLYMORPH)	SPECIALIST	GENERALIST	GENERALIST
FINE GRAIN	SPECIALIST	SPECIALIST	GENERALIST	GENERALIST

Figure 12.1 Niche width theory predictions of relative fitness of specialists and generalists

However, Levins' theory implies that uncertainty favors generalists over specialists only when variations have "coarse grain," that is, when typical durations in a patch are long relative to the typical lifetimes of the organizations.

As we noted in Chapter 5, Levins' theory concerns only equilibrium distributions under an evolutionary process. In previous chapters we expressed doubt that processes of organizational change often reach equilibrium. Rather than rely on dubious assumptions of equilibrium, we recast Levins' theory in dynamic terms. In doing so we specialize the theory in several ways. First, we consider implications only for mortality processes. Second, we consider only the case of concave fitness sets, meaning those situations in which the environmental variations are large relative to the adaptive capacities of organizations. Third, we confine discussion to specialist and (monomorph) generalists. In other words, we do not consider the case of polymorphism. We do this by modeling the impacts of environmental variations on the mortality rates of organizational forms with specialist and generalist characteristics, leaving moot the question of whether populations of polymorphs have higher or lower mortality rates.

The ecological literature discusses effects of both variability and unpredictability of variations. Although both uncertainty and variability conceivably affect niche width, the existing literature is not very clear on this subject. For example, Levins did not draw a distinction between these two components of environmental fluctuations. We concentrate on only one of them—variability.[1] We argue that variability constrains niche width,

1. We decided not to specify the model in terms of uncertainty because the certainty of variations depends on an organization's information processing capacity as well as on the pattern of fluctuation. Introducing considerations of certainty will tend to shift the focus toward decision-making. We want to emphasize the role of environmental forces rather than adaptation by individual organizations. Therefore, we focus on variability of environments rather than the certainty of variations.

whether or not it is predictable. However, in analyzing the niche width of semiconductor firms, we consider variability around temporal trends, which shades into measuring uncertainty.

The most important step in operationalizing niche theory is specifying the precise forms of environmental effects. Levins considered situations in which the environment fluctuates between only two kinds of patches; we extend his treatment to the case where environments fluctuate over continua. Let μ denote the mortality rate of an organization. We propose that

$$(12.1) \quad \mu = \exp(\alpha + \beta G + \gamma GV + \delta GC + \zeta GVC),$$

where G is a dummy variable that tells whether the organization is a generalist, V records the variability of the environment, and C is a dummy variable that equals one if the environment has coarse grain. This model can be reduced to each case in Figure 12.1 by setting some combination of parameters to zero, as we now show.

The simplest way to interpret the model in equation (12.1) is in terms of relative mortality rates of generalists and specialists,

$$\Delta = \frac{\mu_g}{\mu_s},$$

where μ_g and μ_s are the mortality rates of generalists and specialists, respectively. The baseline for all comparisons is the mortality rate for specialists, obtained by setting $G = 0$ in equation (12.1):

$$\mu_s = \exp(\alpha).$$

The mortality rate for generalists, obtained by setting $G = 1$ in (12.1), is

$$\mu_g = \exp(\alpha + \beta + \gamma V + \delta C + \zeta VC).$$

The ratio of the rates for generalists and specialists is

$$(12.2) \quad \Delta = \exp(\beta + \gamma V + \delta C + \zeta VC).$$

Niche theory makes one global prediction and several specific ones. The global prediction is that selection processes for organizations differ in fine-grained and coarse-grained environments:

Hypothesis 1: $\delta \neq 0$ and $\zeta \neq 0$.

Our specific hypotheses are predictions about how selection processes differ with grain. In the case of fine grain, niche theory implies that specialism is optimal at all levels of variability (see Figure 12.1). Setting $C = 0$ in the mortality function for generalists gives $\Delta(f)$, the relative death rate in fine-grained environments, as

$$\Delta(f) = \exp(\beta + \gamma V).$$

Our formulation of niche theory implies that $\Delta(f)$ exceeds unity over the range in V. This requires

Hypothesis 2a: $\beta > 0$

and

Hypothesis 2b: $\beta + \gamma V > 0$ over the range of V,

and Hypothesis 2b requires either that

$\gamma > 0$

or, if $\gamma < 0$, that

$$|\gamma V_{max}| < |\beta|,$$

since V is a variance and cannot be negative.

Hypothesis 2a, that stable environments favor specialist organizations over generalists, is common to all well-known theories about relationships of organizations and environments. Hypothesis 2b is distinctive to the model that we have proposed. The more conventional view holds that increasing variability increases the relative advantage of generalists, that γ is *negative*.

The case of coarse grain is more complex. Figure 12.1 tells that specialists are favored over generalists when coarse grain combines with low variability, but that generalists are favored when coarse grain combines with high variability. When C equals unity, the ratio of the mortality rates of generalists and specialists, $\Delta(c)$, has the form

(12.3) $\Delta(c) = \exp[\beta + \delta + (\gamma + \zeta)V].$

As we just stated, niche theory implies that specialists are favored over generalists when variability is low, but that generalists are favored when variability is high. In terms of the model, this means that

$$\text{Hypothesis 3:} \quad \Delta(c) > 1 \text{ for } V_{min} \quad \text{but} \quad \Delta(c) < 1 \text{ for } V_{max},$$

where V_{min} and V_{max} denote the minimum and maximum levels of environmental variability. That is, the values of the four parameters must imply that the expression in brackets in the equation for $\Delta(c)$ changes from positive to negative within the observed range of V.

We explore these questions using data from two of our studies. A large portion of the chapter concentrates on the analysis of restaurant populations, which were studied precisely because they allow relatively uncomplicated tests of niche width. The general approach used in analyzing restaurant ecology is then applied to the population of semiconductor manufacturing firms.[2]

Niche Width and Mortality of Restaurants

For a number of reasons discussed below, we decided that populations of restaurant establishments were nearly ideal candidates for analysis of niche width and mortality. Because our study of restaurants was designed to test hypotheses from one kind of model, it is the most narrowly focused of the data sets. It is also the only design that uses a *prospective* observation plan.

Although the restaurant industry is huge in terms of employment and sales, individual restaurants are neither large nor powerful. Why study restaurants rather than the large firms and government bureaus that have preoccupied organizational research? The choice of restaurants offers several advantages for testing our version of niche width theory. First, restaurants are small enough that most cities have many of them. Hence it is feasible to estimate the distributions of effects of environmental variations on restaurants. And restaurants have diverse forms. For example, fast-food forms, many types of ethnic restaurants, coffee shops, luxury dinner

---

2. Carroll (1985) has already reported estimates of models of niche width for American newspapers. We do not report any analyses here of the niche width of labor unions because we have been unable to reconstruct reasonable series on environmental variability at the industry level over a sufficiently long period of the 150-year history to do justice to the problem.

houses, and natural food restaurants can readily be identified. Moreover, an obvious spectrum of specialism/generalism underlies the variety of forms. Some restaurants, such as sandwich shops and night clubs, specialize to a narrow price range; others span much of the range. Similarly, some restaurants, such as doughnut shops and luncheonettes, specialize to one part of the day; others operate 24 hours a day. Finally, some restaurants specialize in a narrowly defined cuisine while others provide a broad array of menu items. Overall, there appears to be great variability in terms of specialism/generalism.

Restaurants supposedly have much shorter life expectancies than many other kinds of firms. If disbanding rates are sufficiently high, observation over short periods can yield enough failures to permit meaningful survival analysis. We chose to study restaurants partly for the reason that geneticists study *drosophila*: both turn over rapidly enough that one is not restricted to retrospective analysis.

Finally, it is easy to find reasonably complete listings of restaurants in urban areas. Since restaurants depend on local consumer environments, they usually purchase listings in the *Yellow Pages*. This publication provides a convenient universe from which to sample restaurants.

Research Design

We conducted prospective analysis because following establishments forward in time increases the likelihood of recording events for short-lived organizations. As we have noted repeatedly, we wanted to avoid the common practice of sampling only the most successful members of an organizational population.

The unit of observation here is the individual establishment. Our design goal was to maximize variation in grain and variability of sales among establishments. However, we knew nothing about the environments of particular establishments before sampling. Therefore, we used information about variation in sales among cities in designing a plan for sampling establishments. We analyzed time series of aggregate restaurant sales by quarter for the 200 largest cities in California for the period 1974–1977 and chose 18 cities that fell toward the extremes of the joint distribution of seasonality and variability of aggregate sales. Sampling establishments within these cities should maximize variation in grain and variability, and minimize the correlation between them.

In 1977 we sampled up to 50 establishments in each city. In cities with more than 50 restaurants we took a random sample; in smaller cities we selected the whole population. Establishments that had already closed or that refused to participate were replaced with a randomly chosen alternative when the local population had not been exhausted.[3]

We conducted telephone interviews with owners or managers to obtain information about each restaurant's history and current operations. The interviews were repeated in 1978 and 1979. In later interviews, we added establishments to replace those that had failed. In an effort to obtain more variation in life-cycle characteristics, we oversampled newly listed restaurants in the second and third waves. In all, we sampled 985 establishments.[4]

The period of observation ranges from one to three years because restaurants were added in the second and third years of the study. This feature of the design requires use of a method of analysis that adjusts properly for differential length of exposure to the risk of having an observed disbanding, as we discussed in Chapter 8.

Although most establishments in the sample were independently owned local establishments, 128 were branches of large chains. We suspect that the contingencies of selection differ for local establishments and members of chains. For one thing, chains operate in many local markets. Since we have information only on local environments, we restrict attention to organizations that operate completely within the city; this restriction leaves us with 810 observations. Eighty-one of these cases had missing data on seasonality or age. Excluding these cases, the effective sample size is 729. Of these, 102 (14 percent) closed during the observation period and 91 (12 percent) were sold. We treat closure as the event of interest and sale of the establishment as an independent competing risk. Cases in which a restaurant is sold are treated as censored at that time with respect to the risk of closure.[5]

Measurement

A restaurant can specialize in many ways: type of cuisine, style of service, hours of operation, price range, diversity of menu items, or range of ser-

3. The refusal rate for the three years of study was 6 percent.
4. This excludes establishments that appeared following the sale of an original sample member at the same address. In an earlier report (Hannan and Freeman 1982) we analyzed the full set of 1,097 establishments. However, this number is somewhat deceptive since we lack complete data on almost all of these new entrants. Therefore, we decided to concentrate here on the original sample members.
5. In Freeman and Hannan (1983) we report that none of the variables used in the analysis here had significant effects on the sale rate.

vices. We use a single measure of specialism that reflects our understanding of the main strategic choices involved in attempting to establish a
restaurant. Some attempt to appeal to a narrow range of the population of
potential customers. Others try to appeal to the "average" consumer who
occupies the middle of the market range reflecting quality and price. After
studying the completed interviews and advertisements in the *Yellow
Pages*, we classified establishments into 33 forms. This coding relied heavily on menu specialization; it also took into account the hours of operation,
number of entrees, and staff composition. We distinguished cafés, steak
houses, coffee shops, health food restaurants, taco stands, and Basque
restaurants, to name only a few.

The distinction used in this chapter collapses the 33 forms into three:
generalist, fast-food establishment, and other specialist. To be coded a
generalist, a restaurant had to meet three criteria: (1) offer a fairly general
menu, not limited to items such as pizza or hamburgers and not dominated
by a specific ethnic cuisine; (2) offer seating; and (3) employ at least one
person in the differentiated role of chef or cook.[6] Thirty-one percent of the
restaurants in the sample are generalists. The fast-food form contains establishments that specialize in one of the following: pizza, hamburgers, hot
dogs, fried chicken, tacos, doughnuts, or ice cream. Thirty-four percent of
the establishments fall in this category. The remaining thirty-five percent,
the specialists, tend to feature ethnic cuisine or have a very limited menu.

In our first analyses of these data (Hannan and Freeman 1982; Freeman
and Hannan 1983) we established that the dynamics for the fast-food and
for the specialist forms do not differ substantially. So we collapse this
distinction here. With this revision, roughly two-thirds of the population
are specialists, and a third are generalists.

In preliminary analysis we learned that specialists tend to be slightly
older than generalists but have slightly lower average sales (Freeman and
Hannan 1983, table 1). The fact that these differences are small suggests
that we are not comparing generally successful organizations with generally unsuccessful ones when we compare specialists with generalists.

We assume that these broad forms respond differently to changing demand—that they have different fitness functions. Demand for restaurant

---

6. Many restaurants do not have staff with the formal role of chef or cook. This is true
particularly of those that offer a very limited menu that can be mastered by most employees (such as sandwiches). Investment of resources in employing chefs and cooks is one
of the fixed costs of generalism in the restaurant business. The value of having such staff
is that they can prepare a wide variety of menu items and can shift production as tastes
change.

services has many distinguishable components, such as the business lunch trade, family dining, tourism, meetings, and banquets. We assume that the various components do not change proportionately each time aggregate sales rise or fall. Generalists are presumably less sensitive to fluctuations in aggregate demand because they offer a greater range of services to more diversified populations of consumers. They achieve this reduced sensitivity at least partly by maintaining the excess capacity of employing a chef.

Since many respondents were reluctant to reveal detailed financial information, we could not measure variability in sales over time for individual establishments. It is not clear, however, that this would have been appropriate. Extreme fluctuations in sales for a particular establishment may be confounded with disbanding. As business failure threatens, restaurants may manipulate their prices, hours of operation, quality of food or service, and other features of their operations in ways that temporarily influence sales. Therefore, for both practical and theoretical reasons, we do not measure variability at the establishment level. Instead we give each establishment the variability score for the city in which it is located. We used the time series of quarterly gross sales by city mentioned earlier. Our measure of variability (denoted by V) is the coefficient of variation of each city's gross restaurant sales by quarter over the period extending from the fourth quarter of 1976 to the first quarter of 1980. This measure ranges from a low of .058 to a high of .252.[7]

The second important dimension is grain. It is not obvious a priori whether a particular patch size is large or small for a class of organizations. Should we analyze weekly variations in demand? Quarterly variations? Yearly variations? Our understanding of the economics of the industry is that restaurants can average over variations from one week to the next, but that several months of low sales create serious problems. This view suggests that *seasonal* variations in sales ought to be considered coarse-grained for restaurants. Therefore, for our purposes a restaurant has a coarse-grained environment when its sales variations have a strong seasonal component.

We have tried two approaches to measuring coarseness of grain. The first is the strength of the seasonal component in the time series of aggre-

7. Our earlier reports from this study (Hannan and Freeman 1982; Freeman and Hannan 1983) used this measure multiplied by 100. Herriot's (1987) questions about our procedures caused us to reexamine the data, and we found that there were several miscoded observations. However, we showed that correcting these errors did not make much difference in the qualitative pattern of findings (Freeman and Hannan 1987). The analysis reported here uses the corrected measure of variability.

gate sales for the city in which the establishment is located. This is the same method used to stratify the sample. The second method uses a self-report from each establishment about the seasonality of its sales. We obtain sharper results with the self-reports. The patterns of estimates are similar with the two measures, but the standard errors of estimates are considerably smaller with the self-report. This is not surprising, because there are likely to be important differences among subenvironments in each city. For example, restaurants located near highway interchanges probably face opposite seasonal patterns from those in central business districts. Moreover, the calendar quarters used in official statistics do not square well with the seasonal patterns actually faced by restaurants in some cities.[8] Therefore, we use self-reported seasonality as our measure of coarseness of grain (denoted by C) in the analysis that follows. Twenty-three percent of the establishments report a highly seasonal pattern of sales.

It turns out that generalism and coarseness of grain are not correlated— the χ^2 statistic for independence in this four-fold classification is only 0.02. Generalism has a weak correlation with variability ($r = 0.02$), and the correlation between variability and coarseness of grain is 0.33. Restaurants in coarse-grained environments tend to be slightly older than fine-grained ones and to have slightly higher sales.

Use of our adaptation of Levins' model in analyzing the relative mortality rates of specialist and generalist restaurants requires that we establish the likely shape of the fitness functions of restaurant populations. Are the fitness sets of populations of restaurants convex or concave? We concentrate on the effects of variations in demand for services. Restaurant sales fluctuate with seasons, business cycles, and consumer income cycles. They also respond to purely local events and to fashions and fads. Are typical demand variations large relative to the adaptive capacities of restaurants? Most restaurants seem to operate close to the margin, suggesting that they are sensitive to even small fluctuations in demand. This means that the fitness sets of restaurants are concave with respect to typical variations in demand. The rest of our argument depends on this assumption.[9]

---

8. For example, the ski season in Lake Tahoe falls in two quarters, as does the spring season in Palm Springs.

9. When fitness sets are convex, variable environments favor generalists regardless of grain. Thus if restaurants have convex fitness sets, grain will not play any role in affecting mortality rates. Our hypotheses will fail.

Results

We began our analysis by exploring the effects of various control variables, including measures of the size of the establishment (number of employees, number of seats, number of meals served per week), its age, the logarithm of its gross sales, and characteristics of its local environment such as total restaurant sales, sales per establishment, and measures of growth and decline in aggregate sales. Only the age at time of first observation and the log of gross sales[10] had systematic effects on mortality rates. Given the theoretical and empirical importance of age dependence in mortality rates, we concentrate on results of models that include this factor. Readers interested in findings without age (which allows use of a slightly larger number of cases) and with effects of size (which limits the number of cases considerably) may consult Freeman and Hannan (1987).

With these preliminaries, we arrive at our specification:

$$(12.1) \qquad \mu_{ic} = \exp(\alpha + \beta G_{ic} + \gamma G_{ic} V_c + \delta G_{ic} C_{ic} + \zeta G_{ic} V_c C_{ic} + A_{ic}),$$

where A contains the main effects of V and the effect of age.[11] The subscripts in equation (12.1) are a reminder that coarseness of grain, generalism, and age vary among establishments (indicated by the subscript i) but that variability varies only between cities (indicated by c).

Table 12.1 reports ML estimates of this model.[12] The first hypothesis is that mortality processes differ by grain. A likelihood ratio test rejects the hypothesis that the two parameters indexing the effects of grain are zero at the .01 level. So the data agree with this broad hypothesis.

---

10. Many respondents refused to divulge information about finances. In such cases we estimated gross sales by taking the product of the average number of meals served per week and the midprice of the main courses on the menu.

11. We have also introduced an interaction between V and C. We do not report the results of models with this term because we have not always obtained convergent solutions. However, in those cases in which the iterative maximum likelihood routine does converge, we find that the VC interaction is small and not significantly different from zero. More important, presence of a VC interaction does not change the qualitative patterns of effects reported later in this section (including levels of significance).

12. Because we recorded data in waves of yearly interviews, we learned at each interview after the first either that a restaurant was still in business or that it had closed or been sold. We did not learn the dates of such events. We have used this information to calculate maximum likelihood estimates of parameters of constant rate models, using the "change data" specification in Tuma's (1980) program RATE.

Table 12.1.   ML estimates of niche width model of restaurant
disbanding rate

Independent variable	Parameter	Model		
		(1)	(2)	(3)
Intercept	—	−8.53[c]	−8.53[c]	−7.96[c]
Variability (*V*)	—	1.50	1.01	−.44
Coarse grain (*C*)	—	.10	.25	.42
Generalism (*G*)	β	.37	−.23	−.53
*G*V*	γ	−3.94	4.73	8.70[a]
*G*C*	δ	—	2.72[a]	2.68[a]
*G*V*C*	ζ	—	−35.30[a]	−37.00[a]
Age	—	—	—	−.042[c]
Number of spells		788	788	729
Number of events		104	104	102
χ^2 (vs. constant rate model)		1.45	13.0	27.2
Degrees of freedom		5	7	8

a. $p < .10$.
b. $p < .05$.
c. $p < .01$.

The two point estimates are relevant to the specific hypotheses about fine-grained environments. Hypothesis 2a, that $\beta > 0$, tells that specialists are favored in fine-grained (non-seasonal) environments. This hypothesis receives no support: $\hat{\beta}$ does not differ significantly from zero.[13] Hypothesis 2b, that $\beta + \gamma V > 0$, means that specialism is favored over generalism over the full range of environmental variation in fine-grained environments. This hypothesis is supported in this analysis. The point estimates imply that the mortality rate of generalists exceeds that of specialists over almost the entire range of *V*. However, the ratio of the two mortality rates is close to unity at the minimum observed level of *V*. Perhaps more important is the fact that the point estimate of γ differs significantly from zero in the direction predicted. So these results suggest that specialists are favored in fine-grained environments that fluctuate greatly, contrary to the conven-

13. We report two-tailed tests for all parameters, for consistency with our practice in other chapters. However, signs are predicted for most of the parameters and, accordingly, the probabilities should be halved.

tional view noted at the beginning of the chapter (see also Freeman and Hannan 1983).

Next consider the case of coarse grain, that is, seasonal environments. The estimated relative mortality rate of generalists to specialists (see equation 12.3) is

$$\hat{\Delta}(c) = \exp(-.529 + 2.68 + [8.7 - 37]V).$$

The expression in parentheses is positive for small observed values of V and negative for large observed values of V, as predicted. The expression in parentheses changes sign when V equals 0.08, which falls within the observed range. According to these estimates, the relative mortality rate of generalists to specialists at V_{min} equals 1.66. In other words, the mortality rate of generalists exceeds that of specialists by two-thirds in stable, coarse-grained environments. But in extremely variable environments (when $V = V_{max}$), the relative mortality rate is .01, which means that the mortality rate of generalists is only a hundredth as large as that of specialists.

Because coarseness of grain and variability are correlated, estimates of effects at the extremes are unlikely to be precise. Nonetheless, the qualitative pattern implied by the model appears to hold. Not only are the implied differences in mortality rates of specialists and generalists large, but in addition, both $\hat{\delta}$ and $\hat{\zeta}$ differ significantly from zero at the .05 level.

Our model makes several predictions about the effects of environmental variables on the relative mortality rates of specialist and generalist organizations. The global prediction is that the patchiness of environmental variation affects the selection process. Analysis of this problem in terms of seasonality of demand confirms the prediction. Establishments that report seasonal sales patterns are affected differently by variability in aggregate sales.

The model also predicts how the relative mortality rates vary by grain. The predictions are confirmed for the case of fine grain: the signs of estimated parameters agree with the predictions. The usual argument is that any kind of environmental instability favors generalist strategies, but our estimates imply that this is not so in fine-grained environments. In particular, our estimates imply that specialists are actually favored in fine-grained environments with high variability. This finding agrees with the prediction of niche width theory.

The second case, involving coarse-grained environments, gives strong support to the model. The implied relative mortality rate shows the predicted reversal over the range of V. The parameters associated with this pattern differ significantly from zero in the predicted direction.

Niche Width and Exit Rates of Semiconductor Firms

We turn next to discussion of our attempt to replicate these findings using data on the mortality of firms in the semiconductor industry.

Measurement

We use the same definition of mortality reported in previous chapters: exits from the market, as tracked through references to listings in the *Electronics Buyer's Guide*. We record for each firm by year whether it was listed in each of the 85 product categories that appeared at one time or another in the *Guide*. We counted the number of categories existing in each year. For each firm, we counted the number of categories in which it markets products in each year. We measure *generalism* as the percentage of products sold in a given year that are sold by the firm in question. This measure varies among firms at a point in time and over time for each firm.

We measured *variability* and *coarseness of grain* using data on yearly North American sales in nine aggregate categories. We conducted spectral analysis of the yearly series of sales for each category using the *SAS* procedure PROC SPECTRA (SAS Institute 1984). The first step in this analysis was to detrend the series on sales. We tried various specifications of a regression model to accomplish this, using R^2 as the criterion for choosing among them. We found that logarithmic transformations of the series improved the fits substantially. Then we regressed each value (of the log-transformed series) on the previous year's value and its square. This quadratic specification was used to take the accelerating growth in sales into account. The resulting R^2 values ranged from 0.92 to 0.98. The residuals from these time-series analyses are the bases of our measures of both variability and coarseness of grain.

The decision to focus on seasonality in the restaurant study was a substantive one. It seemed reasonable to treat the market in a unitary way, rather than trying to estimate fluctuation in demand by kind of food. In the semiconductor study, we knew a priori that the families of products do not appear at the same time and that each has its own product life cycle. Transistors, for example, are one of the older product families; over time the technology for producing these products has become highly standardized. Others, such as MOS integrated circuits, are newer (and, therefore, have shorter time series). At the time of the study, these products were still accelerating in sales and the technology was still evolving. Finally, semiconductor products are integral parts of larger systems; they are rarely sold directly to end users. Consequently, the business cycles for each product family are driven by the business cycles for the systems in which they are inserted. In order to accommodate these differences, we analyzed each product group separately.

To measure coarseness of grain, we used spectral analysis to estimate the strength of cycles of different frequencies. The time series of any variable may have high-frequency cycles nested within low-frequency cycles. Spectral analysis provides estimates of the contribution to variance in the series of cycles of varying lengths (frequencies). The spectral density associated with each frequency is analogous to an R^2; it reflects the share of total variation in the detrended time series which can be attributed to that cycle. For each sales vector, we noted the frequency of the cycle with the highest spectral density. This allowed us to distinguish product groups in which deviations for the growth trend concentrated in short-term cycles from those in which deviations had longer-term fluctuations.

We computed a measure of the *coarseness* of the environmental grain of each firm using information on the cyclical behavior of the product groups in which the firm participated. We noted the product families in which the firm sold products each year. We also noted for each product group the frequency that had the highest spectral density. Then we computed the mean of the frequencies for the product families in which the firm was active in each year as a measure of coarseness of grain (C) for each firm.

Of course the vectors of yearly sales may exhibit highly cyclical patterns of variation, or there may be virtually no cycles in the data. Variation composed of all frequency cycles in equal proportion, once long-run trends are removed, is called "white noise." The relative amount of white noise in the various sales vectors is the basis of our measure of variability (V). Fisher's Kappa is used to measure the white noise in the time series of residuals (Fuller 1976). The mean of Kappa across the product families in which a firm produces devices is the measure of V used here. It varies among firms and over time for individual firms as they enter and leave product families. Kappa ranges from 1.97 to 3.65.

In the analysis of restaurants we defined variability in terms of the temporal variation in circumstances affecting the life chances of a given form of organization. Variability was described in terms of variation about a mean. In this study, that mean is a shifting average defined in least-squares terms. This is tantamount to assuming that semiconductor firms are not exposed to uncertainty by the orderly expansion of the markets in which they operate. Their managers know what this expansion is likely to be; what they know much less well is when cycles will reach turning points. Being well adapted to all the circumstances that the pronounced semiconductor business cycle represents is virtually impossible. Firms must counterbalance the long-run advantage of continuing to invest in the most current technology against the short-run risks attending financial losses in a period in which orders fall. Firms that invest little when times are lean may survive the current conditions only to fall behind in either product design or manufacturing technique. This suggests that no single form of organization can dominate the others in all circumstances. If this is true, fitness sets are concave. We proceed on the assumption that they are, and note that if we are wrong, our model should not fit the data well.

Results

We begin by reporting estimates of a model that parallels the one whose estimates are reported in the first column of Table 12.1. Column 1 of Table 12.2 reports a simple model with just the effects of the three components generalism, variability, and coarseness of grain, and the interaction effect of generalism and variability. (Since we are using partial likelihood estimation, there is no intercept.) Column 2 adds the other two interaction effects, which allows estimation of δ and ζ and a joint test of hypothesis 1, that fine-grained and coarse-grained selection environments differ. Adding the two interactions in column 2 increases the fit significantly. Moreover, both $\hat{\delta}$ and $\hat{\zeta}$ differ significantly from zero at the .01 level. This result supports the first hypothesis.

Column 3 adds the effect of log time since entry. We expected this variable to have a negative effect and it does, as we discussed in previous chapters. None of the other variables changes its sign when we control for time since entry, and none loses statistical significance. So we evaluate the hypotheses involving point estimates using the estimates in column 3.

Hypotheses 2a and 2b pertain to fine-grained environments. They concern the claim that specialist organizations fare better than generalists over the range of variability in such environments. The first subhypothesis, 2a, pertains to fine-grained environments with low variability. It holds that specialists are favored in these conditions, which in our notation means $\beta > 0$. In the case of the semiconductor population, as for the restaurant population, this hypothesis fails. In fact, $\hat{\beta}$ is positive and significantly different from zero at the .01 level. So in our data, fine-grained environ-

Table 12.2. PL estimates of niche width model of semiconductor firm exiting rate

Independent variable	Parameter	Model		
		(1)	(2)	(3)
White noise (V)	—	−.056	.299[c]	.152
		(.135)	(.156)	(.153)
Coarse grain (C)	—	−.629[c]	−1.715[c]	−1.176[c]
		(.224)	(.276)	(.274)
Generalism (G)	β	−20.421[c]	−20.036[b]	−20.385[b]
		(6.189)	(10.227)	(10.009)
$G*V$	γ	6.034[c]	3.738	4.586
		(2.116)	(3.602)	(3.526)
$G*C$	δ	—	100.279[c]	98.302[c]
			(31.719)	(30.234)
$G*V*C$	ζ	—	−28.513[c]	−29.406[c]
			(10.564)	(10.092)
Log of time since entry	—	—	—	−.108[c]
				(.006)
Number of spells		6,856	6,856	6,856
Number of events		895	895	895
χ^2		121.5	164.1	445.9
Degrees of freedom		4	6	7

Note: Figures in parentheses are asymptotic standard errors.
a. $p < .10$.
b. $p < .05$.
c. $p < .01$.

ments with low variability do not favor specialists; they favor generalists rather strongly.

Hypothesis 2b concerns the relative mortality rates of specialists and generalists in fine-grained environments with moderate or high levels of variation. Specialists are favored over the full range of variation if $\gamma > 0$. This is the case in all three columns in Table 12.2. However, the estimated parameter does not differ significantly from zero in the second and third columns. Thus we conclude that this hypothesis also fails.

Our third hypothesis pertains to coarse-grained environments. It states that when variability is low, the mortality rate of generalists should exceed that of specialists, but when variability is high, specialists should have the advantage and their mortality rate should be relatively lower than generalists. Our data strongly support this hypothesis. The estimated ratio of mortality rate of generalists over specialists is

$$\hat{\Delta}(c) = \exp(-20.39 + 98.30 + [4.59 - 29.41]V).$$

The expression in parentheses changes sign when V equals 3.14. The range of V is from 1.97 to 3.65. So when grain is coarse, generalists maintain their advantage except when V is near its maximum.

For continuity with the previous chapter, we present Table 12.3, which shows how the niche width model adds to the fit provided by the models developed in the previous chapters. The model of exit rates from Chapter 11 includes density dependence, dependence on prior rates of entry and exit, dependence on time since entry to the industry, the subsidiary/independent organizational difference, and the effects of historical periods and business conditions. To aid comparison, we reproduce the results from Table 11.4, column 4. Column 2 adds the variables and interactions relevant to niche width dynamics. This addition improves the fit of the model in column 1 significantly.[14] The log-likelihood rises from $-7,474.2$ to $-7,427.7$, a difference that is significant at the .01 level with six degrees of freedom.

In fact, although we made no predictions about the first-order effects, all three columns in Table 12.2 show a negative first-order effect of coarseness of grain, and all three are statistically significant. However, the interaction effects in the niche width model no longer differ significantly from zero individually. We should not be greatly surprised by this, however, since the model we are supplementing already has twelve parameters. If we ignore the lack of individual statistical significance and examine the hypotheses of the niche width model, we find the same pattern of results reported in Table 12.2: hypothesis 2 is not supported, but hypotheses 1 and 3 are supported.

The failure of hypothesis 2 reflects the fact that generalist firms appear to have an overall advantage. Why would generalism offer such persistent advantages? One answer lies in the fact that we have been unable to measure the size of the organizations in the population. Generalism, as we

14. A likelihood ratio test of the model in column 2 against the model in column 1 equals 93 with six degrees of freedom, which is significant at the .01 level.

Table 12.3. PL estimates of expanded niche width model of semiconductor firm
exiting rate

Independent variable	Parameter	Coefficient	Standard error	Coefficient	Standard error
$N(t)$	—	$-.037^c$	.005	$-.046^c$	.005
$N(t)^2/1000$	—	$.097^c$	.012	$.116^c$	.012
Log of time since entry	—	$-.110^c$	.006	$-.097^c$	.006
Exits (t)	—	$.031^c$	.007	$.030^c$	.007
Exits $(t)^2/1000$	—	$-.337^c$	.054	$-.341^c$	.054
Entries (t)	—	$.046^c$	.015	$.037^b$	.015
Entries $(t)^2/1000$	—	$-.647^c$	.183	$-.536^c$	.184
DIV	—	$-.605^c$	.092	$-.450^c$	.093
Period 2 (1960–1984)	—	1.101^c	.349	1.344^c	.347
Period 3 (1970–1984)	—	$-.683^c$	.128	$-.761^c$	.132
Aggregate sales (billions of dollars)	—	$-.360^c$	.047	$-.331^c$	.047
Interest rate	—	$.303^c$	.050	$.272^c$	.050
V	—	—	—	.047	.153
C	—	—	—	$-.846^c$	.277
G	β	—	—	-15.500	9.711
$G*V$	γ	—	—	3.697	3.414
$G*C$	δ	—	—	44.340	29.724
$G*V*C$	ζ	—	—	-13.610	9.801
Number of spells	—	6,856	—	6,856	—
Number of events	—	895	—	895	—
χ^2	—	580.6	—	673.7	—
Log-likelihood	—	$-7,474.2$	—	$-7,427.7$	—
Degrees of freedom	—	12	—	18	—

a. $p < .10$.
b. $p < .05$.
c. $p < .01$.

have measured it, is very likely to be confounded with large size. A big
firm, such as Texas Instruments, is likely to offer a broad range of products, while a very small firm could not do so. Large size may very well
operate like generalism. A big firm has greater reserves of resources with
which to ride out difficult conditions.

We believe that we have exposed our theory to an unusually stringent test. Although it was not fully supported, we do think the data support it well enough to encourage further research.

Comparisons and Contrasts

Our model of niche width and mortality appears to work reasonably well for semiconductor firms as well as for restaurants. Two more different organizational forms would be hard to imagine. The differences between the restaurant and semiconductor studies are substantial. In the former, disbandings are used to define mortality; in the latter, exits were studied. Individual restaurants are on average small organizations, and they are run by sole proprietors for the most part. Semiconductor companies are sometimes billion-dollar enterprises, but they are sometimes as small as all but the smallest restaurants. The owners of both kinds of organizations intend them to be profitable, but the technologies used to generate their products stand at the opposite extremes of sophistication. In a comparison of these two studies, "high technology" meets "low technology."

Restaurant environments were conceptualized as either facing strong seasonal variations or not having them; other kinds of cycles were not studied. In the semiconductor data, we were able to consider a much more complicated pattern of temporal variation in the environment. But in both cases aggregate measures of environments were used for measures of variability. The units of aggregation were quite different, however. Restaurants were presumed to operate in a geographically localized environment, which confronted each of them in the same way regardless of form. So a highly unstable pattern of quarterly sales for a town was assumed to operate as a uniform stimulus, provoking different reactions from restaurants manifesting different forms. Among semiconductor producers, the unit of aggregation was the North American market for a product family. It was assumed that geography was of limited significance, and, indeed, convenience and accuracy of data were the reasons for using North American sales rather than worldwide sales. Research focusing on the industry in more recent years would have to use worldwide data since the industry became a truly global business in the later seventies and eighties.

The restaurant study was prospective, whereas the semiconductor study was retrospective. Consequently, the spans of time covered by the two studies were quite different. Indeed, the short time period and the small number of observations made over time precluded the use of restaurant data for the analyses in Chapters 9, 10, and 11. Although the semiconductor study was not planned primarily as a study of niche width, we did have an advantage in carrying it out, namely the previous experience with the restaurant research. Among other things, this permitted measurement of variables as continua that had been measured as binary variables in the restaurant study (that is, coarseness of grain and generalism). This change and the greater number of uncensored observations undoubtedly helped improve the model's fit.

Given these great differences between the kinds of organizations under study, and in the designs of the research projects themselves, it is remarkable how consistent the results were.

13 | Conclusions

Our treatment of organizational ecology has ranged widely, emphasizing theory and empirical applications in roughly equal measure. As we stated at the outset, one of our goals is to bring the sociological study of organizations back into the mainstream of sociology. This means reorienting theory and research on organizations so that they speak once again to fundamental problems of social organization and change. The population ecology of organizations brings about this reorientation by (1) shifting the focus to the population level, (2) moving from a static to a dynamic approach, (3) recognizing the strong limits on the speed with which existing organizations can adapt to rapidly changing environments, and (4) examining change in diverse but internally homogeneous organizational populations over their full histories.

A closely related goal is to develop sociological propositions about organizational change that hold over time and space and across organizational forms. There is currently much pessimism in the social sciences about the prospects for finding any social laws. We do not think that such pessimism is warranted in the case of change at the level of organizational populations.

At each step we have emphasized connections between theory and empirical research. We have sought to develop a theory of organizational change that leads directly to empirical formulations and to comparative research on organizational populations. Our comparative research on diverse populations bears directly on core theoretical concerns. Of course, not all of the important connections have yet been made. Some of the theories discussed in Part I have not yet been addressed in empirical research; and each empirical analysis reported in Part III raises new theoretical questions. So the work reported in this book represents the first steps in a program of theory and research.

Implications of the Research

We have found regularities in processes that shape the vital rates of organizational populations: rates of entry and exit. As we noted in Part I, we have concentrated on these rates because they are fundamental to long-term change in populations and communities of organizations. In our formulation, these vital rates are affected by several general processes and also by numerous processes that are idiosyncratic to organizational forms in particular social and historical contexts (sometimes called "historically grounded" factors). The general processes include (1) competition within and between populations for capital, members, and other limited resources; (2) legitimation; (3) aging, in the case of mortality; and (4) environmental abundance and constraint. The idiosyncratic factors include legal and technical developments that bear specifically on certain organizational populations, such as legal protection for union organizing or the development of new technologies for producing semiconductor products; they also include institutional rules that are specific to time periods or national contexts. Empirical analysis of organizational ecology necessarily blends the general and particular processes since efforts to uncover general processes are likely to fail unless the most important idiosyncratic processes are considered. The approach we have developed incorporates both types of factors or processes in a natural way.

Our modeling strategy begins with baseline models of the effect of density on vital rates, with density conceptualized as the number of organizations in the population. It assumes that processes of competition and legitimation can be usefully represented as functions of density. This approach, which has generated controversy in organizational sociology, has obvious advantages and disadvantages. The main disadvantage follows from its indirect nature—it does not rely on measurements of competition and legitimacy. Rather, it infers the operation of these processes from estimates of parameters of models of density dependence. In so doing, it follows a long tradition in population ecology. And just as many field biologists and naturalists have derogated mathematical models of bioecology for oversimplifying processes of competition, students of any one kind of organization may think that our models greatly oversimplify the nature and sources of legitimacy and localized competition.

But such simplifications, if they are not extreme, provide considerable analytic advantages in the present context. By abstracting from much of the detail, we have been able to develop parametric models that can be used successfully to study many different organizational populations. In addition to the four populations we have studied (unions, semiconductor manufacturers, newspapers, and restaurants), other researchers are currently applying these models to populations of telephone companies (Barnett and Carroll 1987), medical imaging companies (Mitchell 1987), wineries (Delacroix and Solt 1988; Delacroix, Solt, and Swaminathan in press), social service agencies (Tucker et al. 1988), ethnic and linguistic newspapers in the United States (West and Olzak 1987), and social movements against drunk driving (McCarthy et al. 1988).

Ease of application to dissimilar populations facilitates learning about the generality of the core processes. It also permits these models to serve as building blocks for studies of the interrelationships of social structures and organizations. Of course these potential advantages do not amount to much if the processes turn out to differ greatly among populations. Fortunately, this has not turned out to be the case so far.

We have found considerable similarity in qualitative patterns of density dependence in founding and mortality rates for three quite different populations: national labor unions, semiconductor manufacturing firms, and newspapers. So the modeling strategy has paid an initial dividend, exposing consistencies that were not obvious at the outset. The consistent finding is that founding rates and mortality rates in the three populations depend on density in a non-monotonic fashion. The qualitative patterns of density dependence agree with our model of legitimation and competition processes.

Our modeling strategy also allows use of a long time perspective in empirical research. As our research on labor unions and newspapers illustrates, data on density and vital events can be collected for complete populations over long historical periods for which it would be extremely difficult—if not impossible—to reconstruct detailed and subtle measures of changing levels of legitimacy and local competition. Gaining a longer perspective conveys strong advantages in attempts to understand the social processes that have shaped populations of organizations. To continue the example of unions and newspapers, the most important changes in the demographic structure of these populations seem to have occurred during the nineteenth century. Research that excludes this period in an effort to reconstruct detailed measures would have missed virtually the whole story. Moreover, lengthening the period of observation increases the value of organizational research to work on macro social change, as we noted at the outset of the book. So this modeling strategy facilitates connections with macrosociology.

There is a second reason for valuing an approach that allows systematic empirical analysis over long periods. As we noted some time ago (Hannan and Freeman 1977), time scales in empirical research on organizational ecology must be commensurate with the vital rates of the populations under study. Studies of populations of small, short-lived organizations like restaurants can be done usefully over a reasonably few years, as we have demonstrated. But studies of the ecology of large, powerful, and long-lived organizations like commercial banks, research universities, and some national labor unions require a time scale of a century or longer. Some critics have misunderstood this methodological point; they have confused several instances of application of ecological theory to populations of short-lived organizations like restaurants with the general approach, and have concluded that organizational ecology applies mainly to small, insignificant organizations (see, for example, Perrow 1986, pp. 211–212). This is not so, as we have shown in this book. Studies of populations that contain large, powerful organizations (with links to the state and ability to mobilize considerable resources in crises) require use of a long time perspective. So the modeling strategy we have developed is particularly appropriate for the study of such populations.

A second area of progress involves theory and research on the niche structure of organizational populations. The concept of the niche serves as an organizing principle in much of ecology; it summarizes the effects of opportunity and constraint in the environment and in the structure of localized populations. Thus the niche is the focal point at which concerns with environments and concerns with organizational events meet.

There is a duality between the notion of a finite niche and that of density dependence. If a niche is finite, then the growth rates of organizational populations must vary with density. So our analyses of density dependence in vital rates have implications for the structures of niches. Indeed, our research reveals that the dynamics of adjustment to niche constraints are more complicated for populations of organizations than for biotic populations. The added complexity is due to the presence of second-order effects of density in the vital rates for the populations we studied.

We have also used niche theory to study selection processes that control the distributions of specialist and generalist organizations. Using a variation on a model developed by Levins, we have shown that the life chances of populations of specialist and generalist organizations depend on the combination of the variability and coarseness of grain in environments for populations as different as those of restaurants and semiconductor manufacturing firms. Since a great many issues in organization–environment relations can be cast in terms of specialism versus generalism, this approach has the potential for broad application.

A third area of progress involves attempts to link the vital rates of interacting populations. Recall that a major thrust of general ecological theory, developed in the spirit of Lotka–Volterra models, is to understand the consequences of positive and negative links between populations for the diversity of ecological communities. Previous work in organizational ecology has followed this lead. Nielsen and Hannan (1977) used a linearized Lotka–Volterra model to study the interactions of populations of primary, secondary, and tertiary educational organizations in affecting expansion of national educational systems. Carroll (1981) repeated this analysis using the full nonlinear model. Brittain and Wholey (1988) have used Carroll's approach to study the fluctuations in numbers of various subpopulations in the semiconductor manufacturing industry. And McPherson (1983) and McPherson and Smith-Lovin (1988) have used the equilibrium implications of the Lotka–Volterra model to analyze competition among voluntary associations. Each of these analyses has moved organizational population ecology in the direction of answering questions about *communities* of organizations.

We used a different approach in this book. As we have emphasized, the Lotka–Volterra model, which forms the basis of much modern population ecology, assumes *linear* density dependence in growth rates. But both our theory and empirical research indicate that density dependence in vital rates is *non-monotonic*. So we have attempted the more complicated task of introducing links between the growth rates of populations with the assumption that each population's vital rates are non-monotonic functions of density. We used models of such processes to study the links between the most important subpopulations in the population of labor unions (craft and industrial unions) and semiconductor manufacturing firms (independent firms and subsidiaries of other firms). In each case we found evidence of strong but asymmetric links between subpopulations. We think that our approach has potential value for addressing a wide variety of issues involving social structure and organizations. In particular, it provides a way of analyzing relations of dominance within a set of interacting populations.

At each stage in empirical analysis we have considered the effects on growth rates of environmental conditions and events whose relevance is idiosyncratic to particular organizational forms. Thus, for example, in studying vital rates of semiconductor firms, we specified models in which rates of entry and exit change discontinuously at the times of crucial technological changes. We have also estimated effects of environmental factors such as interest rates that change more smoothly. And we have learned that the various kinds of environmental factors have had powerful effects on vital rates. Moreover, we have learned that political, social, and economic environments do not always affect founding rates and mortality rates symmetrically. By breaking growth rates into components reflecting foundings and failures, we obtain sharper results about environmental dependencies.

We believe we have found a way to combine idiosyncratic and general elements in analyzing change in organizational populations. Our approach allows the analyst to tailor models and research designs to the peculiarities of organizational forms, historical periods, and sociopolitical contexts without losing the analytic power to evaluate general processes of change. Our initial efforts (along with those of other researchers cited throughout this book) suggest that the dynamics of organizational populations are indeed subject to strong general processes. We hope that other investigators continue to explore the generality and strength of these processes. We also hope that social scientists interested in macro social change make use of the population ecology approach in linking the dynamics of populations of organizations with changes in social and economic institutions.

Problems for Analysis

Lest we give the impression that the main analytic problems concerning the dynamics of organizational populations have been solved, we close with a discussion of promising directions for future research. Empirical study of adaptation is needed to explore our claim that radical change in core features of an organization's form increases its risk of mortality in the short run. We had planned to conduct such research with the populations discussed throughout this book. However, we found that radical change in strategy and structure was exceedingly rare in the populations we studied. For example, only a handful of national labor unions shifted from the craft to the industrial form (or vice versa) without going through a merger. As a result, we did not have enough evidence to study the causes and consequences of major adaptive changes. It would be interesting to collect data on populations in which such changes are thought to be common in an effort to resolve some of the debates about the role of strategic change in shaping populations of organizations. It may well turn out to be the case that our experience with a few populations is not unusual—that adaptive change typically takes the form of merger and acquisition rather than gradual change in existing routines, roles, and strategies. If so, the approach we have used, treating merger as a life event, applies to the main sources of adaptation. If not, then more complicated dynamic theories, like the one sketched in Chapter 4, are needed.

Such research would also provide empirical information on another key issue: the relative time scales of changes in environments, population composition, and strategies and structures of typical organizational populations. To what extent are organizational populations shaped by sudden disruptive shocks in the environment, as contrasted with routine changes such as those reflected in business cycles? We need to learn more about the role of shocks like wars, revolutions, and financial panics in shaping the key features of organizational populations. Comparison of the ecologies of organizational populations in social systems in which such events are common, as in parts of the Third World, with those of more stable systems would be particularly illuminating.

A related issue concerns selection for *r*-strategies and *K*-strategies, as discussed in Chapter 6. One way to think about such life-history strategies in the case of organizations is in terms of variations in speed of founding. It would be interesting to learn whether the selective advantage to quick-to-build organizational forms varies systematically with the coarseness of grain and severity of change in the local environment. This kind of issue can also be best addressed by research that compares the distributions across populations in different national and regional contexts, especially when the average levels of resources differ less than their volatility among environments. Such comparative work has begun with populations of newspapers in four countries: Argentina and Ireland (Carroll and Delacroix 1982; Delacroix and Carroll 1983), the United States (Carroll 1987; West and Olzak 1987), and Finland (Amburgey et al. 1988).

One of the earliest treatments of organizational ecology, by Blau and Scott (1962, pp. 214–221), noted that individual organizations have the potential to expand indefinitely. They suggested that such unlimited potential for growth makes it useful to consider a model of dominance in a system of specialized organizations as an alternative to the equilibrium model employed by classical economists. Following the lead of Hawley (1950), they suggested that symbiotic relationships between diverse kinds of organizations may come to replace competition between similar organizations under such a model. Community ecology gains relevance as a

result of the skewed size distributions resulting from competition and organizational growth.

An issue that we have not pursued in depth is the relationship between
population growth and organizational growth. Clearly, the expansion of
the resources available for organizing will often lead both to growth of
individual organizations and to growth in the populations of organizations
using those resources. The relationships between the two kinds of growth
processes are unknown.

In addition, it seems likely that organizational forms differ substantially
in growth potential. Family firms face stronger internal limits to growth
than publicly traded corporations, for example. These limitations include
the shortage of managerial resources available from the labor supply in the
family and difficulty in access to capital markets. In contrast, franchised
retail organizations can grow rapidly because they use the credit resources
of those who purchase franchises, and they do so by reproducing retail
units according to a form that is designed to be easily reproducible. So we
can expect organizational forms to differ greatly in speed of growth.

A further point is that many organizations change form as they grow. As
Caplow (1957) argued many years ago, social relationships change as organizations move from small groups to large corporations, and such changes
may serve as the basis for defining the concept of size. Much of the literature on stages of growth and organizational life cycles (for example, see
Kimberly and Miles 1980) identifies discontinuities in patterns of organization and in sets of managerial problems as organizations grow large. Such
arguments support the contention that there may be small-form and large-
form variants of many organizational forms. Such discontinuities, if they
exist, suggest a variety of research issues for ecological study. Among
them are the possibility that mortality rates are particularly high for inter-
mediate-size organizations, and that growth from small to large variants is
hazardous as a result. Similarly, large organizational forms may result
from processes other than growth as conventionally defined. Merger and
acquisition are two related means of assembling a large organization, and
they almost certainly differ dramatically in their survival implications compared with the situation of simply adding to the organization's resource
base and to its level of human participation.

Consideration of absolute and relative size of organizations as it affects
industrial concentration has been the preoccupation of industrial–organization economics. Our work presents opportunities for convergence with
economic analyses of organizational change, but it also implies differences. There are at least two issues here: the role of efficiency and the role

of self-interested actors in producing change in populations of organizations.

As we noted in earlier chapters, influential economic analyses of organizational structure such as Williamson's (1975, 1985) transaction cost theory of organizational boundaries and Nelson and Winter's (1982) evolutionary theory of the firm assume that efficiency, that is, cost minimization, drives the process of change. These two lines of work diverge in one crucial way. Williamson assumes that the world of organizations usually approximates an efficient equilibrium, that the set of boundaries around firms are those that actually minimize the costs of completing the entire set of transactions that characterize the system. Nelson and Winter doubt that equilibrium is common and instead assume that populations of firms evolve locally (by satisficing rather than maximizing globally) in the direction of higher aggregate efficiency. Still, these lines of argument retain the economic focus on efficiency as the key to understanding organizational change.

We have expressed reservations about the power of efficiency in dictating change in the world of organizations. Although we recognize that considerations of efficiency have powerful consequences for many kinds of organizations, we feel that they do not obviously override institutional and political considerations. But we lack anything resembling a full-fledged theory of the interactions of these various social and economic processes in shaping change in populations and communities of organizations. Theory and research that address these connections are sorely needed.

The second point of contact with the economic tradition concerns the role of self-interested actors in shaping change in the macro features of organizational populations. Mancur Olson (1986, p. 176), in commenting on our work, suggested that: "Some organization theory is a little bit like a murder mystery in which the victim is killed for no reason at all. That is to say, one doesn't get any sense of the reasons or individual motives." This characterization is correct as far as it goes. As we have stressed, we have tried to develop theories at the population level that are robust with respect to assumptions about individual motivation. In this respect, our goal is to develop theories like Darwin's theory of evolution, which continues to have value despite great changes in our understanding of the detailed genetic processes upon which processes of biotic evolution depend. A macro theory is robust with respect to assumptions about individual motivations if the theoretical structure does not have to be reassembled each time a micro assumption is changed.

Still, we have not established the robustness of our theories and models.

What are the consequences of alternative assumptions about individual actors in our framework? Attempting to answer this question will clarify the relation of our approach to that of many others in the social sciences whose main business is specifying and testing propositions about individual action.

Some of the most interesting yet most complicated issues for empirical research are those that concern boundary dynamics. In Chapter 3 we proposed empirical research on the subprocesses of most sociological interest. We think it would be particularly productive to pursue our notions of the role of social networks in creating and maintaining boundaries in the organizational world. We suggest following the lead of two lines of work. The first line begins with McPherson's (1982) use of survey responses to count overlaps in organizational memberships as a way to measure overlaps among voluntary organizations. An interesting application of this approach is McPherson and Smith-Lovin's (1987) analysis of sex segregation in populations of voluntary associations. The second related line of research begins with Breiger's (1981) approach to inferring the presence of class boundaries from patterns of movements of individuals among sets of occupations. The key idea is to use movement and the absence of movement to measure boundaries. This work has broad potential application to the issues we raise because, like McPherson's, it makes explicit links to the rapidly growing corpus of methods for analyzing data on social networks. We think it would be extremely useful to exploit these links in conducting research on the processes that segregate collections of organizations into populations with unitary character.

We also need to learn much more about the detailed structure of the niches of diverse populations. Exactly what are the factors that limit the expansion of populations of various forms of organizations? How much variability in niche width actually obtains in various interesting communities of organizations? Does the distinction between specialists and generalists cut the same way across many different dimensions of environments? That is, are some organizational forms highly specialized to many different environmental dimensions, or does the classification of organizations in terms of degree of specialism depend greatly on the environmental dimension?

Many obvious extensions of our work shade naturally into the community ecology of organizations. This branch of study concerns the system-level consequences of the dynamics of interacting populations. Although, we and some other researchers have begun to explore such links empirically, we have barely scratched the surface. We would like to close by pointing to two potentially productive extensions to community ecology.

Our analyses of foundings (and entries) within populations take as given the time of the first founding or entry. That is, these analyses condition on the time of founding of the *population*. The next step is to analyze the origins of populations. The natural question is whether the growth of numbers in other populations affects the likelihood that some particular population will be founded. For instance, did the growth in the number of firms in the United States in the early nineteenth century affect the timing of the founding of the first *national* labor union? Answering such questions forces the analyst to consider the effects of the composition of organizational communities on the rates of creation and demise of entire populations.

A second set of questions about community-level processes concerns the consequences of links between organizations in a single population or in multiple populations. Our empirical analysis has treated each organization in a population as an independent actor subject to common constraints. But this is obviously an oversimplification. Members of organizational populations commonly form associations for mutual defense, strategic planning, and lobbying, as we have noted in discussing the evolution of national labor unions. These associations in turn form alliances with other corporate actors such as political parties or government agencies. Many sociologists think that the existence of such associations implies the absence of selection pressures on the members of the population—that federated populations can change their environments in ways that guarantee survival of the members. We suggested earlier (Hannan and Freeman 1977) that nonindependence of organizations does affect selection processes, not by eliminating competition and selection but by shifting these processes to a higher level of analysis. So, for instance, members of an industry often successfully pressure national governments to provide protected markets, thereby improving the life chances of each member firm. Yet, as we have seen repeatedly in recent years, such protection sustains inefficient producers and inefficient production practices. Eventually the cost of the political protection grows sufficiently that the survival of the entire national industry is threatened. In some cases national industries dwindle in scope as the world economy reallocates the production to other nations; in other cases, the protected status of the industry is removed and intense selection occurs. In either case, nonindependence of organizations in the population has altered the time path of selection. But this complication does not rule out ecological analysis along the lines we have suggested. It does mean that analysts must consider processes at the national and international level in order to understand the dynamics of many kinds of organizational populations.

References

Aalen, Odd. 1978. "Nonparametric Inference for a Family of Counting Processes." *Annals of Statistics* 6: 701–726.

Aldrich, Howard E. 1979. *Organizations and Environments*. Englewood Cliffs, N.J.: Prentice-Hall.

Aldrich, Howard E., and Jeffrey Pfeffer. 1976. "Environments of Organizations." *Annual Review of Sociology* 2: 79–105.

Aldrich, Howard E., and Udo Staber. 1988. "Organizing Business Interest: Patterns of Trade Association Foundings, Transformations, and Deaths." In Glenn R. Carroll, ed., *Ecological Models of Organizations*. Cambridge, Mass.: Ballinger.

Amburgey, Terry L. 1986. "Multivariate Point Processes in Social Research." *Social Science Research* 15: 190–207.

Amburgey, Terry L., Marjo-Ritta Lehisalo, and Dawn Kelly. 1988. "Suppression and Failure in the Political Press: Government Control, Party Affiliation and Organizational Life Chances." In Glenn R. Carroll, ed., *Ecological Models of Organizations*. Cambridge, Mass.: Ballinger.

Arrow, Kenneth J. 1974. *The Limits of Organization*. New York: Norton.

Astley, W. Graham. 1985. "The Two Ecologies: Population and Community Perspectives on Organizational Evolution." *Administrative Science Quarterly* 30: 223–241.

Astley, W. Graham, and Andrew Van de Ven. 1983. "Central Perspectives and Debates in Organization Theory." *Administrative Science Quarterly* 28: 245–273.

Averitt, Robert T. 1968. *The Dual Economy*. New York: Norton.

Ayer, N. W. *American Newspaper Directory Annual*. Philadelphia: Ayer Press.

Barnard, Chester I. 1938. *The Functions of the Executive.* Cambridge, Mass.: Harvard University Press.

Barnett, William P., and Glenn R. Carroll. 1987. "Competition and Commensalism among Early Telephone Companies." *Administrative Science Quarterly* 30: 400–421.

Baron, James N., and William T. Bielby. 1984. "The Organization of Work in a Segmented Economy." *American Sociological Review* 49: 454–473.

Barth, Fredrik. 1956. "Ecologic Relationships of Ethnic Groups in Swat, North Pakistan." *American Anthropologist* 58: 1079–1089.

—— 1969. "Introduction." In Fredrik Barth, ed., *Ethnic Groups and Boundaries.* Boston: Little, Brown.

Becker, Gary S. 1975. *Human Capital,* 2nd ed. New York: Columbia University Press.

Becker, Howard S. 1982. *Art Worlds.* Berkeley: University of California Press.

Bell, Wendell. 1954. "A Probability Model for the Measurement of Ecological Segregation." *Social Forces* 32: 357–364.

Benson, J. Kenneth. 1977. "Organizations: A Dialectical View." *Administrative Science Quarterly* 22: 1–21.

Berk, Richard. 1983. "An Introduction to Sample Selection Bias in Sociological Data." *American Sociological Review* 48: 386–399.

Blau, Peter M., and Otis Dudley Duncan. 1967. *The American Occupational Structure.* New York: Wiley.

Blau, Peter M., and Richard A. Schoenherr. 1971. *The Structure of Organizations.* New York: Basic Books.

Blau, Peter M., and W. Richard Scott. 1962. *Formal Organizations.* San Francisco: Chandler.

Bonacich, Edna. 1976. "Advanced Capitalism and Black/White Relations in the United States: A Split Labor Market Interpretation." *American Sociological Review* 41: 34–51.

Boyd, Robert, and Peter J. Richardson. 1985. *Culture and the Evolutionary Process.* Chicago: University of Chicago Press.

Braun, Ernest, and Stuart MacDonald. 1978. *Revolution in Miniature: The History and Impact of Semiconductor Electronics.* Cambridge: Cambridge University Press.

Braverman, Harry. 1974. *Labor and Monopoly Capital: The Degradation of Work in the Twentieth Century.* New York: Monthly Review Press.

Breiger, Ronald L. 1981. "The Social Class Structure of Occupational Mobility." *American Journal of Sociology* 87: 578–611.

Brittain, Jack, and John Freeman. 1980. "Organizational Proliferation and Density-Dependent Selection." In John R. Kimberley and Robert H. Miles, eds., *Organizational Life Cycles.* San Francisco: Jossey-Bass.

Brittain, Jack, and Douglas R. Wholey. 1988. "Competition and Coexistence in Organizational Communities: Population Dynamics." In Glenn R. Carroll, ed., *Ecological Models of Organizations*. Cambridge, Mass.: Ballinger.

Brooks, R. R. 1937. *When Labor Organizes*. New Haven, Conn.: Yale University Press.

Burawoy, Michael. 1979. *Manufacturing Consent: Changes in the Labor Process under Monopoly Capitalism*. Chicago: University of Chicago Press.

Burns, Tom, and George M. Stalker. 1961. *The Management of Innovation*. London: Tavistock.

Burrell, Gibson, and Gareth Morgan. 1979. *Sociological Paradigms and Organizational Analysis*. London: Heinemann.

Caplow, Theodore. 1957. "Organizational Size." *American Sociological Review* 1: 484–505.

Carroll, Glenn R. 1981. "Dynamics of Organizational Expansion in National Systems of Education." *American Sociological Review* 46: 585–599.

——— 1983. "A Stochastic Model of Organizational Mortality: Review and Reanalysis." *Social Science Research* 12: 303–329.

——— 1984. "Organizational Ecology." *Annual Review of Sociology* 10: 71–93.

——— 1985. "Concentration and Specialization: Dynamics of Niche Width in Populations of Organizations." *American Journal of Sociology* 90: 1262–1283.

——— 1987. *Publish and Perish: The Organizational Ecology of Newspaper Industries*. Greenwich, Conn.: JAI Press.

——— 1988. Editor. *Ecological Models of Organizations*. Cambridge, Mass.: Ballinger.

Carroll, Glenn R., and Jacques Delacroix. 1982. "Organizational Mortality in the Newspaper Industries of Argentina and Ireland: An Ecological Approach," *Administrative Science Quarterly* 27: 169–198.

Carroll, Glenn R., and Michael T. Hannan. 1988. "Density Dependence in the Evolution of Newspaper Populations." Paper presented at the annual meetings of the American Sociological Association, Atlanta.

Carroll, Glenn R., and Yanchung Paul Huo. 1986. "Organizational Task and Institutional Environments in Evolutionary Perspective: Findings from the Local Newspaper Industry." *American Journal of Sociology* 91: 838–873.

——— 1988. "Organizational and Electoral Paradoxes of the Knights of Labor." In Glenn R. Carroll, ed., *Ecological Models of Organizations*. Cambridge, Mass.: Ballinger.

Cavalli-Sforza, Luca, and Marcus Feldman. 1981. *Cultural Transmission and Evolution*. Princeton, N.J.: Princeton University Press.

Chandler, Alfred D., Jr. 1977. *The Visible Hand: The Managerial Revolution in American Business*. Cambridge, Mass.: Harvard University Press.

Child, John. 1972. "Organizational Structure, Environment, and Performance: The Role of Strategic Choice." *Sociology* 6: 1–22.

Child, John, and Alfred Kieser. 1981. "Development of Organizations over Time." In William Starbuck and Paul Nystrom, eds., *Handbook of Organizational Design*, vol. 1. New York: Oxford University Press.

Chow, Garland. 1978. "The Cost of Trucking Revisited." *Motor Carrier Economic Regulation: Proceedings of a Workshop*. Washington, D.C. : National Research Council.

Christie, Robert A. 1956. *Empire in Wood: A History of the Carpenter's Union*. Ithaca, N.Y.: New York State School of Industrial and Labor Relations Press.

Clawson, Dan. 1980. *Bureaucracy and the Labor Process*. New York: Monthly Review Press.

Clegg, Stewart. 1979. *The Theory of Power and Organization*. London: Routledge and Kegan Paul.

Coleman, James S. 1964. *Introduction to Mathematical Sociology*. New York: Free Press.

—— 1974. *Power and the Structure of Society*. New York: Norton.

Commons, John R., et al., eds. 1927. *History of Labor in the United States*, 4 vols. New York: Macmillan.

Cooper, A. C. 1972. "Incubator Organizations and Technical Entrepreneurship." In *Technical Entrepreneurship: A Symposium*. Milwaukee: Center for Venture Management.

Cox, D. R. 1972. "Regression Models and Lifetables." *Journal of the Royal Statistical Society* B34: 187–220.

—— 1975. "Partial Likelihood." *Biometrika* 62: 269–276.

Cox, D. R., and D. Oakes. 1984. *Analysis of Survival Data*. London: Chapman and Hall.

Cyert, Richard M., and James G. March. 1963. *A Behavioral Theory of the Firm*. Englewood Cliffs, N.J.: Prentice-Hall.

Daggett, Emerson (supervisor). 1939. *History of Journalism in San Francisco*, vols. 1–6. San Francisco: Works Project Administration Project 10008, O. P. 665–08–3–12.

David, Paul A., and Peter Solar. 1977. "A Bicentenary Contribution to the History of the Cost of Living in America." *Research in Economic History* 2: 1–80.

Delacroix, Jacques, and Glenn R. Carroll. 1983. "Organizational Foundings: An Ecological Study of the Newspaper Industries of Argentina and Ireland." *Administrative Science Quarterly* 28: 274–291.

Delacroix, Jacques, and Michael E. Solt. 1988. "Niche Formation and Foundings in the California Wine Industry." In Glenn R. Carroll, ed., *Ecological Models of Organizations*. Cambridge, Mass.: Ballinger.

Delacroix, Jacques, Michael E. Solt, and Anand Swaminathan. In press. "Density Dependence vs. Population Dynamics: An Ecological Study of Failings in the California Wine Industry." *American Sociological Review*.

DiMaggio, Paul J. 1983. "State Expansion and the Structuration of Organizational Fields." In R. L. Holland and R. Quinn, eds., *Organizational Theory and Public Policy*. Beverly Hills, Calif.: Sage.

—— 1986. "Structural Analysis of Organizational Fields: A Blockmodel Approach." In Barry Staw and Lawrence Cummings, eds., *Research in Organizational Behavior*. Greenwich, Conn.: JAI Press.

DiMaggio, Paul J., and Walter W. Powell. 1983. "The Iron Cage Revisited: Institutional Isomorphism and Collective Rationality in Organizational Fields." *American Sociological Review* 48: 147–160.

Dobzhansky, Theodosius. 1951. *Genetics and the Origin of Species*, 3rd ed. New York: Columbia University Press.

Downs, Anthony. 1967. *Inside Bureaucracy*. Boston: Little, Brown.

Duncan, Otis Dudley, David Featherman, and Beverly Duncan. 1972. *Socioeconomic Background and Achievement*. New York: Seminar Press.

Durkheim, Emile. [1893] 1933. *The Division of Labor in Society*. Glencoe, Ill.: Free Press.

Edwards, Richard. 1979. *Contested Terrain: The Transformation of the Work Place in the Twentieth Century*. New York: Basic Books.

Efron, Bradley. 1977. "The Efficiency of Cox's Likelihood Function for Censored Data." *Journal of the American Statistical Association* 72: 557–565.

Eisenstadt, S. N. 1958. "Bureaucracy and Bureaucratization: A Trend Report and Bibliography." *Current Sociology* 7: 99–164.

Elton, Charles. 1927. *Animal Ecology*. London: Sidgwick and Jackson.

Etzioni, Amitai. 1961. *The Comparative Analysis of Complex Organizations*. Glencoe, Ill.: Free Press.

Finance, Maurice. 1894. *Les Syndicates Ouvriers aux États-Unis*. Paris: Imprimerie Nationale.

Fink, Gary, ed. 1977. *National Labor Unions*. Greenwood, Ala.: Greenwood Press.

Fisher, R. A. 1930. *The Genetical Theory of Natural Selection*. New York: Dover.

Foner, Philip. 1947–1975. *History of the Labor Movement in the United States*. Vol. 1, 1947; vol. 2 (2nd ed.), 1975; vol. 3, 1964; vol. 4, 1972. New York: International Publishers.

Fortune. 1986. "Who Will Survive the Microchip Shakeout." January 6: 82–85.

—— 1987. "Silicon Valley Phoenixes." November 23: 128–135.

Freeman, John. 1978. "The Unit of Analysis in Organizational Research." In Marshall Meyer et al., eds., *Environments and Organizations*. San Francisco: Jossey-Bass.

—— 1982. "Organizational Life Cycles and Natural Selection Processes." In Barry Staw and Lawrence Cummings, eds., *Research in Organizational Behavior*, vol. 4. Greenwich, Conn.: JAI Press.

—— 1986a. "Data Quality and the Development of Organizational Social Science: An Editorial Essay." *Administrative Science Quarterly* 31: 298–303.

—— 1986b. "Entrepreneurs as Organizational Products: Semiconductor Firms and Venture Capital Firms." In Gary Libecap, ed., *Advances in the Study of Entrepreneurship, Innovation and Economic Growth*. Greenwich, Conn.: JAI Press.

Freeman, John, and Warren Boeker. 1984. "The Ecological Analysis of Business Strategy." *California Management Review* 26: 73–86.

Freeman, John, and Jack Brittain. 1977. "Union Merger Processes and Industrial Environments." *Industrial Relations* 16: 173–185.

Freeman, John, Glenn R. Carroll, and Michael T. Hannan. 1983. "The Liability of Newness: Age Dependence in Organizational Death Rates." *American Sociological Review* 48: 692–710.

Freeman, John, and Michael T. Hannan. 1975. "Growth and Decline Processes in Organizations." *American Sociological Review* 40: 215–228.

—— 1983. "Niche Width and the Dynamics of Organizational Populations." *American Journal of Sociology* 88: 1116–1145.

—— 1987. "The Ecology of Restaurants Revisited." *American Journal of Sociology* 92: 1214–1220.

Friedman, Milton. 1953. *Essays in Positive Economics*. Chicago: University of Chicago Press.

Fuller, Wayne A. 1976. *Introduction to Statistical Time Series*. New York: Wiley.

Galenson, Walter. 1940. *Rival Unionism in the United States*. New York: American Council on Public Affairs.

—— 1960. *The CIO Challenge to the AFL: A History of the American Labor Movement 1935–1941*. Cambridge, Mass.: Harvard University Press.

Gamson, William. 1975. *Power and Discontent*. Homewood, Ill.: Dorsey.

Gause, G. F. 1934. *The Struggle for Existence*. Baltimore: Williams and Wilkins.

Gibson, J. L. 1970. "An Analysis of the Location of Instrument Manufacture in the United States." *Annals of the Association of American Geographers* 60: 352–367.

Gifford, Courtney D. 1985. *Directory of U.S. Labor Organizations 1984–1985*. Washington, D.C.: Bureau of National Affairs.

Gordon, David M., Richard Edwards, and Michael Reich. 1982. *Segmented Work, Divided Workers*. Cambridge: Cambridge University Press.

Gould, S. J., and N. Eldridge. 1977. "Puncutated Equilibria: The Tempo and Mode of Evolution Reconsidered." *Paleobiology* 3: 115–151.

Greene, William. 1986. "LIMDEP Manual." Unpublished mimeo.

Gregory, Winifred, ed. 1937. *American Newspapers 1821–1936*. New York: H. W. Wilson.

Griffin, Larry J., Michael Wallace, and Beth Rubin. 1986. "Capitalist Resistance to the Organization of Labor before the New Deal. Why? How? Success?" *American Sociological Review* 51: 147–167.

Gutman, Herbert. 1976. *Work, Culture and Society in Industrializing America*. New York: Vintage.

Hage, Jerald, and Michael Aiken. 1970. *Social Change in Complex Organizations*. New York: Random House.

Hannan, Michael T. 1979. "The Dynamics of Ethnic Boundaries in Modern States." In John W. Meyer and Michael T. Hannan, eds., *National Development and the World System*. Chicago: University of Chicago Press.

—— 1980. "The Ecology of National Labor Unions: Theory and Research Design." Technical Report 1, Organizations Studies Section, Institute for Mathematical Social Sciences, Stanford University.

—— 1986a. "Uncertainty, Diversity and Organizational Change." In Neil J. Smelser and Dean R. Gerstein, eds., *Social and Behavioral Sciences: Discoveries over Fifty Years*. Washington, D.C.: National Academy Press.

—— 1986b. "A Model of Competitive and Institutional Processes in Organizational Ecology." Technical Report 86-13. Department of Sociology, Cornell University.

—— 1988a. "Social Change, Organizational Diversity, and Individual Careers." In Matilda White Riley, ed., *Social Structures and Human Lives*. Beverly Hills, Calif.: Sage and the American Sociological Association.

—— 1988b. "Age Dependence in the Mortality of National Labor Unions: Comparisons of Parametric Models." *Journal of Mathematical Sociology* 14: 1–30.

Hannan, Michael T., and John Freeman. 1974. "Environment and the Structure of Organizations." Paper presented at the annual meetings of the American Sociological Association, Montreal, Canada.

——— 1977. "The Population Ecology of Organizations." *American Journal of Sociology* 82: 929–964.

——— 1978. "Internal Politics of Growth and Decline." In Marshall Meyer et al., eds., *Environments and Organizations*. San Francisco: Jossey-Bass.

——— 1982. "Organizational Niche Width: Test of a Model." In Wolfgang Sodeur, ed., *Mathematische Analyse von Organizationsstrukturen und - Prozesen*. Dusisburg, FRG: Verlag der Sozialwissenscaftlichen Kooperative.

——— 1984. "Structural Inertia and Organizational Change." *American Sociological Review* 49: 149–164.

——— 1986. "Where Do Organizational Forms Come From?" *Sociological Forum* 1: 50–72.

——— 1987. "The Ecology of Organizational Founding: American Labor Unions, 1836–1985." *American Journal of Sociology* 92: 910–943.

——— 1988. "The Ecology of Organizational Mortality: American Labor Unions, 1836–1985." *American Journal of Sociology* 94: 25–52.

Hawley, Amos. 1950. *Human Ecology*. New York: Ronald Press.

——— 1968. "Human Ecology." In David Sills, ed., *International Encyclopedia of the Social Sciences*. New York: Macmillan.

——— 1986. *Human Ecology: A Theoretical Essay*. Chicago: University of Chicago Press.

Heckman, James J. 1979. "Sample Selection Bias as Specification Error." *Econometrica* 45: 153–161.

Herriot, Scott. 1987. "Fitness Set Theory in Population Ecology of Organizations: Comment on Freeman and Hannan." *American Journal of Sociology* 92: 1210–1213.

Hirsch, Paul. 1975. "Organizational Effectiveness and the Institutional Environment." *Administrative Science Quarterly* 20: 327–344.

Hodson, Randy, and Robert L. Kaufman. 1982. "Economic Dualism: A Critical Review." *American Sociological Review* 47: 727–739.

Hrebiniak, Lawrence G., and William F. Joyce. 1985. "Organizational Adaptation: Strategic Choice and Environmental Determinism." *Administrative Science Quarterly* 30: 336–347.

Hutchinson, G. Evelyn. 1957. "Concluding Remarks." *Cold Spring Harbor Symposium on Quantitative Biology* 22: 415–427.

——— 1959. "Homage to Santa Rosalia, or Why Are There So Many Kinds of Animals?" *American Naturalist* 93: 145–159.

——— 1978. *An Introduction to Population Ecology*. New Haven, Conn.: Yale University Press.

Huxley, Julian. 1944. *Evolution: The Modern Synthesis*. London: George Allen.

Industrial Commission. 1901. *Report*. Washington, D.C.: Government Printing Office.

Johnson, Norman L., and Samuel Kotz. 1970. *Distributions in Statistics: Continuous Univariate Distributions*, vol. 2. Boston: Houghton Mifflin.

Kahneman, D., P. Slovic, and A. Tversky. 1982. *Judgement under Uncertainty: Heuristics and Biases*. Cambridge: Cambridge University Press.

Kalbfleisch, John D., and Ross L. Prentice. 1980. *Statistical Analysis of Failure Time Data*. New York: Wiley.

Kanter, Rosabeth Moss. 1983. *The Change Masters: Innovations for Future Productivity in the American Corporation*. New York: Simon and Schuster.

Kaplan, E. L., and P. Meier. 1958. "Nonparametric Estimation from Incomplete Observations." *Journal of the American Statistical Association* 53: 457–481.

Karlin, Samuel, and Howard M. Taylor. 1975. *A First Course in Stochastic Processes*, 2nd ed. New York: Academic Press.

Katz, Daniel, and Robert L. Kahn. 1966. *The Social Psychology of Organizations*. New York: Wiley.

Kaufman, Herbert. 1976. *Are Government Organizations Immortal?* Washington, D.C.: Brookings Institution.

Kaufman, Robert L., Randy Hodson, and Neil D. Fligstein. 1981. "Defrocking Dualism: A New Approach to Defining Industrial Sectors." *Social Science Research* 10: 1–31.

Kimberly, John R., and Robert H. Miles, eds. 1980. *Organizational Life Cycles*. San Francisco: Jossey-Bass.

Ladde, G. S., and D. D. Šiljak. 1976. "Stability of Multispecies Communities in Randomly Varying Environments." *Journal of Mathematical Biology* 2: 165–178.

Langton, Nancy. 1984. "Mortality of Unions in the Service Sector." Ph.D. diss., Stanford University.

Lawrence, Paul, and Jay Lorsch. 1967. *Organization and Environment*. Cambridge, Mass.: Harvard University Press.

Lescohier, Don D. 1910. *The Knights of St. Crispin, 1867–1874. Bulletin of the University of Wisconsin*, no. 355. Economic and Political Science Series. vol. 7, no. 1.

Levin, Simon A. 1970. "Community Equilibria and Stability: An Extension of the Competitive Exclusion Principle." *American Naturalist* 104: 413–423.

Levins, Richard. 1968. *Evolution in Changing Environments*. Princeton, N.J.: Princeton University Press.

Lewontin, Richard C. 1974. *The Genetic Basis of Evolutionary Change*. New York: Columbia University Press.

—— 1978. "Adaptation." *Scientific American* 239: 212–230.

Lieberson, Stanley. 1969. "Measuring Population Diversity." *American Sociological Review* 34: 850–862.

Lipset, Seymour Martin, Martin A. Trow, and James S. Coleman. 1956. *Union Democracy*. Glencoe, Ill.: Free Press.

Lorrain, François, and Harrison C. White. 1971. "Structural Equivalence of Individuals in Social Networks." *Journal of Mathematical Sociology* 1: 49–80.

Lotka, Alfred J. 1925. *Elements of Mathematical Biology*. New York: Dover Publications.

MacArthur, Robert H. 1972. *Geographical Ecology: Patterns in the Distribution of Species*. Princeton, N.J.: Princeton University Press.

MacArthur, Robert H., and Richard Levins. 1964. "Competition, Habitat Selection and Character Displacement in a Patchy Environment." *Proceedings of the National Academy of Sciences* 51: 1207–1210.

March, James G. 1982. "Footnotes on Organizational Change." *Administrative Science Quarterly* 26: 563–597.

March, James G., and Johan P. Olsen. 1976. *Ambiguity and Choice in Organizations*. Bergen, Norway: Universitetsforlaget.

March, James G., and Herbert A. Simon. 1958. *Organizations*. New York: Wiley.

Marrett, Cora B. 1980. "Influences on the Rise of New Organizations: The Formation of Women's Medical Societies." *Administrative Science Quarterly* 25: 185–199.

May, Robert M. 1974. *Stability and Complexity in Model Ecosystems*, 2nd ed. Princeton, N.J.: Princeton University Press.

Mayo, Elton. 1945. *The Social Problems of an Industrial Civilization*. Boston: Graduate School of Business Administration, Harvard University.

McCarthy, John D., Mark Wolfson, David P. Baker, and Elaine Mosakowski. 1988. "The Founding of Social Movement Organizations: Local Citizen's Groups Opposing Drunken Driving." In Glenn R. Carroll, ed., *Ecological Models of Organizations*. Cambridge, Mass.: Ballinger.

McKelvey, Bill. 1975. "Guidelines for the Empirical Classification of Organizations." *Administrative Science Quarterly* 20: 509–525.

—— 1982. *Organizational Systematics*. Berkeley: University of California Press.

McKelvey, Bill, and Howard E. Aldrich. 1983. "Populations, Natural Selection and Applied Organizational Science." *Administrative Science Quarterly* 28: 101–128.

McPherson, J. Miller. 1982. "Hypernetwork Sampling: Duality and Differentiation in Voluntary Associations." *Social Networks* 3: 225–249.

—— 1983. "An Ecology of Affiliation." *American Sociological Review* 48: 519–535.

McPherson, J. Miller, and Lynn Smith-Lovin. 1987. "Homophily in Voluntary Associations: Status Distance and the Composition of Face-to-Face Groups." *American Sociological Review* 52: 370–379.

—— 1988. "A Comparative Ecology of Five Nations: Testing a Model of Competition among Voluntary Organizations." In Glenn R. Carroll, ed., *Ecological Models of Organizations*. Cambridge, Mass.: Ballinger.

Merton, Robert K. 1957. *Social Theory and Social Structure*, 2nd ed. Glencoe, Ill.: Free Press.

Merton, Robert K., Ailsa P. Gray, Barbara Hockey, and Hanan P. Selvin, eds., 1952. *Reader in Bureaucracy*. Glencoe, Ill.: Free Press.

Meyer, John W., and Brian Rowan. 1977. "Institutionalized Organizations: Formal Structure as Myth and Ceremony." *American Journal of Sociology* 83: 340–363.

Meyer, John W., and W. Richard Scott. 1983. *Organizational Environments: Ritual and Rationality*. Beverly Hills, Calif.: Sage.

Meyer, Marshall W. 1972. "Size and the Structure of Organizations: A Causal Analysis," *American Sociological Review* 37: 434–441.

Michels, Robert. [1915] 1949. *Political Parties*, trans. Edward Cedar Paul. Glencoe, Ill.: Free Press.

Miles, Robert H. 1982. *Coffin Nails and Corporate Strategies*. Englewood Cliffs, N.J.: Prentice Hall.

Miles, Robert H., and W. A. Randolph. 1980. "Influence of Organizational Learning Styles on Early Development." In John R. Kimberly and Robert H. Miles, eds., *The Organizational Life Cycle*. San Francisco: Jossey-Bass.

Mitchell, Will. 1987. "Dynamic Tension: Theoretical and Empirical Analyses of Entry into Emerging Industries." Paper presented at the Stanford Asilomar Conference on Organizations.

Mittleman, Edward B. 1927. "Trade Unionism (1833–1839)." In John R. Commons et al., eds., *History of Labor in the United States,* vol. 1. New York: Macmillan.

Monod, Jacques. 1971. *Chance and Necessity*. New York: Vintage.

National Industrial Conference Board. 1956. *Sources of Union Government Structures and Procedures*. New York: NICB.

Nelson, Richard R., and Sidney G. Winter. 1982. *An Evolutionary Theory of Economic Change*. Cambridge, Mass.: Harvard University Press.

Nelson, W. 1972. "Theory and Application of Hazard Plotting for Censored Data." *Technometrics* 14: 945–965.

New Jersey Bureau of Labor Statistics. 1898. *Annual Report*.

Newsweek. 1972. "The Last Soldier." February 7: 41–42.

Nielsen, François. 1986. "Structural Conduciveness and Ethnic Mobilization: The Flemish Case." In Susan Olzak and Joane Nagel, eds., *Competitive Ethnic Relations*. Orlando, Fla.: Academic Press.

Nielsen, François, and Michael T. Hannan. 1977. "The Expansion of National Educational Systems: Tests of a Population Ecology Model." *American Sociological Review* 42: 479–490.

Nystrom, Paul C., and William Starbuck. 1981. "Designing and Understanding Organizations." In William Starbuck and Paul C. Nystrom, eds., *Handbook of Organizational Design*, vol. 1. New York: Oxford University Press.

Oakey, Ray. 1984. *High Technology Small Firms: Innovation and Regional Development in Britain and the United States*. New York: St. Martin's Press.

Olson, Mancur. 1986. "Discussion." In Siegwart Lindenberg, James S. Coleman, and Stefan Novak, eds., *Approaches to Social Theory*. New York: Russell Sage Foundation.

Olzak, Susan. 1983. "Contemporary Ethnic Mobilization." *Annual Review of Sociology* 9: 355–374.

——— In press. "The Changing Job Queue: Causes of Shifts in Ethnic Job Segregation in American Cities, 1870–1880." *Social Forces*.

Oster, George F., and Edward O. Wilson. 1978. *Caste and Ecology in the Social Insects*. Princeton, N.J.: Princeton University Press.

Ouchi, William G. 1981. *Theory Z*. Reading, Mass.: Addison Wesley.

Paige, Jeffrey. 1975. *Agrarian Revolutions*. Berkeley: University of California Press.

Parsons, Talcott. 1960. *Structure and Process in Modern Society*. Glencoe, Ill.: Free Press.

Perrow, Charles. 1961. "The Analysis of Goals in Complex Organizations." *American Sociological Review* 26: 854–866.

——— 1967. "A Framework for the Comparative Analysis of Organizations." *American Sociological Review* 32: 194–208.

——— 1986. *Complex Organizations: A Critical Essay*, 3rd ed. Glencoe, Ill.: Scott Foresman.

Peters, Thomas J., and Robert H. Waterman. 1982. *In Search of Excellence*. New York: Harper and Row.

Peterson, Florence. 1944. *Handbook of Labor Unions*. Washington, D.C.: American Council of Public Affairs.

Pfeffer, Jeffrey. 1983. "Organizational Demography." In Lawrence Cummings and Barry Staw, eds., *Research in Organizational Behavior*. Greenwich, Conn.: JAI Press.

Pfeffer, Jeffrey, and Gerald Salancik. 1978. *The External Control of Organ-*

izations: A Resource Dependence Perspective. New York: Harper and Row.

Poor's Register of Corporations, Directors and Executives, United States and Canada [various years].

Pugh, D. S., D. J. Hickson, C. R. Hinings, and C. Turner. 1969. "The Context of Organization Structures." *Administrative Science Quarterly* 14: 91–114.

Roethlisberger, F. J., and William J. Dickson. 1939. *Management and the Worker*. Cambridge, Mass.: Harvard University Press.

Roughgarden, Jonathan. 1979. *The Theory of Population Genetics and Evolutionary Ecology: An Introduction*. New York: Macmillan.

San Jose Mercury. 1984. "Intel Finds Marital Bliss with IBM." January 9: 1C–10C.

SAS Institute Inc. 1984. *SAS/ETS User's Guide, Version 5 Edition*. Cary, N.C.: SAS Institute.

—— 1985. *SAS User's Guide: Statistics, Version 5 Edition*. Cary, N.C.: SAS Institute.

—— 1986. *SUGI Supplemental Library User's Guide, Version 5 Edition*.

Schudson, Michael. 1978. *Discovering the News*. New York: Basic Books.

Scott, W. Richard. 1987. *Organizations: Rational, Natural, and Open Systems*, 2nd ed. Englewood Cliffs, N.J.: Prentice-Hall.

Scott, W. Richard, Ann Barry Flood, Wayne Ewy, and William H. Forrest, Jr. 1978. "Organizational Effectiveness and the Quality of Surgical Care in Hospitals." In Marshall Meyer et al., eds., *Environments and Organizations*. San Francisco: Jossey-Bass.

Selznick, Philip. 1948. "Foundations of the Theory of Organization." *American Sociological Review* 13: 25–35.

—— 1957. *Leadership in Administration*. New York: Harper and Row.

Šiljak, D. D. 1975. "When Is a Complex Ecosystem Stable?" *Mathematical Bioscience* 25: 25–50.

Simon, Herbert A. 1957. *Administrative Behavior*, 2nd ed. New York: Macmillan.

—— 1962. "The Architecture of Complexity." *Proceedings of the American Philosophical Society* 106: 67–82.

Singh, Jitendra, Robert J. House, and David J. Tucker. 1986. "Organizational Change and Organizational Mortality." *Administrative Science Quarterly* 31: 587–611.

Singh, Jitendra, David J. Tucker, and Robert J. House. 1986. "Organizational Legitimacy and the Liability of Newness." *Administrative Science Quarterly* 31: 171–193.

Stacy, E. W. 1962. "A Generalization of the Gamma Distribution." *Annals of Mathematical Statistics* 33: 1187–1192.

Stanley, S. M. 1979. *Macroevolution: Pattern and Process*. San Francisco: Freeman.

Stewart, Estelle. 1936. *Handbook of American Trade Unions*. Washington, D.C.: Bureau of Labor Statistics.

Stinchcombe, Arthur L. 1959. "Bureaucratic Craft and Administration of Production: A Comparative Study." *Administrative Science Quarterly* 4: 168–187.

———— 1965. "Social Structure and Organizations." In James G. March, ed., *Handbook of Organizations*. Chicago: Rand McNally.

———— 1968. *Constructing Social Theories*. New York: Harcourt, Brace and World.

———— 1983. *Economic Sociology*. New York: Academic Press.

Stinchcombe, Arthur L., Mary Sexton McDill, and Dollie R. Walker. 1968. "Demography of Organizations." *American Journal of Sociology* 74: 221–229.

Taft, Philip. 1964. *Organized Labor in American History*. New York: Harper and Row.

Taylor, Frederick W. [1911] 1970. *The Principles of Scientific Management*. New York: Harper.

Tewksbury, D. G. 1932. *The Foundings of American Colleges and Universities before the Civil War*. New York: Teachers College, Columbia University.

Thompson, James D. 1967. *Organizations in Action*. New York: McGraw-Hill.

Thorp, Willard L., and Wesley C. Mitchell. 1926. *Business Annals*. New York: National Bureau of Economic Research.

Tilly, Charles. 1978. *From Mobilization to Revolution*. Reading, Mass.: Addison Wesley.

Tilton, J. 1971. *International Diffusion of Technology: The Case of Semiconductors*. Washington, D.C.: The Brookings Institution.

Tomlins, Christopher. 1985. *The State and the Unions: Labor Relations, Law and the Organized Labor Movement in America, 1880–1960*. Cambridge: Cambridge University Press.

Troy, Leo. 1965. *Trade Union Membership, 1887–1962*. New York: National Bureau of Economic Research.

Tsiatis, A. 1981. "A Large Sample Study of Cox's Regression Model." *Annals of Statistics* 9: 93–108.

Tucker, David J., Jitendra Singh, Agnes G. Meinard, and Robert J. House. 1988. "Ecological and Institutional Sources of Change in Organizational Populations." In Glenn R. Carroll, ed., *Ecological Models of Organizations*. Cambridge, Mass.: Ballinger.

Tuma, Nancy Brandon. 1980. "Invoking RATE." Menlo Park, Calif.: SRI International.

Tuma, Nancy Brandon, and Michael T. Hannan. 1984. *Social Dynamics: Models and Methods*. New York: Academic Press.

Tushman, Michael L., and Philip Anderson. 1986. "Technological Discontinuities and Organizational Environments." *Administrative Science Quarterly* 31: 439–465.

Tyack, David B. 1974. *The One Best System*. Cambridge, Mass.: Harvard University Press.

Ulman, Lloyd. 1955. *The Rise of the National Trade Union*. Cambridge, Mass.: Harvard University Press.

U.S. Bureau of the Census. 1975. *Historical Statistics on the United States; Colonial Times to 1970*. Washington, D.C.: Government Printing Office.

U.S. Bureau of Labor Statistics. 1926. *Handbook of American Trade Unions*. Washington, D.C.: Government Printing Office.

Van de Ven, Andrew H. 1980. "Early Planning, Implementation, and Performance of New Organizations." In John R. Kimberly and Robert H. Miles, eds., *The Organizational Life Cycle*. San Francisco: Jossey-Bass.

Volterra, Vito. [1927] 1978. "Variations and Fluctuations in the Number of Coexisting Species." In F. M. Scudo and J. R. Ziegler, eds., *The Golden Age of Theoretical Ecology: 1923–1940*. New York: Springer-Verlag.

Wall Street Journal. 1983. "Deregulation of Banks Stirs Confusion, Splits Fed and White House." July 1: 7.

Wallace, Michael, and Arne L. Kalleberg. 1982. "Industrial Transformation and Decline of Craft: The Decomposition of Skill in the Printing Industry 1931–1978." *American Sociological Review* 47: 307–324.

Wallerstein, Immanuel. 1974. *The Modern World System*. New York: Academic Press.

Warren, Roland L. 1967. "The Interorganizational Field as a Focus for Investigation." *Administrative Science Quarterly* 12: 396–419.

Weber, Max. [1924] 1947. *The Theory of Social and Economic Organization*, ed. by A. H. Henderson and Talcott Parsons. Glencoe, Ill.: Free Press.

——— 1968. *Economy and Society: An Outline of Interpretive Sociology*, 3 vols. New York: Bedmeister.

Wedervang, F. 1965. *Development of a Population of Industrial Firms*. Oslo: Universitetsforlaget.

Weick, Karl. 1979. *The Social Psychology of Organizing*, 2nd ed. Reading, Mass.: Addison Wesley.

West, Elizabeth, and Susan Olzak. 1987. "The Ecology of Ethnic Newspapers in the United States, 1870–1915." Paper presented at the annual meetings of the American Sociological Association, Chicago.

Wheeler, Jean French. 1973. "Historical Directory of Santa Clara County Newspapers 1850–1972." Occasional Paper no. 1, Sourriseau Academy for California State and Local History, San Jose State University.

White, Harrison C. 1963. *Anatomy of Kinship*. Englewood Cliffs, N.J.: Prentice-Hall.

White, Harrison C., Ronald L. Breiger, and Scott A. Boorman. 1976. "Social Structure from Multiple Networks: I. Blockmodels of Roles and Positions." *American Journal of Sociology* 81: 730–780.

Williamson, Oliver E. 1975. *Markets and Hierarchies: Analysis and Antitrust Implications*. New York: Free Press.

—— 1985. *The Economic Institutions of Capitalism*. New York: Free Press.

Wilson, Edward O., and William H. Bossert. 1971. *A Primer of Population Biology*. Stamford, Conn.: Sinauer Associates.

Wilson, Kenneth, and Alejandro Portes. 1980. "Immigrant Enclaves: An Analysis of the Labor Market Experiences of Cubans in Miami." *American Journal of Sociology* 86: 295–319.

Wilson, Robert W., Peter K. Ashton, and Thomas P. Egan. 1980. *Innovation, Competition, and Government Policy in the Semiconductor Industry*. Lexington, Mass.: D. C. Heath.

Woodward, Joan. 1965. *Industrial Organization: Theory and Practice*. New York: Oxford University Press.

Wright, Sewell. 1968. *Evolution and the Genetics of Populations*, vol. 1. Chicago: University of Chicago Press.

Wyckoff, D. Daryl, and David H. Maister. 1977. *The Motor Carrier Industry*. Lexington, Mass.: D. C. Heath.

Zucker, Lynne. 1983. "Organizations as Institutions." In Samuel Bachrach, ed., *Research in the Sociology of Organizations*. Greenwich, Conn.: JAI Press.

Name Index

Aalen, Odd, 181, 183, 247
Aiken, Michael, 30
Aldrich, Howard E., 39, 42, 48, 60, 82
Amburgey, Terry L., 175, 192, 337
Anderson, Philip, 298
Arrow, Kenneth J., 67, 69, 72
Ashton, Peter K., 164, 175, 229
Astley, W. Graham, 15, 38n, 40, 64, 91
Averitt, Robert T., 46, 47, 47n
Ayer, N. W., 176

Barnard, Chester I., 32
Barnett, William P., 333
Baron, James N., 47
Barth, Fredrik, 53, 54n
Becker, Gary S., 80
Becker, Howard S., 58
Bell, Wendell, 104, 128
Benson, J. Kenneth, 34
Berk, Richard, 279
Bielby, William T., 47
Blau, Peter M., 31, 33, 63, 72, 92, 337
Boeker, Warren, 44
Boorman, Scott A., 52
Bossert, William H., 101
Boyd, Robert, 21
Braun, Ernest, 175
Braverman, Harry, 34
Breiger, Ronald L., 52, 340
Brittain, Jack, 55, 90, 103, 119n, 132,
    167, 171, 233n, 335
Brooks, R. R., 157

Burawoy, Michael, 11, 12, 34
Burns, Tom, 29, 29n, 54
Burrell, Gibson, 40

Carroll, Glenn R., 11, 15, 58, 64, 103,
    115, 138, 141, 142, 175, 176, 188, 191,
    205, 214, 238, 238n, 240–242, 242n,
    245, 246, 255, 270n, 306, 307, 314n,
    333, 335, 337
Cavalli-Sforza, Luca, 21
Chandler, Alfred D., Jr., 6, 24, 25, 40,
    41, 74, 124
Child, John, 32, 85
Chow, Garland, 63
Christie, Robert A., 278
Clawson, Dan, 34
Clegg, Stewart, 34
Coleman, James S., 3, 73, 178, 274
Commons, John R., 25, 154, 158
Cooper, A. C., 129
Cox, D. R., 179, 197, 198, 249
Cyert, Richard M., 10, 29

Daggett, Emerson, 176
Darwin, Charles, 18, 21, 35–38, 50, 92,
    339
David, Paul A., 210, 281
Delacroix, Jacques, 138, 141, 142, 175,
    205, 214, 240, 333, 337
Dickson, William J., 29n
DiMaggio, Paul J., 11, 14, 35, 46, 52, 58,
    124

Dobzhansky, Theodosius, 18
Downs, Anthony, 79, 82, 87
Duncan, Beverly, 31
Duncan, Otis Dudley, 31
Durkheim, Emile, 125, 126, 140

Edwards, Richard, 11, 34, 46, 47
Efron, Bradley, 198
Egan, Thomas B., 164, 175, 229
Eisenstadt, S. N., 125
Eldridge, N., 38
Elton, Charles, 95
Etzioni, Amitai, 63

Featherman, David, 31
Feldman, Marcus, 21
Finance, Maurice, 158
Fink, Gary, 158, 276
Fisher, R. A., 18, 324
Fligstein, Neil D., 47
Foner, Philip, 158, 276
Freeman, John, 5, 11, 34, 39, 42, 44, 48,
    51, 55, 57, 62, 67, 79, 83, 90, 92, 93,
    103, 106, 113, 119n, 132, 167, 171, 188,
    207n, 209n, 211, 246, 283n, 301, 310,
    316n, 317, 318n, 320, 322, 334, 341
Friedman, Milton, 36
Fuller, Wayne A., 324

Galenson, Walter, 278, 279
Gamson, William, 25
Gause, G. F., 97, 102
Gibson, J. L., 129
Gifford, Courtney D., 158
Gordon, David M., 11, 46, 47, 167
Gould, S. J., 38
Greene, William, 196
Gregory, Winifred, 176
Griffin, Larry J., 288

Hage, Jerald, 30
Hannan, Michael T., 5, 8, 11, 20n, 25,
    31n, 34, 39, 42, 48, 51, 54, 62, 67, 79,
    83, 92, 93, 103, 106, 113, 133, 142, 179,
    188, 207n, 209n, 211, 238n, 242n, 246,
    249, 264n, 280n, 283n, 306, 310, 316n,
    317, 318n, 320, 322, 334, 335, 341
Hawley, Amos, 79n, 93, 126, 337
Heckman, James J., 26, 279
Herriot, Scott, 318n

Hirsch, Paul, 56
Hodson, Randy, 47, 47n
House, Robert J., 46, 148, 156, 188, 191
Hrebiniak, Lawrence G., 42
Huo, Yanchung Paul, 191, 240–242, 255,
    307
Hutchinson, G. Evelyn, 92, 95–97
Huxley, Julian, 18

Johnson, Norman L., 185
Joyce, William F., 42

Kahn, Robert L., 310
Kahneman, Daniel, 41, 68
Kalbfleisch, John D., 179, 189, 190, 196
Kalleberg, Arne L., 47, 277
Kanter, Rosabeth Moss, 26, 27
Kaplan, E. L., 180, 181
Karlin, Samuel, 202n
Katz, Daniel, 310
Kaufman, Herbert, 126
Kaufman, Robert L., 47, 47n
Kieser, Alfred, 85
Kimberly, John R., 338
Kotz, Samuel, 185

Ladde, G. S., 88
Lamarck, Jean Baptiste Pierre Antoine
    de Monet, 22
Langton, Nancy, 191, 254
Lawrence, Paul, 12, 29, 310
Lescohier, Don D., 278
Levin, Simon A., 102
Levins, Richard, 98, 106, 107, 110, 114,
    118, 310–312, 319, 334
Lewontin, Richard C., 17, 21
Lieberson, Stanley, 104
Lipset, Seymour Martin, 274
Lorrain, François, 52
Lorsch, Jay, 12, 29, 310
Lotka, Alfred J., 51, 99–101, 117, 141,
    335

MacArthur, Robert H., 92, 104, 118
MacDonald, Stuart, 175
Malthus, Thomas R., 100
March, James G., 10, 12, 29, 69, 86
Marrett, Cora B., 132
Marx, Karl, 11, 36, 61, 96, 288
May, Robert M., 88

Mayo, Elton, 29n
McCarthy, John D., 333
McKelvey, Bill, 48, 49
McPherson, J. Miller, 46, 51, 335, 340
Meier, P., 180, 181
Mendel, Gregor, 50
Merton, Robert K., 29, 77
Meyer, John W., 11, 12, 14, 33, 34, 56, 94, 123, 124, 136
Meyer, Marshall, 11, 12, 14, 33, 34, 56, 94, 123, 124, 136
Michels, Robert, 6, 11, 28, 273–275, 293
Miles, Robert H., 24, 32, 33, 33n, 147, 281, 338
Mitchell, Wesley C., 210, 281, 333
Mitchell, Will, 210, 281, 333
Mittleman, Edward B., 156
Monod, Jacques, 48
Moore, Gordon, 167
Morgan, Gareth, 40
Mouzelis, Nicos P., 29n

Nelson, Richard R., 22, 37, 49n, 76, 80, 181n, 225n, 339
Nelson, W., 22, 37, 49n, 76, 80, 181n, 225n, 339
Nielsen, François, 142, 143, 335
Nystrom, Paul C., 127

Oakes, D., 179, 198, 249
Oakey, Ray, 129n
Olsen, Johan P., 12
Olson, Mancur, 339
Olzak, Susan, 53, 104, 333
Oster, George F., 19
Ouchi, William G., 27

Paige, Jeffrey, 31
Parsons, Talcott, 78
Perrow, Charles, 29, 43, 82, 91, 334
Peters, Thomas J., 26
Pfeffer, Jeffrey, 12, 14n, 30, 39, 310
Portes, Alejandro, 8
Powell, Walter W., 11, 14, 35, 58, 124
Prentice, Ross L., 179, 189, 191, 196
Pugh, D. S., 30

Randolph, W. A., 147
Reich, Michael, 11, 46, 47
Richardson, Peter J., 21

Roethlisberger, F. J., 29n
Rogers, T. J., 294
Roughgarden, Jonathan, 19n, 102, 107, 110
Rowan, Brian, 34, 123, 124, 136
Rowell, George P., 176
Rubin, Beth, 288

Salancik, Gerald, 12, 30, 310
Schoenherr, Richard A., 33
Schudson, Michael, 25
Scott, W. Richard, 11, 12, 14, 28, 29, 34, 39, 46, 63, 69, 72, 79, 82, 92, 94, 123, 124, 337
Selznick, Philip, 6, 32
Šiljak, D. D., 88
Simmel, Georg, 140
Simon, Herbert A., 29, 88, 90, 120, 121
Singh, Jitendra, 46, 148, 188, 191
Smith-Lovin, Lynn, 335, 340
Solar, Peter, 210, 281
Solt, Michael E., 138, 333
Spencer, Herbert, 36
Staber, Udo, 42
Stacy, E. W., 190
Stalker, George M., 29, 29n, 54
Stanley, S. M., 38
Starbuck, William, 127
Stewart, Estelle, 158
Stinchcombe, Arthur L., 14n, 15, 16, 38, 54, 56, 61, 71, 73, 80, 81, 113, 114, 122, 125, 245, 246, 256, 265

Taft, Philip, 210, 214, 276, 282, 285
Taylor, Frederick W., 29n
Taylor, Howard M., 202n
Tewksbury, D. G., 24
Thompson, James D., 12, 29, 54, 72, 78, 310
Thorp, Willard L., 210, 281
Tilly, Charles, 3, 31, 274
Tilton, J., 174, 175
Tomlins, Christopher, 210
Trow, Martin A., 274
Troy, Leo, 158
Tsiatis, A., 198
Tucker, David J., 46, 148, 188, 191, 333
Tuma, Nancy Brandon, 20n, 25, 31n, 103, 179, 280n, 320n
Tushman, Michael L., 298

Tversky, Amos, 41, 68
Tyack, David B., 24

Ulman, Lloyd, 278

Van de Ven, Andrew H., 40, 91, 147
Volterra, Vito, 51, 99–101, 117, 141, 335

Wallace, Michael, 47, 277, 288
Wallerstein, Immanuel, 31
Warren, Roland L., 14
Waterman, Robert H., 26
Weber, Max, 6, 11, 24, 28, 58, 73, 74,
  96, 125, 126
Wedervang, F., 25
Weick, Karl, 31

West, Elizabeth, 333
Wheeler, Jean French, 176
White, Harrison C., 52
Wholey, Douglas R., 103, 335
Williamson, Oliver E., 25, 55, 72, 119,
  339
Wilson, Edward O., 19, 101
Wilson, Kenneth, 8
Wilson, Robert W., 164, 175, 229
Winter, Sidney G., 22, 37, 49n, 76, 80,
  114, 225n, 339
Woodward, Joan, 30, 54
Wright, Sewell, 17

Zucker, Lynne, 56

Subject Index

Absorption, 160; rate of absorption of labor unions, 259–264
Accountability, 73–75, 80, 90, 245, 246
Adaptation, 21–33, 40–44; theories of, 12, 29–30, 66
Adaptive function, 107, 110
Affiliations, 8, 163
Age dependence, 244–270, 279–280; models of, 188–192
American Federation of Labor, 256, 278
Arrival processes, 193, 202
Authority, 77–79, 168

Bankruptcy, 82, 149–150, 167–168
Barriers to entry and exit, 68
Blending processes, 54, 57, 60, 62
Blockmodels, 52
Boundaries of forms, 53–60
Breweries, 138
Bureaucracy, 6, 28–29, 77, 96, 113–114, 126–127

Capital investment, 211, 282, 288, 290
Careers: and diversity, 8–9, 73; in semi-conductor industry, 267
Carrying capacity, 51, 100–102, 131–137, 204
Censoring, 160, 179, 185
Cessation of operations, 150
Classification of forms, 46–53, 62–64
Closure of social networks, 55
Clustering, 52, 63

Coexistence, 97–98, 101–103
Collective action: and organizations, 3, 5, 71–72, 80–81, 154–155; and boundaries of forms, 56–57
Commensalism, 97
Community ecology, 14, 15, 92, 337, 340
Competing risks, 87, 182, 183
Competition, 51, 61, 91–92, 97–104, 132–141, 202, 233–235, 271–275, 278, 290–293, 302, 309, 341; competition theory, 97, 103; competition coefficients, 101–104
Competitive exclusion, 61, 97–98, 102; principle of, 97, 102
Concentration, 9–10, 115, 121, 131, 338
Conflict, 82, 103, 140
Constant rate model. *See* Exponential model
Construction industry, 104, 113–114
Contingency theory, 12, 30
Conventional definitions of forms, 50, 62–63, 89, 310
Core structures, 67, 79–80
Counting processes, 192–194
Coupling of intentions and outcomes, 23; loose coupling, 94

Darwinism, 17–23, 35–38, 50, 92; Darwinian change, 22–23
Decision-making, 7, 29, 41, 73, 75, 77, 79, 149, 323
Deinstitutionalization, 59
Demography of organizations, 14

Density, 129–131, 207–209, 211–212, 225–227, 238–239, 332–335; density dependence, 131–141, 202–206, 212–219, 229–231, 233–242, 286–298, 306–308; cross-effects, 141, 205
Determinism, 39–40
Disbanding, 25, 142, 149–151, 160; rate of, 135–139; of labor unions, 250–259, 273–293
Disorganization, 150
Dissimilarity index, 105
Dissolution, 149
Diversity of organizations, 7–9, 11, 15–17, 60–62, 75–76, 125–127, 154–157, 310, 335; diversity dependence, 141–143
Division of labor, 125–126
Dominant leader, 81
Dualism, 46–47
Duration, 179, 186, 193, 197–198; duration dependence, 188–192, 215–216
Dynamics, 24–26, 60–62, 143–144, 187, 201; dynamics of selection, 143

Economic catastrophes, 281
Economics and organizational ecology, 10, 19, 339–340
Educational system, 4
Efficiency and organization, 10, 30, 34–35, 67, 72, 106, 120, 124, 338–339; hyperefficiency, 36–37; efficient producers, 37, 119; efficient boundaries, 55
Employer offensives, 210, 215, 276, 282
Ending events, 149–153, 160
Endogenous sampling. *See* Sample selection bias
Entrepreneurs, 37, 57, 167, 233, 293–294
Entry into semiconductor industry, 168–170, 224–229; rate of entry, 229–238
Environment, 91; environmental uncertainty, 12, 118, 311; organization-environment relations, 13–16, 29–30, 34–35, 45, 91, 93–95; environmental constraint, 68–69, 78, 85–86, 123–129; environmental variability, 106–114, 209–211, 214–215, 226–230, 281–282, 288–290, 299, 311–314, 318, 320–330
Equilibrium: assumption, 20, 25, 31, 51, 311; punctuated, 38

Ethnic boundaries, 53
Event histories, 179; event history analysis, 180–198
Evolution of organizational populations, 17–24, 60, 118–120, 122, 143–144
Excess capacity, 106, 318
Exit from semiconductor industry, 169, 269, 293–296, 323, 327, 329, 332, 336; rate of exit, 268–270, 296–305, 325–329
Experience, 298–299
Exponential model (constant rate model), 184–185
Extreme value distribution, 184–185

Failure. *See* Mortality of organizations
First mover, 118–120
Fitness, 19, 21, 36, 96, 110; fitness function, 50–51, 98–99, 107–108, 319; fitness set, 107–112, 311, 325
Founding, 147–149, 159; rate of, 124–129, 131–135, 141–143, 192–194, 201–224; of labor unions, 207–224; of newspaper publishing firms, 238–243

Gamma model, 189–190; generalized gamma model, 190–191
Generalism, 76, 103–116, 310–330
Genetics, organizational, 48–50
Gestation period, 121–123
Goals, 5–6, 13, 71–72
Gompertz model, 187–189
Gradualism, 37–38
Grain of environmental variation, 106–107; coarse grain, 106; fine grain, 106–107
Growth rates, 96–101; variations in intrinsic growth rates, 117–120; growth potential, 338

Half-life, 186–187
Hazard function, 180; integrated hazard function, 180–181; Aaalen estimator, 181; actuarial estimator, 249, 267
Heterogeneity: environmental, 94–95; unobserved, 190, 215, 254, 260, 267
Hierarchy, 88–89, 120–121

Immigration, 276, 282, 288
Inbreeding, 55–56

Inequality, 9, 11, 36, 115
Inertia, structural, 32–33, 66–68, 70–71,
    75–82, 84, 87–90, 278
Instantaneous transition rate, 182–183
Institutionalization, 56–57, 75, 80–81,
    124–125, 129, 132, 212; institutional
    rules, 3, 56, 123, 124, 332; institutional
    theory, 11, 34–35
Intentions, 5–6, 23, 33, 77, 152
Interactions among populations, 96, 100–
    103, 205, 219–224, 233–238, 273, 290–
    293, 301–305
Interunion rivalry, 278
Iron law of oligarchy, 274
Isomorphism, 93–95; institutional, 34, 94,
    124; principle of, 93

K-strategy, 100, 118–120, 337
Knights of Labor, 163, 191, 255

Labor unions, 153–164; industrial unions,
    97, 156, 293; craft unions, 105, 155–
    157; labor history, 275–279
Lamarckian change, 22
Legitimacy, 34, 69, 81, 131–134, 136–138
Liability of newness, 81, 85–86, 122,
    245–270
Logistic population growth, 100
Log-logistic model, 191
Lotka-Volterra (LV) model, 101–103, 335

Makeham model, 188
Managerialism, 32
Marxian theory, 35, 61
Maximum likelihood (ML) estimation,
    194–197
Mendelian inheritance, 18–19
Merchant producers. *See* Semiconductor
    devices, industry
Merger, 139, 150–152, 159; equal-status
    merger, 160; rate of merger of labor
    unions, 264–266
Microprocessors. *See* Semiconductor
    devices
Military organizations, 75, 150
Modern synthesis (of genetics and evolu-
    tion), 18
Moore's Law, 167
Mortality of organizations, 15–16, 25,
    83–88, 115, 135–141, 149–153, 244–

246, 271–273; lingering death, 149–151;
    labor unions, 160, 247–273; semicon-
    ductor manufacturing firms, 169, 267–
    270, 293–305, 323–329; newspaper
    publishing firms, 175–176, 305–308;
    restaurants, 314–323
Multiplier of the rate (defined), 186, 206
Mutualism, 234

Natural selection. *See* Selection pro-
    cesses
Newspaper publishing firms, 142, 175–
    176, 201, 224, 238, 246, 272, 305, 307,
    309; definition of newspaper, 175
Niche, 50–52, 95–98, 102–106, 113–116,
    310–314, 322–323, 325–330; duality of
    niche and form, 50–51; fundamental
    niche, 96–98; realized niche, 97; niche
    overlap, 97–98, 103–104; niche width,
    104–116, 310–314, 322–323, 325–330

Optimization, 19–20
Organizational change, perspectives, 10–
    13, 33–35, 69–70
Organizational forms, 16–17, 24–25, 45–
    60, 62–65, 79, 311, 329, 331–332, 336–
    338, 340; definitions of, 48–53; of labor
    unions, 154–157, 161, 207–209; of
    semiconductor manufacturing firms,
    164–165, 170–174; of restaurants, 316–
    318

Partial likelihood (PL) estimation, 197–
    198
Patch size, 106, 107, 110, 311–312, 318
Period effects, 187, 203–204; in analysis
    of semiconductor manufacturers, 174;
    in analysis of labor unions, 209–210
Peripheral structures. *See* Core struc-
    tures
Poisson process, 193–194, 202; Poisson
    regression, 194, 196
Politics: internal, 5–6, 23, 30, 67–68;
    external, 37, 79, 126–127, 136, 276;
    political turmoil, 240, 242, 305, 307
Polymorphs, 113–114, 311
Population thinking, 15–17, 28
Power and organizations, 6, 12, 30–31,
    34, 47, 56–57, 81, 82, 115, 125, 127,
    142, 150–153, 274–276

Predator-prey interactions, 97, 129, 140
Punctuational change, 37–38

r-strategy, 100, 118–120, 122–123, 184, 337
Random drift, 58
Random transformation theories, 12–13
Rate dependence, 141–143, 205, 215–216, 232, 237, 273, 299, 302
Rationality, 37, 41–42, 73, 74; norms of, 11, 73, 125
Reliability, 72–75, 80, 83, 85, 90, 105–106, 245–246
Reorganization, 7–8, 41, 67–68, 70, 82–87, 89
Reproducibility, 75–77, 80–81, 84, 90
Resources, 50–53, 67, 69, 71–74, 76–78, 93–97, 100–106, 125–127, 131–132, 142, 177, 204–205; resource dependence, 12, 30, 69, 71, 81, 122; resource mobilization, 71, 73, 81, 122, 148
Restaurants, 64, 122, 314–319, 329, 333–335
Routines, 49, 76, 245

Sample selection bias, 26–27, 32, 279
Seasonality, 315–316, 319, 322–323
Secession from labor unions, 159, 256, 259, 262, 264, 280, 285
Second source, 234, 304
Segregating processes, 54, 56–58, 60, 61
Selection processes, 13–24, 25–26, 35–37, 74, 77, 82, 118, 122–124, 143–144, 341; theories, 11–12
Semiconductor devices, 54–55, 165–170, 238; industry, 42, 54, 107, 119, 128, 139, 225–226, 267, 293–294; manufacturing firms, 164–175, 233–238
Silicon Valley, 54, 57, 128, 129
Size: and scope of application of organizational ecology, 39, 82, 153, 334; and structural change, 81–84, 338; and mortality rates, 83–84, 88, 256–259, 262–267; and inertia, 87–88; conceptualizing the size of populations, 129–131
Skill level, 156, 161–162, 208–209
Slack. See Excess capacity
Social Darwinism, 35–36
Social movements, 3, 273–275
Social networks, 54–55, 340

Social revolution, 125–126
Social service agencies, 46, 333
Specialism. See Generalism
Spectral analysis, 323–324
Starting event, 147–149, 150, 159–160
Strategy, 22, 30, 32, 41–44, 107–110, 304–305; life history strategy, 118–120; labor union organizing strategy, 161–163
Strikes, 75, 154, 240, 275–277, 282
Structural equivalence, 52
Subsidiary, 165, 169
Survivor function, 180; Kaplan-Meier estimator, 181
Symbiosis, 97, 140

Taxonomy. See Classification of forms
Technology, 55, 78–79; and structure, 29–30, 34, 54–55; technological change and innovation, 71, 119, 128–129, 162, 166–167, 174–175, 238, 277–278, 282, 293–294, 298–299
Transaction costs, 41, 55, 339
Transformation, 11–13, 17, 66, 81, 87, 125–127, 160, 168, 181, 323
Transmission (mechanisms and processes), 18–21, 49, 164

Uncertainty: and diversity, 9; and adaptation, 22–23, 29–30; and reliability, 72–73; and generalism, 310–311; contrasted with variability, 311–312, 324–325
Unemployment rate, 281, 288
Unit: of analysis, 13, 16, 167–168, 192, 315; of observation, 159, 175
Unitary character of populations, 45, 48, 66
Universities, 29, 46, 49, 68–69, 77–78, 113, 128–129, 334

Voluntary associations, 51, 255, 335, 340

Waiting time. See Duration
Weibull model, 188–189
Wineries, 59, 138, 333

Yule process, 202–203; generalized, 203